Berliner Ensem[

BERTOLT

Bertolt Brecht was born in Augsburg on 10 February 1898 and died
in Berlin on 14 August 1956. He grew to maturity as a playwright in
the frenetic years of the twenties and early thirties, with such plays
as *Man Equals Man*, *The Threepenny Opera* and *The Mother*. He left
Germany when Hitler came to power in 1933, eventually reaching
the United States in 1941, where he remained until 1947. It was
during this period of exile that such masterpieces as *Life of Galileo*,
Mother Courage and her Children and *The Caucasian Chalk Circle*
were written. Shortly after his return to Europe in 1947, he founded
the Berliner Ensemble, and from then until his death mainly directed
and supervised productions of a wide variety of plays, including his
own.

David Barnett is Reader in Drama, Theatre and Peformance at the
University of Sussex. He has published monographs on Heiner Müller
(1998) and Rainer Werner Fassbinder (2005, paperback 2009), and
has co-edited a volume and edited a special issue of *Contemporary
Theatre Review* on contemporary German theatre. He is the author
of *Brecht in Practice: Theatre, Theory and Performance* (2014) and
A History and the Berliner Ensemble (forthcoming).

Berliner Ensemble Adaptations

The Tutor
Coriolanus
The Trial of Joan of Arc at Rouen, 1431
Don Juan
Trumpets and Drums

Edited and introduced by
DAVID BARNETT

With notes by
JOHN WILLETT

Series Editor
TOM KUHN

B L O O M S B U R Y
LONDON · NEW DELHI · NEW YORK · SYDNEY

Bloomsbury Methuen Drama

An imprint of Bloomsbury Publishing Plc

50 Bedford Square	1385 Broadway
London	New York
WC1B 3DP	NY 10018
UK	USA

www.bloomsbury.com

Bloomsbury is a registered trade mark of Bloomsbury Publishing Plc

First published 2014
Bloomsbury Methuen Drama Series Editor for Bertolt Brecht: Tom Kuhn

© Bertolt-Brecht-Erben / Suhrkamp Verlag 2014
Introduction © Bloomsbury Methuen Drama 2014
The Tutor, original work entitled *Der Hofmeister* © 1951
Coriolanus, original work entitled *Coriolan* © 1959
The Trial of Joan of Arc at Rouen, 1431, original work entitled *Der Prozess der Jeanne
D'Arc zu Rouen, 1431* © 1959
Don Juan, original work entitled *Don Juan* © 1959
Trumpets and Drums, original work entitled *Pauken* and *Trompeten* © 1959
Edited and introduced by David Barnett
With notes by John Willett

British Library Cataloguing-in-Publication Data
A catalogue record for this book is available from the British Library.

ISBN: PB: 978-1-4725-1438-7
ePDF: 978-1-4725-0664-1
ePub: 978-1-4725-1285-7

Library of Congress Cataloging-in-Publication Data
A catalog record for this book is available from the Library of Congress.

Typeset by RefineCatch Limited, Bungay, Suffolk
Printed and bound in India

Contents

Contents

Introduction: Adaptations for the Berliner Ensemble

Bertolt Brecht is celebrated as a dramatist in his own right, but he was also involved in literary collaborations for the duration of his career as a writer. He gathered a group of friends around himself as a young man in Augsburg to exchange ideas and discuss their literary work, and the practice continued with different writers, directors and dramaturges until his death in 1956. Another form of collaboration, however, is to be found in Brecht's relationship with the work of other playwrights. His first full-length play, *Baal*, was a direct and critical engagement with Hanns Johst's *The Lonely Man*, yet, over the years, Brecht also developed more intimate relationships to source texts in the form of adaptations. His approach was not dictated by a standard approach but by complex responses to the dramatic material in question. Brecht's *The Life of Eduard II of England*, for example, was a radical dismemberment and reassembly of Marlowe's play, while Brecht preserved many important elements of John Gay's *The Beggars Opera* in *The Threepenny Opera*. *Round Heads and Pointed Heads* began as an adaptation of *Measure for Measure* before taking a completely different direction and leaving little more than a passing resemblance to Shakespeare's play. However, once Brecht had a theatre of his own, the Berliner Ensemble (BE), his approach to adaptation began to take its lead from a series of political and aesthetic principles, as we shall see below. The adaptations in this volume, which were written between the BE's first season (1949–50) and the last one Brecht would experience (1955–6), conform to these principles, but, as will become evident, their application did not lead to standardized output by any means. In order to understand this shift to a different, more focused form of adaptation, we need to appreciate what having his own theatre meant to Brecht and how this affected the work he sought to bring to it.

* * * * *

Brecht, together with his wife, Helene Weigel, and their children, had been in exile in a number of countries since the Nazis came to power in 1933. During this period Brecht had very little access to the theatre and instead devoted most of his creative energy to writing plays, poems and theoretical texts. Having left the USA in October 1947, after a not untraumatic hearing at the hands of the McCarthyite House Un-American Activities Committee, he journeyed on to Zurich via Paris, and contemplated a return to active theatre-making. At this time, it was by no means certain that he would settle in the Soviet zone of Berlin. Although the Soviets had offered him incentives, he flirted with relocating to Salzburg and Munich but these plans came to nothing.

By late 1948 Brecht finally decided to return to Berlin, the site of his only major triumph to date, *The Threepenny Opera*. Yet the theatre in which it premiered under the direction of Erich Engel in 1928, the Theater am Schiffbauerdamm, was already occupied by a company under the leadership of Fritz Wisten. Indeed, there seemed to be no room at all in what would become East Berlin for Brecht and a new ensemble; it looked like he had arrived in Germany too late. So, with this lack of free space in mind, he sought to attach the new ensemble he proposed, at least for the short term, to an existing theatre. The East German government was planning to rebuild another major theatre, the Volksbühne, with a view to moving Wisten and his troupe there and allowing Brecht to return to the Schiffbauerdamm. Estimates concerning the building project were hopelessly optimistic, however. In the meantime, the BE, with Weigel as general manager and Brecht as artistic director, was supposed to spend just one season at Wolfgang Langhoff's Deutsches Theater. As it turned out, they remained there until 1953.

After much to-ing and fro-ing between the various institutions that ran Berlin before the foundation of the German Democratic Republic (GDR) on 7 October 1949, Weigel finally signed a contract with the Department of People's Education that brought the BE into existence on 1 September. The initial question that confronted the new company was what it was going to perform. Brecht certainly had enough plays of his own and, indeed, opened the new season on 12 November with *Mr Puntila and his Man Matti*. However, he was reluctant to turn his company into a vehicle solely for realizing his own dramas and wanted a greater mix, including contemporary and classic plays, that could make an active contribution to the cultural life of the city and its citizens.

While Brecht was interested in attracting other directors to work at the BE, he was also keen to develop his own theorized practice now that he had regular access to a proper stage. This he could not do alone and so he re-activated old contacts, such as Erich Engel and his school friend, the set-designer Caspar Neher. Yet these were collaborators of Brecht's generation, and one of the BE's missions was to test out and disseminate a new way of making theatre. Consequently, Brecht recruited a team of young assistants who were to learn from him, not by spending hours in the archive reading his unpublished theories, but by observing him at work, making suggestions, and reflecting on the work they observed in their own detailed and analytical rehearsal notes. Brecht created a circle of enthusiastic, committed theatre-makers with whom he could collaborate and advance his ideas. Yet the tasks he set them extended well beyond the rehearsal room.

In a bid to build the BE's repertoire, Brecht returned to the practice of adaptation, but also exploited the *process* of adaptation as a means of developing his young assistants. That is, he was able to focus his assistants' nascent interests and abilities by encouraging them to edit and, indeed, to adulterate existing texts while reserving his own place as editor-in-chief and writer of additional material. But the repertoire was not merely to comprise a collection of Brecht's favourite plays; Brecht was profoundly aware that he had opted to live in the first (and, as yet, last) socialist state on German soil and set about fashioning a repertoire worthy of that state. So, while he implemented ideas that had fermented during his long exile – from developing an active ensemble on stage to assembling a dynamic team he envisaged as able successors in due course – he did not neglect the material his predominantly young cast and crew were to perform. The adaptations, which would become something of a staple at the BE, were written in such a way that they would exemplify the social aims of the company, and these can be seen in the criteria Brecht set down for his young assistants.

*   *   *   *   *

The first text Brecht selected for adaptation was *The Tutor*, written by J. M. R. Lenz in 1774. Lenz was one of a disparate group of energetic young writers who would collectively be known as the 'storm and stress' movement, or *Sturm und Drang*. His dramatic output is marked by its bold themes and formal innovation; indeed his play *The Soldiers* can be read as a precursor to Brecht's epic theatre in that it regularly features scenes in which characters comment explicitly on the action rather than participate in it, like Brecht's narrators. *The Tutor*, a play that is today regarded as a classic of the 'storm and stress' period, was, in 1949, little-known and ripe for rediscovery. However, Brecht was not prepared to direct it as it stood and engaged his assistants in the process of adaptation. In the following extract, we can see the sort of tasks he set. This systematic approach to adaptation may have been implicit to his own practices previously but the overt statement of its tenets signalled a set of principles which informed both his thoughts about the nature of dramatic source texts and how they might be realized at the BE.

First, he asked his assistants to trim 30 minutes off the total running time. He then wanted them to:

2. establish clearly the central *Fabel* (the account of the real events) so that it is easily understandable, while retaining the elegance of the sequence of the scenes,
3. arrange the subplots around the central *Fabel* so that they illuminate and explicate the latter smoothly without interrupting it,
4. eliminate the untypical, accidental or purely pathological features in the motivation of the action and the characters.

The instructions point to several important aspects of an adaptation for Brecht. Items 2 and 3 put an unmistakable emphasis on clarity. The organization of the main plot and the subplot had to serve the purpose of drawing clear through-lines in the complicated course of events. Lenz, who, like other storm-and-stress playwrights, was influenced by Shakespeare, wanted to give his play the richness and liveliness associated with Shakespeare's dramas. Brecht, however, sought to impose order upon the various plots as a way of deepening the treatment of the central themes, rather than taking in too many extraneous meanderings, as he saw them. It should be noted, however, that this formal reorganization was not to interfere with the beauty of the play's flow. Brecht was not suggesting a utilitarian butchering of the play's form; instead he wanted to combine his aims with the qualities that made Lenz's play so attractive to him in the first place. This respect towards the unique appeal of all the source texts in this volume is one factor that prevented the adaptations from becoming mechanical or repetitive: each work had to be confronted on its own terms and only then could adaptation proceed.

Item 4 deals more specifically with issues concerning Brecht's political aims for the adaptation as the basis for a successful performance. The direction to eliminate certain elements again concerns itself with clarity. In addition, the three elements also tell us about the type of material that was not admissible in a text designed to engage the audience's critical faculties to the full. Eliminating the untypical meant that spectators could contemplate characters and events which were not in some way out of the ordinary but ones which would have concrete significance for them. Similarly, the accidental relied too much on chance to offer an audience material from which it could make meaningful connections about the world and the way it worked. Brecht maintained here that the representation of the world on stage had to be exemplary – it could not simply follow the foibles of everyday life but had consciously to aim to reproduce actions that were important and intelligible to an audience. If spectators were to learn anything, then exceptional or accidental material could not be included. The prohibition on 'pathological features' indicates another area Brecht deemed beyond the remit of a politically committed drama, in that such conditions were innate and thus unchangeable. While scholarly work has subsequently posited links between mental illness and the mechanisms of society, at that time, socialist states considered psychoanalysis and psychotherapy bourgeois and alien to working people.

The three items thus show how Brecht's formal adaptation process focused on offering material to the audience defined by its usefulness. The unswerving drive towards clarity should not, however, be mistaken for a desire to make things easy for the audience. Brecht's theatre was based on posing questions which only the spectators could answer. 'Clarity', then, involved articulating these questions as clearly as possible. The questions came in the form of on-stage contradictions. In *The Tutor*, for example, the audience was confronted with the central issue of why an intelligent tutor had to sell his services and demean himself in order to survive in the society of the time. Brecht thus sought to make the articulation of that difficult contradiction clear while the responses to it were complex and a matter for the audience.

Adaptation was not only a business that concerned the form of a play. Certain aspects of the original's themes were also important. For example, Lenz's play contains a reformist streak, suggesting that class and educational systems were capable of repair under feudalism. Brecht disagreed with this position and both deleted the first scene from Lenz's second act and rewrote the main voice of reform, Major von Berg, in order to expunge this suggestion from the play. As a Marxist, Brecht wanted to point to the failings of the system itself and suggest that only revolution was the appropriate solution. However, the accuracy of the depiction of feudalism and those involved in it should equally demonstrate just how difficult it would be to engineer such social and political upheaval.

Formal and thematic adaptation served to heighten the central theme of the play in Brecht's reading: the German 'misère'. Broadly speaking, this term refers to the German people's inability to bring about a successful social revolution, unlike the French in 1789. The Peasants' Revolt of the early sixteenth century and the bourgeois uprising of 1848 both came to nothing and the patchwork of German states retained their class-based hierarchy. Brecht also noted in the unpublished introduction to *Turandot* that even in the most terrible days at the end of World War Two, the German proletariat had not seized the moment and risen up against the Nazis. To Brecht, *The Tutor* was an object lesson in servility and deference to one's social 'superiors', and he wanted the production to use comedy as a way of pointing to this attitude with a view to overcoming it.

Adaptation was also much more than merely cutting and reworking the text into a finished product; it was an ongoing process that ran through rehearsals. Several drafts of *The Tutor* exist and chart the ways in which practical work affected the architecture and feel of the new script. Rehearsal would reveal just how successful the current draft had been and the rhythm of lines, speeches, dialogues and scenes would change in accordance with the effects generated on stage. It is worth noting that this was an experimental process: actors were not required merely to perform what they found on the page but to plumb the text's depths and make discoveries which may not have been apparent to the adapters. The discoveries would then inform the next draft. The lack of a definitive end point for the script, for example, is betokened by the fact that Brecht wrote the epilogue to *The Tutor* very late in the day. Up until then, the cast had used the more general epilogue to *The Good Person of Szechwan*. This shows how the team were not working towards this end from the outset; on the contrary, the epilogue took the material developed previously and made its own concluding remarks.

*   *   *   *   *

I have dwelt on the adaptation of *The Tutor* at length because it offers a model for how the other adaptations in this volume also developed. The emphasis on clarity, the social rather than the individual dimension, and the idea that text can only be properly developed in rehearsal runs through the BE's work under Brecht's leadership. The one adaptation which did not make it to rehearsal in Brecht's lifetime was *Coriolanus*. As a result, the text we have is incomplete, especially, as Ralph Mannheim notes, around the battle scenes at the end of Act One. However, it should not be overlooked that rehearsal itself might well have revealed more about the initial adaptation and that the final version might have looked very different from the version Brecht in fact left after he stopped working on it in 1953. Indeed, when the BE finally staged the play in 1964, the directors Manfred Wekwerth and Joachim Tenschert spent much time with a battery of assistants adapting the adaptation. The final BE script contained roughly 10 per cent of material added after Brecht's death.

It was a logical progression for Brecht to move from Lenz to Shakespeare, and he said as much in a *Journal* entry of 22 December 1949. Brecht rated Shakespeare as the greatest realist of the bourgeois stage, yet realism here does not denote the faithful reproduction of everyday appearances, as is the case with plays by Chekhov, for example, or Arthur Miller. What Brecht meant was that Shakespeare understood how characters behaved and acted under the pressure of their historical situation – this was the 'reality' Brecht sought beneath surface appearances. The characters' language may, of course, be poetic and metaphorical – nobody actually talks like that. To Brecht, it was the attitudes towards reality encoded in such speeches that rendered them 'realistic'. Performing such realism was not easy and so *The Tutor*, inspired by Shakespeare's dramaturgy, offered the BE, and particularly its young actors, an opportunity to develop the skills demanded by Brecht's realistic theatre before the cast and crew confronted the master of the genre.

As much as Brecht admired Shakespeare, he still felt that there were characters and events that required further adaptation. The 'Study of the first scene of Shakespeare's *Coriolanus*' (to be found on p. 450 of this volume) demonstrates the ways Brecht interrogated the material he found. The 'study' is not a verbatim account of a meeting, in which Brecht is represented by a 'B'; he rewrote it in order to emphasize certain salient points. B's role here is to stimulate dialogue by asking questions and making observations about the text as it stands. On occasion, he notes that Shakespeare was writing for a different kind of theatre, one of a class society. Brecht and the BE, on the other hand, were planning a production in a socialist state, and this shift of context provided the main reason for an adaptation. Brecht sought to undermine the prejudices against the working people of Rome that pervaded Shakespeare's time and to undermine the implicit dominance of the patricians. In response, the people's tribunes became more credible characters in their own right than mere intriguing politicians who have a personal problem with Coriolanus himself. The common people were also recast. Shakespeare's IV iii became Brecht's IV i, for example, and the scene was completely rewritten. Rather than making the banishment of Coriolanus the focus, two men, a Roman and a Volscian, consider how the world is safer without Coriolanus, but they are more concerned with their common social plight away from the tribal wrangles. The workers of this world most certainly unite, because they understand that they share a common set of problems defined by their place on the lower rungs of the social ladder.

The last scene also presents a very different finale: rather than the dramatic murder of Coriolanus at the hands of Aufidius and his men, the audience is returned to a more tranquil and understated setting, the Roman Senate. Life goes on and the politicians are going about their legislative business when news of Coriolanus' death arrives. Menenius asks that the vanquished general's name be inscribed in the Capitol but the politicians continue their meeting. The family is also denied the honour of wearing public robes of mourning for ten months, a decision that inverts the ending of Shakespeare's play. This final scene is also interesting in that it features senators, a consul, and the tribunes. That is, the defeat of Coriolanus and the relegation of his importance has not suddenly led to social revolution: the noble senators are still present in the legislature. However, the tribunes are the ones who reject the two proposals to memorialize the man who ultimately betrayed Rome, despite his victories earlier in the play. Power is shifting, but is not in the tribune's hands yet.

Brecht was also troubled by the figure of Coriolanus himself because he represented one of Shakespeare's 'great individuals'. These characters appeared to be imbued with character traits that resisted social categorization, that is, they were seemingly 'given' naturally, something Brecht found difficult to accept. Instead he read Coriolanus as a specialist in war who overestimated his own value. Viewing himself above and apart from society, he mistakenly believed he was indispensable. Brecht showed how the people of Rome went on to arm themselves against further attack from the Volscians under Coriolanus in order to point out Coriolanus' more peripheral status. His tragedy in Shakespeare is his pride; in Brecht he falls because of his individualism, a category which is social as well as personal. He fails to realize that the upper echelons of Roman society indulge him his individualism when he is in favour but that the people, in the form of the tribunes, reject it when he fails to play his role in the political process. Brecht thus retained the element of tragic pride but re-contextualized it in the power networks of Roman society.

*   *   *   *   *

The social element also provided the focus when Brecht and Benno Besson adapted Anna Seghers' *The Trial of Joan of Arc at Rouen, 1431*. The original radio play mostly emphasized the trial, yet the adapters sought to bring in the on-stage audience far more prominently as a way of creating a fuller picture of French society under English rule. Besson, who directed the production, acknowledged that this was his first show in which he clearly understood the way socially defined contradictions manifested themselves on stage and changed as events changed. The new script thus allowed him to construct contradictions, resolve them and develop them with new ones. Indeed, the expansion of the crowd scenes led to experiments with the staging, in that Besson used approaches taken from Stanislavsky in order to individualize the representative crowd more 'realistically'. The BE found that Stanislavsky could be integrated into the BE's working methods as long as the focus of the work remains social rather than psychological. The individuality brought out from the members of the crowd emphasized details of their social origins and attitudes, and made plain how these factors altered as new information and relationships emerged in the light of the trial.

Don Juan initially started as a project commissioned by another theatre, the Volkstheater Rostock. Besson had been out of favour at the BE because he had lost the rehearsal notes to *The Tutor* and was invited independently of Brecht to direct any play of his choice. Having been involved in the adaptation process at the BE, he chose Molière's play because he considered it formally weak in comparison to the rest of the French playwright's *oeuvre*. He was particularly concerned by the way the action seemed to drag in the original's final two acts and so he conflated them into what is the final act of the adaptation, Act Four. Elsewhere we notice again the introduction of new characters and situations in a bid to expand the social reach of the play.

Besson reported that he and Brecht's long-standing collaborator Elisabeth Hauptmann started translating and adapting the text when Brecht got wind of the project and that Brecht then took a leading role. A transcript of a meeting that Brecht chaired, which appears to be verbatim rather than the edited text on *Coriolanus* discussed above, again shows how actively Brecht sought to problematize the texts staged by the BE. In this discussion, he particularly focused on what comedy meant in *Don Juan*, but rather than offering his own theses, he employed an interrogative mode, persistently posing questions to tease out the meaning of the genre in the context of the Don Juan myth, which is usually considered tragic. His constant questioning did not settle on the answers given by his collaborators but used them only to probe further.

Again the central figure proved problematic and Brecht was keen to process the reviews the production garnered in Rostock in order to correct some of its perceived flaws and to improve upon them. Brecht objected to the position that Don Juan's atheism was in some way progressive (see 'Don Juan as a character', p. 478 of this volume). He preferred to view it as a mark of Don Juan's decadence in a decadent court, an absence of faith rather than the militant championing of a cause. Again, social contradiction is central to Brecht's thought: Don Juan's hedonism makes him lazy, and his hedonism is an index of the state of the court in pre-revolutionary France. Brecht wanted Besson to bring out these aspects as comic and laughable. This Besson did when he directed the play afresh as the curtain-raiser when the BE finally moved to the Theater am Schiffbauerdamm in early 1954. That Brecht chose to open the new venue with a play written by another dramatist and directed by one of his assistants and not himself shows how he was happy not to hog the limelight but to promote the talent of others. Brecht certainly played a major role in both the adaptation and the direction. As he told Besson afterwards, he was happy to help, but he would have staged the production quite differently and so he wanted Besson to take the credit as sole director.

Brecht followed up the success of the adapted *Don Juan* with another comedy, taken from a different tradition. George Farquhar's Restoration Comedy *The Recruiting Officer* formed the basis of *Trumpets and Drums*. One of the most obvious changes is historical: Farquhar's original settings taken from his own time, the beginning of the eighteenth century, shift forward to the American War of Independence, much later that century. This decision appears to have been taken in a bid to make the action more accessible for the German audience. Spectators would have found it easier to understand the tensions associated with imperialism, although this could have led to a political issue concerning the positive portrayal of the Americans at a time when they played the role of imperialist aggressor in GDR cold-war propaganda.

As it happened, this was not the case. Instead, the ruling Socialist Unity Party (abbreviated in German to 'SED') had more pragmatic concerns. As John Willett notes in 'Adapting Farquhar', p. 490 of this volume, the main work on the adaptation took place between March and April 1955, yet the play was only premiered in September. The reason for this was that the cultural functionaries were concerned that the play, which has a critique of press-ganging as its theme, could be construed as pacifist. The Federal Republic of Germany was remilitarizing and founded the *Bundeswehr* a month after the premiere, and the GDR followed suit in 1956 with the formation of the *Nationale Volksarmee* (National People's Army). The SED thus viewed pacifism as a position that undermined the planned establishment of its armed forces and did not want its most famous theatre producing work that could be interpreted as critical of the policy. In the period between adapting *The Recruiting Officer* and putting it on the stage, the BE set about insulating the text from any charge of pacifism by focusing its critique on the issue of *imperialist* warmongering and the lengths to which the British would go to fight their war of subjugation, rather than as a blanket condemnation of military action.

* * * * *

This, however, was not the only occasion on which the SED intervened in the BE's plans regarding adaptations. Indeed, adaptations were much contested because of their implication in a major aspect of GDR cultural policy. The SED viewed the GDR as the inheritor of a progressive German tradition and used this usurped authority as a way of distancing the GDR as a socialist republic from the catastrophe of Nazism. The way in which this political definition of the nation affected culture was in the treatment of the German cultural heritage. Productions of classic works were obliged to emphasize positive aspects in the plays in order to connect the present with those chosen and preferred parts of the past. It is thus not a little peculiar that the SED neither publicly nor privately censured *The Tutor*. Staging the 'misère' pointed out, after all, a deep-rooted historical inability of the German people to shape history in its own interests, and the production's ironic happy ending would not have protected the BE against the charge of pessimism. To Brecht, on the other hand, the play and its ending were an example of a 'negative example', one in which the audience was confronted with the parody of an ideal with a view to suggesting its own improvements. The lack of pointers towards a brighter future would not have sufficed as a valid conclusion to the authorities, who banned Hanns Eisler's *Johannes Faustus* in 1953 for its negative portrayal of Faust, the SED's most cherished figure from the German canon.

The question then arises as to why the SED did not move against *The Tutor* in 1950. It is likely that three main factors led to the production failing to register with the SED's cultural organs. First, *The Tutor*, as already noted, was not that well known. It would have been difficult to raise the Party's hackles if it could not refer to an official line on the play. Similarly, the audience would have encountered performances 'afresh' with few, if any, preconceived notions about the play, its themes or its forms. That Brecht and his collaborators had made great changes may not have been all that noticeable, especially given the second item in the list of tasks for the adapters: that the play should retain 'the elegance of the sequence of the scenes'. Second, the production was a great success. Audiences and reviewers alike praised its precision, its beauty, its lightness and its humour. The young ensemble had demonstrated how well it could function as a unit, and the production's critique of an oppressive society was lively and engaging, not leaden and propagandistic. Third, the SED itself was uncertain how to wield its new power. The regime was still in a process of bedding down and culture was administered by a range of different agencies, ranging from the Central Committee, through the recently established Ministry of People's Education, down to more local Berlin authorities. It is possible that the Party was not confident enough to launch an attack on a work that was at once unfamiliar and remarkably popular.

The same could not be said of *Coriolanus*. By 1951, the SED was firmly in control and had turned its opinions on the cultural heritage and other aspects of cultural policy into dogma. The Party officially adopted positions on various cultural matters at a conference held between 15–17 March 1951. After this date, it sought to impose its will more heavy-handedly, and, in a meeting in August 1951, it banned further work on the Shakespearean adaptation. The combination of the world's most famous dramatist, whom the Germans had been calling 'our Shakespeare' since at least the eighteenth century, and a protagonist, who had certain affinities to Stalin, was enough to alert the Central Committee to the potential dangers of a production. Brecht did continue to work on the play, but kept the further adaptation quiet, partly for political reasons, partly because he could not secure a suitable male lead for the eponymous hero.

Another BE adaptation, not included in this volume, also came in for official criticism. In 1951, the company staged a fusion of two plays by Gerhart Hauptmann that featured the same lead character, one each side of the interval. *The Beaver Coat* is a full-blooded comedy, *Red Hen* a tragi-comedy; their joining did not make for great theatre, and the production was not well received despite the much-lauded performance of one of Germany's most accomplished actors, Therese Giehse, in the main role of Mother Wolffen. The SED was not concerned about the success or failure of the production; it found the process of adulterating two classic plays by transforming them into one evening's theatre at odds with its ideas on the purity of the cultural heritage and sought to remove the mongrel from the repertoire. In this case, however, the SED was beaten to its goal by Hauptmann's estate which unknowingly shared the Party's view and withdrew the rights after a mere fourteen performances. The estate explicitly objected to the act of adaptation because it had only granted permission for what it called a 'dramaturgical arrangement' of the material.

It is telling that the BE's most controversial production in this early period of GDR history was deliberately kept 'un-adapted'. The BE staged Goethe's *Urfaust*, the early drafts of what would become the first part of *Faust*, in 1952 in Potsdam and 1953 in Berlin. After the diktats on *Coriolanus* and other works scheduled for the BE, Brecht was naturally wary. Nonetheless, he supervised the *Urfaust* production, which was directed by assistant Egon Monk, and approached it in much the same way he would any other production. That is, he mined it for contradictions and conferred on it a lively new reading, away from the orthodoxies of the day. The first production, which portrayed Faust as a charlatan and seducer, was initially praised in the local press but a letter from the Party group at the theatre that hosted the production was merciless in its critique of how the BE had betrayed the German cultural heritage. An adaptation would have merely given the Party more grist to its mill, in that Brecht would have been accused of 'perverting' the text to suit his ends. The preservation of the original text meant that he was only working with the material he found. The second attempt to stage the play in Berlin was deliberately toned down, in the light of the public criticism. Faust no longer had the negative traits that he had had in Potsdam; his tragic contradiction was predicated upon the position that he had to engage in a pact with the devil in order to pursue his more progressive ends. This radical shift in interpretation could not, however, save a production already sullied. The head of the Deutsches Theater, Wolfgang Langhoff, did not allow *Urfaust* to be performed to audiences as an evening show, and consigned it to matinees. After seven of these passed, and with no prospect of entering the normal repertoire, the production vanished, never to be seen again, although, ironically enough, young film-maker Hans-Jürgen Syberberg captured some of the rehearsals on his 8mm camera in 1953.

The Trial of Joan of Arc and *Don Juan* did not attract any adverse criticism. One can only speculate about why this was the case, but *The Trial* was, like *The Tutor*, a little-known work, and it was written by Anna Seghers, a socialist writer of impeccable credentials. Brecht's additions were not controversial – they mostly expanded the crowd scenes to involve the Party's hero of choice, the common people. *Don Juan* was being rehearsed on one of the most traumatic days in the GDR's history: 17 June 1953. This was the day when workers went on strike and protested against the SED's economic policies. With support from the West, the protests became an uprising in which the masses on the streets called for the removal of the SED from power. Soviet tanks rolled into Berlin and order was restored, yet the SED was given the bloodiest of noses and was forced to dilute its hard-line position on a variety of fronts. What followed for the cultural sector was something of a thaw. It is difficult to know whether *Don Juan* would have attracted censure in the first place – Molière was not as problematic as Goethe or Shakespeare, and to call a possibly progressive aristocrat decadent was hardly incendiary. It is more likely that the authorities felt severely restricted in their ability to intervene and this particular play offered so little offence that it would not have been worth criticizing the work.

* * * * *

Adaptations, it would seem, were an important part of the BE's repertoire, yet the BE's two attempts at *Urfaust* raise an important question regarding the necessity of adaptations at Brecht's theatre at all. With the SED firmly applying pressure to *Coriolanus*, Brecht decided to trust his own approaches to making theatre rather than risk a ban on a play he considered important. Brecht's stagecraft was concerned with activating the audience and he developed a range of ideas and practices to achieve this. At their base was the desire to do away with a harmonic union of signs transmitted from the stage to the auditorium. For example, Brecht did not necessarily want lines about, say, happiness to be delivered in a happy voice, or for music to tell the same story as a song's lyrics. Similarly, an actor's body could articulate something different from what he or she was saying. Such moves were designed productively to unsettle the spectators and ask them why the theatre was saying two different things at once. In short, Brecht was keen for his audience to question what it saw and heard, and to ask what might be motivating it. And with his customary emphasis on the social, contributory factors tended to emanate from society rather than the characters.

So Brecht had envisaged modes of performing which criticized or at least modified the material being performed. His theatre of juxtaposed signs deferred ultimate interpretation to the audience. Performance was thus taking on some of the qualities identified in the adaptation discussed above: it pointed to areas one might consider questionable and invited constructive responses. Brecht said as much shortly before his death in 1956: 'if I were putting him [Shakespeare] on today, it is only small changes I would have to make in the production, changes of emphasis'. Sadly, we do not know how Brecht would have directed *Coriolanus* or any other classic play after this pronouncement, but perhaps he had realized by then that the stage could offer a forum for creative challenges to dramatic works to dislodge the centrality of the written adaptation. Regardless of this late position, the BE continued to adapt plays, including those by Brecht that were as yet unperformed, such as *Arturo Ui* and *The Days of the Commune*.

Whether Brecht planned to shift from adapting texts to staging them more radically will never be known. The adaptations in this volume, however, give a clear sense of Brecht's theatrical interests and the directions he sought to pursue upon arriving back in Germany and taking control of an ensemble of his own. The need to make socially useful theatre runs through the adaptations, and the dramaturgical 'corrections' he introduced point to a need to readjust older plays for a more complete picture of society represented on stage. From a new role for the common people to the relativisation of seemingly autonomous central characters, the plays give the audience more to consider in terms of the interaction between the individual and society. This expansion of the social palette was matched by an almost iron resolve to achieve clarity on stage. The social contradictions could not be blurred or mistaken for something else, otherwise the audience would not be able to make informed decisions. The adaptations strove to include only salient material. This did not mean that society was in some way reduced to simple tensions; rather the adaptation process was concerned with bringing out the complexities of society in a clear fashion. Merely observe the dynamic modulations that run through the crowd scenes in *The Trial of Joan of Arc*, for example, to understand how changes in situation affect different social strata in different ways.

The adaptations draft a vision of socially committed drama to act as a corrective to plays that suggest we are prisoners of our psychology and unable to influence our environment. Brecht and his collaborators set about probing the texts in question to expose how people got trapped in the seemingly unchangeable structures of society and to ask in whose interests such structures functioned. Hasty, the eponymous tutor, is no fool but finds himself suffering at the hands of a system loaded against him. While he can hardly be said to triumph at the play's conclusion, the audience, armed with more knowledge about the social set-up, can speculate about how Hasty and others like him might seek to escape their fate.

The BE was a hothouse that produced innovative ways of conceptualizing and realizing theatre. The adaptations in this volume represent one of the strands Brecht developed to change the theatrical landscape of Germany. While they are one of many, they endure today as documents that reflect important directions for a new kind of theatre. And while reading them is one thing, they also invite theatre-makers to take up their challenge and realize productions that present a world which may not be easy to change, but is changeable all the same.

The Tutor

Jakob Michael Reinhold Lenz

Adaptation

Collaborators: R. Berlau, B. Nesson, E. Monk, C. Neher
Translators: Ralph Manheim and Wolfgang Sauerlander

Characters*

Hasty, a tutor
Pastor Hasty, his father
Privy Councillor von Berg
Fritz, his son
Major von Berg
Mrs. von Berg, his wife
Gussie, their daughter
Leopold, their son
The von Bergs' Maid
Wenceslas, a village schoolmaster

Lisa, his ward
Count Vermouth
Squint and Buttress, students
Mrs. Blitz, a landlady
Miss Swandown
Caroline Squint
Miss Cotton
Miss Miller
Miss Gosling

* See note, p. 410.

Prologue

In which the tutor introduces himself to the audience.

Ladies and gentlemen, the play you're about to see
Was written in the eighteenth century.
A household tutor is the part I play
Ancestor of our teachers of today.
I'm still a servant of the nobility
Teaching their offspring for a meager fee
A little manners, the Bible more fully
And how to sneer and sham and bully.
I myself, though I've had a higher education
Am and remain of humble station.
Of course the times have been changing of late
The middle class is rising in the state.
Unless I read the portents wrong
I'll be serving it before too long.
Adept at toeing any line
I'm sure that I will suit it fine.
With all their trimming, clipping, drilling
Those nobles made me only too willing
To teach what suits the ruling class—
A habit that will never pass.
But what I really do, you'll see
Is spell out the sorry state of Germany.

Act One

1

Insterburg in Prussia. Outside Privy Councillor von Berg's ornamental garden.

Privy Councillor. Major.

Major Things aren't doing too well at the farm, William. No horses to be had, not for love nor money. Zounds! The country still hasn't recovered from the war—seven years of it.—There comes that starveling again, I can't take a step without running into him.

*(**Hasty** passes, bowing and scraping four times. His greetings are not acknowledged)*

Hasty Oafs! The devil take you!

Privy Councillor Who's that lickspittle?

Major They tell me his name is Hasty, a pastor's son. My wife asked him to call, she needs a tutor for Leopold; I suppose he'll do as well as anyone.

Privy Councillor I remember that name. His father's been pestering me to do something for him. He wanted a position at the town school. But he's not trained for it. His father's purse gave out before his finals. What is he to teach your son?

Major Drum a little knowledge and good manners into him, so he can grow up to be a soldier like me.

Privy Councillor He may be good enough for that, Frederick. *(He enters the garden, preceding the major, and stops in front of a plant)* Farra communis, the common fern, oldest plant on earth.— But tell me, brother, about this Hasty, do you know what sort of man you'll be taking into your house? What about his ethical maturity? My own inquiries have not been too thorough. I haven't looked into his past.

Major   All I know is that he's not overcharging. And what with the war and the high cost of living . . .

Privy Councillor   I wouldn't want anything cheap. That's why I'm sending my boy Fritz to the university in Halle.

Major   'Sblood! Enough about that lout. We were talking about your fern here.

Privy Councillor   The fern whose remote ancestor, the horsetail, can be traced back to the ice age . . .

2

Gussie's room.

Gussie. **Fritz von Berg**.

Gussie   Fritz! How far is Halle?

Fritz   Three hundred miles or three miles—as you like. If I can't stay here, Gussie, and you're unattainable in any case, what difference is there between three miles and three hundred?

Gussie   And you'll be in Halle and . . .

Fritz   With you heart and soul! But you won't write to me and I shall cease to exist.

Gussie   Then you think it won't be a separation when you get into the coach, not a real separation?

Fritz   We'll always be together in spirit. Take this, Gussie!
(He gives her Klopstock's Odes)

Gussie   Klopstock! *(Reads)*

"The drunken joy of the long wept-for,
Almost too blissful hour
Which tells the lover that he is loved!"
"And now two beauteous souls, ennobled, feel
Wholly, for the first time wholly, the fullness of their being!"
Oh!—But Uncle will marry you off to that ungodly Count Vermouth long before I take my degree. My three years at the university will be a long time in your life!

Gussie   Three years or thirty, as you like.—I hear my father and my uncle in the hall. Let's go out into the garden.

Fritz   No, they're gone. But I'll come back. Wait, Gussie, read just this: "Hermann and Thusnelda." The return of the Cheruscan.

Gussie *(reads)*

"Ah, there he comes, covered with sweat, with
Roman blood and the dust of battles. Never was
Hermann so beautiful! Never did such flames
Flash from his eyes.

Come, I tremble with desire, hand me the eagle
And thy blood-drenched sword! Come, breathe here and rest
In my embrace
From the too terrible battle."
Wait, let's go out to the summer-house.

Fritz   No, no, Papa's outside. Go on reading.

Gussie *(reads)*

"Rest here that I may wipe the sweat from thy brow
And from thy cheek the blood. Thy cheek's on fire!
Hermann, Hermann, never before
Has Thusnelda loved thee so!"

Oh, Fritz!

"Not even when first in the shade of the oak thou
Seizedst me impetuously in thy tawny arms!
Fleeing I stayed and saw upon thee
The mark of immortality."

Fritz   Gussie . . .

Gussie   Would you—no, I mustn't ask you.

Fritz   Ask for my life, for my last drop of blood.

Gussie   We were going to swear an oath together.

Fritz   Yes, let us. Magnificent. Let us kneel down here beside the bed. You raise your finger like this and I raise mine.—Tell me now, what shall I swear to you?

Gussie   That you'll always fly to the arms of your Gussie at holiday time and come back from the university in three years and make Gussie your wife, no matter what your father says.

Fritz   And what will you promise in return, my angelic . . .

(Kisses her)

Gussie   I swear that I will never, never marry anyone but you, not even if the Tsar of Russia himself should come and ask me.

Fritz   I swear a thousand oaths—

(The **Privy Councillor** *comes in: both jump up with loud screams)*

Privy Councillor   Make a clean breast of it. What have you two been up to? For shame, I thought I had a sensible son. You want to study law, and you can't even teach yourself how to behave? Come here, both of you. I choose to see no wrong. If you like to be with your cousin, Fritz, I have no objection, but now it's off to Halle with you to become a beacon to humanity. To make yourself worthy of her. And to learn the meaning of true freedom. Which distinguishes man from the animals. Stallions and mares have to do it, but human beings are free not to. Understand, son? *(* **Fritz** *nods shamefacedly)* Consequently I want you to take leave of each other at once, without constraint, pursuant to your better judgment, voluntarily. No letters to be exchanged, except unsealed. Promise? *(* **Fritz** *and* **Gussie** *nod)* Thoughts are free, but writing will be censored. Now, say good-bye in my presence—and refrain of your own free will from doing anything that cannot be done in the presence of witnesses. *(* **Fritz** *makes a bow to* **Gussie***, she curtsies to* **Fritz***)* Yes, children, reason is a hard taskmaster.

3

Mrs. von Berg's parlor.

Mrs. von Berg *at the spinet,* **Hasty** *stands beside her in a deferential attitude,* **Leopold** *stands catching flies.*

Mrs. von Berg   I've spoken to your father; he suggested a salary of three hundred ducats and we've settled on a hundred and fifty. In return I must ask you, Mr.—what was the name?—Mr. Hasty, to keep yourself in clean clothes and not to disgrace our house. As to your daily schedule, you will take your chocolate at seven with the young master and see to it that he eats properly; his health is delicate. School from eight to twelve. Afternoon: a walk in the public park and be sure never to let go of his hand, he's a very spirited boy. From six until dinner time you may sit by the bay window and pursue your own studies. In the evenings I shall expect you to entertain our guests. I trust you've got a tongue in your head. I expect you to show good taste and to be honorable as well. The last tutor had to be dismissed for stuffing his pockets with pears.—Do you skate? Could you teach Leopold?—And are you proficient in dancing?

Hasty   I hope your ladyship will be pleased with me. In Leipzig I never missed a ball, I must have had at least five dancing masters.

Mrs. von Berg   Indeed? Won't you show me? A figure from the minuet. Make me a *compliment*. Don't be nervous, Mr. . . . Hasty. Don't be nervous! My son hates books as it is; if his tutor turns out to be a simpleton, that will be the end of him. Just to give me an idea.—Well, well, not bad. Now, if you please, a *pas*.—You'll do. You'll get into the spirit once you've attended one of our soirées . . . Are you a musician?

Hasty   I play the violin and I can get by on the spinet.

Mrs. von Berg   Splendid! I've always had to sing for the dear children when they wanted to dance. That will be a great improvement.

Hasty Your ladyship, you overwhelm me. Is there any virtuoso in the whole world who would dare match his instrument against your ladyship's voice?

Mrs. von Berg Ha, ha, ha, you haven't even heard me yet. . . . Wait, do you know this minuet? *(She sings)*

Hasty Ah . . . Ah . . . You must forgive my enthusiasm. *(Kisses her hand)*

Mrs. von Berg I happen to be enrhumée, I'm sure I sound like a crow. Vous parlez français, sans doute?

Hasty Un peu, madame.

Mrs. von Berg Avez-vous déjà fait votre tour de France?

Hasty Non, madame . . . Oui, madame . . .

Mrs. von Berg Vous devez donc savoir, qu'en France on ne baise pas les mains, mon cher . . .

Maid *(enters)* Count Vermouth.

Mrs. von Berg One of my daughter's suitors . . .

*(**Count Vermouth** enters. After a few silent bows he sits down on the sofa)*

Count Vermouth Has your ladyship seen the new dancing master who just arrived from Dresden? A marchese from Florence, by the name of . . . In all my travels I have only seen two who might have been compared to him.

Mrs. von Berg Only two? You do arouse my curiosity. I know what exquisite taste Count Vermouth has.

Hasty Pintinello . . ., isn't it? I saw him dance at the theater in Leipzig. With no great distinction . . .

Count Vermouth He dances—on ne peut pas mieux.—As I was saying, your ladyship, in Petersburg I saw Beluzzi, who may have been better. But this one has a nimbleness in his feet, there's something so free, so divinely negligent about his stance, his arms, his turns—

Hasty   Last time he appeared at Koch's Theater, they booed him.

Mrs. von Berg   Be advised, my friend, that domestics do not intervene in conversations between persons of quality. Go to your room. Who asked your opinion?

(**Hasty** *goes toward the door)*

Count Vermouth   The new tutor, I presume?

Mrs. von Berg   Fresh from the university.—Off with you! Don't you hear you're being talked about? All the less reason to stand there listening.

(**Hasty** *goes out.* **Mrs. von Berg** *and* **Count Vermouth** *take their chocolate)*

Mrs. von Berg   It's intolerable that one can no longer get the right kind of person for one's money. Think of it. Five hundred ducats a year! Isn't it dreadful?

Count Vermouth   As I was saying, this Pintinello dances like a god. My passion for the dance has cost me some thirty thousand ducats, but I'd gladly pay twice as much if . . . *(He sighs)* How is Mademoiselle Gussie?

Mrs. von Berg   So, so, la la. She's been looking a bit pale these last few days.

4

At the skating rink.

Miss Cotton, **Miss Gosling**, *and* **Miss Miller**, *skating. To one side* **Hasty** *is giving* **Leopold** *a skating lesson.*

Miss Miller   I love listening to Pastor Detzer. Those passages in his sermons.

Miss Cotton   About sinning in secret!

Miss Miller   He's a thunderer, but only by allusion. *(Imitating him)* "You think no one sees it, no one is present, it can never come to light. But I say unto you, the devil lies in wait for those that eat of the fruit in secret."

Miss Gosling   There's the new one. He's doing figure eights!

(**Hasty** *skates past)*

Miss Miller   You mean him? He's the new tutor at Major Berg's. Don't stare!

Miss Cotton   He's wondering whether to greet us.

Miss Gosling   He's a fine, upstanding fellow.

Miss Miller   So they say.

Miss Cotton   Who says? Don't be oracular, Miller.

Miss Miller   All right, go over to him, let him greet you. I say no more.

Miss Gosling   Shall we skate past him or . . .

Miss Cotton   I'm for it. *(They skate past* **Hasty***)*

Miss Gosling *(nose in the air)*   Methinks there's a whiff of snow in the air.

Miss Cotton *(bursts out laughing)*   Why not ask your tutor when it's going to thaw?

Miss Miller   That's enough now. Don't be childish. I don't want him to join us. Before long he'll be as notorious as a yellow dog.

Miss Cotton   How so?

Miss Miller   Last Sunday he tried to make up to that Beck girl. But she didn't let him, and she's not choosy, far from it, the hussy! *(They whisper together)*

Miss Gosling   But what is he to do if no decent girl will go near him?

Miss Cotton   If one of us were seen with him, everyone would know it wasn't just for fun.

Miss Miller   When you go with Hans next door, no one says a word. He may be a whoremaster, but he's not a stranger. But a stranger—why on earth would you want to go with him? Just drinking a cup of chocolate with somebody like that would ruin your reputation in Insterburg for the rest of your life.

Miss Cotton   Here he comes.

(**Hasty**, *without* **Leopold**, *has followed them and now doffs his hat. They stand stiffly without acknowledging his salutation)*

Miss Miller   There. Now he knows where he stands.

Miss Cotton   'Tis a pity. There aren't many like him in these parts.

(**Hasty** *has angrily skated back to* **Leopold** *who pulls him to the ground by his clumsiness. The young ladies laugh)*

5

Hasty's room.

Hasty, *writing "agricola" on the blackboard*. **Leopold** *at his desk.*

Leopold *(reads, with incorrect stress)* —cola.

Hasty *(loathingly correcting the stress)* Agricola. *(The major walks in)*

The Major *(reads, with wrong stress)* Agricola. That's fine, that's the way I like it. Busy, busy—and if the rascal doesn't get it, Mr. Hasty, just hit him on the head with the book till he forgets how to get up. Look at him now—making faces again. So touchy when your father speaks to you. I'll make a man of you yet, if I have to whip you till your guts split open, you little sneak! And you, sir, keep after him. I demand it. This essay about the Hero-King that I've been reading is rather sloppy, I should say. The list of his enemies is incomplete. He defied not only the Saxons, the Austrians, the French, and the Russians, he also addressed the British in no uncertain terms. If you leave them out, it's not clear that he was on the brink of disaster—and then the glory doesn't come through.

Hasty I beg your pardon, major. I am at fault. I didn't paint the picture black enough.

Major Are you pulling my leg? Or shielding this little sneak?

—Let's see if he knows his Cornelio. Back straight, boy! Chin up! *(He straightens him)* Egad, get your head out of your shoulders or I'll break every bone in your body.

Hasty Beg your pardon, major, but he hardly knows any Latin.

Major What? Has the little rascal forgotten it all? The last tutor told me his Latin was perfect, perfect . . . I'll beat the stuffing out of you *(boxes him on the ear)*—and now you're doubled up again like a question mark. He simply never listens—go away, out of my sight, leave the room! I'll teach you to shake a leg. Out, I say! *(He stamps his foot,* **Leopold** *goes out. The major sits down on* **Leopold's** *chair. To* **Hasty***)* Sit down, Mr. Hasty. I wanted a word with you, that's why I sent the boy away. Sit down, all the way! Egad, you'll break the chair if you keep teetering on the edge . . . A chair is for sitting on. Don't you even know that after all your travels?—Now, listen. I regard you as a clean-cut, decent young man, Godfearing and obedient. Otherwise I wouldn't do what I'm doing for you. I promised you a hundred and forty ducats, did I not?

Hasty   A hundred and fifty, major.

Major   A hundred and forty.

Hasty   But with your gracious permission, major, her ladyship promised me a hundred and fifty ducats.

Major   Pshaw! What do women know? A hundred and forty ducats, that would come to three—let's see now—three times a hundred and forty, how much is that?

Hasty   Four hundred and twenty.

Major   Are you sure? Really, as much as that? Very well, to round it out, I'm setting your salary at four hundred Prussian thalers. Egad, that's more than I get from my land. Four hundred thalers.

Hasty   But a hundred and fifty ducats equal exactly four hundred and fifty thalers, and those were the terms I agreed to.

Major   Four hundred thalers, monsieur. In good conscience you really can't ask for more. Your predecessor was as happy as a lark with two hundred and fifty. And, upon my soul, he was a learned man. You have a long way to go before you can hold a candle to him. I'm only doing this out of friendship for your father, and for your own sake too, of course, if you work hard.—Now, listen: I have a daughter. She knows her Christianity inside out, but you see she's coming up for communion soon, and you know what our pastors are like, so I want you to do a bit of Christianity with her every morning.

Hasty   Yes, major.

Major   I'm paying you four hundred, and that includes religion for my daughter. An hour every morning; you'll go to her room.

Hasty   Yes, major.

Major   Properly dressed, if you please; not like the young swine we once had here who insisted on coming to table in his dressing-gown. None of that, eh? Do we understand each other?

Hasty   Major, would it be too bold of me to make a most humble request—in connection with your last proposition and in view of the fact that it's difficult for me to meet people and make friends in Insterburg and that living in a big city has become almost a habit with me, because city people are not so standoffish toward strangers . . .

Major   Come to the point!

Hasty   If once every three months, no more, I might be granted the use of a horse to ride to Königsberg for two or three days? . . .

Major   Hm. That might be considered.

Hasty *(jumps up and makes several bows)*   Oh, most gracious major—

Major   Anyhow it can't be until spring. It's an impossible ride in this winter weather.—Can you draw too?

Hasty   A little, your worship.—May I show you a few things?

Major *(inspecting them)*   Charming, charming!—Very nice. This one's quite good. You shall teach my daughter drawing too. My resources don't allow me to keep a whole battalion of sinfully expensive tutors on my payroll. But see here, Mr. Hasty, for heaven's sake, don't be hard on her. The little girl is different from the boy. She's my only solace. And she's been rather droopy lately, if you know what I mean. I see the child wasting away, losing her health, her beauty, and so on, and there's nothing I can do about it. It breaks my heart.—I'm telling you this because I want you to be gentle with her.

Act Two

6

Halle in Saxony.

Fritz von Berg, Squint *in shirtsleeves, sitting at the table.* **Buttress** *lying on the bed,* **Mrs. Blitz.**

Buttress Three months in Halle and I still haven't spoken to a girl!

Fritz After all we have certain ties back home.

Squint You've got a girl there?

Buttress Hic Rhodus, hic salta! The gentleman from Insterburg seems to be forgetting his physiology. A man doesn't go to bed with a girl because he loves her, he loves her because he wants to go to bed. You just wait till March!

Squint You must be getting the glooms without a girl. Why not move in with us, that will cheer you up. What's the sense in staying with that pastor? That's no place for you.

Fritz How much do you pay here?

Squint We pay—what do we pay, Buttress?

Buttress Nothing.

Squint Honest to goodness, brother, I don't know. Mrs. Blitz writes it all down, the rent, the coffee, the tobacco, whatever we ask for. We pay the bill once a year when our allowance comes.

Fritz Do you owe her much right now?

Squint We paid up last week.

Buttress His allowance is due.

Squint It will all be yours when it comes. If it ever does, Brother Buttress!

Fritz   You help each other out? That's very decent of you.

Squint   We go halves. I couldn't afford it myself. This time they've cleaned me out. I had to fork over my whole allowance, didn't I, Buttress? And my coat that I hocked last July is still at the pawnshop. Heaven knows when I'll be able to redeem it.

Fritz   How do you manage in the meantime?

Squint   Me?—I'm sick. This morning I received an invitation from Councillor Hamster's wife, and I went straight to bed.

Fritz   But how can you sit home all the time, in this lovely winter weather?

Buttress   Why not? He reads his favorite philosopher, Immanuel Kant.

Fritz   What does he do about his girl? We mustn't neglect our physiology.

Buttress   With girls it's not our coats that count, it's . . .

Squint   Our heads, Berg. In my case it doesn't really matter, because my girl doesn't know me.

Fritz   You mean it's all imagination?

Buttress   He dreams about her. And his bed sheet gets it all. What I say is: Tell me the girl you dreamed about and I'll tell you the girl you didn't sleep with. But now we've invited Insterburg for coffee. Where in blazes is the coffee? *(He stamps his foot)* Mrs. Blitz! Damn it, Mrs. Blitz, we paid you, didn't we?

*(***Mrs. Blitz*** comes in with a serving of coffee)*

Buttress   Where on earth have you been, ma? Mr. Squint has been waiting for an hour.

Mrs. Blitz *(to* **Squint***)*   What? You good-for-nothing tramp, you alley-cat! What are you hollering about? I'll take the coffee away this minute, I'll—

Buttress   Biscuits.

Mrs. Blitz   There aren't any. *(Referring to* **Squint***)* Do you think I have nothing else to do than give that bald-headed lout his biscuits every afternoon?

Buttress   Why him? I need biscuits! You know I never touch coffee without biscuits—what am I paying you for?

Mrs. Blitz *(hands him biscuits out of her apron)*   Now are you satisfied, you trombone? Mr. Buttress has a voice like a whole regiment. *(To* **Squint***)* Put your books away, they're no good anyway. All those beautiful, expensive books and you still don't know which way is up! Well, is the coffee all right? Is it? Tell me this minute or I'll tear the last hair out of your bald head.

Squint *(drinks)*   Incomparable! Really, I never had better in all my life.

Mrs. Blitz   You see, you young rascal. If Ma Blitz didn't take care of you and give you food and drink you'd starve by the wayside. Just look at him, Mr. von Berg, the way he goes around, without a coat to his name and his dressing-gown looking as if he'd been hanged in it and fallen off the gallows. This is the fourth year he's failed in philosophy. Why? Because he just can't get that stuff into his head. I feel sorry for his mother. She's a widow too. And now all the widows' and orphans' pensions have been reduced because of the glorious war. But you seem to be a nice, well-bred gentleman, I don't see how you can be friends with that lout. Well, I suppose it's coming from the same district that makes for a kind of family feeling. That's why I keep saying that Mr. von Berg should move in here. Then we might make something of you. That's what I say. *(Goes out)*

Squint   You mightn't think so, Berg, but she's really a good soul.

Fritz   What's this about your failing all the time, Squint?

Squint   I'm studying under Professor Wolffen. He detests Mr. Kant of Königsberg. And Kant is my man.

Buttress   Your Mr. Kant is a muddlehead. Listen to this—*(he picks up a book)*—"When peace is concluded after a war, it might not be amiss for a nation to let the thanksgiving celebrations be followed by a day of repentance, on which day the people, in the name of the state, would implore heaven's forgiveness for the great sin which mankind persists in committing—the utilization of the barbaric instrument that is war."—Imagine teaching stuff like that at a German university.

Fritz   It doesn't seem so wrong to me.

Buttress   Altogether wrong. Take the title: "Eternal Peace." If we stopped fighting old Blitz for one day, her coffee would be pure barley. For four years now our friend here has been reeling off Mr. Kant's absurdities in Wolffen's classroom. Naturally he flunks. Repeat after me: Mr. Kant is an idiot.

Fritz   Couldn't you say it just to get your degree?

Squint *(has carved something on the table top with his pocket knife)*   Here, read what I've carved.

Fritz   "No."

Squint   I'll say it a fifth time if I have to. And my "No" applies equally to every aspect of German servility. As long as Germans find their only happiness in obeying orders, they will go on serving, preferably as soldiers, and sacrificing themselves to some supreme leader.

Buttress   I call it strength of character. You appall me. Squint, the upright! Squint, the fearless!

Squint   Who is Wolffen anyway? He hates Kant's writing on freedom as the capon hates the cock's crow.

Fritz   I take it, Mr. Buttress, that you're not interested in these battles of minds.

Buttress   No. I'm going to be a tutor, I'll be shut up in some god-forsaken hole. In the meantime I've got to get in a lifetime of loving.

Fritz   This coffee tastes like barley.

Buttress   What's that? *(He tastes it)* So it does. With the biscuits I hadn't—*(Looks into the pot)* God damn it! *(Throws the coffee* *things out the window)* Barley coffee for five hundred guilders a year! It's an insult to Squint the upright!

Squint   Buttress, you're raving, my dear Buttress!

Mrs. Blitz *(rushes in)*   What's this? What in the devil is going on? *(To* **Squint***)* Are you raving, sir, or has the devil got into you?

Squint   Calm down, ma, I'll pay for it.

Mrs. Blitz *(with a horrible scream)*   Where are my coffee things? Heavens alive, out the window!—I'll scratch your eyes out!

Squint   There was a spider in the coffee; in my fright I threw it—is it my fault if the window was open?

Mrs. Blitz   I wish you'd choked on that spider. If I sold you and all your belongings, it wouldn't pay for my coffee set, you worthless dog! Rack and ruin is all I get from you. I'll have you prosecuted, I'll have you locked up.

Squint   Let it go for once, Mrs. Blitz. It won't happen again. Please, Mrs. Blitz.

Mrs. Blitz   And what's that on my table, you monster? Don't cover it up. He's been carving. Some obscenity. "No."

Squint   It's in reference to Immanuel Kant.

Mrs. Blitz   On my table! I'll call the constable. I—

Buttress   That'll do, Ma Blitz. Don't frighten Squint the fearless. The coffee was inadequate. Get thee hence, woman!

Mrs. Blitz *(intimidated)*   Well, I must say—throwing my coffee set out in the snow drifts . . . *(Goes out)*

Squint   I fear nothing but that woman. She is devoid of understanding.

Buttress   What would you do without Buttress? You'd pay through the nose and starve to death.

Fritz   I'm thinking of taking up philosophy myself.

Buttress   Mr. von Berg, I only hope philosophy can stand it. Everybody's taking up philosophy. I'll have to change now, I'm going to the new comedy tonight. They're playing *Minna von Barnhelm*. I have a weakness for actresses.

Fritz   Can I come along? It's a nice play. If only I could take my Gussie to see it.

Squint   I wish I could go too. But I haven't got a coat!—So her name is Gussie? I'll be glad to show you my girl. Now I really need a coat.

Buttress   You haven't got one, though. So I'll show him your girl. She's the daughter of Swandown the lutenist. She gets a free place in the standing room, thanks to her father. A footnote to the history of the war. Let's go, Berg. And mind you, don't neglect your physiology. *(**Buttress** and **Fritz** go out)*

7

Insterburg, in March. Gussie's room.

Gussie, **Hasty**.

Gussie   I believe that God created me.

Hasty   If only He hadn't! *(Helping her along)* And all . . .

Gussie   And all other creatures . . .

Hasty   And has given me . . .

Gussie   And has given me, and keeps my body and soul . . .

Hasty   Body too . . .

Gussie   Eyes, ears, and all my limbs, my reason and all my senses . . .

Hasty   And that . . .

Gussie   And that he bestows upon me each day clothing and shoes, meat and drink, house and home, wife and child, fields and cattle, and all my goods . . .

Hasty   And supplies in abundance all needs and . . .

Gussie   Necessities of my . . .

Hasty   Body . . .

Gussie   And life . . .

Hasty   And protects me . . .

Gussie   From all perils, and guards and defends me from all . . .

Hasty   Bodily harm . . .

Gussie   What's the matter with you?

Hasty   Without any merit or worthiness in me.

Gussie   Amen.

Hasty   Weren't we supposed to draw from nature? You had a good laugh, didn't you, at the thought of that silly tutor waiting for you at the mill. And how many more fine March mornings will there be? *(Hasty slaps his palm with the ruler)*

Gussie   Ha, ha, ha, my dear tutor. Really, I had no time.

Hasty   Don't be cruel.

Gussie   But what *is* the matter with you? I never saw you so deep in thought. And I've noticed that you don't eat.

Hasty   You have? Really? You're a paragon of compassion.

Gussie   Oh, Mr. Hasty—

Hasty   Would you care to draw from nature this afternoon?

Gussie *(touches his hand)*   Oh, dearest tutor, forgive me for disappointing you yesterday. It was quite impossible for me to come. I was so amazingly enrhumée.

Hasty   I suppose it's the same today. Perhaps we had better stop drawing from nature altogether. It doesn't amuse you any more.

Gussie *(half in tears)*   How can you say that, Mr. Hasty? It's the one thing I like to do.

Hasty   Or find yourself a drawing master. Because I believe I shall ask your father to remove the object of your aversion, your hatred, your cruelty, from your sight. I can see that instruction from me is becoming more and more repellent to you.

Gussie   Mr. Hasty—

Hasty   Let me be. I must find a way of putting an end to this miserable life, since death is denied me.

Gussie   Mr. Hasty—

Hasty   You're torturing me. *(He tears himself away and rushes out)*

Gussie   Oh, how sorry I feel for him!

8

Privy Councillor von Berg's ornamental garden.

Privy Councillor, Pastor Hasty, Hasty.

Privy Councillor   I'm sorry for him and even more sorry for you, reverend. But intercede with my brother on behalf of your son—no!

Pastor   But think of it, only three hundred thalers! Three hundred miserable thalers! The major promised him four hundred. Then, after the first six months, he paid him a hundred and forty. And now, at the beginning of the second half year, while more and more work is being piled on my son, he speaks of two hundred as his annual wage. That is unjust. Begging your pardon.

Privy Councillor   Why? A tutor! What does he do? Lolls about and gets paid for it. Wastes the best hours of the day with a young master who doesn't want to learn anything and has no need to. Spends the rest of his time bowing to madame's whims or studying the lines in the major's face. Eats when he's full and fasts when he's hungry, drinks punch when he wants to piss and plays cards when he has the colic. Without freedom life goes backward. Freedom is to man what water is to fish. A man who forfeits freedom poisons his noblest impulses, smothers the sweetest joys of life in their bloom, and murders himself.

Pastor   But—oh my! Those are the things a tutor must put up with. No one can do what he likes all the time, my son understands that, but—

Hasty   It was about the horse, your worship.

Privy Councillor   So much the worse if he puts up with it, so much the worse. Blast it, reverend, you didn't raise your son to be a common servant. And what is he now but a servant?

Pastor   But, your worship! Goodness gracious!

Hasty   Stick to the horse, father.

Pastor   Good God, sir! There have to be tutors in this world.

Privy Councillor   In my opinion tutors are not needed in this world. Worthless trash, that's what they are.

Pastor   Your worship, I didn't come here to be insulted. I was a tutor myself once. Good day.

Hasty   Father!

Pastor   I'm not a hot-headed man, but how can I listen to such absurdities? Tutors are useless, you say. I hear your son is studying at the university of Halle. Who taught him sense and good manners?

Privy Councillor   Why, I had the good judgment to send him to public school. And the few principles he needs to conduct himself as a scholar and a gentleman, he got from me. We talked it over at the dinner table.

Pastor   I see—*(takes out his watch)*—alas, your worship, I haven't time for prolonged disputations. I'm a plain pastor, a shepherd of souls, and when once in a blue moon I come all the way from Ingelshausen I have errands to do.

Hasty   Your worship, couldn't you . . .

Pastor   Forget it, son. Come along!

Hasty   The horse. Couldn't you put in a word with your brother? The worst of it is that I never get away from Insterburg. For six whole months—I'm coming, father—I haven't left . . . I was promised a horse to ride to Königsberg every three months!

Privy Councillor   What do you want to go to Königsberg for?

Hasty   Visit the libraries, your worship.

Privy Councillor   The brothels seems more likely. Been feeling your oats? *(The **Pastor** goes out)*

Hasty   Your worship . . . Something terrible may happen . . .
(Follows his father)

Privy Councillor *(calling after them)*   My brother hasn't enough
horses for his farm, and here you are, wanting one for your
dissipations.

Act Three

9

Halle.

Squint, **Fritz**.

Fritz   Look what she's sent me. She copied it out of the
Klopstock I gave her:
"Oh thou, to find thee I learned love,
Which has exalted my swelling heart
And now, in ever sweeter dreams,
Is wafting me to Paradise."

And this one:

"Great, O Mother Nature, is the glory of thy invention On every
field and meadow . . ."

And now she's drawing from nature. But what are you brooding
about?

Squint   A metaphysical problem, brother, a philosophical
problem. I'll dissect it for you. Let us assume that a woman's body
and senses are directed toward an object—a particular man—and
so likewise are her soul and mind—in other words that the thought
of her mind and the desires of her body coincide, then everything
is as it should be and without philosophical interest. Agreed?

Fritz   Agreed. But what are you driving at?

Squint   That it becomes of philosophical interest when she loves
one man A and desires, or gives her body to, another man, B.

Fritz   Is that an actual case?

Squint   A hypothetical case. But what is the solution? Is it
the body or the spirit that counts? You see that the problem is
philosophical.

Fritz   You mean: should we say that she loves A or that she's
sleeping with B?

Squint   Precisely: And what's the answer?

Fritz   I suppose you want me to say that the spirit counts. But why are you trembling? Has it anything to do with you?

Squint   Berg, there are times when I feel almost weary of philosophy. *(He bursts into tears)* Oh, Buttress, Buttress! Why did you have to take my place at the meeting with Miss Swandown? Why did you take her to the shooting gallery to put in a word for me? If only I had had a coat! It was for me, for me that you fondled her and got her with child!

Fritz   So that's it. Has Buttress confessed? Poor Squint.

Squint   Poor Squint! Doubly poor, for he lacks the wherewithal to help the unhappy creatures. Poor Squint, always flunking, ruined by his perseverance in antagonizing Professor Wolffen. So that now he is unable to do his duty.

Fritz   What duty?

Squint   Don't you see? The surgeon wants twenty thalers.

Fritz   But good Lord, not from you. It wasn't you that . . .

Squint   But it was done for my sake and no one else's. I'm the one she loves. If he hadn't gone in my stead, she'd never have . . . Her tear-drenched face haunts my dreams: when Buttress brought her to me, she took my hand and whispered: "We talked of nothing but you the whole time." How can I abandon her?

Fritz *(embraces him)*   Magnanimous Squint. I understand. What will you do? What shall we do? Yes, we. Am I not your friend? Your duty is my duty. Command my purse.

Squint   Fritz, oh Fritz, can it be true? Is the earth peopled by a race of philosophers?

Fritz *(gives him money)*   Quick, take it. I had it on me because I was going to Insterburg for the holidays.

Squint   Then I won't accept it. Your Gussie! I shouldn't wonder if she needed you badly, straining her eyes for the sight of you.

And no Fritz appears to embrace her. He sacrifices his travel money for Miss Swandown . . .

Fritz   Forget it, Squint, let's say that I am not overcome by emotion but guided by reason. My girl expects me for the holidays, she says so in her letter. *(Reads)* "In your Easter holidays you will find a bolder Juliet!" Frankly, Squint, those words frightened me. No, believe me, I shall do better not to go home this year. I'm not the chaste Joseph I used to be. I too have developed in this Halle of yours.

Squint   How can I ever repay you, brother?

Fritz   By teaching me more about your rebellious Immanuel Kant during the holidays. I'll have got the better of the bargain.

Squint   I will—though his rebellion is limited to the realm of ideas. *(The doorbell rings)*

*(***Squint*** *leaps to the window)*

Squint   Here they are!

(Enter **Buttress** *and* **Miss Swandown***)*

Buttress   Well, we're back. The Hunold woman wants thirty thalers.—Miss Swandown is indisposed. A glass of water would help.

Squint   My dear, adorable child, you find me—my friend here too, he knows all—overcome with tenderness.

Buttress   Tenderness is all very well, but how about some cash?

Squint   Everything will be all right. But first that glass of . . .

Buttress   All right, you say? You'll cough up? You've got money? Don't run away! You've got it?

Squint   Miss Swandown, I won't keep you in suspense another minute. I shall do my duty without reserve or delay.

Buttress   Twenty thalers?

Squint *(counts out the money on the table)*   Rendered liquid by the profound influences of philosophy!—Twenty thalers!

Miss Swandown   You're very kind, Mr. Squint, seeing you didn't get anything out of it for yourself.

Buttress   Don't say that. But you've done a good deed. Kiss her, honest Squint, you deserve it.

Squint *(with a deep bow)*   Your humble servant, Miss Swandown.

*(**Buttress** and **Miss Swandown** leave)*

Squint   There must be something good in Buttress, or he wouldn't be so crude. He's eating his heart out. *(Returns the purse to **Fritz**)* You have acted on the principles of Immanuel Kant, Brother Berg. *(Looks for something in a book)* "So act that you can will the maxim of your action to become universal law." Writings on Morals, Part One, Fundamental Principles of the Metaphysics of Morals, Chapter Two.

10

Insterburg, Gussie's room.

Gussie *and* **Hasty***, in bed.*

Hasty Your father's been to blame from the start. Why did he have to scrimp on a teacher for you? Then in the same burst of avarice he reduced my pay. And now he wants to cut me down to a hundred and twenty thalers for next year. I shall have to quit.

Gussie But what will I do then?

Hasty Get them to send you to my father's rectory in Ingelshausen.

Gussie My uncle would never let my father send me to your father's house.

Hasty Confound his beastly nobleman's pride!

Gussie *(takes his hand)* Don't be angry, Hermann! *(Kisses him)* Oh, dear teacher, how does your pupil look? As pale as death?

Hasty As fit as a fiddle. Now, I need your advice.—Yesterday your brother slapped my face again.

Gussie You must bear it for my sake.

Hasty Then maybe I needn't regret my failure to control myself. I suppose I'm being fed too well for a slave. The celery, the turkey, the chocolate—how can a body so pampered help succumbing to sin?

Gussie Faugh! Is that the language of love? It was fate, my dear teacher.

Hasty *(as she continues to raise his hand intermittently to her lips)* Let me think . . . *(Sits up in thought)*

Gussie *(in the pantomime described)* Oh, Romeo, if this were thy hand!—Why hast thou abandoned me, ignoble Romeo? Dost not thou know that thy Juliet is dying for love of thee—hated, despised, rejected by all the world, by her whole family? *(Presses his hands to her eyes)* Cruel Romeo!

Hasty *(looks up)*   What are you raving about?

Gussie   It's a soliloquy from a tragedy that I like to recite when I'm upset.

Hasty   I don't care for tragedies.

Gussie   Oh, Halle, worlds away!—Maybe I shouldn't blame it all on you. Your father forbade you to write to me—but love surmounts all obstacles.—You've forgotten me . . .

Hasty *(suspiciously)*   Even in bed I have to decipher everything you say.

Gussie *(kisses **Hasty***'s *hands with abandon)*   Oh, heavenly Romeo!

Hasty *(crossly)*   I'm not Romeo, I'm Hasty, if you don't mind. (**Gussie** *turns to the wall, weeps.* **Hasty** *remorsefully kisses her hand and gazes at her for a while)* What happened to Abelard could happen to me. I seem to recall that you've read the romance, Miss von Berg. Would you recapitulate what you know of Abelard and Héloïse?

Gussie   When it became known that Abelard and Héloïse had secretly married, her uncle, Monsignor Fulbert, canon in Paris, had him seized and deprived of his manhood.

Hasty   I hear footsteps in the hall!

Gussie   My father—Oh God—you've stayed three-quarters of an hour too long. (**Hasty** *hurries away)* Oh Fritz, my love!

11

Mrs. von Berg's parlor. August.

Mrs. von Berg, **Count Vermouth**, *the* **Major**.

Mrs. von Berg *(at the spinet)* Ah, dear count, so many talents are doomed to hide their light. They find no scope in this narrow world. Oh, to be a singer! With the candles shining on me, perhaps even the footlights. It's denied us, our station doesn't permit of such liberties. Do you like this one? *(She sings a languishing air)*

Count Superb!

Mrs. von Berg Flatterer! I'm not in good voice today. This one . . . *(Sings another)*

Count A natural talent. Some have it, some don't. And if they don't, nothing helps.

Mrs. von Berg Believe me, it's training and hard work as well. Sheer will power.

Count I wish Miss Gussie had inherited such genius. Where is she?

Mrs. von Berg Ah, yes. *(Hums)* I see I'm keeping you. Is there anything more ghastly than an artist—however talented—who doesn't know when to stop? Just one more, may I? *(She sings)*

Count Charming. But, madame, am I never to see Miss Gussie again? Has she been well since the hunt the other day?

Mrs. von Berg Thank you for asking. She had a toothache last night, that's why she must keep out of sight today. And your stomach, count, after the oysters?

Count Oh, I'm used to it.—I must say that Miss Gussie has developed magnificently—blossomed out like a rose since last fall.

Mrs. von Berg These modern young girls . . . they change from day to day. Those sentimental books they read give them consumptive shadows under their eyes; but then a little drawing from nature brings back the bloom . . . I always say that proper health begins at forty.

Count   And health is the true source of beauty. *(Mrs. von Berg plays the spinet again)* If Miss Gussie were to come down, I should like to take a stroll in the garden with her. I can't ask you, dear madame, because of the fontanelle on your leg.

Mrs. von Berg   If only certain people were as concerned about my well-being . . . Since the war the major has had only one interest, his damnable farm. All day he's in the fields, and when he comes home he sits there like a stick.—Oh, dear count . . . A few days ago he took it into his head to sleep with me again, but in the middle of the night he jumped out of bed and started . . . ha, ha, ha, I shouldn't be telling you this, but you know how ridiculous my husband can be . . .

Count   Started . . .?

Mrs. von Berg   Poring over his account books. And groaning something dreadful. I could hear him down in his study. But his foolishness is nothing to me. Let him turn Quaker or Pietist if he wants to. It won't make him any uglier or more amiable in my eyes than he is now. *(She looks roguishly at the count)*

Count *(chucks her under the chin)*   What wicked things you say!
—But where is Gussie? I'd really like to take a stroll with her.

Mrs. von Berg   Hush! Here comes the major . . . Why don't you go out with him, count? He'll show you his hothouse.

Count   Fancy that!—But it's your daughter I want to see.

Mrs. von Berg   I dare say she's not dressed yet. The girl is insufferably lazy.

*(**Major von Berg** comes in, his coat bespattered with mud)*

Mrs. von Berg *(plays Handel's* Largo *on the spinet)*   Well, husband? What have you been up to now? I don't lay eyes on you from morning to night, and now look at him, count. Doesn't

he look exactly like Terence's Self-Tormentor in Madame
Dacier's edition? I do believe you've been carting manure,
Major von Berg.

Count   It's true, major, you've never looked so horrible. I'd never
have expected farming to go to your head like this.

Mrs. von Berg   Avarice, pure, execrable avarice. He thinks we'll
starve if he doesn't go burrowing in the muck like a mole. He
spades, he plows, he harrows. If you must turn peasant, couldn't
you find me another husband first?

Major   Zounds, woman, you forget that wars have to be paid for.
But it's true, I never see you ladies any more. Where's Gussie?

Mrs. von Berg *(still playing)*   Gussie! Gussie! Gussie! That's all
I ever hear! The mole, there's nothing else left in his head. Only
Gussie. His Gussie, always his Gussie.

Major   Yes, and you keep her away from me because you're
jealous of her.

Mrs. von Berg   How the man speaks to me! As if I kept her
locked up. I'm sick of it. She should come down when there are
visitors. *(Goes out)*

Count   I am embarrassed, Major von Berg. Permit me to take my
leave.

Major   Just hang around.

Count *(after a pause)*   Speaking of economics, have you seen a
gazette recently? There's been quite a stir about the king founding
a bank in Berlin on the French . . .

Major   Berlin!

Count   Don't say anything against Berlin. We are definitely
making progress, all Europe is watching us. First the ballet and
now the bank, à la bonne heure!

Major   A bank! It's a rotten business, count, take it from me. We
can perish like Sodom without any need for banks and such-like
novelties, indeed we can.

Count   But think of the ballet. Between you and me, major, I've always felt that a brief excursion to Sodom now and then is good for the blood.

(Mrs. von Berg rushes in)

Mrs. von Berg   Help! Help! Husband—we're lost—the family! The family!

Count   Madame, what on earth . . .?

Mrs. von Berg   The family—the infamy—oh, I can't go on. *(Falls on a chair)* Your daughter!

Major *(goes toward her)*   What's happened? Out with it! Speak up or I'll wring your neck!

Mrs. von Berg   Your daughter—the tutor—hurry! *(She faints)*

Major   Has he made a whore of her? *(Shakes her)* Is this what I burrow in the earth for? What's the good of collapsing? This is no time to collapse. Made a whore of her? Is that it? All right. Let them turn the whole world into a whore, with ballets, banks and spinets. And you, Berg, take up your pitchfork. *(To his wife)* Come on, you're a whore too! Watch me! *(Tears the doors open)* I'll set an example. That's what God has preserved me for to this day—to make an example of my wife and children.—Burn it all, burn, burn, burn! *(Carries his wife, who is still in a faint, off the stage)*

Count   Parbleu!

12

Village school near Insterburg.

Wenceslas, **Hasty**, **Lisa**.

Wenceslas *(sitting at a table, spectacles on his nose, ruling sheets of paper)*　Who's there? What is it?

Hasty *(who has rushed in breathlessly)*　Help! Save me! Dear schoolmaster! They'll kill me!

Wenceslas　Who are you?

Hasty　The tutor at the castle. Major von Berg is after me with all his servants. He wants to shoot me.

Wenceslas　God forbid!—Just sit down quietly.—You'll be safe with me, here's my hand on it. Tell me all about it while I write out these exercises.

Hasty　Let me collect my wits first.

Wenceslas　All right. Get your breath. But tell me this—tutor—*(puts his ruler aside, takes off his spectacles and looks at him for a while)* what on earth can have made your master so angry at you?—Would you kindly pass me the sand box?—You see, I have to rule out the lines for my boys, because nothing is harder for them to learn than to write, straight, to write evenly.—The main thing, I always say, is to write not elegantly or quickly, but straight, because handwriting has its effect on everything else, morals, thought, in short everything, my dear Mr. Tutor. A man who can't write straight, I always say, can't act straight either.—Where were we? Would you put these sheets over there?

Hasty *(who has done so)*　May I ask you for a glass of water?

Wenceslas　Water?—You shall have beer. But—yes, what were we talking about?

Hasty　About writing straight.

Wenceslas   No, about the major. Ha, ha, ha. Now let's see. Do you know, Mr.—what is your name?

Hasty   Name—my name is—Midge.

Wenceslas   Mr. Midge.—Forgotten it, hadn't you? Strange how our thoughts can give us the slip.

Hasty   May I open the window? Oh God, there's Count Vermouth.

Wenceslas *(severely)*   I need the sand box again, if you please. *(***Hasty***, shaking, hands it to him.* **Count Vermouth** *comes in with some servants brandishing pistols.* **Hasty** *dashes into another room)*

Wenceslas   Nervi corrupti!

Count   I'm looking for a certain Hasty. A student with a brown braided coat.

Wenceslas   Sir, in our village it is customary to remove your hat when addressing the master of the house.

Count   The matter is urgent.—Is he here or not?

Wenceslas   What can the man have done that you should be looking for him with pistols? *(The* **Count** *is about to enter the side room;* **Wenceslas** *blocks the door)* Stop, sir. That is my room. Leave my house this instant, sir, or I shall pull the bell cord and half a dozen sturdy peasants will beat you to a pulp, pistols and all! If you behave like a bandit, you shall be treated like a bandit, sir! The way out is the same as the way in, but in case you've forgotten—*(He takes him by the hand and leads him out the door)*

Hasty *(peeps out of the side room)*   Happy man! Enviable man! I admire you . . .

Wenceslas   Now sit down and have some knackwurst and potato salad after your fright. Lisa! *(***Lisa** *comes in)* Bring Mr. Midge a pitcher of beer. *(***Lisa** *goes out)* She's my ward.—While you're waiting for your beer, you may as well earn your supper and help me to rule these sheets. It will improve your morals. *(***Hasty** *sits down to do the ruling)* Who was that rude fellow who wanted you?

Hasty   A certain Count Vermouth, the major's son-in-law to be.
He's jealous of me, because the young lady can't stand him.
That's all.

Wenceslas   But what's the sense in it? What does the young lady
want of you, monsieur ladykiller? Better get that sort of thing out
of your head and stick to knackwurst. Go ahead, eat! But don't
make grease spots. And draw the lines evenly, if you please.—I
dare say there's a difference between the major's table and
mine. But when schoolmaster Wenceslas eats his supper, a clear
conscience helps him digest it, and when Mr. Midge was eating
pheasant with mushroom sauce, his conscience prompted moral
qualms that drove every bite he swallowed back into his throat.

Hasty   Very true, but that's not all. You don't realize how
fortunate you are. Have you never seen a slave in a braided coat?
Oh, freedom, golden freedom!

Wenceslas *(motioning him back to his ruling)*   That churl wanting
to break into my room without so much as a by-your-leave! Just
let him come back, with all the majors in the world! Zooks! Now
you've finished your knackwurst, and the beer isn't here yet.—
Won't you smoke a pipe with me?

Hasty   I'll be glad to try. I've never smoked in all my life.

Wenceslas   Of course not, you fine gentlemen, it discolors your
teeth, is that it? I started smoking when I was barely weaned.
Exchanged my mother's nipple for the mouthpiece. Ha, ha, ha.
Smoke is good for foul air, and for foul cravings as well. Here's
my program: on rising, cold water and a pipe, school till eleven,
then another pipe until the soup's ready. My Lisa's soup is as good
as any French chef's. Then another pipe, then school until four.
Then I write out exercises until supper time. Most usually I have a
cold supper, sausage with salad, a piece of cheese, or whatever the
good Lord may provide. And then a last pipe before bed.

Hasty   God help me, I've come to a smoking den!

Wenceslas   And with all that I'm fat and healthy and cheerful,
and I haven't even begun to think about death.

Hasty   You earn good wages, I presume?

Wenceslas   Wages? That's a stupid question, Mr. Midge.
Forgive me, did you say wages? My wages are from God, a good
conscience. Have you any idea what it means to be a schoolmaster?
(He struts awesomely to and fro) I shape human beings in my
own image. German heroes! Healthy minds in healthy bodies, not
French monkeys. On the one hand, as it were, mental giants, on
the other hand, good subjects. And what does that mean? Does it
mean subjected giants or gigantic subjects? It means: reach for the
stars, but God help you if you kick against the pricks!—Won't you
have a smoke? Go on, have a pipe. Conquer yourself—no, not you,
the German hero—if you would conquer the world. I'll take the
cane to you if ever you . . . Oh dear *(he snatches the goose quill
which* **Hasty** *has been picking his teeth with)* what are you doing!
A grown man! Haven't you even learned to take care of your own
body? Picking the teeth is suicide. There. If something gets stuck
in your teeth *(takes water and rinses his mouth)* this is the thing to
do, if you want to have sound teeth. Go on, do it! *(**Hasty** does so)*

Hasty   He's going to schoolmaster me to death.

Wenceslas   You don't care for the pipe? Just spend a few days with
old Wenceslas, and I'll wager this hand will shape you so you won't
know yourself.—I assume, young man, that without a reference
your tutoring days are over. And you can't hope for a position in a
village school because the king, now that his war is over, is putting
in his disabled sergeants as schoolmasters. Yes, that's how it is.
You're probably weak in Latin, but as a tutor you must have a likely
handwriting. You could lend me a hand in the evening. It's time I
began to spare my eyes. You could write out the exercises for my
boys. But you will have to work hard, I can tell you that!

Hasty   The humiliation!

(The **Major**, *the* **Privy Councillor** *and* **Count Vermouth** *enter
with servants)*

Major *(with pistol drawn)*   The deuce . . .! There he sits like a
rabbit in the cabbage patch. *(He shoots and hits* **Hasty** *in the arm.*
Hasty *tumbles from his chair)*

Privy Councillor *(has vainly tried to restrain the* **Major***)*
Brother! *(Pushes him angrily)* Now you've done it, you fool!

Major   Hey! Are you dead? Speak to me! Where is my
daughter?

Wenceslas   Your lordships! Is the last judgment on its way? *(He
reaches for the bread knife)* I'll teach you to assault a Christian in
his own house!

Hasty   Don't, I implore you!—It's the major. I deserved it for
what I did to his daughter.

Privy Councillor   Worthy schoolmaster, is there a surgeon
in the village? He's wounded in the arm. I want to have him
cared for.

Wenceslas   Cared for! You bandits! Do you think you can shoot
people down because you're rich enough to have them cared for?
He's my assistant. He's been in my house exactly one year. A quiet,
peaceful, industrious man. And you barge in and shoot down my
assistant before my very eyes!—I'll be avenged!

Privy Councillor *(motions a servant to bandage* **Hasty***)*   What's
the good of lying, my dear man? We know the whole story. *(To
the* **Major***)* I shall send Fritz to Italy, he must never hear of this.—
He'll bleed to death. Run for a surgeon!

Wenceslas   Nonsense! If you make wounds, you can heal them
yourselves, you bandits! I'm not running to get the surgeon, I'm
running to ring the tocsin. *(Leaves)*

(Servants put **Hasty** *back on his chair.* **Hasty** *comes to)*

Major   And now to you! If it takes red-hot pincers: Where is my
daughter?

Hasty   If your worship had only granted me a horse to ride to
Königsberg, as you agreed to!

Major   What's the horse got to do with it, you scoundrel?
Where's my daughter?

Hasty   I don't know.

Major   You don't know? *(Draws another pistol)*

Lisa *(comes in with the beer)*   Don't shoot! Poor Mr. Midge!
(Throws herself in front of **Hasty***)*

Privy Councillor *(snatches the pistol from the* **Major** *and fires
it out the window)*   Do we have to put you in chains, you . . .
(To **Hasty***)* Answer us!

Hasty   I haven't seen her since I escaped from your house. I
swear to God before whose judgment seat I may soon stand.

Major *(about to assault him again)*   Another charge of powder
wasted! Swine, I wish it had gone straight through your body,
seeing we can't get any sense out of you!

Privy Councillor   Berg!

Lisa   Are you Major von Berg? Oh, your grace, there was a lady
at the inn, she ordered coffee. As she was paying she said to the
landlord, "If my father comes asking for me, don't tell him I went
to the pond by the elm trees. Tell him, good people, that I send him
my love."

Major   To the pond? To the pond! To the pond! *(Goes out)*

Privy Councillor   The man can't swim.

Count   If only I could!

Privy Councillor   I mustn't lose sight of him. *(Throws* **Hasty** *a
purse)* Use it to get well and remember you wounded my brother a
good deal worse than he wounded you.

(The **Privy Councillor** *and the* **Count** *leave quickly)*

Hasty *(with bitterness)*   What's the horse got to do with it! My
vita sexualis can go hang!

13

Near Insterburg.

Gussie *at the edge of a pond surrounded by bushes.* **Major**, **Privy Councillor**, **Count Vermouth**, *servants*.

Gussie   Nobody's coming. Must I die here? Fritz, oh Fritz! Why didn't you come home for the holidays? Then I was still . . . Clouds are passing over the moon. No one will ever find me.

Major *(from a distance)*   Gussie! Gussie!

(Gussie *puts down her shoes and wades into the pond, her face turned back)*

Major *(appears, followed by the* **Privy Councillor** *and* **Count Vermouth***)*   Heigh-ho! Somebody's gone into the pond—there, look, it's a woman. After her, Berg! I'll save her or go to hell. *(Wades after her)*

Privy Councillor   God Almighty, he's going to drown too.

Count   Let's hope it's shallow.

Privy Councillor   To the other side! *(To the servants who are carrying long poles)* After them, fellows!—I think he's grabbed her . . . There . . . back there, by the bushes.—Don't you see? He's wading along the shore. God preserve our wits! On the other hand, can one help being moved by human . . .

(The servants probe the pond with their poles)

Major *(backstage)*   Help! This way! It's my daughter!

Privy Councillor *(to* **Count Vermouth***)*   The tragedy of it all! The tragedy! The poor man; for all we know, he's saving two lives.

Count *(to* **Privy Councillor***)*   I feel so helpless. Those crude fellows *(pointing at the servants)* are better at it.

Major   Odds bobs, zookers and bodkins! Give me a pole! The plague . . .

Privy Councillor *(kicks a servant in the behind, making him fall in the water)*   Get out there, you rascal. Don't just think of yourself!

*(**Major Berg** carries **Gussie** on to the stage)*

Major   There! *(Puts her down and kneels down beside her)* Gussie! Why did you do it?—If only you had breathed a word to me. I'd have bought the swine a title, then you could have crawled into bed with him to your heart's content.—For God's sake, do something. She's only fainted.

Privy Councillor   I wish I knew where that goddam surgeon was.

Gussie *(in a feeble voice)*   Father!

Major   What do you want?

Gussie   Your forgiveness.

Major   Forgiveness be damned, you spoiled brat.—No, don't collapse. I forgive you—and you forgive me. I've put a bullet through that scoundrel's brains.

Privy Councillor   I think we'd better carry her.

Major   Let her be! What concern is she of yours? Worry about your own flesh and blood at home! *(Carrying her in his arms)* There, my girl—really, I ought to walk back into the pond with you *(swings her toward the pond)*—but maybe we shouldn't try to swim until we've learned how.—*(Presses her to his heart)* Godless hussy! *(Carries her out)*

Interlude

To the accompaniment of a music box which misses a few notes, the stage revolves to show the passing of a year and how our characters are spending it. Winter: Fritz von Berg strolling under lemon trees in Italy; spring: Squint marrying his Caroline in Halle; summer: Gussie sewing diapers in Insterburg; autumn: Hasty still writing out exercises at the village school.

Act Four

14

Village school.

a)

Stormy night in November. **Hasty** *is correcting papers.* **Lisa** *comes in.*

Lisa   I've frightened you. I only wanted to ask you if you— needed anything, Mr. Midge.

Hasty   Me? Need anything? Why, I never do. What should a wretch like me need? I have everything. And I'll be going to bed soon.

Lisa   I shouldn't have disturbed you. I'll go, Mr. Midge. You're always writing.

Hasty   Heavenly apparition!

Lisa   I thought the lamp might be smoking.

Hasty   I see.

Lisa   But it isn't.

Hasty   You're cold, my child. Let me put my scarf on you. Now go.

Lisa   A pot of coffee, Mr. Midge, to keep you warm?

Hasty   No. Yes, make some coffee. *(Lisa goes out)* Have I gone mad? What has happened to me? This innocent creature. This angel of kindness. And I, in these few minutes assailed by contemptible instincts! Whence this hurricane rising from a mere nothing? She shows an innocent solicitude—is my lamp smoking?—I requite her with carnal lust! Under my benefactor's own roof, in sight of the objects—this chair, this bed—with which he has surrounded me in his loving kindness. That is how I repay the man who taught me what it is to teach. Monster that I am, shall I never mend my ways?

Is it to start all over again? Haven't I already . . .? My head's in a whirl. Ravished. Fished out of the pond by a despairing father, pushed in by me. And now, is it to be Lisa? Never! Never! *(He bars the door)* Midge, get back to work! *(He works again)* Write straight, live straight. What am I coming to with this hurricane in my heart? How long does it take to make a pot of coffee? Grade papers, correct spelling, a bodice is made for concealment, stop trying to look through it. Scoundrel without a reference, without a future. *(A knocking at the door)* Don't move! The latch will hold. Angel, turn back! *(He opens the door)*

Lisa *(comes in with a pot)*   Why do you lock yourself in? No evil-doer would come this way at night. Here's your hot drink.

Hasty   Thank you. *(Takes it from her and pushes her out)* That's done. *(Sinks onto a chair)* Go in peace, Lisa, you're saved. *(Another knock)* The latch! *(**Lisa** comes in)*

Lisa   I'm back again, Mr. Midge. Do you mind?

Hasty   Yes, I mind.

Lisa   I've come because you said there would be no catechism tomorrow—because you—that's why I've come—you said—I've come to ask if there'd be catechism tomorrow.

Hasty   Oh!—Those cheeks, angels of heaven! See how they burn with the fire of innocence, then condemn me if you can —Lisa, why are your hands trembling? Why are your lips so pale and your cheeks so red? What do you want?

Lisa   To know if there'll be catechism tomorrow.

Hasty   Come, Lisa, sit down.—Who puts your hair up when you go to church? *(Makes her sit down on a chair beside him)*

Lisa *(wants to get up)*   Excuse me. My cap must be crooked. There was such a wind when I went to the kitchen.

Hasty *(takes both her hands in his)*   Oh you are—How old are you, Lisa? Have you ever—what was I saying—have you ever been courted?

Lisa *(gaily)* Oh yes, and Greta at the Sheepshead Inn was envious. "How can he be so interested in that stupid girl?" that's what she used to say. And then I knew an officer too, before you came here.

Hasty An officer?

Lisa Oh, yes. And most distinguished, with three stripes on his arm. But I was too young, my mother wouldn't let me have him.

Hasty And then?

Lisa Because of the life soldiers lead, always moving about, and in the end they have nothing.

Hasty And me? What have I got?

Lisa But you're in trouble, Mr. Midge.

Hasty Would you—would you really—*(slaps his hand with the ruler)*

Lisa Oh yes, with all my heart. *(**Hasty** throws himself on her and kisses her hand. **Lisa** takes it away)* Oh, you mustn't. My hand is all black from the stove.—Shame on you, what are you doing? You know, I always thought I wanted a clergyman. Even as a child I liked educated gentlemen, they're so gentle and polite, not slam-bang like soldiers, though in a way I like them too, I can't deny it, because of their gay coats. If clergymen wore such gay coats, really it would be the end of me.

Hasty *(leaps at her and seizes her)* Oh, Lisa! You don't know how unhappy I am.

Lisa For shame, sir, what are you doing?

Hasty Once more. And then never never again! *(Kisses her)*

Lisa No, no, no . . .

Wenceslas *(bursting in)* What's going on? Is this the attention you owe to your flock? A rabid wolf in sheep's clothing? Seducing the innocence it's your duty to protect!

Hasty Master Wenceslas!

Wenceslas   Not a word! You've shown your true colors. Leave my house, you seducer!

Lisa *(kneels before* **Wenceslas***)*   Dear godfather, he's done me no wrong.

Wenceslas   He's done you more wrong than if he were your worst enemy. He has seduced your innocent mind.

Hasty   I confess my guilt.—But how could anyone resist such charms? Unless you tear the heart out of my body . . .

Wenceslas   Do you mean to go on seducing innocent girls? Is that your plan?

Hasty   No, no. God is my witness, if I sealed these innocent lips with my kisses, it was only to stop them from inciting me to far greater crimes with the magic of their speech.

Wenceslas   And how would you support her, you pauper?

Hasty   That's what I told her.

Wenceslas   Do you think that will keep her fed? You, get up, innocent victim. You're a disgrace to your profession. Where are your references? Where can you show your face? Out of my sight, you reprobate! *(Takes the copy books away)* You will corrupt my good children no longer. Tomorrow morning you leave my house! *(He drags* **Lisa** *out)*

b)

Hasty*, at the open window.*

Hasty   There I go again!—Roar, ye night winds! And you, unworthy fiend, out into the storm with you! Did you think you could shape little children in your own image? Behold your face in this window glass, and tremble! Does a nurseryman pull up his seedlings? Guardian, where is your guardian? All your life you've been an outcast. After what you have done will you go to him and say: Unfortunate man—unfortunate because you trusted me—give me the hand of your ward whom I have abused. You can ruin her, but can you feed her? And yet, is it so reprehensible to be human?

Carnal or not, are such impulses unnatural? A curse on nature for
not making me a stone in the presence of her creation! What's
wrong with me? A stablehand is allowed to be a man. Not I. Shall
I pluck out the eye that offends me? Shall I stand up to you, spirit
of creation, and say: I reject your purposes? The face you gave me
is disfigured, I myself disfigured it because it did not fit. And say to
the wind, when you come back tomorrow, I shall be here no longer.
So be it. I must. I will set an example to make you tremble! *(Tears
off his coat)*

c)

Hasty, *in bed.* **Wenceslas** *comes in.*

Wenceslas   Holy God! What is it now? Why have you called me
away from my work? This room!—It looks like a battlefield. Why
are you still in bed? I've told you to leave my house. You should
have been on your way to Heidebühl long ago.

Hasty   I believe I'm on my way somewhere else.

Wenceslas   Why those fearful glances? They make my blood
run cold. Frigidus per ossa—What is it?—As if you had killed a
man.—Why are you making such a face?

Hasty   Master Wenceslas, I don't know if I've done right.—
I've castrated myself.

Wenceslas   What?—Emasculated?—But that's . . .

Hasty   I hope you'll grant me a few more days under your
desecrated roof.

Wenceslas   Say no more. You shouldn't have done it. Why,
you're a second Origen! Let me embrace you, young man, oh
precious chosen vessel. A deed like this can make you a beacon of
the school system, a shining star of pedagogy. I congratulate you.
Wenceslas salutes you with a Jubilate and Evoë—my spiritual son!

Hasty   And yet, dear schoolmaster, I regret it.

Wenceslas   What, regret it? Not for one moment, my dear
colleague! Will you darken your noble deed with foolish regrets

and sully it with sinful tears? Do I see tears welling up in your eyes? Swallow your tears and intone a joyful song: I have freed myself from vanity, and need but wings to fly. Are you going to behave like Lot's wife, looking back at Sodom when you've already reached the peace and safety of Zoar? No, no. I prefer our blessed Doctor Luther: Whatsoever rises is for our dear Lord, whatsoever descends is for Beelzebub.

Hasty   I'm afraid my motives were of a different kind . . . Repentance . . . Concern for my livelihood.

Wenceslas   That's taken care of now. Who can be better fitted for a teaching career than you? Now you have the highest qualifications of them all. Haven't you destroyed your rebellious spirit, subordinated everything to duty? No longer will your private life deflect you from shaping human beings in your own image. What more could you have done? As to your future, don't let it worry you. You've done your duty. Your prospects are of the brightest.

Hasty   I've written a letter to Major von Berg. It's there on the table, beside the knife. Would you read it and send it off if you approve?

Wenceslas (reads)   ". . . And so, by my own decision—a cruel one, I can assure you—I have eliminated any danger that may have arisen from my manhood . . . Between Scylla and Charybdis, between nature and my profession, I have chosen my profession, and venture to hope that you will most mercifully vouchsafe me a testimonial permitting me the exercise of that profession. All the more so, most gracious lord, as I shall endeavor must dutifully, in all other respects as well—I repeat, in all respects—to do and to teach exactly what is desired of me, for my own good and that of my fellow men . . . I am, most gracious etc. . . . . Your most humble and obedient servant . . . Postscript: Furthermore I promise always to teach the martyrdom of our Hero-King without omissions."

Hasty   Is it still storming?

Wenceslas   No.

Hasty   No.

Wenceslas   Everything's covered with snow.

Hasty   Safely tucked away.

Wenceslas   Great-hearted sufferer, any teaching position, I assure you, any teaching position in the district is open to you.

Act Five

15

Halle, winter.

Squint *in slippers, smoking his pipe.* **Fritz** *in traveling habit.*

Squint Let me quote what Immanuel Kant has to say: "Matrimony (matrimonium) is a contract between two persons providing for the lifelong use of each other's sexual organs." And here: "Hence, though based on the supposition of pleasure through the mutual use of the sexual attributes, that is to say, the sexual organs, the marriage contract is no arbitrary contract, but one made necessary by the laws of mankind, that is, if man and woman desire to derive pleasure from one another in accordance with their sexual attributes, they must of necessity marry, and this necessity follows from the laws prescribed by pure reason." You see.

Fritz I thought you'd given up Kant.

Squint Only in public. How else could I have obtained a teaching position? And without a position, how could I have married my Caroline—you haven't met her yet, the dear. And as you see right here, I had to.

Fritz So your favorite philosopher has proved to you that you had to give him up, and you've given him up by following his precepts. What a world!

Squint An antinomy, that's all. He could have resolved it in a twinkling.

Fritz What was the subject of your thesis?

Squint I was clever, Berg. I left philosophy well alone. "War, Father of all Things"—still, I managed to slip in a suitably obscure phrase implying that the paternity is not always demonstr . . .

Fritz Speaking of Caroline, what became of Miss Swandown?

Squint   She sank lower and lower.—Caroline is very different. She was made for marriage. Incidentally, she's the rector's daughter.

Fritz   So the two of you live here beside the stove, happy.—Do you ever see Buttress?

Squint   I find that I've rather cooled toward him, Berg. Now that we're both schoolmasters. There's some good in him, but . . . Caroline finds him attractive and I've forbidden her to see him. Women have got to be kept in hand, Berg . . . How was Italy?

Fritz   Divine. It's made a man of me.

Squint   Half a year in Italy!—There's a father after Rousseau's own heart.

Fritz   I don't know, Squint. Sending me to Italy like that and giving me that curious piece of advice, not to write to Gussie—I was too excited about the trip to wonder why. Down there, among the lemons and olives, I began to worry, but consoled myself with the thought that he was putting our love to the test. And then in Pompeii a sudden fear sent me flying back—covering as much as eighty miles a day. Here in Halle the same emotions made me interrupt my headlong journey. It seemed to me that perhaps I had better not return too quickly to my beloved Insterburg. And here I find this letter, I'm afraid to open it. My hand shakes every time I try to break the seal. You break it, brother, and read it to me. *(Throws himself into an easy chair)*

Squint   Who is it from? Is it your father's hand?

Fritz   No, it's from a certain Soapbubble. A neighbor.

Squint *(reads)*   "In view of the friendship I have had the honor of enjoying in your father's house—" *(Stops)* the fellow's spelling is insane! *(Reads on)* "—I feel obliged, considering that having long been out of communication with our delightful Insterburg you can hardly be aware of the incident concerning the tutor who has been put out of your esteemed uncle's house . . . *(Stops)*

Fritz   Go on!

Squint   ". . . for ravishing your cousin, whereby her spirits were so shaken that she jumped into a pond, which calamity threw your family into the utmost . . ." *(Fritz faints)* Berg! What's the matter? *(Pours lavender water on him)* Berg, Berg, speak to me!—Damn letter, if only I hadn't . . . It must be a fabrication—Berg! Berg!

Fritz   Leave me alone. It will pass.

Squint   Shall I get someone to bleed you?

Fritz   Faugh! Don't be so French! Read it again.

Squint   Certainly not.—It's a disgusting, malicious letter, I'll . . . *(Tears it up)*

Fritz   Ravished—drowned—*(Strikes his forehead)* My fault. All my fault.

Squint   You're out of your mind.—Is it your fault if she lets that tutor seduce her?

Fritz   Squint, I swore to go back home for the holidays! And I went to Italy. Damn picturesqueness! She despaired of me. Grief. You know her melancholy bent. Loneliness, disappointed love. It's as plain as day: I'm a villain. I'm to blame for her death. *(Throws himself back into the chair and covers his face)*

Squint   Pure imagination!—It's not true, it wasn't like that at all. *(Stamps his foot)* 'Sblood! How can you be stupid enough to believe all this, she can't have been all that innocent. Women! We know what they are. They don't want it, but they do it. When they itch, they look for someone to scratch them.

Fritz   I beg of you, Squint, she is no more.

Squint   Berg, look me in the eye and tell me women are not as I say.

*(**Caroline Squint** comes in)*

Squint   Here she is, my beloved wife. This is Berg, an old school friend.

Caroline   I've heard about you. You're a companion. of Squint's rebellious youth.

Squint   Yes, indeed. Make him some coffee, he needs it. He's just had a terrible letter from home.

Caroline   Oh, it can't be so terrible that a good cup of coffee . . .

Fritz   Please, don't trouble. I must hurry home. My friends, my place is at a grave-side. *(Leaves)*

Squint   Sad.—But it's no concern of ours. Come, Caroline, come and warm yourself by the stove.

16

Insterburg, Mrs. von Berg's parlor.

Mrs. von Berg, *the* **Major**, **Gussie**, **Privy Councillor**, **Leopold**. *A baby in a cradle.*

Privy Councillor   My dear sister-in-law, my dear brother, dear Gussie, dear Leopold! Let us drain a glass of grog in honor of St. Nicholas and the first snow that decks the streets so gloriously. But first it seems fitting to ask the servants in to share the hot spirits with us and admire the landscape so beautifully transformed.

Gussie   I'll call them. *(Leaves)*

Privy Councillor   Oh yes, there's a letter for you from Hasty, in which he proclaims his contrition and swears to change for the better. He encloses a medical certificate to the effect that he, with his own hands, has so corrected his God-given corpus as never again to be a menace to his female pupils.

Mrs. von Berg   Disgusting!

Privy Councillor   I agree, sister-in-law. And he asks you, dear Berg, in exchange for his certificate to give him a reference that will enable him to pursue his profession.

Major *(laughs)*   He ought to be all right now.

Privy Councillor   Say what you will, he's a man of principle.

Major   A rare disciplinarian!

Privy Councillor   A true pedagogue, by the grace of God.

Major   He shall have his reference.

Privy Councillor   Thou shalt not muzzle the ox—ha, ha, ha, the ox—when he treadeth out the corn. *(They laugh uproariously)*

Mrs. von Berg   Disgusting!—

(**Maid** *comes hurrying in*)

Maid   Sir! Madame! The young master. *(She sobs)*

Major   Which young master?

Maid   Master Fritz!

Privy Councillor   Fritz back from Italy?

Maid   He's downstairs. What a thing to happen! They'll put it in the gazette. He comes in in his traveling clothes. He sees Miss Gussie. Stares at her like she's a ghost. Cries out: "Gussie, you're not dead? My own Gussie, not dead?" She's in his arms. "Oh Fritz, you've come?" And all is love. But then: "Poor me, don't touch me, I'm your Gussie no longer." And he, you should have heard his voice . . . "Oh yes, you are!"—and she: "No, you don't know." And him so loud they could hear him in the kitchen: "I know all about it, and all I want is—to beg your forgiveness. My Gussie!" Oh, here they come.

Mrs. von Berg   Gussie and Fritz?

Major   'Ods bodkins!

(**Fritz** *and* **Gussie** *enter*)

Fritz   Father! And my second parents! I'll fight for my Gussie to the last drop of blood.

Major   You mean you want to marry her? In spite of everything?

Fritz   In spite? No, not in spite, because of. Let me tell you, Gussie, how a strange experience in Halle opened my eyes to the glory and weakness of your sex. A young lady, to make a long story short, was in love, passionately in love, with a splendid fellow, conscientious, devoted to philosophy, though perhaps somewhat unworldly. Nevertheless—perhaps, my friends, I should say for that very reason—she gave herself to a man of far less consequence. But while in his arms she never for one moment— she told me so herself—thought of anyone but the man she truly loved. Yes, dear father, you may not understand it but I do, and now more than ever; in reality, in spirit, she gave herself to her true beloved. Nothing, my friends, would have happened to Gussie, if oddly enough because of my involvement in this very affair, I hadn't stayed away during the holidays.

Privy Councillor   Or if a certain young scoundrel had been given a horse.

Gussie   Oh, Fritz, that's how it was, just like that.

Fritz   Papa, I thought she was a ghost when I saw her on the stairs. But she's real.

Privy Councillor   Always stick to reality—isn't that what I've always taught you?—unless it contradicts the inner image.

Major   Come! *(Takes **Fritz** to the sofa)* Are you a philosopher?

Mrs. von Berg *(referring to the baby)*   Do you recognize this?

Privy Councillor   My son, having justified the cause, you must not shrink back from the effect. Having climbed a tall tree, will you climb down again to retrieve your hat that has blown away? What have you studied logic for?

Fritz *(kisses the baby and hands it to **Gussie**)*   Now the child is mine too. I love it already. It has your angelic features.

Gussie   Fritz!

Privy Councillor   You're right!

Mrs. von Berg   Oh dear!

(The servants appear)

Major   Don't gape, you people, don't gossip, don't judge. Join a happy father in a drink. To the young couple!

Leopold   And to the little one!

Mrs. von Berg   Leopold!

Privy Councillor   And to the first snow!

Mrs. von Berg   Berg, I suspect you would like me to contribute something in the popular vein. *(She sings at the spinet while all others drink)*

Oh silent winter snow
That cloaks the earth below.
Men sit and idly gaze
Upon the snow-clad days.
And in the barn the silent cows
Hark to the silence as they drowse.

17

Village schoolhouse.

Wenceslas, **Hasty**, *both dressed in black.* **Lisa**.

Wenceslas What did you think of my sermon, colleague? Did you find it edifying?

Hasty Oh yes. Yes indeed. *(Sighs)*

Wenceslas *(takes off his wig and puts on a nightcap)* That won't do.—Tell me what part of it your heart most favored. Listen to me—sit down—I have something to say to you: in church just now I saw something that troubled me. Your gaze as you sat there was so shifty that, to tell you the truth, I felt ashamed of you in the eyes of the congregation. Several times I nearly lost the thread of my discourse. I said to myself: Is this the young warrior who fought so bravely and triumphed, as it were, in the hardest of battles?—And I must confess, you made me angry. I saw the direction of your thoughts, I saw it only too clearly. Toward the center door, down by the organ. Did you for one moment hear what I was saying? Can you repeat one word of my sermon? It was all for your benefit, you know, designed to fit your particular case.—Oh, oh, oh!

Hasty I was delighted with your idea that the rebirth of our souls can be likened to the raising of flax and hemp, and that just as hemp must be freed of its husks by vigorous beating, so our spirits must be prepared for heaven by suffering, hardship, and the eradication of all sensuality.

Wenceslas It was designed to fit your case, my friend.

Hasty However, I can't deny that your list of the devils expelled from heaven and the whole story about the revolt and about Lucifer regarding himself as the most beautiful strikes me as sheer superstition—our age has outgrown all that!

Wenceslas   That's why this rational world of ours will go to
the devil. Take the devil away from the peasant and he'll turn
against his master like a devil, so proving that devils exist. But
enough of that—what was I saying? Yes. Just tell me, whom
were you looking at all through my sermon? Don't deny it. You
certainly were not looking at me, or you'd have had to squint
disgracefully.

Hasty   I don't know what you mean.

Wenceslas   You were looking down toward the girls who get their
catechism from you.—My dear friend, can a pinch of the old Adam
have lingered in your heart? I ask you—the very thought makes
my hair stand on end—what will become of you if you yield to the
old evil promptings when you lack the means of satisfying them?
(Embraces him) I beg you, my dear son, by these tears that I'm
shedding out of the most heartfelt concern for you: Don't go back
to the fleshpots of Egypt when you have come so close to Canaan!
How can you keep leering at my ward as if you were dying of
thirst? As if she would content herself with a capon.

*(**Lisa** steps forward)*

Lisa   Oh yes, dear godfather, I'm perfectly content with him.

Hasty   Woe is me!

Lisa   Believe me, dear godfather, I shall never let him go.

Wenceslas   Oh.—The devil—Lisa, you don't understand—Lisa, I
can't tell you why, but you can't marry him, it's impossible.

Lisa   Why is it impossible, dear godfather? You always said I
might marry a clergyman some day.

Wenceslas   The devil take you, he can't—God forgive me my
sins, can't you take my word for it?

Hasty   Maybe that's not what she's asking for.—Lisa, I cannot
sleep with you.

Lisa   But you can wake with me. If only we can be together in the
daytime and smile at each other and kiss each other's hands now

and then, because, by God, I'm fond of you. God knows, I'm fond of you.

Hasty   You see, Master Wenceslas! All she wants of me is love. Does a happy marriage really require the satisfaction of animal lusts?

Wenceslas   Heaven help us.—Be fruitful and multiply, says the Good Book. Where there is marriage there must be children.

Lisa   No, dear godfather. I swear that I want no children as long as I live. You've got plenty of ducks and chickens for me to feed every day: must I feed children too?

Hasty *(kisses her)*   My divine Lisa!

Wenceslas *(pries them apart)*   I declare! What's this? Before my very eyes?—All right, go ahead, crawl into bed, it's better to marry than to burn.—But, Mr. Midge, it's all over between you and me. The high hopes I set in you as a paragon without compare—the expectations aroused by your heroism—merciful heavens! To me you're just another hybrid, neither fish nor flesh. *(Goes out)*

Hasty   And I feel sure their lordships at Insterburg will help me— in my present state—to find a good position that will enable me to support my wife.

Epilogue

Spoken by the actor who played the tutor.

That's the conclusion of our play
We hope it's brought you some dismay.
You've seen the sorry state of mind
To which the Germans were resigned
A hundred years and even ten years ago—
It still prevails in many parts, you know.
You've seen a tutor of the German school
Led to his calvary of ridicule—
Poor devil whom they so browbeat
He can't distinguish hands from feet.
Enacting a parable bigger than life
He finally has recourse to the knife
Exterminating his virility
Which only brought him misery.
For when he did as nature meant
The higher-ups were not content
And when he crawled as best he could
They cut down on his livelihood.
His sterling value they proclaimed
Only when he was cut and maimed.
His backbone broken, he would do
His duty by breaking his pupils' too.
The German schoolmaster, if one reflects
Is the product and origin of our defects.
Pupils and teachers of this century:
Consider his servility
And let it teach you to be free.

Coriolanus

William Shakespeare

Adaptation

Translator: Ralph Manheim

Characters

Caius Marcius, later called **Coriolanus**, a Roman general
Volumnia, his mother
Virgilia, his wife
Young Marcius, his son
Menenius Agrippa, his friend
Cominius, Titus Lartius, generals against the Volscians
Sicinius Velutus, Junius Brutus, tribunes of the people
Valeria, friend of Virgilia
Virgilia's Servant
The Man with the Child
Tullus Aufidius, general of the Volscians
One of Aufidius' Captains
Romans and Volscians: (Senators, Consuls, Aediles, Patricians, Citizens—Plebeians—Officers, Soldiers, A Herald, Attendants, Servants, Messengers)

Act One

1

Rome. A public square.

Enter a group of rebellious **Citizens** *to whom clubs, knives, and other weapons are distributed; among them a man with a child; the man is carrying a large bundle.*

First Citizen   Before we go any further, let me speak.

Citizens   Speak, but be brief.

First Citizen   Are all of you resolved to die rather than starve?

Citizens   Resolved. Resolved.

First Citizen   Are you prepared to stand fast until the senate agrees that it's us citizens who decide the price of bread?

Citizens   Yes. Yes.

First Citizen   And the price of olives?

Citizens   Yes.

First Citizen   Caius Marcius will meet us with force of arms. Will you run away or will you fight?

Citizens   We'll knock him dead.—He's the people's main enemy. No need to ask us that.

First Citizen   Because if you're not prepared to see this thing through, you can count me out. Why have you brought that sack? And the child?

The Man with the Child   I want to see how far you get. If you fail, I'm going to leave Rome with those people from the third district.

First Citizen   Regardless of the fact that the plain where they're going to settle is as arid as stone?

The Man with the Child   Regardless. We'll have water, fresh air and a grave. What more is there for us plebeians in Rome? At least we won't have to fight rich men's wars. *(To the child)* Will you be good, Tertius, if there's no goat's milk for you? *(The child nods)*

First Citizen   You see, that's the kind of people we've got. He fears Caius Marcius more than the wilds of the Allegi Mountains. Aren't you a Roman citizen?

The Man with the Child   Yes, but a poor one. They call us plebeians the poor citizens, but they call the patricians the good ones. The unnecessary food the good citizens stuff into their bellies could save us from starvation. Even if they gave us their leftovers, we'd be saved. But they don't even think that much of us. Their food tastes better when they see us starving. *(To the child)* Tertius, tell him you don't want to be a citizen of such a city.

(The child shakes his bead)

First Citizen   Then make off quickly, you cowardly dog, but leave the child here; we'll fight and make a better Rome for Tertius.

Citizens   What's that shouting?—The sixth district has risen.— And we hang around here, squabbling among ourselves. To the Capitol! Who's this?

*(Enter **Menenius Agrippa**)*

First Citizen   It's Menenius Agrippa, the senator and silver-tongued orator.

Citizens   Not the worst of them.—He has a weakness for the people.

Menenius
My dear fellow citizens, what's this? Where are you going With bats and clubs? What's wrong, I pray you?

First Citizen   Our business is not unknown to the senate. They've been hearing rumors of it for a fortnight. Your Caius Marcius says our smell takes his breath away. He says poor pleaders have strong breaths; he'll see that we have strong fists too.

Menenius
Citizens, my good friends and honest neighbors
Are you determined to destroy yourselves?

First Citizen   We can't do that, sir. We're destroyed already.

Menenius
I tell you, friends, the senate has for you
Most charitable care. For your grievances—
The rising cost of food—you may as well
Strike at the heavens with your staves as lift them
Against the senate; you see, the soaring prices
Come from the gods and not from man. Alas
Your misery is driving you to greater
Misery. You remind me of a babe that
Bites at the empty breast of its unhappy
Mother. You curse the senate as an enemy
And yet it cares for you.

First Citizen   Cares for us! A likely story! They've never cared for us. Leave us to starve when their storehouses are crammed full of grain. Issue decrees against usury that benefit no one but the usurers! Every day they repeal another good law against the rich and every day they grind out another cruel regulation to chain the poor. If the wars don't eat us up, they will. That's all the love they bear us.

Menenius
Either you must
Confess yourselves wondrous malicious
Or be accused of folly. I shall tell you
A pretty tale. It may be you have heard it
But it's appropriate. Well, will you listen?

First Citizen   It's hardly a time for stories. But I for my part have long wished to learn how to make a pretty speech. And that can be learned from you, Agrippa. Fire away!

Menenius
There was a time when all the body's members
Rebelled against the belly, thus accused it:
That only like a gulf it did remain

In the midst of the body, idle and inactive
Yet storing up the victuals, never bearing
Equal labor with the rest, whereas the other organs
Did see and hear, devise, instruct, walk, feel
And, mutually participating, minister
Unto the appetite and affection common
To the whole body. The belly answered . . .

First Citizen
Well, sir, what was the belly's answer?

Menenius
Sir, I shall tell you. With a kind of smile
That came not from the heart, a dismal smile—
For you see, I can make the belly smile
As well as speak—it tauntingly replied
To the discontented members, the mutinous parts
That envied its receipts . . .

First Citizen

What did he say?

The lazy belly, sink and cesspit of
The body? What did he say?

Menenius
What? No—how!
That is the crux of the matter.

First Citizen
No, tell us what your gluttonous belly said.
What could he say?

Menenius

You soon shall hear.

First Citizen
With you "soon" means "tomorrow."

Menenius
Your most grave belly was deliberate
Not rash like his accusers, and thus answered:
"It is true, my incorporate friends," he said
"That I am the first to receive the general food

You live upon, and this is necessary
Because I am the storehouse and the shop
Of the whole body. But if you will remember
I send it through the rivers of your blood
And through the corridors and pantries of the body.
The strongest sinews and the finest veins
From me receive their proper sustenance.
And though, my friends, you may not all at once"—
This is the belly speaking, mind you . . .

First Citizen
Stop, sir.

Menenius
                           "Though you may not see all at once
What I deliver out to each of you
Still, my account books show that I
Distribute to you all the finest flour
Retaining only the bran." Well then, what do
You say to that?

(Enter, unnoticed except by **Menenius**, **Caius Marcius** *escorted by armed men)*

First Citizen
An answer of sorts. But now the moral?

Menenius
The senators of Rome are this good belly.
You are the mutinous members. Think!
That's all you have to do. Think, think, think, think!
Then you will fathom how the worthy fathers
Intent upon the common weal, distribute
The public bounty to each citizen.
Whatever you receive is given you
By them alone. Well, what do you think now?
You, the great toe of this assembly?

First Citizen
I the great toe? Why the great toe?

Menenius
Because you, the lowest, basest, poorest
Of all this rabble, take the lead.
You scoundrel, you infectious rotten apple, you
Self-seeking bandit—very well, swing your clubs!
Rome will make war upon its rats. Once and
For all it will . . . Hail, noble Marcius!

Marcius
Thanks. What's the matter? Got the itch again?
Scratching your old scabs?

First Citizen
                                              From you we can
Always expect a gracious word.

Marcius
                                                        You curs
That like nor peace nor war. War frightens you
Peace makes you insolent. Anyone who trusts you
Finds hares when he wants lions, geese when he looks
For foxes. You hate the great because they are great.
To depend upon you is to swim with fins
Of lead and hew down oaks with rushes. Hanging's
The only hope! You've got the appetite
Of a sick man who devours what makes him sicker.
You curse the senate who with the help of the gods
Maintain some little order. If they didn't
You'd feed upon each other.

Menenius
                                              They're demanding
The right to set the price of grain. They say
The granaries are overflowing.

Marcius
                                              They say! Hang 'em!
They sit by the fire and presume to know
What's happening on the Capitol, what there is
And what there isn't. Waste grain on them!

If only the senate dropped its moderation
For which I have a very different name—
They say there's grain!—they'd get their answer
From my sword. And with my lance I'd measure
Not grain but their corpses by the bushel
In the streets of Rome.

Menenius
Let be. I've won these fellows over, stopped them
With a fairy tale. Though to be sure, it was not
The sword of my voice but rather the voice of your sword
That toppled them. But what of the other troop?

Marcius
Dissolved. I broke it up. Hang 'em! Damnation!
They shouted they were hungry, bellowed slogans
That hunger breaks stone walls, that dogs must eat
That bread is made for mouths, that the gods don't send
Fruit for the rich alone. And more such nonsense.
And when I fell upon them, while retreating
They shouted: "Then we'll emigrate." And I
Wished them a pleasant journey.

(A **Messenger** *enters)*

Messenger   Where's Caius Marcius?

Marcius
Here. What's the matter?

(The **Messenger** *whispers in his ear)*

Marcius
                                    Menenius, in the forum
They're tossing up their caps into the air
As if they wished to hang them on the moon:
The senate has allowed them their demand.

Menenius
Allowed them what?

Marcius
                                    Two tribunes

To represent the wisdom of the rabble.
The one is Junius Brutus, then Sicinius
And heaven knows who else. I'd sooner
Have seen the rabble tear the city's roofs off
Than granted that. They'll be
More insolent than ever. Soon they'll threaten
Revolt for every pound of olives.

Menenius

It is strange.

*(A **Citizen** comes running)*

Second Citizen   Long live Junius Brutus! The senate has granted
all our demands! Two tribunes appointed! With the right to attend
all sessions and veto decisions!

Citizens
Hurrah for Junius Brutus!

Second Citizen

And Sicinius Velutus!

Marcius
Go home, you fragments!

Menenius

The worthy fathers!

Marcius
And the newly baked
Tribunes are coming too. With faces
Such as you'd cut down from the gallows!

*(Enter **Cominius**, **Titus Lartius** and other **Senators**, **Brutus**, and
Sicinius)*

Citizens
Long live Sicinius!—And Junius Brutus!

Marcius
Most worthy fathers, I've heard ugly news
And I see an ugly sight . . .

First Senator

Noble Marcius

The Volscians are in arms, encouraged by
Reports of shortage and rebellion here.

Cominius
War!

Marcius
I'm glad to hear it.
That ought to help us here in Rome
To use our surplus that is growing moldy.

First Senator
Tullus Aufidius is leading them.

Marcius

                                        I know him.

Comenius
You've fought together.

Marcius

                            An enemy like him

Makes the whole war worth fighting.

First Senator
You will fight under Cominius.

Cominius

                            As you once promised.

Marcius
Agreed. And Titus, what of you?
Stiff in the joints? Will you stay home?

Lartius

                                Never, Marcius.
I'll lean upon one crutch and fight with the other
Before I miss this business.

First Senator

                                    To the Capitol!

Lartius
Lead on, Cominius.

Cominius

After you.

Lartius

You first.

Marcius
After you.

First Senator

Citizens, go home.

Marcius

No, let them follow.
The Volscians have much grain; take these rats with you
To gnaw their garners. Worshipful mutineers
Your courage can now prove itself. Do follow!

(All go out except for the tribunes and **Citizens***)*

Brutus
Follow him, friends. Inscribe your names in the lists!
Be valiant soldiers for a better Rome.
As for the struggle waged within its walls
Over grain, olives, and the remission of debt
We will keep watch while you are in the field.

Citizens
The Volscians are in arms!—War!

(The **Citizens** *go out)*

Brutus
We'll have to. Did you see Marcius' eye
When we, the tribunes of the people, approached him?

Sicinius
I heard him speak. A man like him's a greater
Danger to Rome than to the Volscians.

Brutus
I don't believe that. The valor of his arm
Outweighs his vices and makes good their harm.

(Both go out)

2

Rome. The house of Caius Marcius.

Volumnia *and* **Virgilia** *are standing on the balcony looking after the departing* **Soldiers**. *Martial music.*

Volumnia   If my son were my husband, I should rejoice more in an absence that won him honor than in the fondest embraces of his bed. When he was still tender of body, the only son of my womb, when the comeliness of his youth attracted every eye, when a king might have entreated me all day before I'd have let him out of my sight for an hour, I bade him seek danger where he was likely to find fame. I sent him to a cruel war. He came back crowned with oak leaves. I tell you, daughter, I didn't leap more for joy at first hearing he was a man-child than on the day when he first proved himself to be a man.

Virgilia   But if he had died in the battle, madam, what then?

Volumnia   I tell you sincerely that if I had a dozen sons, none less dear to me than your Marcius and mine, I would rather see eleven die on the battlefield than one wallow in peace.

Virgilia   Heaven protect my husband from Aufidius.

(Enter a **Serving Woman***)*

Volumnia
Virgilia, I seem to hear your husband's drum.
I see him slaughter this Aufidius and go
His way like a reaper after a day's work.
Upon his neck, as it says in the *Iliad*
He sets his bloody foot.

Virgilia
Oh no, no blood!

Serving Woman   Valeria.

(Enter **Valeria**. *The servant woman goes out)*

Valeria   How is your little son?

Virgilia   Thank you, my dear; he is well, my dear.

Volumnia   He would rather look at swords and hear a drum than listen to his teacher.

Valeria   Every inch his father. A darling child. On Wednesday I watched him for half an hour on end. What a resolute little boy! I saw him run after a gilded butterfly. And when he caught it, he let it go again. And over and over again he caught it and let it go. Then he fell down. And perhaps because his fall made him angry, or something else, he suddenly set his teeth and tore it apart. My word, he tore it into little pieces!

Volumnia   One of his father's rages!

Virgilia   A lively lad, madam.

Valeria   You must play grass widow with me this afternoon.

Virgilia   No, my dear. I have no wish to go out.

Valeria   No wish to go out?

Volumnia   She shall. She shall.

Virgilia   No, by your leave, I won't set foot over the threshold until my lord returns from the wars.

Valeria   Faugh! It's not reasonable to shut yourself up like that. She wants to be another Penelope. But they say all the yarn she spun in Ulysses' absence only filled Ithaca with moths. Leave her alone; in her present mood she would only spoil a pleasant evening.

(All go out)

3*

a)

Before Corioli.

Enter with drums and banners **Marcius**, **Titus Lartius**, **Captains**, *and* **Soldiers**. *To them a messenger.*

Marcius
A messenger. I wager they have met.

Lartius
My horse to yours they haven't.

Marcius

Done.

Lartius

Agreed.

Marcius
Say, has our general met the enemy?

Messenger
They are in view, but haven't spoken yet.

---

* For scene 3, Act One of his adaptation Brecht intended to combine
Shakespeare's scenes 4–10 into a big battle scene. He planned to write this
new scene 3 in the course of production because he thought it necessary to
study the positions and movements of the actors in rehearsal. He did not
live to do this work. Consequently Shakespeare's scenes 4 to 10 are given
here in Dorothea Tieck's translation as scenes 3 a–g. (Note to German
edition.)

In the English of these scenes Shakespeare's text is somewhat modified
to accord with the style employed in the translation of the rest of the play.
(R.M.)

Lartius
Then the good horse is mine.

Marcius

I'll buy him from you.

Lartius
No, I won't sell or give him, I'll lend him to you For fifty years.—
Call on the city to yield.

Marcius

How far away are the armies?

Lartius

Less than a mile and a half.

Marcius
Then we shall hear their trumpets, and they ours.
Now Mars, I pray you, help us to work quickly
And then with smoking swords we shall march off
To aid our embattled friends! Come, blow your blast!

*(They sound a parley. Enter two **Senators**, with others on the walls)*

Tullus Aufidius, is he within your walls?

First Senator
No, nor any man who fears you less than he,
Which is less than little. *(Drum afar off)* Hear that!

Our drums

Are calling out our youth. We'll break the walls
Rather than let them close us in. Our gates
Which still seem shut, are only pinned with rushes;
They'll open of themselves. *(Alarum far off)* Listen out there.
That is Aufidius. Hear what he is doing
To your divided army.

Marcius

Ha, they're at it!

Lartius
Their noise will keep us informed. Ladders, ho!

Marcius
They're not afraid. They're coming out to meet us.
Now put your shields before your hearts and fight
With hearts more staunch than shields. Advance, brave Titus!
I never expected to see them despise us so;
It makes me sweat with rage. Come on, men. If
Any of you retreat, I'll take him for a Volscian,
And he shall feel my sword.

(Alarum. The **Romans** *are beaten back to their trenches. Re-enter* **Marcius***, cursing)*

Marcius
All the contagion of the south light on you,
You shame of Rome! You herd of . . .! Boils and plagues
Plaster you over till you can be smelled
Further than seen, and one infect another
Against the wind a mile! You souls of geese,
That bear the shapes of men, how can you run
From slaves that apes could beat! Pluto and hell!
Wounded behind! Backs red and faces pale
With flight and palsied fear! Turn back and charge,
Or, by the fires of heaven, I'll leave the foe
And make my war on you. Look to it; come on!
If you'll stand fast, we'll beat them to their wives
As they have beaten us to our trenches.

(Another alarum. The **Volscians** *fly, and* **Marcius** *follows them to the gates)*

The gates are open; now show yourselves good soldiers.
Fortune has widened them for the pursuers,
Not for the fugitives. Watch me, and follow.

(He enters the gate)

First Soldier
The man's insane; not I.

Second Soldier

Nor I. *(***Marcius** *is shut in)*

First Soldier
Look, they have shut him in. *(Alarum continues)*

All
That's the end of him, I warrant.

*(Re-enter **Titus Lartius**)*

Lartius   What has become of Marcius?

All

Killed, sir, doubtless.

First Soldier
Pursuing the fugitives at their very heels,
With them he enters; whereupon they
Suddenly slam the gates. He's left alone
To fight the entire city.

Lartius

O noble soldier!

Who sensibly outdares his senseless sword,
And when it bends stands straight. You are lost, Marcius;
The purest diamond, as big as you are,
Would not be so rich a jewel. You were a soldier
After Cato's heart, not fierce and terrible
Only in blows; but with your grim looks and
The thunder-like percussion of your sounds,
You made your enemies shake, as if the world
Were feverish and trembling.

*(Re-enter **Marcius**, bleeding, assailed by the enemy)*

First Soldier

Look, sir.

Lartius

O, it's Marcius!

Let's carry him off, or stay and die with him.

(They fight and all enter the city)

b)

Corioli. A street.

Enter certain **Romans** *with loot.*

First Roman   I'll carry this to Rome.

Second Roman   And I this.

Third Roman   A plague on it! I took this for silver.

(They go out. Alarum continues still far off)

(Enter **Marcius** *and* **Titus Lartius** *with a trumpeter)*

Marcius
Look at these thieves whose hours are no more worth to them
Than a cracked drachma! Cushions, leaden spoons,
Halfpenny irons, doublets that the hangman would
Bury with those that wore them, these base slaves
Pack up before the fight is done. Cut them down!
But listen to the general's battle cry!
And there's the man I hate, Aufidius,
Piercing our Romans; therefore, brave Titus, take
What numbers you may need to hold the city;
While I, with those who have the spirit, will hurry
To help Cominius.

Lartius
                                    Worthy sir, you're bleeding.
Your exercise has been too violent
To let you fight again.

Marcius
                                    Sir, do not praise me,
My work has not yet warmed me; fare you well,
The blood I drop is far more curative
Than dangerous to me. Now I'll go
To fight Aufidius.

Lartius
                                    May the fair goddess Fortune
Fall deep in love with you, and her great charms

Misguide your opponents' swords! Brave Marcius, may
Prosperity attend you.

Marcius

And be your friend no less
Than those she places highest. So, farewell.

(Marcius goes out)

Lartius
O worthiest Marcius!
Go, sound your trumpet in the marketplace
And summon all the officials of the town:
There they shall know our mind.

c)

Near the camp of **Cominius**.

Enter **Cominius**, *as though in retreat, with soldiers.*

Cominius
Rest awhile, friends. Well fought. We have come off
Like Romans, neither foolhardy in our standing
Nor cowardly in retreat. Believe me, sirs,
We'll be attacked again. While we were fighting,
At intervals, borne by the wind, we heard
The battle cry of our friends. O Roman gods!
Lead them to victory and ourselves as well
That both our armies may meet with smiling faces
And give you thankful sacrifice.

(Enter a **Messenger***)*

Cominius

Your news?

Messenger
The citizens of Corioli have sallied
And given battle to Marcius and Titus;
I saw our party driven to their trenches,
And then I came away.

Cominius

The truth perhaps
But most unwelcome. How long ago was that?

Messenger
More than an hour, my lord.

Cominius
It's not a mile; we heard their drums a moment.
How could you take an hour to cover a mile
And bring your news so late?

Messenger

Volscian scouts
Pursued me, forcing me to make
A three or four mile circuit. Otherwise
I would have been here half an hour since.

(Enter Marcius)

Cominius

Who's that,
Looking as if they'd flayed him? Gods above!
He has the stamp of Marcius, and I've seen
Him looking thus before.

Marcius

Am I too late?

Cominius
A shepherd would sooner take thunder for a tabor
Than I mistake the sound of Marcius' voice
For that of any lesser man.

Marcius

Am I too late?

Cominius
Yes, if you come not in the blood of others
But mantled in your own.

Marcius

O, let me clasp you
In arms as sound as when I wooed, in heart

As merry as when our wedding day was done
And tapers burned to bedward.

Cominius

                                        Flower of warriors,

How is it with Titus Lartius?

Marcius

As with a man who's busy with decrees:
Condemning some to death and some to exile;
Mercifully ransoming one, threatening another;
Holding Corioli in the name of Rome,
As one holds a fawning greyhound in the leash,
To let him slip at will.

Cominius

                                        Where is that slave

Who told me that he beat you to your trenches?
Where is he? Call him.

Marcius

                                        Let him alone.

He told the truth. But for our gentlemen,
The rank-and-file—a plague! Tribunes for them?
A mouse never fled from a cat as those knaves ran
From rascals worse than they.

Cominius

                        But how did you come through?

Coriolanus

Is this a time for telling? I think not.
Where is the enemy? Are you lords of the field?
If not, why stop until you are so?

Cominius

                                        Marcius,

We've fought at a disadvantage. We retired
To win our purpose.

Marcius

What is their battle order? Do you know
On which side they have placed their trusted men?

Cominius

In the vanguard, Marcius, I believe they've placed
The Antiates, their best troops, led by Aufidius,
Their very heart of hope.

Marcius

Then I beseech you,
By all the battles you and I have fought,
By the blood we've shed together, by the vows
Of friendship we have made, that you directly
Set me against Aufidius and his Antiates.
Delay no longer, but let us,
Filling the air with clashing swords and darts,
Attempt our chance at once.

Cominius

Although I wish
You might be taken to a gentle bath
And balms applied to you, I would never dare
Refuse your asking. Take your pick of those
Who best can aid your action.

Marcius

Those are the most willing. If any such be here—
It would be a sin to doubt it—who love this paint
You see me smeared with; if any of you fear
Harm to his person less than ignominy;
If any think brave death outweighs bad life,
And that his country's worth more than himself;
Let him alone, or all that are so minded,
Wave thus to express his disposition,
And follow Marcius.

(They all shout and wave their swords, take him up in their arms and throw up their caps)

O, me alone! Come, make a sword of me!
If this is not an outward show, which of you
Isn't equal to four Volscians? Each of you
Is able to oppose to the great Aufidius
A shield as hard as his. I thank you all,
Yet I must choose a certain number from

Your ranks; the rest will fight another time
As occasion may require! forward, friends!
And four of you, whichever prove the fittest
Shall be my captains.

Cominius

March off, men,

Make good your boast, and all of you
Shall share with us alike.

(They go out)

d)

The gates of Corioli.

Titus Lartius, *having set a guard upon Corioli, going with drum and trumpet toward* **Cominius** *and* **Caius Marcius**, *enters with a lieutenant, other soldiers, and a scout.*

Lartius
So, let the gates be guarded; do your duties
As I have ordered. If I send word, dispatch
Those companies to our aid; the rest will serve
To hold here briefly. If we lose the field,
We cannot keep the city.

Lieutenant

You can trust me.

Lartius
Go then! And shut the gates behind us.
Come, guide; and lead us to the Roman camp.

(They go out)

e)

A battlefield.

Battle cries. Enter **Marcius** *and* **Aufidius** *from different directions.*

Marcius
I will fight none but you, for I hate you
Worse than a perjuror.

Aufidius

We hate alike.
Africa has no serpent I abhor
More than your envied fame. Stand fast.

Marcius
Let the first to yield ground die the other's slave,
And the gods doom him after!

Aufidius

If I run, Marcius,
Hunt me down like a hare.

Marcius

Within these three hours, Tullus,
I fought alone within your Corioli's walls,
And struck what blows I pleased. It's not my blood
You see me masked in; for your revenge
Screw up your power to the utmost.

Aufidius

If you were Hector,
Champion of your boasted ancestors,
You'd not escape me here.

(They fight. Some **Volscians** *come to the help of* **Aufidius***)*

Zealous but not valiant, you have shamed me
With your detested succor.

(They go out)

f)

The **Roman** *camp near Corioli.*

Flourish. Alarum. A retreat is sounded. Enter from one side **Cominius**
with the **Romans***; from the other side,* **Marcius** *with his arm in a sling.*

Cominius
If I should tell you about this day's work,
You'd not believe your deeds; but I'll report it
Where senators will mingle tears with smiles,
Where great patricians hearing it will shrug,

But then be struck with wonder; where ladies thrilled
With fright will ask for more; where the dull tribunes,
Who like the stinking plebs abhor your honors,
Will say despite themselves: "We thank the gods
That Rome has such a soldier."
But you have barely come for the end of this feast,
Having fully dined before.

(Enter **Titus Lartius** *with his men)*

Lartius

                                                        O general,

Here is the steed, we the caparison.
If you had seen . . .

Marcius

                                Come, come. No more. My mother,
Who is entitled to extol her blood,
Annoys me with her praises. I have done
What you have done, to wit, my best; induced
As you have been by love of country.
Anyone who has done his utmost
Has done as well as I.

Cominius

                                                        You shall not

Stifle your glory; Rome must know
The value of her own. It would be concealment
Worse than a theft, no less than a betrayal,
To hide your doings, and to silence what,
If carried to the pinnacle of praise,
Would still seem slighted; therefore, I beseech you—
In token of what you are, not to reward
What you have done—let me address the army.

Marcius

I have some wounds upon me, and they smart
To hear themselves remembered.

Cominius

                                                        Should they not,

Well might they fester with ingratitude

And plague themselves to death. Of all the horses
We've taken, and we've taken good ones, of all
The treasure captured in the fields and city,
We render you the tenth, to be selected
Before the general distribution, at
Your choice alone.

Marcius

I thank you, general, but
I cannot make my heart consent to take
A bribe to pay my sword. I must refuse it,
I'd rather take an equal share with those
Who only looked upon the doings.

(A long flourish. All cry: "**Marcius! Marcius!**" *and throw up their caps and lances.* **Cominius** *and* **Lartius**, *stand bareheaded)*

Let these same instruments which you profane
Never sound again! If drums and trumpets
Are flatterers in the field of war
Then courts and cities are but lies and sham.
When steel grows soft as the parasite's silk,
Let it no longer serve as a warrior's shield.
No more, I say! Because I have not washed
My nose that bled, or downed some feeble wretch—
As many others here have done unnoticed—
You glorify me with fulsome acclamations,
As if I wished to feed my humble person
On praises spiced with lies.

Cominius

You are too modest,
More cruel to your just repute than grateful
To us who represent you truly. By your leave,
If you are angry at yourself, we'll put you
Like one intent upon his harm, in manacles,
So we can speak with you more safely. Be it known
To all the world as it is to us that Caius Marcius
Has won the laurels of this war, in token of which,
My noble steed, known to the camp, I give him,

With full equipment. And from this time on,
For what he did before Corioli, call him,
With all the applause and clamor of the army,
Caius Marcius Coriolanus! Bear
Your new name forever nobly!

(Flourish. Trumpets sound, and drums)

All
Caius Marcius Coriolanus!

Coriolanus

Now I'll go wash;

And when my face is clean, you'll see
Whether I blush or not. However, thank you;
I mean to ride your horse, and at all times
Show myself worthy of my new name
As best I'm able.

Cominius

Come to our tent

Where, before lying down to rest, we'll write
To Rome of our success. You, Titus Lartius,
Return to Corioli. Send their leaders
To us in Rome, that we may draw up articles
Of peace, for their own good and ours.

Lartius
I will, my lord.

Coriolanus
The gods begin to mock me, I who have just
Declined most princely gifts am compelled to beg
A favor of my general.

Cominius
Take it; it's yours. What is it?

Coriolanus
I lodged some years ago in Corioli
At a poor man's house. He was kind to me.
He called out to me—I saw him prisoner—

But then Aufidius came within my view
And rage overwhelmed my pity. I request you
To give my poor host freedom.

Cominius

A handsome plea!

Were he the butcher of my son, he should
Be free as the wind. Deliver him, Titus.

Lartius
Marcius, his name?

Coriolanus

By Jupiter, forgot!

I am weary; yes, my memory is tired.
Have we no wine here?

Cominius

Let us go to our tent.

The blood upon your face is drying; it's time
Your wounds were cared for. Come.

(They go out)

g)

The **Volscian** *camp.*

A flourish. Trumpets. Enter **Tullus Aufidius***, bloody, with two or
three soldiers.*

Aufidius
The town is taken.

First Soldiers
It will be given back on certain terms.

Aufidius

Terms?

I wish I were a Roman, for I cannot,
Being a Volscian, be what I am. Terms?
What sort of terms can be expected by
The party that sues for mercy. Five times, Marcius,
I've fought with you; five times you've beaten me,

And will continue, I think, if we should fight
As often as we eat. By the elements,
If ever again I meet him face to face
He's mine or I am his. My ambition
Has lost a measure of its honor, for once
I hoped to vanquish him on equal terms,
Sword against sword, but now I'll strike him as
I can; by wrath or craft I'll get him.

First Soldier
He's the devil.

Aufidius
Bolder, though not so subtle. My valor is poisoned
With letting him stain it; for him it will
Bely itself. Neither sleep nor sanctuary,
Being naked or sick; nor temple nor capitol,
Nor prayers of priests nor times of sacrifice—
All obstacles to fury—shall assert
Their worn-out privilege and prerogative
Against my hate of Marcius. Wherever
I find him, even at home under my brother's
Protection, in defiance of the laws
Of hospitality, I'll wash my angry
Hands in his heart. Go now to the city;
Learn how it's held and who are being sent
To Rome as hostages.

First Soldier

Will you not go?

Aufidius
I am expected at the cypress grove. I pray you—
It's south of the city mills—to bring me word
How the world goes, so I may adjust my step
To its pace.

First Soldier

I will, sir.

(They go out)

Act Two

1

Rome. A public place.

Enter the tribunes **Brutus** *and* **Sicinius**.

Brutus   The augurs, I hear, have received news from the field this morning.

Sicinius   The worthy priests do not honor me with more confidences than you, Brutus, but I know the news is bad.

Brutus   Why necessarily bad?

Sicinius   Because either the Volscians have won, and then they will be the masters of Rome, or Caius Marcius has won, and then he will be master.

Brutus   That's the truth. Here comes Menenius Agrippa.

(Enter **Menenius***)*

Menenius   How goes it, herdsmen of the plebeian cattle?

Sicinius   Food is in short supply on the banks of the Tiber. But it seems you have had news.

Menenius   Yes, from Caius Marcius, but you don't love him. Tell me: whom does the wolf love?

Sicinius   The lamb.

Menenius   Yes, to devour him; as the hungry plebeians would the noble Marcius.

Brutus   He's a lamb that roars like a bear.

Menenius   No, he's a bear that lives like a lamb. Do you know how you are judged in the city? I mean by us, the upper classes?

Brutus   Well, how are we judged this morning?

Menenius   As a pair of conceited, violent, unpatriotic rogues, not good enough to serve beer to a fishwife.

Sicinius   Come, sir, come, we know you.

Menenius   You know neither me, nor yourselves, nor anything else.

Brutus *(to* **Sicinius** *as they leave)*   Now it's clear what the news is. Marcius has conquered. Otherwise the fellow wouldn't be so insolent.

(Enter **Volumnia**, **Virgilia**, *and* **Valeria***)*

Menenius   Where are you going, my noble ladies?

Volumnia   Honorable Menenius, my boy is on his way. Don't delay us.

Menenius   Marcius coming home?

Volumnia   Yes, and with the highest honors.

Menenius   Marcius coming home!

Volumnia and Virgilia   Yes, it's true.

Volumnia   Here's a letter from him; the senate has one, his wife has one, and I think there's one at home for you.

Menenius   A letter for me?

Virgilia   Indeed there's a letter for you. I've seen it.

Menenius   A letter for me? That will keep me in good health for seven years; I'll spit in my doctor's face. But—isn't he wounded? Usually he comes home wounded.

Virgilia   Oh no, no, no.

Volumnia   Oh, he's wounded, I thank the gods for it.

Menenius   And so do I, if it's not too bad. Is he bringing victory in his pocket?—If so, his wounds become him.

Volumnia   Yes, on his brows, Menenius. For the third time he's coming home with the oaken garland.

Menenius   Has he given Aufidius a lesson?

Volumnia   Titus Lartius writes that they fought together but Aufidius escaped.

Menenius   Indeed, Caius Marcius is not the man to cross, not for all the chests in Corioli and all the money in them. Has it been reported to the senate?

Volumnia   Ladies, we must go. Yes, yes, yes. The senate has received letters from the general, giving my son full credit for the capture of Corioli.

Menenius   Splendid!—Where is he wounded, ladies?

Volumnia   In the shoulder and in the left arm. There will be large scars to show the people when he runs for office. And in the battle against Tarquin he received seven body wounds.

Menenius   One in the neck and two in the thigh. That makes nine that I know of.

(Trumpets)

Menenius   They're coming.

Volumnia
And under the step of the mighty
The same earth trembles both in fear and joy.
And many are no more, and home comes the victor.

(Enter **Cominius** *and* **Titus***; between them, crowned with an oaken garland,* **Coriolanus***)*

Herald
To all and sundry be it known
That Caius Marcius fought his way unaided
Into the fortified city of Corioli.
For which deed, his name and title
Shall henceforth be Coriolanus.

Menenius
Welcome to Rome, renowned Coriolanus!

Coriolanus
No more of that, I beg you.

Cominius
Look, sir, your mother.

Coriolanus
Oh!

(Goes to her)

I know you have petitioned all the gods
For my success.

(He kneels down before her)

Volumnia
No, stand up, soldier. My dear Caius
My worthy Marcius, and—what was it, how
Son, must I call you now? Ah yes, Coriolanus.
But oh, your wife!

Coriolanus
                                              Hail, my dear silence!
Would you have laughed if I'd come home in a coffin,
That you weep to see me triumph? Ah, my dear
The widows in Corioli have such eyes
And the mothers who lack sons.

Menenius
                                              Now the gods crown you.

Coriolanus
You still alive? *(To* **Valeria***)* Forgive me!

Menenius
A hundred thousand welcomes! I could weep
And I could laugh, I am light and heavy. Welcome!
Rome ought to deify all three of you
But even now we've got some crab trees here
That no amount of grafting will make sweet
To your taste.

Cominius
                                              The old man hasn't changed.

Coriolanus
Still the old Menenius, eh? *(To* **Volumnia** *and* **Virgilia***)* Your hand!
And yours.

Volumnia

                    I've lived to see my wishes granted.
There's only one thing wanting, and now Rome
Will give you that.

Coriolanus

                                        Good mother,

I'd rather be their slave in my own way
Than their master in theirs.

Cominius

                                    To the Capitol!

(All go out except the tribunes)

Sicinius
What a to-do!
As if a god had come down on the earth!
Believe me, he'll be consul before you know it.

Brutus
For us tribunes that would be good night.

Sicinius
His mission was to turn away the Volscians.
No more. You might as well command the wolf
To chase the fox away from the chicken house
And stop at that. He's taken Corioli.

Brutus
And by so doing stirred the Volscians up
Against us for years to come.

Sicinius
Now listen how a city drunk with triumph
Echoes the praises of that lawless man!
Today every saddler's boasting to his wife
That Corioli's been given him as a bonus.
How will he ever find room for three or four
Patrician villas in his cellar? That's all
They want to know. And we're just spoil-sports.

Brutus

On the other hand
He breaks the rules of every game he plays.
I've heard that if he deigns to stand for consul
He will not speak in the market as customary
Or show himself in a worn-out toga, or
Display his wounds to the people. That, he says
Would be to beg for votes. Yet if he did it
He'd likely hit the mark.

Sicinius

                                        I hope he stands
By his proud purpose.

(Enter a **Messenger***)*

Brutus

                                        What's the matter?

Messenger

You're summoned to the Capitol. Everyone thinks
That Marcius will be consul. I have seen
The deaf crowding to see him, the blind
To hear him. Ladies are flinging gloves
Young girls are tearing off their scarves and tossing
Them down upon him. The patricians
Are bowing to him as if he were Jupiter's statue.
The commoners are clapping their rough hands.
I never saw the like.

Brutus

                                        To the Capitol!

(All go out)

2

Rome. The Capitol.

Attendants *are laying cushions.*

First   Come, come, they'll soon be here. How many are standing for the consulate?

Second   Three, so they say; but everyone thinks Coriolanus will carry it off.

First   A good man, but damnably proud; he has no love for the common people.

Second   There have been great men who flattered the people more, yet didn't love them. And there are some that the people have loved, without knowing why. In other words, when they love, they don't know why, and they hate for no better reason. Consequently, if Coriolanus doesn't care whether they love him or hate him, it only shows his intelligence. They're coming.

(Enter **Cominius**, *the* **Consul**, **Menenius**, **Coriolanus**, **Senators**, **Sicinius**, *and* **Brutus**)

Menenius

Now that the matter of the Volscians is settled
The main business before this second session is
To glorify the man who conquered them
For Rome. Permit, then, noble elders, that
The present consul and recent general
Should say a few words of the warlike valor
Displayed by our Caius Marcius Coriolanus.

Senator

Speak, consul, and your words need not be few.
Tribunes, lend ear, and presently in the assembly
Of the people, argue to obtain approval
Of what is here decided.

Sicinius

We are here

Amicably disposed, not disinclined
To honor and support the object of
This session.

Brutus

Most particularly if he shows

A little more respect for the common people
Than hitherto.

Menenius

That's out of place.

You'd have done better to say nothing. Would
You hear Cominius speak?

Brutus

Most willingly.

And yet my warning was more pertinent
Than your rebuke.

Menenius

He loves your people surely.

Just don't press him to be their bed-fellow.
Speak, Cominius.

(**Coriolanus** *stands up and wants to go*)

Come, come, sit down.

Senator

Don't be afraid to hear

Of things that you were not afraid to do.

Coriolanus

Forgive me, I would rather cure my wounds
Than hear tell how I came by them.

Brutus

I hope

My words are not driving you away, sir.

Coriolanus

No, sir. Often

When blows have made me stay, I've fled from words.
Since you don't flatter me, you don't offend
Me either. And as for your people, I love them
As much as they deserve.

Menenius

Come, be seated.

Coriolanus
I'd rather have someone scratch my head in the sun
When the alarm is sounded, than sit idly
While such a fuss is made about my nothings.

*(***Coriolanus*** goes out)*

Menenius
You see the kind of man he is.
He'd rather venture all his limbs for honor
Than risk an ear to hear about it. Proceed, Cominius.

Cominius
My voice will be inadequate. In times
Like these such deeds as Coriolanus does
Should not be uttered feebly. At sixteen
When Tarquin marched on Rome, he went to battle.
With beardless chin he drove the bristled lips
Before him. At an age when he might have played
The parts of women on the stage, he won
The crown of oak. Then, grown to manhood
He bore the brunt of seventeen battles
And robbed all swords of the garland. To his prowess
Before and in Corioli, I cannot
Do justice. Those who were taking to their heels
He stopped, and by his rare example made
The last of cowards exult in war as a sport.
Like rushes before a vessel under sail
Battle lines swayed and fell before his prow.
He was a bloody instrument, whose every movement
Brought cries of death. Alone, he entered
The deadly city gate, almost unaided

Returned, and then with sudden reinforcement
Struck Corioli like a meteor.

Menenius

There's a man!

Senator
In fullest measure he deserves the honors
That we propose.

Cominius

He kicked away the spoils
As other men would kick the dust from their path.

Menenius
Call him! Call him!

Senator

Call Coriolanus.

(An attendant brings **Coriolanus** *in)*

Menenius
Coriolanus, the senate unanimously
Elects you consul.

Coriolanus

I still owe them
My life and service.

Menenius

Then you have only to
Address the people.

Coriolanus

I beseech you
Let me omit that custom. I cannot
Unbutton my coat, stand naked and entreat them
To elect me for my wounds. I beg you
Let me forgo that usage!

Sicinius

Sir, the people
Must have their voice, and they will not forgo
One jot of ceremony.

Menenius
Incline please to the custom. Do as all
Consuls have done before you.
No more nor less.

Coriolanus

It's a part

I blush to play. The people should be made
To do without such spectacles.

Brutus

Did you hear that?

Coriolanus
To stand before them bragging: I did this
And that could not have been done without me.
And show my mended wounds and say: My friends,
I came by these to make you vote for me.

Menenius
Better give in. Now, tribunes of the people
Make our decision known.—To the new consul
We wish all joy and honor.

Senators

All joy and honor!

(The Senators go out with Coriolanus)

Brutus
You see how he means to treat the people.

3

Rome. The Forum.

Enter **Citizens**.

First Citizen   Once and for all: if he asks for our votes, we can't deny them.

Second Citizen   We can if we want to, friend.

First Citizen   Yes, we have the power, but it's a power we haven't the power to use. Because if he shows us his wounds and tells us his noble exploits, we've got to show a certain amount of noble appreciation. He's indispensable.

Second Citizen   Like a neck with a goiter.

First Citizen   What do you mean by that?

Second Citizen   A neck is indispensable even if it has a goiter. The goiter is his pride.

First Citizen   I still say that if he were friendlier there'd be no better man.

Second Citizen   Here he comes.

First Citizen   And in a plain toga as the law requires.

Second Citizen   Let's see how he behaves.

First Citizen   Let's wait until he stops and then pass by him singly or by twos or threes. He will have to make his request of each one of us, and then each one of us will give him his vote.

Second Citizen   If he wants to.

*(***Coriolanus** *has entered with* **Menenius Agrippa***)*

Menenius

No, sir, you are not right. You're well aware
The greatest men have done it.

Coriolanus

What must I say?

Please, sir! No, damn it, my tongue
Sticks in my throat. Look, sir, my wounds.
I got them in my country's service, when
Some of you fellows howled and fled
From the sound of your own drums.

Menenius

Ye gods, not that!

Don't take that tone. Remind them of your deeds
Not your opinions!

Coriolanus

Let them forget me as

They've always forgotten honor and gratitude.
Hang 'em!

Menenius

Don't spoil it all, I beg you.

Speak to them. And please, please, speak sensibly.

Coriolanus

Tell them to wash their faces
And clean their teeth.

(Menenius goes out)

Well, here comes

The first batch.
You know, friends, why I'm standing here?

First Citizen   Yes, sir, we know. Tell us what brought you to it?

Coriolanus   My own merit.

First Citizen   Your own merit?

Coriolanus   Yes, not my own desire.

First Citizen   What? Not your own desire?

Coriolanus

No, it was never my desire
To beg from the poor.

Second Citizen   The poor?

First Citizen   To beg? Don't let that worry you. If we give you something, it's because we hope to get something in return.

Coriolanus
Very well, then what's the price of the consulship?

Second Citizen
The price is that you ask for it politely.

Coriolanus
Politely?
Sir, let me have it. I have wounds
That I can show you in private. Sir, your vote!
Well, what's your answer?

First Citizen

You shall have it, sir.

Coriolanus
Is it a deal, sir?
There, that's two worthy voices begged.
I've got your pennies! So good-bye!

First Citizen
This is very odd.

Second Citizen
If I had to give again . . . But never mind.

(Both go out. Enter **The Man with a Child***)*

Coriolanus
Sir, I should like to be consul.

The Man *(pointing out* **Coriolanus'** *toga to the child)*   That's the plain toga, Tertius, they've got to wear it when they plead in the marketplace. It has no pockets, that's to keep him from buying votes, ha ha ha. Otherwise, you see, he might buy them. Ha ha ha. But he'll get my vote because he's taken one more city for Rome. He'll get it. *(Goes out)*

Coriolanus   Many thanks, sir.

(Enter two citizens)

A word, sirs. It's the regulation
That all should see how for a high honor
I wear my shoes out in the market place . . .

Third Citizen   I'm glad to see that, sir, if only because of my trade.

Coriolanus   What is your trade, sir?

Third Citizen   To tell you the truth, sir, it's mere patchwork
compared to yours.

Coriolanus   What is your trade then?

Third Citizen *(archly)*   A trade I can practice with a clearer
conscience than certain noble lords can practice theirs. It consists
in improving the wretched walks of life.

Coriolanus   Your trade.

Fourth Citizen   Begging your pardon, sir, he's a shoemaker. And
you have his vote because war raises the price of shoes and you are
the living embodiment of war, sir.

(Another citizen joins them)

Coriolanus   Ha ha ha! I'm studying the trades here. This
gentleman is a shoemaker, and what are you, sir?

Fifth Citizen   I'm a gardener, sir.

Coriolanus   And what does your trade teach you about the state?
Because you are being asked to make a decision concerning the
state.

Fifth Citizen
My garden, sir, that little realm
Of flowerbeds and turnip patches, has taught me
That even the noble rose of Corinth must
Be pruned of undue pride of growth, or else
It cannot thrive. Moreover, it must humble
Itself to having leeks and cabbages and
Such plants of low descent, but passing useful
Watered and cultivated by its side.

Coriolanus
What does all that mean, vote?

Fifth Citizen
It seems to me the garden would grow wild
If one thought only of the royal rose.

Coriolanus
Thanks for the lesson. But just one thing more:
Your vote! Your vote!

(Three more citizens have joined them)

Good day, gentlemen! If you have no objection to my face,
I'd like to be consul. I'm wearing the customary dress.

Sixth Citizen   You've deserved nobly of your country, and you
have not deserved nobly.

Coriolanus   The answer to your riddle?

Sixth Citizen   You've been a scourge to her enemies and a rod
to her friends. To put it plainly, you haven't loved the common
people.

Coriolanus   I love them according to their deserts. But you hold
that I haven't made myself common with my love for the common
people. I understand. There are certain needs, and to meet them
you need public establishments and public men. However, if you
set more store by my hat than by my heart, I will tear out my heart,
remove my hat, and pray you humbly: let me be consul.

Third Citizen   You have received many wounds for your
country?

Coriolanus   I won't bother you to look at them. But if you
demand entertainment, I can sing you a song about the gratitude of
the she-wolf. *(To the tune of a bagpiper who has begun to play for
small coins)*

Here stands C. Marcius Coriolan
Trying to please the common man
He's selling the Roman eagle here
(Don't fight over the feathers, children dear!)

Gentlemen, my wounds. These. And these.
Look closely. Touch them if you please.
I'll serve you for a penny; I'll dance
Attendance. Gather round! Step up! Last chance!

(More citizens step up)

Here come more votes.
Your votes! I went to battle for your votes.
Stood sleepless for your votes. For your votes
I've got two dozen scars. I've fought
In eighteen battles. For your votes I've done
All manner of things and not done others.
Give me your votes and I'll be consul.

Third Citizen *(frightened)*   Of course. Of course. Calm down.

Fourth Citizen   Let him be consul if that's what he wants.
Bravery is the one thing that counts in these warlike times.

Fifth Citizen   Amen.

(Coriolanus *bows low)*

(Enter **Senators** *and tribunes)*

Menenius

You've carried out the program.

Coriolanus

                                                        Then I'm through?

Sicinius
You've pressed your candidacy singly and
In person, no objection has been raised.
The senate and the tribunes can confirm you.

Coriolanus
Where? In the senate?

Sicinius
Yes.

Coriolanus
But can I change
This toga now?

Sicinius

Yes, that you may. One thing perhaps
Remains: before the assembled people to
Question the candidate concerning
His program and his general opinions.

Menenius

No!

That's not provided in the charter.

Sicinius

The tribunes

Aren't mentioned in the charter either. The people
Have won a new law in the field, and now
In victory they want to use it, sirs.

Fifth Citizen
That's right.

Sicinius

Coriolanus

You are descended from the noble house
Of Marcius, from which house sprang also
That Ancus Marcius, Numa's daughter's son
Who followed great Hostilius as our king.
Of the same house were Publius and Quintus
Who brought us our best water with their conduits.
And now, before I put my questions in
The people's name, I ask you to look back
Most earnestly upon your beloved ancestors.
Coriolanus, ships from conquered Antium
Have just put into port. Their cargo is grain
Tribute and booty taken in the bloody
War with the Volscians. Noble Marcius, what
Will you do with this grain if chosen consul?

Menenius
Easy does it, Marcius.

Coriolanus

This is a plot.

Brutus
Call it a plot! The people are crying for grain.
When free grain was apportioned to the people
Some seven months ago, you, Marcius, literally
Reviled all those who took it as lazy scoundrels.

Coriolanus
Yes, yes, it's long since known.

Sicinius

But not to all.

Coriolanus
Then tell the others!

Menenius

Easy now.

Cominius
You're stirring up the people!

Coriolanus
Speaking to me of grain! Would it please you
To hear it again? It would? Then I'll repeat it.

Menenius
Not now. Not here.

Cominius

Not now and in this heat.

Coriolanus
Here and at any time. I say what I think.
You don't feed virtue when you give free grain.
You're feeding disobedience, fattening it
For insurrection, for with every wish
You satisfy, you give the filthy rabble
New wishes.

Fifth Citizen

Oho!

Menenius

Let well enough alone.

Sicinius

Let me ask you this: why should the people vote
For a man who speaks of them like that?

Coriolanus

Was it then children's votes I got by my begging?

Cominius

Keep calm!

Brutus

You've not yet been confirmed in office.

Coriolanus

Whoever suggested that the granaries
Be emptied free of charge, as may perhaps
Be customary in Greece . . .

Brutus

Where the people

Are really consulted, and not just on paper!

Coriolanus

In Greece? Then go to Greece.
This city's name is Rome.

Cominius

Enough!

Sicinius

And then some.

Coriolanus

No, I'll give you something more

For your constituents. It's free. I happen
To know that when war threatened this city
With sudden doom, the scum who live in
The stinking districts by the lower Tiber
Demanded grain before they'd take up arms.

Some people thought the time had come to feather
Their nests by blackmailing the state.

Cominius
No more, I beg you, sir.

Fourth Citizen
Instead of blackmail, certain others steal.
Where, Coriolanus, are the spoils
Of Corioli?

Menenius

Be still!

Coriolanus
That's dual sovereignty, where one part
Despises with good ground and the other part
Flings groundless insults, where greatness, power and wisdom
Can't move a step without the yes or no
Of the unreasoning mob.

Citizens

It's us he means.

Brutus
He's said enough.

Sicinius

He's spoken as a traitor.
He'll answer for it as a traitor should.

Coriolanus
You dogs, you crippled sons of turmoil
Because you were confirmed in time of turmoil
When not what's right, but only what cannot
Be helped becomes the law. But now that Rome
No longer has the Volscians at its throat—
And thanks to me—Rome will know how to laugh
And wash away this scurf.

Brutus
Manifest treason!

Sicinius

This a consul? Never!

Brutus

The aediles, ho!—Arrest this man.

Sicinius

Summon the people. In their name
I apprehend you as an innovator
Rebel and enemy of the state.

(Brutus goes out)

Coriolanus

Go away, old goat!

Menenius

Hands off, old man!

(Coriolanus takes Cominius' shortsword)

Coriolanus

Or else I'll shake your bones
Out of your clothes.

Citizens

Careful, Sicinius!—Watch out for his sword!

Coriolanus

A plot, I knew it, to end
The rule of the patricians.

Sicinius

This way!

(Brutus re-enters with Aediles and Citizens)

Brutus

He's drawn the shortsword now!

Cominius

Stand back!

Here stands the victor of Corioli.

Senator

Put that sword away.

Sicinius
Here stands a usurper of the people's sovereignty.

Menenius
On both sides more respect.

Brutus

Seize him, aediles!

Citizens   Down with him.—Down with the grain robber!—
Weapons, weapons!

(The **Patricians** *crowd around* **Coriolanus***)*

Patricians
You'll take him over our dead bodies!—
Lead him away!—Menenius
You speak to them!—Away!

Menenius

I can't.

Tribunes, speak to the people.
Coriolanus, quiet! Speak, friend Sicinius!

Sicinius
Hear me, citizens! Quiet!

Citizens
Hear the tribune!

Sicinius

The man you see before you has outraged the tribunes.

Menenius
That's stirring up the fire, not putting it out.

First Senator
That's making war on Rome!

Brutus

Who's Rome? You or

Its people?

Sicinius
For laying hands on a tribune, the penalty

Is death. Take him away. Take him to
The Tarpeian Rock.

Brutus

Aediles, go seize him.

Citizens
Surrender, Marcius.

Menenius

Patricians! Here! Defend our Marcius!

Citizens
Down with him—To the Rock!

First Senator

The man's his own worst enemy!
Quick! Let's be going! Hold him up! Oh, why
The devil couldn't he speak gently!

*(The **Patricians** push the bewildered **Coriolanus** out. The **Citizens** follow)*

Brutus

Seize the viper

Who's ready to depopulate a city
To be its one and all.

Act Three

1

Rome. Coriolanus' house.

Volumnia, **Coriolanus** *and a few friends.*

Coriolanus
Only one thing surprises me, that my mother
Is not more pleased with me. She used to call
Them churlish vassals, creatures made
To sell themselves for pennies, and to stand
Bareheaded in assemblies, yawning and
Scratching their heads in puzzlement when one
Of my rank stood up and spoke for peace or war.
Why would you wish me milder? Would you want me
To make a dovecote of my heart? I play
The man I am, and that's the end of it.

Volumnia
Son, son. I only wish
You'd taken time to put your power on
Before you wore it out.

Coriolanus

                                           Forget it.

Volumnia
You could have been the man you are more fully
If you had shown it less. When once you hold
The power, they'll no longer have
The power to defy you.

Coriolanus

                                          Hang 'em!

Volumnia

                                             Yes,

And burn them too.

*(Enter **Menenius** and **Senators**)*

Menenius
Come, come, you have been too rough, a bit too rough.
Come back with me and make amends.

Senator

It can't be helped.

Our city, if you don't, will break in two
And perish.

Volumnia

Son, my heart is no more faint

Than yours; my brain, however, tells
Me when it's time for anger and when not.
Take my advice.

Menenius

That's it. A little time

Will turn the trick. If not, I'd put
My armor on that I can scarcely carry
Sooner than see you grovel to the mob.

Coriolanus
What must I do?

Menenius

Return to the tribunes.

Coriolanus
Very well. But what then? What then?

Menenius
Repent of what you said.

Coriolanus

To them? To the gods I cannot.

Volumnia
You're too unbending. I have heard you say
That guile and honor are compatible
In war. Why not in peace?

Coriolanus

Be still.

Menenius

> Well questioned.

Volumnia

If in your wars it brings you honor to seem
What you are not—and that you've always done
When great ends could be won by it—then why
Should that same policy dishonor you
In peace?

Coriolanus

> Why do you press me so?

Volumnia

Because your duty now is to address
The people, to speak to them with words
That bubble from the surface of your tongue
Bastards, mere sounds and syllables
That bear no kinship to your heart.
It will dishonor you no more
Than with soft words to take a city
Against which you would otherwise be forced
To tempt your luck and risk great loss of blood.
Be reasonable. Your friends and family are
In danger. That's the honorable course.
But you would rather show this stinking rabble
How splendidly you frown than smiling cheat
Them of their votes, and save what otherwise
Will go to ruin.

Menenius

> Come, go with us.

Just a few friendly words. That's all.

Volumnia

> Son,

I beg you, go to them. Just stand bare-headed
Holding your hands out so (see, here you are)
Your knees nearly touching the pavement (for in such cases
Posture counts more than words) and wag your head.

Just tell them you're a soldier, reared in the noise
Of battle, unaccustomed to the gentle
Manners which they, as you must now admit
Have every reason to expect. Then tell them
From this day on they will not find you wanting.

Menenius

If you'd do that, speak as your mother has spoken
By the gods, you'd win all hearts.

Volumnia

I beg you, go. I know you'd sooner follow
Your enemy into a fiery pit than gently
Into a tavern.

Menenius

Cominius!

*(Enter **Cominius**)*

Cominius

I've come from the Forum, Marcius, and advise you
To place a strong guard round your house. Or else
Take flight.

Menenius

A gentle word would do it.

Menenius

Of course it would, if he could squeeze one out.

Volumnia

Son,

I beg you, just say yes, and go.

Coriolanus

Shouldn't

I have my face shaved first? All right, I'll do it.
Why fret about this bag of dust named Marcius?
Scatter it to the wind! Come, to the Forum!
Good-bye, my spirit, let some harlot's spirit
Possess me, let my warlike voice
Pipe like a eunuch's, let my eyes be filled

With schoolboy tears, and let my armored knees
That never bent except in stirrups, bow
Like a beggar's stooped for coins. I will not do it.
I will not cut the truth within me down
Or let base gestures vitiate my mind.

Volumnia
You will decide. I'd call it more dishonor
For me to beg of you, than you of them.
Let ruin fall upon us. Do as you please.
You sucked your courage from my breast, but not
Your pride.

Coriolanus
Calm down. I'm going to the marketplace. Stop scolding.
I'll cheat them of their hearts. When I come back
I'll be the idol of every shopkeeper in Rome
And consul too. Commend me to my wife.

Volumnia
Do as you like. *(Goes out)*

Cominius
                          Come, now the tribunes are waiting.
And arm yourself with mildness. They have heaped up
Still stronger accusations than before.

Coriolanus
"Mild" is the word. Come, let's be going.
Inventive as may be their accusations
My repentance will be more so.

Menenius
                                  Yes, but put it mildly.

Coriolanus
Right. Mildly does it. Mildly, mildly.

(All go out)

2

Rome. The Forum.

Sicinius, Brutus, Citizens, *an* **Aedile.**

Brutus   Are these the chairmen of the electoral districts?

Aedile   Yes.

Brutus   Have you a list of all the voters they represent?

Aedile   Yes, here it is.

Sicinius   And here he comes.

(Enter **Coriolanus, Menenius, Cominius,** *and* **Senators***)*

Menenius
Speak calmly now, I beg you.

Coriolanus
Yes, like a stable boy, who for a tip
Puts up with any insult. May the gods
Keep Rome in safety and its seats of justice
Supplied with worthy men. Let love be our
Rallying cry. Peace to the city!

First Senator
                                                                Hear, hear!

Menenius
A noble greeting.

Sicinius
                                                Chairmen, be seated.

Aedile
                                                                        Hear

Your tribunes!

Coriolanus
                                                        Hear me speak first!

Citizens
Him first! The same old story! Him first!

Sicinius
Very well, speak.

Citizens
                                        First me and then the law!—
The forms be damned.

Aedile
                                             Silence, please.

Coriolanus
Shall I be further prosecuted elsewhere?
Will everything be settled here?

Sicinius
                                                    I must

First ask you this: Do you submit
To the people's voice? Do you recognize
Their representatives? Do you consent
To suffer punishment for such offense
As may be proved against you?

Coriolanus
                                                    I do.

Menenius
Hear that? He does. Consider his services
In war. He speaks here not as a citizen
But as a soldier.

Cominius
                                    That's enough now, friend.

Coriolanus
How comes it that no sooner voted consul
I am dishonored and expelled from office?

Sicinius
You are on trial, not we.

Coriolanus

Well, try me then.

Sicinius
You are accused of trying to overthrow
The tribunes of the people and to seize
A tyrant's power. Hence of treason
Against the people.

Coriolanus

Treason!

Menenius

Easy, now!

Cominius
You promised!

Coriolanus

Let the fires of bottommost hell
Swallow up the people.

Sicinius

Did you hear that?

Coriolanus
Call me a traitor! Why, you dog
Of a tribune, you tribune of dogs. You lump
Of filth! You scoundrel hungry for my death!
You throat clogged fast with lies!

Citizens

Enough!

Sicinius
No need of adding further evidence
To our complaint. What you've just seen . . .

Citizens

To the Rock!

Sicinius
And heard . . .

Citizens

Come. Take him to the Rock!

Sicinius

Beating the tribunes, cursing you, the people
Opposing law with violence, and now
Arrogantly defying those empowered
To judge him. Such offences warrant the
Death penalty.

Citizens

Right! Right! Put him to death.

Brutus

But since he has served Rome well . . .

Coriolanus

What is this talk

Of serving well?

Brutus

I'm saying what I know.

Coriolanus

What you know!

Menenius

Is this the promise

You made your mother?

Cominius

Calm yourself. You know . . .

Coriolanus

Don't tell me what I know. Let them hurl
Me down from the steep Tarpeian Rock, or send
Me off to exile, or whatever else they
Can think of. I'll not buy their mercy with
So much as one soft word, not even a
"Good morning."

Sicinius

That condemns you. In the people's

Name, we the tribunes banish you from Rome
And warn you on pain of being hurled
From the Tarpeian Rock, never again
To enter the city gates.

Citizens

Well done!

(All stand up, to go)

Cominius
Hear me!

Sicinius

He's sentenced. The session's closed.

Cominius
No, let me speak. I have been consul. Rome
Can see the marks of her enemies on me. When
I say . . .

Sicinius

We know what you will say.

Brutus
He's banished. That's the end of it.

Cominius

The end?

Coriolanus
You pack of common curs, I hate your breath
More than the reek of putrid swamps, and value
Your love no more than the carcasses of unburied
Enemies. I banish you!
Stay here in Rome, shaking with fear, shitting
In your pants whenever a plume of unfamiliar
Color appears outside the gates. Maintain,
The power to banish your defenders till
Your ignorance (which sees no farther than
Its nose) sends everyone away but you
Who have always been your cruelest enemies
And in the end delivers you to some

Nation that takes the city without striking
A blow. Despising Rome on your account
I turn my back on it. There's a world
Elsewhere.

*(Coriolanus goes out with **Menenius**, **Cominius**, and **Senators**)*

Citizens
The enemy of the people's gone! He's gone!

(They fling their hats into the air)

3

Rome. Outside the gates.

Coriolanus, Volumnia, Virgilia, Menenius, Cominius, *and* **Senators**.

Coriolanus
Come, come. Don't cry. Good-bye. The many-headed
Beast has butted me out. No, mother
Where's the old pluck? Who was it taught me
That common fortune and misfortune were
For common people? That when the sea was calm
All ships show equal mastery in sailing
But that to bear the hardest strokes of fate
And not get hurt requires noble skill?

Virgilia
O heavens! O heavens!

Coriolanus

                                        Stop, woman, please . . .

Volumnia
A plague on all the guilds of Rome!

Coriolanus

                                        What! What! What!
They'll love me when they need me. No, mother
Remember how you used to say
That if you'd been the wife of Hercules
You'd have done six of his labors and so saved
Your husband all that sweat. Cominius
Chin up. Good-bye. Good-bye, wife. It's nothing, mother.
I'll get along. Take care, Menenius.
At your age tears are saltier than when
You're young; they're not good for the eyes.
You, general, I've known you to be staunch.

Heartrending scenes are nothing new to you.
Tell these sad women that it's just as foolish
To cry at blows that cannot be avoided
As it is to laugh. The dangers I have faced
Have kept you youthful, mother, you know that.
Believe me if you can: although he now
Goes forth like a lone dragon which his cave
Makes feared and talked of more than seen, your son
Will either do uncommon deeds or fall
A victim to the petty treachery of
The common herd.

Volumnia

                              Dear son, where will you go?
Take Cominius with you for a while. Discuss
With him your future course, for fear blind chance
Should be your guide.

Coriolanus

                                          O heavenly gods!

Cominius
I'll stay with you a month. We'll talk things over
Decide where you're to go, so you may hear
From us and we from you.

Coriolanus

                                    Thank you, old man. But
You're not as young as you have been. Too old
To roam the country with a man—forgive me—
Who still has ample plans. Just bring me to
The gate. Come, come! And once outside
We'll smile and say good-bye. As long as I
Remain above the ground you'll hear from me
But only news recalling the old Marcius.

(All go out through the gate)

4

Rome. A street near the gate.

Sicinius, **Brutus**, *and an* **Aedile**.

Sicinius
Send them all home. He's gone. The thing is done.
The nobles who, as we see, have sided with him
Are thrown into confusion.

Brutus

Now we've shown
Our power, we can take a humbler attitude.

Sicinius
Make them go home. Their great enemy
Is gone.

Brutus

Yes, send them home. Here comes his mother.

(Enter **Volumnia***,* **Virgilia***, and* **Menenius***)*

Sicinius
Quick. Let's be going.

Brutus

Why?

Sicinius

They say she's mad.

Brutus
They've seen us. Quick.

Volumnia

Well met. God damn your souls!

Menenius
Sh! Gently, gently. Not so loud!

Volumnia

If only

My tears would let me speak, you'd hear
A thing or two. No, stay. You shall hear. Stay there!

Virgilia
And you stay too. I wish I had the power
To say that to my husband.

Sicinius

Bear up like a man.

Volumnia
She's not a man. That's no disgrace for her.
I only wish that you were not a fox.
Then he would still be here who's struck more blows
For Rome than you've made slanderous speeches. Go
Now. No, I've something more to say. I wish
My son were in Arabia, and you
With all your tribe before him in the desert.

Sicinius
What then?

Virgilia

What then? The entire breed
In wedlock born and bastards, you would all
Be soon exterminated. There's revenge!

Menenius
Be still!

Sicinius

If only he had gone on serving
His country as he did at first.

Brutus

I wish he had.

Volumnia
"I wish he had?" But you stirred up the mob.

Brutus
We'll leave you now.

Volumnia

High as the Capitol

Towers above the meanest hut in Rome
So towers my son (this lady's husband, here
Do you see her?) whom you've banished
Above you all.

Brutus

That may be so. Come let's
Be going.

*(***Brutus***, ***Sicinius***, and the ***Aedile*** go out)*

Menenius

You've sent them packing

And upon my word you had every reason to.
Will you sup with me?

Volumnia

No, not tonight.

Anger's my meat. I'll sup upon myself.
And so shall starve with feeding. Come, let's go.

(All go out)

Act Four

1

Highway between Rome and Antium.

A **Roman** *and a* **Volscian** *meet.*

Roman   Why are you turning back? I've come from Rome, but I'm not a bandit.

Volscian   If it isn't Laetus, the tanner on Sandalmaker Street!

Roman   Piger! Where have you been keeping yourself? *(They embrace)*

Roman   How's the old lady? Still making those millet cakes?

Volscian   Still making them; she can get the raisins, but I've got no hemp for my rope shop. That's what I'm going to Rome for.

Roman   And I'm going to Antium to see if they can use any of my leather hassocks.

Volscian   Did you pass through Corioli—the place you stole from us? How is it?

Roman   You'll see. Hasn't changed much. People eat, sleep and pay taxes. How is it in Antium?

Volscian   We eat, sleep and pay taxes. And in Rome?

Roman   We eat too, and sleep and pay taxes. But we've had an uprising and thrown Coriolanus out.

Volscian   Really? You've got rid of him? I can tell you one thing: that makes me happier about going there.

Roman   I was less worried about leaving.

Volscian   Man, to think we've got peace again!

Roman   Have a good trip, Piger. I hope you make out all right in Rome.

Volscian   I hope you make out all right in Antium, Laetus. *(They take leave and go their ways)*

(A disguised man comes from the direction of Rome. It is **Coriolanus***)*

2

Antium. Outside Aufidius' house.

Enter **Coriolanus** *shabbily dressed and muffled.*

Coriolanus
Not a bad town, this Antium. City, I'm
The man who turned your wives to widows. Many
A citizen would have inherited
A house like this had he not groaned and fallen
In my wars. It's better for you not to know me.
Your women would belabor me with buckets
Your little boys with stones.

(Enter a **Citizen***)*

Good evening, sir.

Can you inform me where the great
Aufidius lives? Is he in Antium?

Citizen
Yes, he's at home and entertaining
The nobles of the city.

Coriolanus

Where is his house?

Citizen
Right here before you.

Coriolanus

This one? Thank you, sir.
Good evening.

(The **Citizen** *goes out)*

O world, your slippery turns! Two loving friends
Who seem to bear one heart within two breasts
Sharing their hours, their bed, their meals, their sports
Inseparable twins, will between twelve and noon

Break into bitterest enmity for less than nothing.
Likewise, the most deep-rooted enemies
Whose hate keeps them awake at night devising
Ways to exterminate each other, will
By some stupid trick of chance, not worth an egg
Be turned to staunchest comrades who betroth
Their children. So it is with me. I hate
My birthplace and I love this enemy town.
I'll enter. If he kills me, it's his good
Right. If he welcomes me, I'll serve his country.

Servant *(stepping out of the house)*   What are you gaping at?

Second Servant   Hey, where's the wine? Call that service? Are you fellows asleep?

*(**First Servant** goes out)*

Third Servant   Cotus! The master's calling Cotus. *(Goes out)*

Coriolanus   A nice house. That dinner smells good too.

Second Servant   What do you want, friend? Where are you from? There's no room for you here. Would you kindly . . .

Coriolanus   All right. I don't deserve a better reception: I am Coriolanus.

First Servant *(comes back)*   You still here? Hasn't the gatekeeper any eyes in his head, letting such people in? Get going now.

Coriolanus   Get going yourself.

First Servant   Me? Let's not be insolent.

Coriolanus   You're getting troublesome, friend.

Second Servant   Sir, you've been asked politely to leave. So leave.

Third Servant *(comes back)*   Who's this character?

First Servant   A freak. I can't get rid of him. Call the master.

Third Servant   Get a move on!

Coriolanus   Just let me stand here. I won't harm your hearth.

Second Servant   But who are you?

Coriolanus   A man of some renown.

First Servant   But very poor.

Coriolanus   Yes, that I am.

Third Servant   May I then ask you, poor man of some renown, to stand somewhere else? In short: clear out!

Coriolanus   Do as you've been told. And make it quick or someone else will eat your scraps. *(Pushes him)*

Second Servant   Get the master!

*(***Third Servant*** *goes out)*

First Servant   Where do you live anyway?

Coriolanus   Under the canopy.

Second Servant   Under the canopy?

Coriolanus   Yes.

First Servant   Where's that?

Coriolanus   In the city of kites and crows.

First Servant   A fool. Then you must live with the feather brains?

Coriolanus   No. I don't serve your master.

First Servant   You . . .!

Second Servant   Have you any business with our master?

Coriolanus   Yes, and you'd better be glad it's with him and not with your wife. You stand here and prattle. Out to your platters!

(Enter **Aufidius** *with the* **Third Servant***)*

Aufidius   Where is the man?

First Servant   Here, sir. I'd have whipped him like a dog but I didn't wish to disturb the company inside.

Aufidius   Where do you come from? What do you want here?

Your name? Why don't you speak? Speak, man. What's your
name?

Coriolanus
A name unmusical to Volscian ears
And harsh to your ears too.

Aufidius

                                    Your looks are rude
And yet there's something in your eye as if
You'd lifted up your voice in times gone by.
The tackle's torn and yet the vessel
Was surely noble.

Coriolanus

                                    Prepare to frown. Do you
Really not know me?

Aufidius

                            I don't know you. Your name!

Coriolanus
My name is Caius Marcius, who has done
To you particularly and to all the Volscians
Great hurt and mischief, as my surname bears
Witness: Coriolanus. That name embodies
My arduous service, the mortal dangers faced
The drops of blood I've shed for an ungrateful
Rome. It must surely waken to your mind
The hate you owe me. Only the name is left.
The cruelty and envy of the people
The cowardice of the nobles, who have all
Betrayed me, have devoured the rest.
The voice of slaves has whooped me out of Rome
And this calamity has sent me to your door
Not hope to save my life—no, don't mistake me—
For had I been afraid of death, it's you
Of all men in the world I'd have avoided.
Sheer hatred, lust to be avenged on all
That rabble brings me here before you. If you

—I don't know you—wish to repay the wrong inflicted
Upon you in particular, and the shameful
Scars to be seen throughout your country
Employ me. Put my misery to use.
Harness the vengefulness that burns my entrails
To your own purposes. Your purposes
Are mine. I'll turn the malignant fury of
My sword against my cankered country.
However, if this venture frightens you
If weariness has tamed your enterprise
Then, in a word, I too am tired of living
I offer you my throat and call you fool
If you hesitate to cut it. I have always
Pursued you with my hatred, I have drawn
Barrels of blood from your country's heart. Therefore
My life must cover you with shame, unless
I live to serve you.

Aufidius

O Marcius, Marcius

Each word you've said has weeded from my heart
A root of ancient envy. Let me now
Vie for your love as formerly
I battled with your valor. A dozen times
You've drubbed me so that ever since I've dreamed
Each night of fighting you, unbuckling helmets
Clutching each other's throats—and waked with nothing.
Worthy Marcius, if we had no other quarrel
With Rome except that they have banished you
We'd muster every man from twelve to seventy
And hurl them at the city. Come in. Come in.
Some senators, my friends.

Coriolanus

O gods, how kind

You are today!

Aufidius

And so, sir, if you wish

To pay your debt in person, take one half
My army, and, since you have the experience
And know the strength and weakness of your country
Proceed as you see fit. Choose if you will
To knock directly on the gates of Rome
Or visit more outlying spots. You know
The rule: first frighten, then destroy. But now
Come in! Let me commend you to my friends
Who will approve your wishes. Come!
A thousand welcomes! More a friend than ever
An enemy. And, Marcius, that is saying
Quite a good deal. Come in!

3

Rome. The Forum.

Sicinius *and* **Brutus**.

Sicinius
No news of him. No need to fear him now.
We've made his friends in the senate blush, to see
The world goes on without the hero. It
Grieves them to hear our bakers, ropers, sandal-
Makers all singing at their work.

Brutus
We struck before it was too late.

Sicinius
Menenius.

Brutus
His manners are improving too.

*(**Menenius** enters. Greetings are exchanged)*

Sicinius
Your Coriolanus isn't greatly missed.
By a few friends perhaps. The state, however
Endures, and even if he hated it far more
Would still endure.

Menenius
Yes, all is well
And might have been still better had he learned
To temporize.

Sicinius
Where is he? Have you heard?

Menenius
No news. His wife and mother have no word of him.

*(A few **Citizens** pass by)*

Citizens
The gods preserve you both!

Brutus

Good evening, neighbors.

Sicinius
Good evening all! Good evening!

First Citizen
Let me say this: our wives and children too
Should get down on their knees and pray
The gods to give you both good health.

Brutus
The gods protect you, neighbors!

(The **Citizens** *go out)*

Sicinius
Aren't we all much better off than in the days
When they detested you?

Brutus

Caius Marcius was
A worthy soldier in the field, but insolent
Puffed up with pride, ambitious beyond measure
Self-loving . . .

Sicinius

Yes, he aimed to make himself dictator.

Menenius
That seems unlikely.

Sicinius

We'd have found out to
Our sorrow, had he been chosen, consul.

Brutus
The gods prevented that. Now Rome
Is breathing easier.

(Enter an **Aedile***)*

Aedile

Tribunes!

A slave—we've thrown the man in prison—reports
The Volscians with two separate armies have
Invaded Roman territory, destroying
Everything in their path.

Menenius

Aufidius

Who, hearing we had banished Marcius
Is putting out once more the feelers that
He'd anxiously retracted when he knew
Marcius was here with us.

Sicinius

Come, come, why bring up Marcius?

Brutus

Have him whipped!

The rumor monger! That's not possible!
The Volscians wouldn't dare to break with us!

Menenius

Not possible? It's more than possible.
Three times it's happened in my lifetime.
Question the man before you punish him
And find out where he heard it. Otherwise
You will be whipping information.

Sicinius

Don't tell

Me that. I know it can't be so.

Brutus

Impossible.

(Enter a **Messenger***)*

Messenger

The nobles are meeting in the senate.
Bad news has come in from the mountains.

Sicinius
That slave again! A provocation! Whip him!

Messenger
No, sir. He told the truth. Except it's worse.

Sicinius
What's worse?

Messenger
                              I don't know if it's true, but all
Reports concur in saying that Marcius
Joined with Aufidius is leading
An army against Rome, and swears to take
Such vengeance on the city that neither young
Nor old . . .

Sicinius
                                                      A likely story!

Brutus
                                              Trumped up to make
Our weaker sisters wish for Marcius'
Return.

Sicinius
                                              No doubt about it.

Menenius
                                              Most unlikely:
He and Aufidius! That's mixing oil and water.

(Enter another **Messenger***)*

Second Messenger
They want you in the senate, sir.
A fearful army led by Caius Marcius
In league with Aufidius is driving on Rome.
Corioli's in flames and fallen to
The enemy.

(Enter **Cominius***)*

Cominius
                                              Good work you've done!

Menenius

What news? What news?

Cominius

You've helped to ravish your own daughters
And melt the leaden roofs on your own heads.

Menenius

What news?

Cominius

And burn your temples down to their foundations.
Now you can take your precious bill of rights
And stuff it in a mouse hole.

Menenius

In the gods' name, what news?
If Marcius should indeed have joined the Volscians . . .

Cominius

If? Why, he's their god. He leads them like a thing
Made by some other deity than nature
That turns out better men. They follow him
With no less confidence than boys pursuing
Summer butterflies or butchers killing flies.

Menenius

Good work you've done! You and your apron men
And garlic eaters, with the mighty voice
Of the Roman working class!

Cominius

He'll shake your Rome
About your ears.

Brutus

But is this true, sir?

Cominius

Yes! "Is this true, sir?" All the cities
Laugh and rebel against us. Those who choose
Not to rebel are mocked for their brave innocence
And die like fools.

Menenius

We're lost unless the great man
Takes mercy on us.

Cominius

But who will plead with him?
The tribunes of the people can't; the people
Deserve his pity as the wolf deserves
The pity of the shepherd. As for his friends
If they should come and say "Be kind to Rome"
They'd merely prove themselves his enemies.

Menenius
That's true. If he were here now with a torch
To set my house on fire, I wouldn't have
The gall to say: "Please don't." This thing will cost you
Your cowhide aprons and your hides as well.

Cominius
We love him, but like stupid cattle we
Betrayed him to you and your salt of the earth.
And when he comes, he'll meet not armed resistance
But a despairing mob.

(Enter a group of **Citizens***)*

Menenius

Here comes the salt.
You threw your greasy caps into the air
To drive him from your city. Now he's coming.
He'll take himself as many heads as you
Threw caps. But all of us are in for it.
If he could burn us all to cinders
I'd say we had it coming. Shall we go to the Capitol?

Cominius
What else is there to do?

*(***Cominius** *and* **Menenius** *go out)*

Citizens
They say he's burning every foot of ground
He steps on.

Sicinius

Don't be discouraged. There are dogs in Rome
Who'd gladly see confirmed what they pretend
To fear. Now go, my friends, I didn't say
Run. Go back to your districts
And show you're not afraid.

Second Citizen

I'd rather have
A sword to show than courage. Was it wise
To banish him?

Sicinius

Yes.

(The **Citizens** *go out slowly)*

To the Capitol!

4

Camp near Rome.

Aufidius *and a* **Captain**.

Aufidius
Are they still flocking to the Roman?

Captain
I can't make out what witchcraft he has in him.
But to your soldiers he is grace before meat
Their talk at table and their thanks before rising.
You are overshadowed in this action, sir
In your own army.

Aufidius

                                                   I can't help that now.

If I should try to, it would halt the whole
Campaign before it's fairly started.

Captain

                                                              Sir

I wish you had not shared the high command
With him, but taken it yourself, or else
Left it to him entirely.

Aufidius
I understand you well. But rest assured
When the time comes to settle up accounts
He doesn't know what I can urge against him
Although it seems, and so he thinks, and so
Do people generally think, that he is
Loyal in all his actions. Still, there's
Something he will not do, and if it's left
Undone, it will break my neck, and that in turn
Will break his neck.

Captain

                                     Do you think he will take Rome, sir?

Aufidius

Cities surrender to him before he even
Lays siege to them. The Roman nobles
Are for him. The tribunes are
No soldiers. He has spread the word in Rome
That to prevent unprofitable slaughter
A smoke cloud sent up from the Capitol
Should signal unconditional surrender.
Smug as the ocean whale he calmly waits
For lesser fish to swim obligingly
Into his jaws, but one thing he forgets:
Once he has Rome, I will have him.
For anything he does then will be wrong
Because he does it. If he's hard on the nobles
He's done for—the Volscian nobles will object.
And if he's easy on the nobles, he's done for—
Then too the Volscian nobles will object.
This man was fortune's child and yet unable
To use his fortune. He could not exchange
The saddle for the seat of government
Or war for peace. His deeds are great
But he dwarfs them by extolling them. Our merit
Depends upon the use our epoch makes of us.
Our power has no tomb so everlasting
As the speaker's platform on which it is praised.
The storm puts out the fire it has fanned
Nail drives out nail and power by power's unmanned.

Act Five

1

Rome. The Forum.

Menenius, **Cominius**, *and other* **Senators**. **Sicinius** *and* **Brutus**.

Cominius
He didn't seem to know me.

Menenius
                                                                His
Former commander!

Cominius
                                        Coriolanus, I said.
He forbade that name and every other, shouted
He was a king of nothing, titleless
Until he forged himself a new name in
The fire of burning Rome.

Sicinius
                                                    Or fails to.

Menenius
Will he be prevented by a pair of tribunes
Expert at bringing down the price of corn cakes?

Brutus
Whereas you are expert
At bringing down the price of Rome. Send up
Smoke from the Capitol, let your crony know
He's welcome. Fall upon your knees before
His tent. No, do it a mile away
And on your knees crawl into his good graces.
Make up your minds! Who wants to see the smoke?

(Pause)

Good. No one. Then distribute arms, or else
Those who reject the little smoke

Will see a big smoke from the blaze of Rome.

(Pause)

*(**Sicinius** and **Brutus** go out)*

Cominius
I pointed out
That mercy is more worthy of a king
The less it is expected. To which he
Replied that coming from a city which
Had banished him, my plea was rather tawdry.

Menenius

                                                            Indeed.

Cominius
I spoke of consideration for his friends.
He said he hadn't time to pick them out
From a pile of noisome musty chaff. He said
It was foolish for one poor grain or two
To leave the heap unburned to go on stinking.

Menenius
For one poor grain or two? I'm one of those.
His mother, wife and child, and this brave man
We are the grains.—They are the musty chaff
That stinks above the moon. And we must burn
On their account. All right, I'll go to him.
You tackled him too early in the morning
He hadn't had his breakfast. That, perhaps
Is why you found him in so sour a mood.
I'll wait till he has eaten.

*(**Menenius** goes out)*

Cominius

                                            He'll never gain a hearing.

2

The Volscian camp near Rome.

Sentries. Enter to them, **Menenius**.

First Sentry
Halt! Where are you from?

Second Sentry

Go back! Go back!

Menenius
I am a messenger of state. I come
To speak with Coriolanus.

First Sentry

You're a Roman?

Menenius

Yes.

First Sentry
You can't go through. Turn back. Our general
Wants no more truck with Rome.

Second Sentry

You'll see
Rome burning long before you speak to him.

Menenius
Men, if you've heard your general speak of Rome
Or of his friends there, I'll lay ten to one
He mentioned my name too—Menenius.

First Sentry
We're glad to hear it, but you can't go through.

Menenius
The general's my friend, I tell you.

First Sentry

Then

Friend of my general, go back!

Menenius   But my dear fellow, haven't I told you my name is Menenius, a member of your general's party from way back.

—Has he had his breakfast? Do you know that? I don't intend to speak to him before he's had his breakfast.

First Sentry   You're a Roman, aren't you?

Menenius   I'm what your general is.

First Sentry   Then you should hate Rome as he does. Let me tell you something. You've driven the man out of your city, the same man who defended it for you. You've thrown your shield to the enemy. Do you think you can stop what's coming now with old women's sighs, with a few virgins wringing their hands, or with the gouty kneeling of a doddering old fool like yourself? Do you, with your weak breath, expect to blow out the fire intended for Rome? Don't make me laugh.

Go back to Rome and wait for your execution!

Menenius   Sir, if your general knew . . .

(Enter **Coriolanus** *and* **Aufidius***)*

Coriolanus   What's going on?

Menenius   Now, fellow, you've got yourself in a fix. Judge by his manner of speaking to me whether or not you're ripe for the gallows.—My son, you are preparing a fire for us. Here's the water to quench it.

*(***Coriolanus** *looks to see if smoke is going up)*

Menenius   I was not easily moved to come here. They know that I alone can move you. Sighs, my son, blew me out of the city gate. And now I beseech you, let Rome live! Turn back, my son!

Coriolanus   Go away!

Menenius   What's this? Go away?

Coriolanus
I don't know you or any other Roman.
What I do now serves others. Moreover
I am entitled to revenge. The power to pardon
Is with the Volscians. Let it rather be
Consigned to forgetfulness that we were friends
Than sorrowfully recalled how much so. Go.
My ears are better fortified against
Your pleas than are your gates against my troops.
And yet, because I loved you, take this letter
I've written you. I would have sent it.
And now, Menenius, not another word.
This man, Aufidius, was dear to me in Rome
And yet you see . . .

Aufidius

You have stood firm.

(Coriolanus and Aufidius go out)

First Sentry   Well, sir, so your name is Menenius.

Second Sentry   It does wonders, doesn't it? You know the way home.

First Sentry   Did you hear how we were raked over the coals for not admitting a messenger of state?

3

Rome. One of the gates.

Cominius *and* **Senators** *are waiting for* **Menenius**. *He enters.*

Menenius   I told you there's no hope. Our throats are sentenced and waiting for the executioner.

Senator   Is it possible that a man can change so in so short a time?

Menenius   This Marcius has changed from man to dragon. His face turns ripe grapes sour. He moves like a war machine and the ground shrinks under his tread. I'm painting him from life.

*(*Sicinius *and* Brutus *have entered. With them* Citizens)

Cominius   The gods take pity on our poor city!

Menenius   No, this time the gods will not take pity on us. When we banished him, we disregarded them, and now that he's coming back, they will disregard us. *(To* **Brutus***)* And it's you we have to thank for all this.

(He goes out with the **Senators** *except for* **Cominius***)*

Brutus   They've gone to pack. They prefer to die on their estates. *(To the* **Citizens***)* It's just as we told you. The city fathers are leaving Rome to its fate. How do things stand in your districts?

A Citizen   The majority have reported for military duty. The ones who were still waiting to see if Menenius would get anywhere with Coriolanus will report now.

Brutus   Good. If the people who live off Rome won't defend it, then we, whom Rome has lived off up to now, will defend it. Why shouldn't masons defend their walls?

Cominius   A few of us are with you. Arms will be distributed. On my responsibility.

Citizens   Long live Cominius!

*(A **Second Citizen** enters)*

Second Citizen   Volumnia, his mother, and four women of the foremost families request a pass to see Caius Marcius. They want to plead with him to turn back.

Sicinius   Request rejected.

Brutus   Granted.

Sicinius   You mean to let those traitors out of the city?

Brutus   A few patrician families are living in fear of being stoned for their connection with him. They seem to have appealed to her. I don't believe the old lady is afraid of us, but I doubt if she wants to see the Volscian senate meeting on the Capitol. She's a patriot in her way: she'd rather see us plebeians trampled on by Romans than by Volscians. What do you think, Cominius?

Cominius   Let them go, but . . . Do you see that cornerstone on the Capitol?

Sicinius   Why, what of it?

Cominius   If you can move it with your little finger, there is some hope that the ladies of Rome will get somewhere with him.

Brutus   Her words may be powerless to move him—though that's not so sure, she will be able to tell him certain things that are new to him. That stone you see there is immovable. Give me an earthquake and perhaps I'll move it after all.

Cominius   There's no more mercy in him than milk in a male tiger.

Sicinius   They say he loved his mother.

Cominius   He loved me too. And he no more remembers his mother now than an eight-year-old horse would remember his.

Brutus   The interview may give us a breathing spell. Tonight and tomorrow we'll be short of men to defend the walls. *(To the* **Citizen***)* They can go. But send one of their serving women with them, one you can trust, to report their conversation. Agreed?

Sicinius   Agreed. Two hard days ahead of us.

Brutus

I have the feeling, shared, I'm told, by many
Others, that Rome's a better place
With that man gone, a city worth defending
Perhaps for the first time since it was founded.

(All go out)

4

The Volscian camp.

Coriolanus, **Aufidius**, *a sentry.*

Sentry
No, sir, no smoke.

Aufidius

How long do you mean to wait?

Coriolanus
We'll camp tomorrow before the walls of Rome.

Aufidius
Why not today?

Coriolanus

You are my partner in this action.
You must inform the lords in Antium
How loyally I've gone about this business.

Aufidius
Of course. Of course. You've been the very soul
Of loyalty.

Coriolanus

That old man now, whom I sent
Back to Rome broken-hearted, loved me more
Than had he been my father, worshiped me as
A god—sending him was their last resort.

Aufidius
Yet even that old man who worships you
Showed no submission, only entreaty and
An invitation to go and hang yourself.

(Shouts backstage)

Coriolanus
What's the noise?

*(A **Soldier** enters)*

Soldier

A delegation, sir
Some ladies of the foremost Roman families
Are here in camp. It may be rumor, but
They say your mother's here, sir, and your wife
And little boy.

Coriolanus *(looking **Aufidius** in the eye)*

Control your feelings! Clench
Your teeth, for fear the gods above will laugh
And say this scene's unnatural. The
Volscians can plow up Rome and harrow Italy
Before you'll see me bow to nature or
Grovel before my instinct.

*(**Volumnia**, **Virgilia** with **Young Marcius**, and four Roman ladies have entered)*

Virgilia

My lord and husband!
*(**Coriolanus** approaches and greets them)*

Coriolanus
Woman, these eyes are not the same as
They were in Rome.

Virgilia

Yes, troubles change a man.

Volumnia
You know this lady?

Coriolanus

Young Publicola's
Illustrious sister. Rome's chaste Luna.
My dear Valeria!

Virgilia
Here's a small extract of yourself, which by
The interpretation of the years may grow
To be entirely like you.

Coriolanus

                                                    Yes, my boy

The gods, I trust, are busy making you
A fighter, who amidst the battle's tumult
Will stand, for all who see you, like a beacon
Invulnerable to shame as well.

Volumnia

                                                    Kneel, child.

Coriolanus *(preventing him from kneeling)*
That's my good boy, and now don't ask me to
Call off my soldiers and negotiate
Again with Rome's bricklayers. And don't tell
Me that my conduct is unnatural.
Aufidius, and you Volscians, listen closely:
We want no private word from Rome. Your business!

Volumnia
If silence were possible, I should keep silent
For then I should say nothing that would stir
You or destroy you. Nor should I waste my words.
For I have not set out like other mothers
To save her child, but rather to corrupt him
That is, if he's still human—and if he's not
He'll turn against me. Son, I cannot pray
The gods to give you victory, as under
Usual circumstances would be my duty
Nor to give victory to our city, as would also be
My duty. I must either forfeit Rome
Our family's cradle, or forfeit you, our mainstay
In Rome. To me the outcome's fatal
In either case, for either you'll be led
Through Rome in chains as a traitor, or else in triumph
You'll tread the orphaned ruins of your city

And thereupon be crowned with bronze for shedding
Your wife's and children's blood. For my part, son
I shall not wait until the war decides which
Misfortune is to strike me. If I can't
Persuade you, you will not set foot in Rome
Before you've trampled on the womb of
The mother who bore you.

Virgilia

And on mine

That brought you forth this boy to keep your name
Living in time.

Young Marcius

You will not trample me.

I'll run away until I'm bigger, then I'll fight.

Coriolanus

Aha!

If you would not turn womanish and mild
Don't look upon the face of woman or child.
I've sat too long.

(He stands up)

Volumnia

Not only in our presence.

Forget my petty trouble, that I'll find
It hard to veil my face from this day on
Whenever I go out, because your father
Never gave me reason to. Enough of
Your childish sentiment. I've something else
To say. The Rome you will be marching on
Is very different from the Rome you left.
You are no longer indispensable
Merely a deadly threat to all. Don't expect
To see submissive smoke. If you see smoke
It will be rising from the smithies forging
Weapons to fight you who, to subject your
Own people, have submitted to your enemy.
And we, the proud nobility of Rome

Must owe the rabble our salvation from the
Volscians, or owe the Volscians our
Salvation from the rabble. Come, we'll go now.
The fellow had a Volscian for a mother
His wife is in Corioli, and this child
Resembles him by chance.

(The women go out)

Coriolanus
O mother, mother! What have you done?

Rome. A guarded gate.

Brutus *and* **Sicinius**. *A* **Messenger**.

Messenger
News!
The Volscians have withdrawn and Marcius with them!

Brutus
The stone has moved. The people takes
Up weapons, and the old earth shakes.

(Both go out)

Corioli. The city gate.

Aufidius *with* **Attendant** *and* **Officers**.

Aufidius
Stand over there and give the senators
This paper when they come to welcome me.
Tell them I'll vouch for the truth of what it says
Before them and before the people. Right
Here at the gate I will accuse him, when
He comes to clear himself with empty words.
Go now.

(The **Attendant** *stands off to one side and gives the arriving* **Senators** Aufidius' *paper)*

Senators

Most welcome home!

Aufidius

Why welcome?
I haven't earned your welcome. Have you read
My message?

First Senator

Yes.

Second Senator

And with dismay. His old
Misdeeds can pass. But stopping where he should
Have started, throwing away the advantage
Leaving us nothing but the bill to pay
That's unforgivable.

Aufidius

He's coming. Hear what he says.

(Enter **Coriolanus** *with drums and banners.* **Citizens** *with him)*

Coriolanus

Hail, gentlemen. I'm back. Your soldier
No more infected with the love of my country
Than when I marched off under your
Supreme command. Through bloody fields I've carried
Your battle to the very gates of Rome.
The spoil that we've brought back accounts for more than
A third of what the campaign cost.

Aufidius

                                      Don't read

The inventory. Tell the traitor he has grossly
Abused your trust, and . . .

Coriolanus

                          Traitor? Why? What's wrong?

Aufidius

Yes, traitor, Marcius.

Coriolanus

                                        Marcius?

Aufidius

                                  Did you think

I'd bow to your theft, your stolen name, and call
You Coriolanus in Corioli?
You lords and senators of this state, this man
Is perjured. He has betrayed your cause. For a
Few drops of salt he has given away your Rome
(Your Rome, I say) to his wife and mother
Breaking his oath like a thread of rotten silk.
Without so much as calling a council of war
At the mere sight of his nurse's tears, he whimpered
And whined away your victory. The drummer
Boys blushed, the men
Looked at each other in silence.

Coriolanus

                                      I whimpered?

Aufidius
Like a milksop.

Coriolanus

Oh, you barefaced liar!
Milksop! Forgive me, gentlemen, I've never railed
Before in public. Worthy gentlemen
I've thrashed such welts into this cur
He'll take them to his grave.

Second Senator

Peace, both of you!

Coriolanus
Cut me to pieces, Volscians. Let the children
Redden their penknives in me. Milksop!
You lying dog! If ever your chronicles
Should tell the truth, they'll say that like
An eagle in a dovecote, I fluttered
Your Volscians in Corioli. Milksop!

Aufidius
Enough! More than enough! Gentlemen
Will you allow this braggart to remind you
Of his luck in battle that was your disgrace?

Officer　That's his death warrant!

Citizens　Tear him to pieces.—He killed my son.—My
daughter.—He killed my cousin Marcus.—He killed my father.

Aufidius
Kill him!

*(**Aufidius'** officers draw and kill **Coriolanus**)*

7

Rome. The senate.

Consul, **Senators**, *tribunes.*

Consul
The tribunes' motion to restore the lands
Taken from the inhabitants of Corioli
To their owners, is enacted into law.

Senator
Motion: that we construct an aqueduct
From the third hill to the eastern gardens.

*(A **Messenger** brings in a dispatch)*

Consul
This message says that Caius Marcius
Was stabbed to death in Corioli
Yesterday morning.

(Silence)

Menenius
Motion: He's dead now, therefore let his name
So great before misfortune fell upon
It, be inscribed in the Capitol
As that of a Roman and a . . .

Brutus
Motion: let the senate proceed
With current business.

Consul

Question:

His family has petitioned that its women
As stipulated in the law of Numa
Pompilius concerning the survivors

Of fathers, sons and brothers, be permitted
To wear mourning in public for ten months.

Brutus
Rejected.

(The senate resumes its deliberations)

The Trial of Joan of Arc at Rouen, 1431

After a Radio Play by Anna Seghers

Collaborator: B. Besson
Translators: Ralph Manheim and Wolfgang Sauerlander

The proceedings were recorded day by day in the Latin language. The original of the trial record was prepared for Bishop Cauchon of Beauvais and is preserved at the Chamber of Deputies in Paris. The radio play is based on these trial records as well as on the testimony and information furnished by contemporaries. Bertolt Brecht used the radio play for his dramatization for the Berliner Ensemble.

A. S.

Characters

Joan of Arc
Bishop Cauchon of Beauvais
Jean Beaupère
Jean De La Fontaine
Jean De Chatillon (Chation)
Guillaume Erard
Nicolas Midi
Guillaume Manchon
Jean D'Estivet
Jean Lefèvre
Jean Massieu
Raoul De Rinel
A Clerk
The Executioner
Nuns
An English Observer
His Adjutant
Guards of Joan of Arc
English Soldiers
Two Peasant Girls

Jacques Legrain
Peasant
Peasant Woman
Son
Sister-in-Law
Child
Fishwife
Dr. Dufour
His Two Nieces
Well-Dressed Gentleman
Loose Woman
Wine Merchant
Innkeeper
Young Curate
War Cripple
Grandfather Breuil and His
    Grandson
Children
People

1

Autumn, 1430. For eight years war has been raging between England and France. Recently France has undertaken two bloody campaigns under the banner of a seventeen-year-old girl, Joan of Arc, in a desperate attempt to ward off the English conquerors who still occupy more than two-thirds of the country. A village in Touraine, in the unoccupied part of France, gets bad news.

In front of a **Peasant** *house in Touraine two young girls are pressing grapes.* **Children** *are helping.*

Young Girls *(singing)*
Oh wondrous maiden of Lorraine
Barely sixteen and daughter of a frugal hearth
Upon your shield the enemy strikes in vain.
War is your strength, your resting place the naked earth.
Your boldness has its equal in your guile
Your enemies fall back in panic fear
None dares to stand, they run full many a mile
And countless eyes look on from far and near.

Second Girl *(to the* **Children***)*   Don't eat them all.—They're worse than woodpeckers.

A Boy   You haven't filled a single vat yet.

The Girls *(sing)*
Many, it's true, are so cast down with woe
They cannot understand the Maid. For he
Who weeps is blinded. Though in the brightest glow
His eyes are powerless to see.
But many now have joined the Maiden's ranks
As though to dance they're marching off to fight
The Loire has shaken the enemy from its banks
The sun of France shines with a clearer light.

First Girl   Where's Jacques?

Second Girl   Gone to town again.

First Girl   He ought to go easy on his leg.

Second Girl   I can't hold him back.—How much more is there to pick in the upper vineyard?

First Girl   Two acres.

The Girls *(sing)*
Oh, all ye villains, traitors all
Suffered too long by this long-suffering folk
You who have fostered England's joy and France's fall
Her poverty and shame and captive yoke:
You have been fighting for an unjust cause.
It's not too late for you to mend your ways.
If you go on supporting France's foes
A bitter end will strike your evil days.

Jacques Legrain *(joins them)*   They've captured her, near Compiègne. They've put her in a cage and they're taking her to Rouen.

First Girl   No?!

Legrain   Get my pack ready.

Second Girl   Where are you going?

Legrain   To Rouen, to buy a pound of mackerel.

2

February 21, 1431. In the market place of English-occupied Rouen a crowd looks on as English noblemen and French renegade churchmen lead the resistance fighter to her trial.

Market place at Rouen. Among the crowd a **Peasant** *family (father, mother,* **Sister-In-Law**, **Son**, *and* **Child**), *a* **Fishwife**, **Legrain** *with his pack, a* **Well-Dressed Gentleman**, *a* **Loose Woman**, *a* **Wine Merchant**, *a physician,* **The Executioner** *in his everyday clothes. Two* **English Soldiers**. *Church bells and drumrolls.*

Well-Dressed Gentleman   That's the Duke of Bedford.

Fishwife   Look at his white horse. As sleek and fat as his master.

Peasant Woman   Hey, Johnny, are you sure she'll come this way?

Son   Or is she already inside?

Fishwife   Don't worry, madame, she's sure to come this way.

Peasant Woman   Eugene, have you got the food parcel?

Child   Who's that all in silk?

Well-Dressed Gentleman   Bishop Cauchon of Beauvais.

Dr. Dufour   A French bishop walking behind an English duke! I'm surprised the Englishman hasn't got him on a leash.

Loose Woman *(sings in an undertone)*
Bishop Cauchon of Beauvais
Is an Englishman now, they say
On sentimental grounds
And for five thousand pounds.

Fishwife   That's no joke for the Maid.

Loose Woman   They say she has voices and visions. I wonder if it's true.

Peasant Woman   Did you hear that? She has visions.

Peasant   Ssh.

Wine Merchant   The learned doctors will see about that.

Well-Dressed Gentleman   The papal nuncio.

*(The **Peasant Woman** crosses herself)*

Loose Woman   Look at his hat!

*(All laugh, including the **Peasant Woman**)*

Sister-in-Law   Too bad about the girl. Nobody likes the English.

Well-Dressed Gentleman   I wouldn't say that too loud, madame, not today.

Peasant   She's always shooting her mouth off.

Loose Woman   Johnny, there's somebody here that doesn't like you.

Fishwife   Forget it, they don't understand French.

Wine Merchant   Maybe it's all for the best. She was a troublemaker.

Fishwife   The English give you plenty of business, don't they?

Dr. Dufour   Well said!

*(**Loose Woman** laughs)*

Well-Dressed Gentleman   I beg your pardon!

Peasant Woman *(to **Child**)*   Isn't it a lovely holiday, Jacqueline?

Wine Merchant   I've already seen one of these witches burnt.

Executioner   When was that?

Wine Merchant   Four years ago, in Beauvais, in the spring of twenty-seven.

Executioner   I see.

Fishwife   That's Monsieur Dujardin, the executioner.

Peasant Woman   Where?

(All turn around to look at **The Executioner***)*

Loose Woman   Dear me!

Well-Dressed Gentleman   Seems like he's taking her measurements.

Dr. Dufour   Look, there are the doctors from Paris.

Son   Why can't the English try her themselves?

Dr. Dufour   They'd rather let the French do it for them.

Son   But the French have no reason to.

Dr. Dufour   All those doctors ought to be able to find one.

Legrain   As long as she answers boldly. That's the main thing.

Sister-in-Law   Boldly! How can a girl stand up against so many?

Loose Woman   What did she have to stick her neck out for? Why didn't she stay home?

(**Well-Dressed Gentleman** *assents)*

Legrain   Because the English came to France. Because the English occupied all France as far as the Loire. Because they're gobbling up the whole country. Because they've dethroned the king. Because before she came along the king was too lazy to defend himself.

Peasant Woman   Because—because—because, is that a reason to get crazy ideas and run around in men's clothes in front of soldiers?

Peasant   Shut up!

Well-Dressed Gentleman   She says she owes it to her country, madame.

Dr. Dufour   Country? What do you mean by country?

Fishwife   Her voices told her to drive the English out of the country, Dr. Dufour.

Dr. Dufour   Country! What difference does it make to the country who's on the white horse that's trampling it into dust? The Duke of Bedford or the Duke of Orléans? What difference does it make to the country who gobbles up its wheat and its wine, its venison and fruit, its taxes and tithes? The Lord of Beauvais or the Duke of Gloucester?

Fishwife   It's easier to give a French lord a piece of your mind. Those English gentlemen don't even understand our curses.

Child   Is that the king?

Sister-in-Law   No, that's an English trumpeter.

(Drumrolls)

Loose Woman   Here she comes! Here she comes!

English Soldier   Move back! Back, I say!

Peasant Woman   Careful with the eggs, Eugene!

Loose Woman   My, she's little.

Sister-in-Law   Those chains must be heavy on her. No bigger than an apple.

*(The **Wine Merchant** laughs)*

Legrain   That little apple had the English on the run.

Dr. Dufour   The Duke of Bedford paid the Duke of Luxemburg twelve thousand pounds for that little apple.

Peasant   Why did he do that?

Fishwife   To make his Englishmen stop running.

3

At the first session of the great ecclesiastical trial in the Chapel
Royal of the castle, Joan cleverly eludes the trick questions of
the churchmen who are out to convict her of heresy, and boldly
reminds them of the wretched state of France.

The Chapel Royal of the castle. The churchmen, **Beaupère, Chation,
La Fontaine, d'Estivet, Manchon, Midi, Lefèvre, Massieu,
Brother Raoul** *and the* **Clerk.** *Enter the* **English Observer** *with*
His Adjutant *and the* **Bishop of Beauvais.** *The churchmen kneel.*

Bishop   Praised be the Lord.

All   For ever and ever. Amen.

The English Observer *(to the* **Bishop***)*   Splendid crowd of
doctors.

Bishop   Thank you.

The English Observer   Pleasant chapel, even if not one of the
oldest.

Bishop   Nor one of the newest. Built by Charles the . . . *(He raises
five fingers)*

The English Observer   Oh, the fifth, I see. Don't let me keep
you.

(All take their seats)

Bishop   We, Bishop Cauchon of Beauvais, and our illustrious
assessors, the noble lords and doctors here present, have gathered
this day to conduct a trial which we hereby declare opened. Milord,
have you conveyed to the accused the summons to appear before
us and answer our questions in accordance with the law?

Adjutant   Said woman has answered the summons and is waiting
outside. She requests, however, to be admitted to confession before
the trial.

*(The **Bishop** consults the assessors. They nod)*

Bishop   The request must be denied. In view of the gravity of the charges and the refusal of the accused to relinquish her male clothing. Monsieur Massieu, bring in the accused.

Massieu   The accused may be brought in.

Adjutant   Bring her in.

*(**Joan** is led in by two **English** soldiers)*

Bishop   This woman now appearing before us, Joan, popularly called the Maid, has been apprehended in the jurisdiction of our diocese. As a suspected heretic she has been turned over to us by our Most Christian Lord, the King of England and France. And inasmuch as rumors concerning her offenses against the faith have spread far beyond our diocese and indeed throughout France and the whole of Christendom, we have brought her before this court in order that she may justify herself. We admonish you, Joan, to touch these Most Holy Gospels and swear to reply truthfully to all questions. Monsieur Massieu!

*(At a sign from **Massieu Brother Raoul** brings the Bible)*

Bishop   Now swear by these gospels. Place both hands on the book.

Joan   But I don't know what you're going to ask me. Maybe you want to know something that I won't tell you.

Bishop   Come, come, just swear to tell the truth in all matters concerning the faith.

Joan   I'll gladly swear to tell you about my family and my home and anything that happened before I came to Chinon, but I will not say one word about my voices and revelations, not even if you cut my head off.

Bishop   Very well, Joan. We ask you only to tell the truth in matters of faith, as the law requires in proceedings of this kind. Go on.

Joan *(kneels)*   I swear to tell the truth in matters of faith. *(She sits down)*

Bishop   Tell us your first and last name.

Joan   At home they called me Jeannette and in France Jeanne. I know of no other name.

Bishop   Where were you born?

Joan   In Domrémy on the Meuse.

Bishop   Who are your parents?

Joan   Jacques d'Arc and Isabeau.

Bishop   How old are you?

Joan   About nineteen, I think.

Bishop   Who instructed you in the faith?

Joan   My mother taught me everything: the Lord's Prayer, the Hail Mary, and the Creed.

Bishop   Say the Lord's Prayer.

Joan   Hear my confession and I'll say the prayer.

Bishop   In men's clothes? Come now, just say the Lord's Prayer.

Joan   I will not say it unless you hear my confession.

Bishop   Joan, we, your bishop, forbid you to leave the prison for whatsoever purpose except by our permission. To do so would be disobedience to the church and a grave offense against the faith.

Joan   I can't accept that ruling. No one can accuse me of breaking my word if I escape, I haven't given it to anybody. What's more, I protest against these chains and shackles you've loaded me down with.

Bishop   You have made several attempts to escape. Hence our severity.

Joan   Naturally I tried to escape. Like any captive. I'd escape right now if I could.

Bishop   Have your voices given you permission to escape from prison whenever you feel like it?

Joan   I've asked their permission more than once, but never received it.

Bishop   I see.

Joan   But then they say that "God helps those who help themselves."

Bishop *(to the* **English Observer***)*   With your permission, my lord. *(To the* **Guards***)* We enjoin you most urgently, you, John Grey, and you, William Talbot, to guard her closely and permit no one to speak to her.

Guards   Yes, sir.

Bishop   Monsieur Jean Beaupère, Professor of the Faculty of Theology at the University of Paris, you may question the accused.

Beaupère *(after having bowed to the* **English Observer***)*   First of all, I must once again exhort you, Joan, to answer my questions with nothing but the truth. Have you learned a trade?

Joan   Yes. Sewing and spinning.

Beaupère   What work did you do at home?

Joan   I did the housework. Sometimes I helped to drive the cows into the fortress to prevent the English from stealing them.

Midi   Monsieur Beaupère, may I interrupt? Are the people of Domrémy loyal to our Most Christian Lord, the King of England and France, or do they follow the man whom you call King of France?

Joan   I know of only one person in Domrémy who's in favor of the English. I'd gladly have seen his head cut off if it had so pleased the Lord.

(Commotion among the assessors)

Bishop   Monsieur Beaupère, pray continue.

Beaupère   When did you first hear what you call your voices?

Joan   When I was thirteen I heard a voice that came from God. That was the first time, and I was really frightened. The voice came to me in my father's garden, one summer afternoon. I heard it somewhere behind me, from the direction of the church. A great light came with the voice.

Beaupère   How could you see the light if it was somewhere behind you?

Joan   When I heard the voice for the third time, I knew it was the voice of an angel.

Beaupère   What did it say?

Joan   It has always protected me. It told me to be good and go to church often. And two or three times a week it told me to leave everything and go to my king. It said I would raise the siege of Orléans.

Beaupère   What was your answer?

Joan   I said: I'm a girl, I've never ridden a horse, I don't know a thing about war. But the voice pressed me cruelly and gave me no peace. It told me to go. So I went.

D'Estivet   Question: Hadn't you left home once before?

Joan   Yes, when the English attacked our village, we all ran away, and then two weeks later we came back. Everything had been burned to the ground.

Bishop   Let's get on.

La Fontaine (*intervenes*)   Was it right to leave secretly? Are we not enjoined to honor our father and our mother?

Joan   Yes, but even if I'd had a hundred fathers and mothers, I'd have gone.

Beaupère   What kind of clothes were you wearing when you arrived in Chinon?

Joan   I went to my king in Chinon in men's clothing. I had a sword, but no other weapons.

Beaupère   Who told you to wear men's clothes?

Joan   Ask me something else.

D'Estivet   Your Eminence, we must insist on being told who advised the accused to wear male attire.

Chation   Absolutely.

Joan   Ask me something else.

Bishop   Don't you know that the Scriptures say: The woman shall not wear that which pertaineth unto man, neither shall a man put on a woman's garment?

Joan   I had the best of advice and I trusted it.

Beaupère   How did you get to this man whom you call your king?

Joan   No trouble at all. I arrived in Chinon around noon and went to an inn. After dinner I went to the castle. I recognized the king right away, with the help of my voice. I told him I wanted to go out and fight the English.

Manchon   May I interrupt?

Bishop *(to* **Beaupère***)*   Monsieur Manchon!

Manchon   Did the king have voices too?

Joan   Ask him, maybe he'll tell you.

Lefèvre   Question: How far away from the king were you standing?

Joan   About a lance's length, I think.

Lefèvre   When you first saw the man whom you call your king was there an angel beside him?

Joan   God forbid, I didn't see one.

Bishop *(to* **Beaupère***, with contempt)*   Monsieur Lefèvre!

D'Estivet   Was there a halo around his head?

Joan   There was a splendid gathering of knights around him. Close to three hundred knights. And about fifty torches were burning, not to mention the spiritual light.

Manchon   By your leave. Do you still hear your voice?

Joan   Not a day goes by without my hearing it and I'm badly in need of it too.

La Fontaine   What do you ask of your voice?

Joan   Victory for my side.

Chation   The day when you fought before Paris was a feast day.

Joan   Possible.

Chation   Was it right to fight on a feast day?

Joan   Ask me something else.

La Fontaine   When you came to Compiègne, before you were taken prisoner, would you have gone on fighting if the voice had foretold that you would be captured?

Joan   With a heavy heart. I would always have done what it told me.

Midi   How long were you a prisoner in the tower of Beaurevoir?

Joan   Four months. When I found out I'd been sold to the English and they were going to take me away, I became very downcast. My voices gave me no counsel and at first I was scared. But then I was more scared of the English, so I forced myself to jump.

Midi   Did you say at the time that you would rather die than fall into the hands of the English?

Joan   I'd certainly rather be in the hands of God than of the English.

Beaupère   When was the last time you heard your voices?

Joan   Today.

Bishop   What did they say?

Joan   They said I should answer you judges boldly. You, Bishop of Beauvais, call yourself my judge. I don't know if that is true. But I must tell you that you will be putting yourself in great peril if you judge me wrongly.

Beaupère   Was it saints that spoke to you, or angels, or God Himself?

Joan   Saint Catherine and Saint Margaret.

Bishop   Anyone else?

Joan   Saint Michael.

Beaupère   Which was the last?

Joan   Saint Michael. He's the one who sent me to Chinon.

Beaupère   What is he telling you now?

(**Midi** *is shaking with repressed laughter*)

Joan   Always to show you a friendly face and to answer you boldly.

Massieu   Was Saint Michael naked?

Joan   Naked? Do you think God can't afford to clothe him?

Lefèvre   Did he wear his hair cut short?

Joan *(for the first time slightly impatient)*   Why should Saint Michael have his hair cut short?

The English Observer   Let her be asked whether Saint Margaret speaks English.

Adjutant *(to **Massieu**)*   My lord wishes to know whether Saint Margaret speaks English.

Massieu *(to **Joan**)*   Does Saint Margaret speak English?

Joan   Why would she speak English when she's against the English?

*(The **English Observer** laughs)*

Chation   How could you be sure it was Saint Michael and not the devil pretending to be Saint Michael?

Joan   By the way he spoke, and because he taught me a lot of good things.

Chation   What did he teach you?

Joan   Most of all that I must come to the help of my people,
which so many have abandoned. And he told me about the great
misery in France.

Beaupère   I see. Did you wear a sword?

Joan   The sword from Vaucouleurs. I had a sheath made for it out
of strong leather.

Beaupère   Did you carry a flag?

Joan   I had a banner, snow-white.

La Fontaine   Which did you like more, your sword or your banner?

Joan   My banner, much more. At least forty times more. Holding
it high, I led the troops against the enemy. I never killed anybody
myself.

D'Estivet   Were you never present when Englishmen were killed?

Joan *(laughing)*   I sure was. You talk like a ninny. On battlefields
there are dead people. They should have stayed home.

Beaupère   Why did you never negotiate with the enemy?

Joan   My side sent word to the English that no delay would be
tolerated, no postponement granted. They should clear out then and
there. I shouted over to them myself to beat it on the spot, without
bothering to dress, with no other baggage than their bare lives.

The English Observer *(pushing the* **Adjutant***)*   Go and tell him.

Adjutant *(aside)*   Your Eminence.

Bishop   What's up?

Adjutant   The Duke of Bedford will be angry; he specifically
asked for a speedy trial. We consider this additional questioning
superfluous.

Bishop   The Duke of Bedford will have to accept the fact that this
is an ecclesiastical court, not a court martial. Not that the Duke of
Bedford has anything to worry about.—Monsieur Beaupère!

Manchon   Question: What do you believe will happen to your side?

Joan   It will win. The English will have to give up every last shred of French soil. Not a single man will remain.

Midi   Remember where you are, girl.

Bishop   How can you know such things unless the devil told you?

Joan   The devil doesn't know anything. I know the English are out to kill me. They figure that once I'm dead they'll conquer the rest of France. But even with a hundred thousand more men, they will never get France.

(The **English Observer** *rises)*

Beaupère   That shouldn't be in the record.

Massieu   It cannot be stricken. I protest, Professor Beaupère.

Beaupère   Do you believe God hates the English?

Joan   Whether God hates or loves the English or what He may have in mind for their souls, I don't know. What I do know is that they're going to be driven out of France, except for the ones who die here.

The English Observer   Incompetent. *(Goes out with* **His Adjutant***)*

Bishop   D'Estivet! I wish the Duke would realize that this trial must proceed strictly according to law. The eyes of the world are upon us. Monsieur Massieu!—Monsieur Beaupère, please continue!—Brother Raoul! Go and advise my lord that we have observers here from all over, from the council at Basel, from Rome, from every chancellery in Europe. *(***Brother Raoul** *leaves)* Monsieur Beaupère!

Beaupère *(peevishly)*   Did God command you to wear male attire?

Joan *(lustily)*   Why do you keep asking about my clothes? Clothes are nothing, they don't matter at all. Why don't you say you want to burn me because I'm against the English?

Beaupère   Did you receive the sacraments in male attire?

Joan   Unarmed, in men's clothes.

Bishop   Hm, in view of what we have just heard, we declare today's session closed. Monsieur Massieu, conduct the accused back to prison.

(**Joan** *is taken away)*

Bishop   Gentlemen, from now on we shall question the accused in her cell, myself and two assessors from our number; the public will be excluded. Make use of your time, gentlemen, and study the transcripts. And I remind you once more that no one is permitted to leave Rouen until the trial is over.—Praised be the Lord.

All   Forever and ever. Amen.

4

Bishop Cauchon of Beauvais visits Joan in the prison of La Tour des Champs and asks her a strange question.

The prison of La Tour des Champs. **Joan** *is lying on a cot. Two* **English Guards** *are playing dice.*

First Guard   Joan!

Joan *(tired)*   What is it now?

First Guard *(mocking her)*   I'm Saint Catherine.

Joan   A very brave soldier, that's what you are.

Second Guard   I'm Saint Margaret.

Joan   You're a swine. Shut up!

Second Guard   It's me, Saint Michael.

(**Joan** *strikes him)*

Second Guard   The bitch. Did Saint Michael wake you like this? Did he hold you like this?

(Enter **Jean de la Fontaine***)*

La Fontaine   What's going on?

(The **Guards** *let* **Joan** *go. She gets up)*

First Guard   Halt! No one can come in here. It's forbidden.

La Fontaine   I'm in charge of this interrogation.—Why are you crying, Joan?

Joan   I'm not crying. Leave me alone.

La Fontaine   How have you been getting along since Saturday?

Joan   You can see for yourself how I've been getting along, Father. As best as I can. The bishop sent me a piece of carp, but it made me sick.

La Fontaine   Oh, I'm sorry to hear that. *(He motions the* **Guards** *to step aside)* Listen to me. You've got to accept my advice; don't be so obstinate. Several among us assessors wish you well. Do you understand?

Joan   No.

La Fontaine   Get ready, Joan, the interrogation is about to start.

Joan   All over again?

La Fontaine   You have no one but yourself to blame if it's taking a long time. Here is your bishop.

(Enter the **Bishop, Massieu** *and the* **Clerk***)*

La Fontaine *(in a low voice to the entering churchmen)*   The conditions here are intolerable. These English guards . . .

Bishop   Tush. The child is used to soldiers' company. I trust she can handle them. Monsieur Massieu!

(At a sign from **Massieu** *the* **Guards** *and the* **Clerk** *leave)*

Bishop   Well then. You have said that we, your bishop, would be putting ourselves in great peril if we called you to account. What did you mean? What would that peril be? For us, your bishop, and the others?

Joan   You'll find out soon enough.

Bishop   Did your voices tell you something about it?

Joan   This has nothing to do with your trial. But it's quite possible that the people who want me out of the world will be leaving it before me.

Bishop   Did your voices promise a turn for the better?

Joan   I've answered that before.

Bishop   When will it be?

Joan   I don't know the day and the hour.

Bishop   The year then.

Joan   I won't tell you just yet.

Bishop   Before Saint John's day?

Joan   Ask me something else.

(**Massieu** *whispers in the* **Bishop's** *ear)*

Bishop   What did you say to Grey of the guards?

Joan   That something might happen to them before All Saints' Day.

Bishop   Monsieur La Fontaine.

(At a sign from **Massieu** *the* **Clerk** *returns)*

La Fontaine *(stepping close to* **Joan***)*   Have your voices promised that you would be rescued from prison?

Joan *(with sudden gaiety)*   My voices promised me help. But I don't know if it means that I'll be rescued from prison, or not until the day of the execution, when a great turmoil will make it possible for me to escape. My voices keep telling me that a great victory will set me free.

La Fontaine   I take it you know that others have claimed to hear voices.

(**Joan** *is silent)*

La Fontaine   You have met a certain Catherine of La Rochelle, have you not?

Joan   I have. She told me a white lady in a golden robe appeared to her; she said the lady commanded her to ask the king for heralds and trumpeters. They were to go from city to city proclaiming that anyone possessing gold or silver or hidden treasures must hand them over at once. She said she could tell who was holding back and find all the treasure anyway. Catherine said she'd use the money to pay my infantry.

La Fontaine   What was your answer?

Joan   I told her to go home to her husband and take care of her house and feed her children. But to make perfectly sure I talked it over with Saint Catherine and Saint Margaret and they said Catherine La Rochelle's talk was nonsense. Nothing in it. I wrote my king a report, telling him just that.

La Fontaine   Did you discuss anything else with her?

Joan   Oh yes. She wanted to go to the English and arrange for peace. I told her I didn't think they'd give us any peace except at lance's point.

Bishop   I see.

Joan   I also asked Catherine if her white lady came every night, because then I'd spend a night with her. I did. I stayed awake until midnight and I didn't see a thing. Then I fell asleep. In the morning I asked Catherine if the white lady had come. Yes, she said, while I was asleep. But she hadn't been able to wake me. I asked her if the lady would come the next night and she said yes. So I slept all day so as to stay awake at night. And I stayed awake all night but I didn't see a thing. I asked her several times if the white lady would come soon. Catherine always answered, yes, soon.

La Fontaine   Then you believe you are in a state of grace?

Joan   If I am not, God will put me in it; if I am, God will keep me in it. I would be the unhappiest creature in the whole world if I knew I wasn't in God's grace.

La Fontaine   But when you jumped from the tower, you wanted to kill yourself, did you not?

Joan   No. To escape.

La Fontaine *(with extreme insistence)*   Then you believe you can never again commit a deadly sin?

Joan   I firmly believe in my salvation.

Bishop   If you are confident of your salvation, why then would you wish to confess?

Joan   A body can never keep her conscience clear enough, bishop.

La Fontaine *(no longer kindly, almost furious)*   Wouldn't you say it was a deadly sin to capture a man by ruse, and then to kill him?

Joan   I never did any such thing.

La Fontaine   You did not? What about a certain Franqué of Arras who was murdered in Lagny at your command?

Joan   Him? He deserved it. By his own admission he was a scoundrel, a thief, and a traitor. I wanted to exchange him for one of our people, a good man, Monsieur de l'Ours in Paris. But the man died on us in the meantime. It would have been stupid to let that no-good Franqué go.

La Fontaine   Did you give money to the man who captured Franqué?

Joan   I have no mint or treasury in France; how would I pay out large sums of money?

Bishop   Joan, in summation, we charge you as follows:

1. You fought before Paris on a feast day.
2. You jumped from the tower at Beaurevoir with intent to commit suicide.
3. You brought about the death of Franqué of Arras.
4. You have worn men's clothes.

La Fontaine   Is it possible that you see no mortal sin in all this? Joan!

Joan   Bishop of Beauvais, you'd better watch what you're doing. This trial of yours is crooked. First, this thing about Paris—what if it was a feast day? Sin or not, it has nothing to do with this trial, the confessional's the place for it. Secondly, I jumped from the tower in hope and not despair.

Bishop   And the men's clothes?

Joan   As long as I'm here, I have to wear them. If you give me women's clothes and let me go back to my mother, I'll put them on and go home.

Massieu   Joan, what would you prefer, to forgo mass or to attend it in women's clothes?

Joan   Dress me in women's clothes like any burgher's daughter, I'll even wear a long train and a big hat if that's the only way I can hear mass. When it's over I'll tear them off. But with all my heart I beseech you, let me be as I am.

Bishop   I have been told that your only reason for not removing your men's clothes is that you have heard of a plan to rescue you.

Joan   I won't answer any more questions. You'll find my answers in the record. *(She throws herself on the cot)*

Bishop   Very well. Let us close the proceedings. Transmit the bill of particulars to the court for engrossment.

5

The weekly market in Rouen.

Two stalls. The **Peasant Woman** *and her* **Son** *are selling cheese, butter, and eggs, the* **Fishwife** *is selling fish. A* **War Cripple** *is playing the bagpipes. Customers, among them* **Dr. Dufour** *and* **His Two Nieces**.

An English *soldier, already loaded down with merchandise, points at the wares in the* **Peasant Woman's** *stall. He makes her sell him twenty eggs, four cheeses, and two prints of butter. He allows the* **Peasant Woman** *to fish the money out of his purse.*

Peasant Woman (counting)   Twenty, twenty-two, twenty-four.

The English Soldier   Stop.

A Shabbily Dressed Woman   Two eggs, madame.

(The soldier lumbers to the **Fishwife's** *stall and buys the biggest fish.*

He takes out his purse, the **Fishwife** *takes out the money)*

The English Soldier   Stop. *(With a friendly grin he leaves)*

Fishwife   Hope it poisons you. *(To* **Dr. Dufour***)* Nice mackerel today, doctor.

Dr. Dufour *(choosing one)*   This one with the soulful eyes. No doubt she heard voices too. I suppose they advised her to take the bait.

First Niece *(from the* **Peasant Woman's** *stall)*   Uncle!

Peasant Woman   People shouldn't joke about religion. The girl is a witch and that's that.

Fishwife   Too bad she's a witch if she's against the English.

Peasant Woman   Her voices come from the devil.

Fishwife   Bah, her voices seem to say what we're all saying. I mean, that the English should get out of France.

Son   She's a saint.

Peasant Woman   You shut up!

Dr. Dufour *(addressing his mackerel)*   You may have been a saint and you may have been a witch, but now you've been caught and you're going to be fried.

Fishwife   Very true, doctor, witch or not, she's being tried because the English want to swallow up the rest of France.

First Niece   Come along, uncle, you'll get into trouble. *(Leaves, anxiously looking over her shoulder)*

Dr. Dufour *(with a negative gesture to his niece)*   Ah, madame, you're against the Maid because she's a witch. If she weren't a witch, Madame Braillard would be for her because she's a good Frenchwoman. Madame, I'm now going to buy one pound of your certified Catholic butter, and a minute ago you saw me buying a certified French fish from Madame Braillard. These opposites, dear ladies, will be united in my frying pan to make a mouth-watering dish.

Fishwife   You never change, Doctor Dufour.

Dr. Dufour   Why should I change, Madame Braillard?

Fishwife   The Maid might be able to tell you why, Dr. Dufour.

Son   They say she's giving the court a hard time.

*(Four priests, **Beaupère**, **d'Estivet**, **Mancbon**, and **Lefèvre**, in conversation, cross the market)*

Manchon   Well, what's next?

Beaupère   It's all over.

Manchon   What do you mean?

Beaupère   The report of the Paris faculty has come in.

D'Estivet   Fuel for the fire, crushing for the accused.

Beaupère   Schismatic and heretical on twelve counts.

Lefèvre   Of course people will say that Paris is occupied by the English, just as much as Rouen.

Manchon   No, Paris is Paris!

Lefèvre   I understand there's another report from old Gerson—favorable to the accused. There's no denying that for years now the man has been Europe's leading luminary. His opinion has been decisive in all ecclesiastical trials.

Beaupère   The old fox has always made his decisions with an eye to the common people. In Constance he sent Hus to the stake, but this time it's a child of the people.

Manchon   Child of the people, indeed! As subtle as ten theologians. How careful she is, for instance, not to say that her voices advised her to wear men's clothes. She knows that would finish her, because it would show incontestably that her voices came from the devil.

Lefèvre   Even then we wouldn't have been able to prove that she's in league with the devil. Maid who doth the devil see can no more a maiden be. I understand that Lady Bedford in person has established her virginity.

D'Estivet   And I understand that her husband, our beloved Duke of Bedford, has done likewise, thanks to an aperture in the floor, made for that express purpose.

(Laughter. They move on)

(Dr. Dufour has whispered to the war cripple. The latter nods and plays the well-known song lampooning Cauchon of Beauvais. Manchon drops him a coin, but is informed by d'Estivet that the song is not intended to be friendly)

D'Estivet *(to the **War Cripple**)*   Scoundrel.

(Indignantly the churchmen leave)

Fishwife *(joins in the singing)*
Bishop Cauchon of Beauvais
Is an Englishman now, they say
On sentimental grounds
And for five thousand pounds.

6

May 9, 1431. In the armory of the royal castle. Joan is threatened with torture.

Armory in the great tower of the royal castle. The **Bishop of Beauvais**, *all the assessors,* **Brother Raoul**, *the* **Clerk**, **The Executioner**, **Joan**, *and the* **Guards**.

Bishop   Praised be the Lord.

All   Forever and ever. Amen.

Brother Raoul   Your Eminence, this is Monsieur Dujardin, the executioner.

*(***The Executioner*** *kneels before the* **Bishop** *and kisses the hem of his cassock. The bishop blesses him)*

Bishop   Monsieur Jean de Chation, Professor at the Theological Faculty of Paris.

Chation   Joan, in humility and moderation, with no thought of vengeance or punishment, solely intent on your salvation and instruction, we shall make a last attempt to save your body and soul.

Joan   Just reel off your speech, then I'll answer you.

Chation   Is that all you wish to say?

Joan   Don't beat about the bush. Read the indictment.

Chation   Joan, we have meticulously examined your acts and deeds as recorded in these minutes. We have found grave trespasses.

Joan   How do I know what extra tidbits you've worked into the minutes?

Chation   Do you mean to say that you do not recognize us as your secular judges appointed by the church?

Joan   Exactly.

Chation   Joan, if as you indicate you refuse to recognize the article Unam Sanctam Ecclesiam Catholicam, the court must send you to the stake.

Joan   Even in the fire I couldn't say anything else.

Chation   Joan, we have shown you how hazardous, nay dangerous it is to direct one's curiosity to things that transcend the capacity of human understanding, to place one's faith in new things and even invent new and unheard-of things, for the demons find ways of insinuating themselves into our curiosity. All the learned masters and doctors of the University of Paris have recognized your statements concerning your voices and apparitions to be pure lies. Heedless of our admonitions, you in your pride have deemed yourself worthy to receive voices and inspirations directly from God. Forgetting that God tempts prideful persons like you with diabolical visions, you yourself have invented these voices. We therefore exhort you to subdue your vanity and cast off your lies. If you will not submit to the church today your soul will be consumed by eternal fire and your body by temporal fire.

Joan   Do you think you can intimidate me with such talk and win me over to your side?

Bishop   Monsieur La Fontaine!

La Fontaine   Joan, dearest sister. I beg you, don't let the worst happen. If you really heard voices, dear sister, accept the opinion of the University of Paris which declares your voices to be imaginings and nonsense. What would you have done if one of your soldiers had said, I refuse to obey the orders of my king's officers? So what can you think of yourself when you refuse to obey the representatives of your church? Abandon your resistance, dear sister, or your soul will suffer eternal torments. Moreover, I am very much in fear for your life. Submit, I implore you, in order that we may save your body and your soul.

Joan   I have submitted to God, isn't that enough?

La Fontaine   You should know, Joan, that we distinguish the church triumphant from the church militant. The church triumphant consists of God, his saints and all redeemed souls; the church militant of the Holy Father, the cardinals, prelates, bishops, priests and all Christians. This church, congregated upon earth, led by the Most Holy Ghost, is infallible. Will you submit to it?

Joan   I won't answer any more questions.

Bishop   Joan, for the last time I ask you, will you submit to the church?

Joan   What *is* the church? No. I will not submit to you judges.

Bishop   Will you submit to the pope?

Joan   Take me to him and I'll tell him.

Bishop   Will you submit to the Council of Basel?

Joan   The Council of Basel? What's that?

Lefèvre   It is an assembly representative of the entire church. In other words, it includes members of the English party as well as your own.

Joan   I think I'd rather submit to them.

Chation   Basel!!

Lefèvre   She has every right to do so.

Chation   It's out of the question.

Beaupère   What an idea!

Bishop   Who has been advising her since our last session?

Massieu   No one.

Manchon   Why, then, is she being asked?

Clerk   Can her submission be recorded as final?

Bishop   No, wait.

Joan   You're not letting him record anything in my favor.

Bishop   Be still!—Inasmuch as you, Joan, are unresponsive to our admonitions and continue to deny the truth, we are obliged to subject you to torture. Monsieur Massieu, show the accused the instruments.

*(The **Guards** lead **Joan** to the table where the instruments are displayed)*

Manchon   Pray answer us, Joan!

Lefèvre   Pray submit!

D'Estivet   Won't you give in, girl?

La Fontaine   You're not helping anyone.

Chation   Joan, the torturers are ready to lead you to the truth by force, for the salvation of your soul.

(Joan faints; she is brought front stage again)

Joan   If you break my bones with these instruments and squeeze my soul out of my poor body, I will not say anything different. And if I do say something different, I'll say afterwards that it was torn from me by force.

Massieu *(in an undertone)*   Should we?

La Fontaine *(in an undertone)*   Let us spare her.

Bishop   *(in a loud voice)* In view of the obstinacy of the accused and the insolence of her answers we, the judges, fear that torture can no longer benefit her. We shall therefore dispense with it. Take her back to prison.

*(**Joan** is dragged out)*

Sunday in the prison of La Tour des Champs. Joan hears a song, but does not understand the words.

Prison. Joan is lying on the cot. The two **English Guards**. *In the distance a bagpipe is playing "* **Bishop Cauchon of Beauvais**. *"*

Joan Why are the people so gay?

Guard Because it's a holiday. Why shouldn't people be gay?

Joan Yes.

Joan thinks the people have forgotten her, But in the markets and taverns they are beginning to understand her.

The "St. Peter's Catch" tavern. The **Peasant** *family from the outskirts are eating their lunch. A young, shabbily dressed curate. The* **Loose Woman**. *The* **Well-Dressed Gentleman**. *The* **Innkeeper**. *Bagpipe music.*

Legrain   I see there are decent people here. Anybody who can read?

Young Curate   What is it?

Legrain   It's a copy of the letter she wrote to the English before she raised the siege of Orléans. I don't know if you'd care to read it.

Young Curate   Does my cassock look as if it were paid for, by English money? *(He reads)* "Jesus Mary! You, King of England, and you, Duke of Bedford, who call yourselves regents of the kingdom of France, and you, William Pole, Earl of Suffolk, John Talbot, Thomas Lord of Scales, who call yourselves lieutenants of the said Duke of Bedford: render His due to the King of Heaven and give back the keys of all the fortified cities of France which you have taken and ravished. The Maid has come in the name of God. She is ready to make peace as soon as you leave France and pay for your presence here. And you, all the rest of you, archers, soldiers, and so on, who are here before our city of Orléans, go back to your country, in the name of God. If you do not, you may expect the Maid, who will visit you very soon to your great grief."

Loose Woman   She's good.

Young Curate   "King of England, wherever I find your men on France's soil, I will drive them away, whether they will or not. And if they will not, I will have them all killed. Wherever we find you we will strike you and raise a clamor the like of which has not been heard in France for at least a thousand years. Written this day, Tuesday of Holy Week . . .

Joan."

Unconquerable.

English Soldier *(comes in and demands a drink)*   Evening. Some wine!

Young Curate   Praised be Jesus Christ.

Peasant *(tipsy, plants himself in front of the* **English** *soldier)*   If you are a servant of the Duke of Bedford, then listen to this: the Duke of Bedford's a drunk.

Well-Dressed Gentleman   Come along, Blanche. *(They leave the tavern)*

Peasant Woman   Guillaume!

Peasant   He drinks from morning to night, and all he ever thinks of is hitting us with taxes and grinding down the people.

(The **English** *soldier leaves, looking back over his shoulder. A roar of laughter)*

Young Curate   Give me the letter.

9

In the chapel of the graveyard of Saint-Ouen. Threatened with the stake and worn down by a feeling of utter forsakenness, Joan signs a recantation. It is May 24, 1431.

The chapel of the graveyard of Saint-Ouen. **La Fontaine**. **Joan** *is carried in.* **Guards** *and an* **English** *officer. Church bells and the noise of a crowd are audible while* **Joan** *is being carried in.*

La Fontaine   Joan, you are in the chapel of the graveyard of Saint-Ouen. Collect yourself, dear sister. Out on the square the stake is ready.

Joan *(barely audible)*   Saint Michael.

La Fontaine *(steps up to her)*   Believe me, Joan, it is not too late for your salvation.

(Enter the **Bishop**, **Maître Erard**, **Massieu**, **Beaupère**, **Brother Raoul**. *Once more bells and the noise of crowds are heard)*

Bishop   Maître Erard, we are obliged to you for postponing your journey. You say you had a better impression of her yesterday?

Maître Erard   God will help.—Her physical condition is not of the best. She keeps asking how the people are reacting to her trial—with sympathy or indifference. Attempts by her partisans to communicate with her have been thwarted: She is upset because her voices have abandoned her. Has it been sufficiently impressed on her that today . . .

La Fontaine   She was told at five o'clock this morning.

Massieu   Here are the three documents. This is the sentence in case she recants. *(Hands it to the* **Bishop** *who gives it to* **Brother Raoul***)* This is the sentence if she fails to recant. *(He keeps it)* This is the recantation. *(Gives it to* **Maître Erard***)* Bid her sign the recantation in order that this sentence *(the document in his hand)* may not become effective.

Bishop   Maître Erard! Monsieur Massieu!

Maître Erard   The ground has all been covered, dear sister. Your king is a heretic; moreover, he has forgotten you. Your apparitions are illusions; the professors have said so and they know; you know nothing. You may as well take off your male attire, nobody has come with a horse to set you free. Your voices have deceived you, and what's more, they have stopped coming. I know they have. Were they here today? Did they come yesterday?

Joan   No, not yesterday.

Maître Erard   And the day before, my child?

Joan   No.

Maître Erard   You see, they have abandoned you, but the stake is ready. And here I have a document; if you submit and sign and recant, you will be released from prison.

Joan *(in tears)*   I have done nothing wrong.

Maître Erard   If you don't recant, it will be the fire, dear sister. *(At a sign from him the door is thrown open and the bells and the noise are heard)*

Maître Erard   Would you not rather stay with your mother, the church, for it is written, "The branch cannot bear fruit of itself, except it abide in the vine."

(Joan does not answer)

Maître Erard   Joan, it's to you I am speaking.

(At a sign from **Massieu** *the door is closed)*

Massieu   Forgive me if I should be mistaken, but I believe I heard her say "Then I will."

(All gather around **Joan***)*

Massieu   She says that if the Council at Basel decides she must sign she will do so.

Beaupère   No, dear sister, you must do it now.

Joan   I can't get up.

Beaupère   I'll help you.

Chation   Sign here.

Joan   I can't write.

La Fontaine   I'll guide your hand.

Chation   Quick, sign.

Joan   I've got to think it over.

Beaupère   The executioner is outside. He's got his torch ready.

La Fontaine   Sign! Sign!

Joan   I feel sick.

La Fontaine   Courage, Joan.

Chation   You must sign.

Joan   Where? I can't see.

(La Fontaine guides Joan's hand. She signs)

Joan   I'd sooner sign than be burned.

Bishop   A great day, my girl. Your body and soul are saved. *(To* **Brother Raoul***)* Give me the sentence.

Beaupère   Your voices led you astray, my child.

Joan   Yes, I guess they deceived me.

Bishop   Give the prisoner women's clothes.

(Two **Nuns** *have entered. A screen is brought in. The* **Nuns** *dress* **Joan***, who is tottering, in female clothes)*

Bishop   Brother Raoul, send a message to my lord that she has recanted. *(Reads the sentence very quickly)* You, Joan, having been repeatedly and patiently admonished by us, have now recanted your errors by word of mouth and publicly abjured them. Consequently, you are hereby readmitted to the church. However, since you have most gravely sinned against the church, we condemn you to imprisonment for life, to the bread of sorrow and the wine of tears, albeit constantly in the shelter of our compassion. This is the final decision of the court.

*(The **English Observer** and the **Adjutant** have come in)*

The English Observer   Goddam! The witch has to be burned at once!

Adjutant   What's going on here?

Bishop   She has recanted.

Adjutant   This is high treason.

Bishop   I'm being insulted. I demand satisfaction.

Adjutant   You're letting the girl get away.

Bishop   That's a lie.

Adjutant   The girl must be executed at once.

Bishop   That decision rests with me.

The English Observer   No. *(Goes out with **His Adjutant**)*

Massieu   Where is she to be taken?

Bishop   Same place you took her from. *(Out)*

Massieu   Take her back to prison. *(Out)*

Joan   But you said I would be free!

Guard   Just come along quietly, little girl. How pretty you look in your nice dress.

10

In the graveyard of Saint-Ouen an expectant crowd hears of Joan's recantation.

Market place in Rouen. A crowd, waiting. **English** *soldiers.*

War Cripple   Are they going to burn her today or not?

(**An English** *soldier shrugs)*

Second Soldier   The time it takes. Do they expect us to eat our dinner out here?

First Soldier   Goddam!

Sister-in-Law   You can't get her down, can you? She holds her head high.

Little Girl   Why have the bells stopped?

Peasant Woman   Don't know.

First Soldier   The "Red Lion" costs more, but at "St. Peter's Catch" they cook with garlic.

Second Soldier   They cook with garlic because they don't want us.

(A third **English** *soldier joins the other two and tells them something. They laugh)*

Sister-in-Law   What are the English soldiers laughing about?

(The soldiers go off, laughing)

Loose Woman   Henry, what's happened?

First Soldier   You can all go home. Your Maid has recanted.

Second Soldier   Not that she is one.

Legrain   Some new piece of skulduggery.

Loose Woman   It's all over. The bells have stopped ringing.

Sister-in-Law   You mean they're not going to burn her after all?

Son   How can she recant the truth? How can she betray us like this?

War Cripple   She's recanted all right.

Innkeeper   To save her skin.

Peasant Woman   Is this the end of it all?

Peasant   She's recanted. Let's go home.

Peasant Woman   Eugene.

Wine Merchant   Ha, ha! Not that she is one. Ha, ha, ha! *(He is jostled by the* **Son***)*

Fishwife   What can they have done to the girl?

11

At the "St. Peter's Catch" tavern, opinions are divided.

The "St. Peter's Catch" tavern. The **Innkeeper**. *The* **Fishwife**. *The* **Well-Dressed Gentleman**. *The* **Loose Woman**.

Well-Dressed Gentleman   I'm not for the English. I only said that it's no good trying to crack a nut with a sledgehammer—you might need the nut. The tripe vendors and sewer workers are full of patriotic fervor, that's fine. Jostling the English guards, splendid. But what will it lead to? After all, there's no great difference between the door of a guardroom and the door of my hotel. The English are boors, not much culture, they've blundered unforgivably in their dealings with the population, I grant you that, but for the moment they are responsible for law and order.

Loose Woman *(to* **Fishwife***)*   Law and order, he says. I like that. He hasn't paid my rent in weeks.

Fishwife *(calms her)*   Take it easy, Blanche.

Well-Dressed Gentleman   We've got to keep cool. What I say is: everything in its place. I don't ask my butcher to cook my supper.

Loose Woman   Pay my rent.

Legrain *(enters)*   Monsieur François, un petit blanc! There's been a riot in the harbor. The stevedores have refused to unload two siege machines from the corvette "Glorious." The Duke of Bedford has let loose his watchdogs, but the dockers are fighting back.

Innkeeper   Maybe I'd better close the place. They've already smashed it up once.

Fishwife *(laughs)*   What will the **Bishop** do now?

Well-Dressed Gentleman   How can you laugh, madame? I've had as much as I can take. I'm telling you straight: This town has got to be cleaned up. Sneers, whispering, dirty looks. Pretty soon it won't be safe for a man to show himself in a clean shirt.

Loose Woman   Especially if the laundress hasn't been paid.

Well-Dressed Gentleman   There you have it! Insurrection.

Loose Woman   You mean you won't pay?

Well-Dressed Gentleman   These people are taking me for all they can get.

Innkeeper   Say!

Loose Woman   You aren't that pretty. You think going to bed with you is a pleasure? And listening to your hogwash day and night? Pay up and clear out. A peasant girl! What does that make me? A dockside whore, I suppose. Pay if you want to have fun, pay, pay, pay!

Well-Dressed Gentleman   Suppose I haven't got it?

Loose Woman   Pluck your hat and sell the feathers, you sissy.

Well-Dressed Gentleman   Let me explain . . .

Loose Woman   Don't explain, pay!

Well-Dressed Gentleman   That's the last straw. There's only one thing to be done with you scum, your Maid included: root out, burn to the ground, drown in blood, hang, crush underfoot, exterminate. *(The* **Loose Woman** *slaps his face. He leaves)*

Fishwife   You shouldn't have done that. He'll give you a bad name in the taverns.

Loose Woman   All this is getting me down.

Innkeeper   You're not the only one, mademoiselle. You're not the only one.

Rioting in Rouen. The Bishop of Beauvais receives distressing news.

In the **Bishop's** *house. The* **Bishop** *at dinner.* **Massieu**.

Bishop   Those English blockheads don't realize how well I've served them. They may know all about invading France, but they fail to understand the French mind.

Massieu   Thanks to your great skill they have one less enemy, and the church has lost a martyr.

Brother Raoul *(entering)*   Your Eminence. The city is in a turmoil. The people are crowding into the harbor and beating up the English sailors. Several guard posts have been attacked. The English are demanding satisfaction.

Bishop   I can't be bothered with street brawls. The English can reinforce their guards.

Brother Raoul   Your Eminence, they're putting the blame on us and the way we conducted the trial. I hear the Duke of Bedford is sick with rage.

Bishop   The Duke of Bedford has all the doctors he needs. Besides, he's always had trouble with his liver. It's the life he's been leading. Anything else?

Brother Raoul   The English report that she put on men's clothes this morning.

Massieu   She must have heard about the riots on her account.

Bishop *(aghast, puts his napkin down)*   Water!

*(***Brother Raoul** *hands him the bowl to wash his hands in)*

The prison of La Tour des Champs. Joan has heard the voice of the people and resumes her struggle.

Prison. Joan, again in men's clothes. Enter the **Bishop of Beauvais** *and* **La Fontaine**.

Bishop   You are wearing men's clothes again!

La Fontaine   Why have you caused us this sorrow? Dearest sister, it's too late to save you. You've broken your promise; you've relapsed, now you're lost forever.

Joan   What did I promise you?

Bishop   Have you heard your voices again?

Joan   Yes.

Bishop   And they told you . . .

Joan   That I betrayed my cause.

Bishop   But you have publicly recanted.

Joan   Yes. Because I didn't know what a public recantation meant. I only recanted because I was afraid of the fire. In battle I was never afraid of fire, because I wasn't alone, I had my men around me. But then I doubted the people; I thought they wouldn't care if I died, and would just go on drinking their wine. But they knew all about me the whole time, and nothing I did was in vain.

Bishop   What does it matter what the coopers and fishwives know?

Joan   Bishop, a day will come when the vintners of Touraine and the sailors of Normandy will sit together, and you people won't be here any more.

Bishop   In other words you are obstinate and guilty of a relapse.

Joan   I am.

Bishop   Joan, you have reverted to your old errors and trespasses as a dog returns to its vomit. The church can no longer defend you. Farewell, farewell! *(Goes out with* **La Fontaine***)*

14

On May 30, 1431, Joan is handed over to the excutioner.

Prison. **Joan**. *In the background* **The Executioner**, *a* **Nun**, **An English** *officer, English soldiers, the two* **Guards**. *Enter* **Massieu**.

Massieu   Joan, the Bishop of Beauvais has sent me to prepare you for death.

Joan   Yes.

Massieu   Are you afraid of death?

Joan   Yes, very much afraid.

Massieu   Then you repent?

Joan   No.

Massieu   Joan, in the face of death do you persist in considering your voices true?

Joan   Yes.

Massieu   But, Joan, haven't those voices promised that you would be freed from prison forever?

Joan   Won't I be freed from prison forever today?

Massieu   Joan, did they not foretell your impending release?

Joan   Am I not being released from the fear of death? Am I not being released from fear of the powerful?

(Solemn entry of the **Bishop of Beauvais** *with all the judges and assessors of the trial)*

Bishop   We have come to the end. Joan, have you anything more to say?

Joan   Yes. If the fire were to be lit right now and the faggots were burning and the executioner fanning the flames, I would say nothing different from what I have always said.

Bishop   Conduct her to the stake.

(The Executioner steps forward)

Massieu   This is irregular, my lord. You must proclaim the reasons for your order.

Bishop   Take her away, take her away!

(The Executioner takes Joan away)

15

In the market place of Rouen, in the presence of an immense crowd, the Maid is burned at the stake.

Market place in Rouen. A large crowd. **English Soldiers**.

Sister-in-Law   She looks so little among the men.

Peasant Woman   Lift the child up!

Son *(to the curate)*   Do you think she's afraid?

Young Curate   We are afraid, she isn't.

Child   It's daylight. Why has that man got a torch?

Older Nun   That's the executioner, little girl. He's ready with his torch to light the fire for the witch.

Fishwife   Look at the Duke of Bedford, he's laughing and enjoying himself. Those twelve thousand pounds for the Maid have paid off.

Son   Cardinals and dukes, birds of a feather. English and French lords, birds of a feather.

Peasant   Hold your tongue.

Soldier   Who was that?

Fishwife *(drops her basket to cover up the flight of the young* **Peasant***)*   My fish, my mackerel!

Wine Merchant *(to the soldier)*   Someone pushed me from behind.

Young Curate   That's right, I saw it myself.

Loose Woman   Henry, go home.

Bishop's Voice   We, Bishop of Beauvais, hereby declare you, Joan, a heretic and relapsed sinner and by this same declaration excommunicate you. At the same time we pray that divine judgment upon you may be mitigated after your death and the imminent destruction of your body.

First Soldier   Took a long time!

(Church bells)

Second Soldier   Don't push. The wood's piled high enough, everybody can see her.

Fishwife   Swine! They've piled it high to make her suffer more.

Second Soldier   Why do they let the people come so close?

First Soldier   Don't worry, you've got a pike. Let them get a taste of the smoke.

Loose Woman   Now!

(**Nuns** *recite the Hail Mary)*

First Soldier   It's all over, let's go home. What are you people gaping at? She can't do any more than burn.

Peasant *(to his wife)*   Don't cry now. She can't feel anything now.

Loose Woman   She's still screaming.

Second Soldier   Got to sound off to the bitter end.

Sister-in-Law   She's stopped screaming.

16

Five years later the ultimate liberation and unification of France is initiated by the revolt of the people in Paris. At the head of the popular movement walks the legendary figure of little Joan of Arc.

The village in Touraine. **Jacques Legrain** *is hammering a wine barrel.* **Grandfather Breuil***, an old man from a neighboring village, steps up, leading a* **Child** *by the hand.*

Grandfather Breuil   Well, Jacques, that was a long visit you had with François at the "St. Peter's Catch." Something like five years.

Legrain   One thing led to another, Grandfather Breuil.

Breuil   A man sets out for Rouen and ends up in Paris, hein? The English are there too, I suppose.

Legrain   Not any more, grandfather, not any more.

Breuil   What do you mean, not any more?

Legrain   The artisans from the suburbs, the drapers and tanners, the vegetable women from the market have driven them out.

Breuil   And fellows like Jacques Legrain, I daresay. I suppose they're still in Compiègne?

Legrain   Not there either. Nor in Rheims or Châlons. They're still in Calais, though, and down in Bordeaux; but not for long.

Breuil *(to the* **Child***)*   Did you hear that? The French are making themselves at home in France.

Child   Did you see her, Monsieur Legrain?

Legrain   I saw her burn, Pierre.

Breuil   She led France.

Legrain   Yes, but France led her as well.

Breuil   I thought she was led by voices.

Legrain   Yes, our voices.

Breuil   What do you mean?

Legrain   Well, it was like this: First she led the people against the enemy, that's how she was captured. Then when they locked her up in the tower in Rouen, she didn't hear from us and became weak like you and me. She even recanted. But when she recanted, the common people of Rouen got so angry at her that they went to the docks and beat up the English. She heard about it, nobody knows how, and her courage came back. She realized that a law court is as good a battleground as the earthworks before Orléans. So she turned her greatest defeat into our greatest victory. After her lips were silenced, her voice was heard.

Breuil   Well, well. The war isn't over yet.

Child   Will the English soldiers come back, grandfather?

Breuil   I doubt it. How's the wine at your place this year?

Legrain   I wasn't there last year, but the girls say it's as sweet as in twenty-eight.

(The Girls are heard singing as they pick the grapes)

Girls *(singing)*
The Maid stood trial for half a year
All France was waiting until May.
And those she spoke to did not hear.
Then she was taken out into the day.
And as they dragged her to the stake
As torches hissed and the wind blew shrill
She cried out: Frenchmen, Frenchmen, wake
And fight for France, for the soil you till!

Legrain   They're singing that song in both halves of France now, ours and theirs.

Don Juan

Molière

Adaptation

Collaborators: B. Besson, E. Hauptmann
Translator: Ralph Manheim

Characters

Don Juan, son of Don Luis Tenorio
Sganarelle, Don Juan's servant
Don Luis Tenorio
Donna Elvira, Don Juan's wife
Don Carlos and **Don Alonso,**
  Donna Elvira's brothers
The Statue of The Commander
Angelica, the commander's
  daughter
Mr. Dimanche, a tailor
Guzman, Donna Elvira's
  equerry

La Violette, servant to Don
  Juan
Ragotin, Don Juan's equerry
Pieter, a fisherman
Berthelot, Angelot, Colin,
  boatmen
Charlotte and **Mathurine,**
  fisher maidens
Marphurius, a physician
A Beggar
Seraphine, Don Juan's
  cook

The action is laid in Sicily.

Act One

Entrance of an elegant town house. In front of it, pieces of baggage.

1

Sganarelle. Guzman.

Sganarelle *(fishes a snuffbox out of* **Don Juan's** *baggage and looks at it)* Whatever Aristotle and the other philosophers may say, there's nothing better than tobacco. It's a passion with the nobility. Ah, they choose their passions wisely! To live without tobacco in this day and age is not to live at all. Not only does it cleanse and rejoice the brain, but above all it confers that divine peace of mind without which a nobleman cannot be a nobleman. Tobacco alone allows a nobleman to forget sufferings, especially other people's. One or two of our farms are on the rocks? We take a pinch of snuff and things don't look half so bleak. A petitioner makes a nuisance of himself, a creditor importunes us? Take a pinch of snuff, my friend, be a philosopher! A pinch of snuff satisfies the giver as well as the taker. The mere gesture of offering: you don't wait to be asked, you anticipate your fellow man's desires—tobacco is what he wants—you satisfy them with a smile. Take a pinch, friend Guzman, help yourself.

Guzman Thank you kindly. But let's get back to the subject. Perhaps I haven't made myself quite clear.

Sganarelle Oh yes you have. Donna Elvira has hurried after us, overpowered by love for my master. She can neither live nor die without him. In short, you are here.

Guzman But tell me this: What sort of reception can we expect?

Sganarelle Shall I tell you what I think? I am afraid that her love will be ill-rewarded, that her journey will do her no good. She would have done better to stay at home.

Guzman Why? Has your master intimated that his love has grown cold so soon? Is that the reason for his sudden departure?

Sganarelle   Oh no! What do you imagine? We never discuss our love affairs. To tell you the truth, I've known him so long, I can see how the land lies without his breathing a word. Sometimes I know better than he does himself. Experience!

Guzman   What! Then this sudden journey of his was merely a contemptible betrayal? And Don Juan has miserably deserted Donna Elvira after only a few weeks of marriage? Without a word of explanation?

Sganarelle *(takes a pinch of snuff)*   Oh! We're still young and short on courage . . .

Guzman   A man of his station!

Sganarelle   Station, my foot! His station won't stand in his way. Do you really think he would deny himself the slightest pleasure for the sake of his station?

Guzman   But the holy ties of matrimony?

Sganarelle   Ah, my dear Guzman, my poor friend! Even holy ties are—ties. You don't know Don Juan.

Guzman   I am beginning to fear that I don't. Those sacred oaths, those ardent letters, his impatience until he had lured her out of her pious refuge at the convent of Santa Regina! How can he abandon her after all that? I don't understand.

Sganarelle   If you knew the fellow, you would know that such things give him no trouble at all. Incidentally, I haven't said a word. I had to come here ahead of him to make certain arrangements, and since his arrival I haven't spoken to him. I don't know anything definite. But to be on the safe side, I'd better inform you that my master, Don Juan, is the biggest scoundrel that ever walked the earth, a madman, a devil, a heathen, who believes neither in heaven nor in hell, who lives like a wild beast, an Epicurean pig, a Sardanapalus! Very well, he married your mistress. To get what he wanted he'd have married you too and the priest and the dog and the cat. What's a marriage to him? It's simply the trap in which he catches them all. He is the greatest of all marriers before the Lord: housewife or virgin; noble or shopkeeper; countess or peasant woman; mayor's wife or novice—nothing's too hot or too cold for him. If I were to list all the women he had married in various parts of the world, we'd still be standing here tomorrow morning. But there's one thing I've got to admit: he attracts women as jam attracts flies. He's a magnet that none can resist. His poor old father endures disgrace after disgrace and wonders how he can go on. And the debts! But what can we do? Nothing. One day heaven in its wrath will crush him.

Guzman   Sh-h! Here he comes. What shall I tell my mistress?

Sganarelle *(shrugs his shoulders)*

Guzman *(goes off in despair)*

2

Don Juan. Sganarelle.

Sganarelle *(reporting)*   The light campaign baggage.

Don Juan   Whom were you talking to just now? Wasn't that Donna Elvira's equerry? Guzman?

Sganarelle   Mm, someone of the sort.

Don Juan *(threatening him with his stick)*   Was it or wasn't it?

Sganarelle   It was.

Don Juan   How long has he been in this city?

Sganarelle   Just arrived.

Don Juan   What brings him here?

Sganarelle   You ought to know.

Don Juan   Our journey?

Sganarelle   He wanted to know the reason for it.

Don Juan   What did you tell him?

Sganarelle   That you hadn't confided in me.

Don Juan   And what is your opinion?

Sganarelle   Mine? Begging your pardon, I think we're after another young lady.

Don Juan   That's what you think?

Sganarelle   Yes.

Don Juan   You're not mistaken. We are. Another has banished Elvira from my thoughts.

Sganarelle   I know my master like my little finger. Your heart is insatiable.

Don Juan   Can it be that you don't approve?

Sganarelle   Well, my lord . . .

Don Juan   Well, what?

Sganarelle   Of course I approve if that's what you want. In that case I haven't a word to say. But if you wanted something different, it might be different.

Don Juan   Never mind that. Just tell me what you think. I authorize you.

Sganarelle   In that case, my lord, I'll put it plainly. This indiscriminate loving is abominable.

Don Juan   What? Would you wish me to chain myself to the first one who comes along and have no eyes for others? Fidelity—what an absurd notion! All the beauties in the world have the right to bewitch us. If in justice to one I succumb to her charms, does it mean that I should be unjust to the others? Is it right that one who has had the good fortune to cross our path should deprive all others of their just claims to our heart? My eyes are open to every woman's qualities; I am resolved to pay each one the tribute that nature imposes. A chair! *(Sganarelle brings him the folding traveling chair. Don Juan sits down)* What ineffable pleasure it is to invent the thousand flatteries that subjugate a young beauty's heart! To take note each day of the progress one has made. How gratifying to lay siege, with protestations, tears, and sighs, to a chaste soul reluctant to surrender. Step by step to overcome her tender resistance, to surmount the pangs of conscience on which she prides herself, and to lead her gently where we want her. Once the fortress is ours, we have nothing more to say or desire: we fall asleep. In this domain, my friend, I have the ambitions of a conqueror, who races eternally from one victory to the next, recognizing no boundary to his wishes. Nothing, nothing can halt my impetuous desires. This heart that beats within me aspires to love the whole world. Like Alexander of Macedon, I long for still other worlds to subject to the power of my love. What do you say to that, Sganarelle?

Sganarelle   Well, my lord . . . your way of life . . . I just don't like the way you live.

Don Juan   What do you mean? How do I live?

Sganarelle   Oh, splendidly. Excellently. Except—well, this business of getting married every few weeks.

Don Juan   But it's delightful!

Sganarelle   Undoubtedly. I wouldn't mind doing it myself if only it weren't so sinful. Making a mockery of such a sacred institution!

Don Juan   Come, come. That's between me and heaven.

Sganarelle   Oh, sir. They say that the vengeance of heaven is terrible. People who mock it . . .

Don Juan   Hold your tongue! Don't you know that I can't abide sermons? Blockhead!

Sganarelle   God forbid. I wasn't referring to you. You can't help it. You have your justifications. Such power to attract! So full of fire! It grieves me to say that there are men who take morality lightly without such excellent justifications. If I had that kind of master, I'd say it to his face: You earthworm, I'd say, you crawling louse, how dare you make a mockery of something that all mankind holds sacred! Do you think because you're a nobleman with a blond, prettily curled wig, and feathers on your hat—that's what I'd say to *him*—do you think because you wear a gold-embroidered coat with dashing red braid that you can do anything you please?—that's what I'd say to *him* . . .

Don Juan *(smiling)*   Rascal.

Sganarelle   It would be my duty to tell that kind of man what I thought of him.

Don Juan   That's enough. We haven't much time. Now we must speak of the beauty who has brought us here . . .

Sganarelle *(aside)*   Brought!

Don Juan   . . . by bringing herself.

Sganarelle   That's just it! Must I remind you that you killed the Commander, Don Rodrigo, here in this province? Aren't you afraid?

Don Juan   What is there to be afraid of? I killed him, didn't I? According to all the rules of the art.

Sganarelle   That is true. He can't complain on that score.

Don Juan   Who's afraid of the dead? Anyway, I was tried, my father interceded for me, I was pardoned. The affair is dead and buried.

Sganarelle   Yes, dead and buried. But there are friends, close relations, a young daughter—do you suppose those friends and relations were overjoyed to see you pardoned?

Don Juan   That's enough. It's time to think of the pleasures that lie *ahead* of us. The beauty I referred to is a young . . . *(He catches sight of* **Donna Elvira***)* Donna Elvira! A most unwelcome sight. Scoundrel! Traitor! Why didn't you tell me she was here?

Sganarelle   You didn't ask me, my lord.

Don Juan   Has she lost her mind? Traveling around in evening dress!

3

Don Juan. **Donna Elvira**. **Sganarelle**.

Donna Elvira Don Juan! May I ask you to recognize me? May I hope at least that you will deign to look my way?

Don Juan My lady, I must own that I am surprised. I wasn't expecting you here.

Donna Elvira Yes, I can see you were not expecting me. Your surprise is not of the kind I had hoped for. It convinces me of what I had refused to believe. And now I am amazed at my simplicity and the folly of my heart that led me to doubt your treachery despite so many proofs. I was good, or rather stupid, enough to deceive myself. I thought up a hundred reasons for your sudden departure. In order to acquit you of the crime of which my reason convicted you, I gave ear to a thousand fantastic whisperings that proclaimed your innocence. But this reception dispels all doubt; your look when you saw me revealed more than I wished to know. And yet I should be glad to hear from your own lips the reasons for your sudden departure. Speak, Don Juan, I implore you. I am curious to see how you will justify yourself.

Don Juan Sganarelle here will tell you why I went away, my lady.

Sganarelle *(in an undertone to* **Don Juan***)* I, my lord? Begging your pardon, sir, I don't know a thing.

Donna Elvira Speak, Sganarelle. It makes no difference from whom I learn the truth.

Don Juan *(motions* **Sganarelle** *to approach* **Donna Elvira***)* Go ahead, tell the lady.

Sganarelle *(in an undertone)* What should I say?

Don Juan Speak up!

Sganarelle   My lady . . .

Donna Elvira   Well?

Sganarelle *(to* **Don Juan***)*   My lord . . . what . . . *(A stern look from* **Don Juan***)* Well . . . my lady . . . the great conquerors . . . Alexander of Macedon . . . and the other worlds . . . were to blame for our departure . . . that's as much as I know.

Donna Elvira   Don Juan, may I ask you to explain your puzzling explanation?

Don Juan   To tell the truth, my lady . . .

Donna Elvira   Heavens, how clumsily you defend yourself! Didn't they teach you anything at court? Couldn't you simply swear that your feelings for me are unchanged, that you still love me with the same matchless ardor, and that death alone can part you from me? Couldn't you tell me that an affair of the utmost importance obliged you to slip away without taking leave of me, that you are compelled, quite against your will, to stay here for a time, that I should return home in the certainty that you will follow as soon as possible, and that in my absence you suffer like a body separated from its soul.

That's how you should defend yourself instead of just standing there!

Don Juan   My lady, I must own that I have no talent for dissimulation. I can only tell the truth. I will not say that I still harbor the same feelings for you, that I am burning with desire to be reunited with you, when it is plain that I fled from you. Not for the reasons you suppose, but for reasons imposed by my conscience. To continue living with you would be a sin. Today I see what I have done through the eyes of my immortal soul. Today I see that in order to marry you I ravished you from the holy seclusion of the convent. That you have broken the vows that bound you to another. Heaven, as everyone knows, is extremely jealous in such matters. I fear, my lady, that our marriage is adultery in disguise. I fear the wrath of heaven for both of us. I am trying to forget you. It is my duty to let you return to your former bonds. My lady, would you oppose so pious a thought? Would you have me, by remaining with you, bring down the wrath of heaven on my head? My lady, our obligation to heaven and our fellow creatures often demands painful sacrifices . . .

Donna Elvira   Ah, scoundrel! Now I know you. To my misfortune, I have come to know you too late. What use is my knowledge to me now? It only hurls me into deeper despair. But know this: your crime will not go unpunished. The heaven you scoff at will avenge me.

Don Juan   Sganarelle. Heaven!

Sganarelle   Heaven, indeed! Do they expect us to fall for that?

Don Juan   My lady . . .

Donna Elvira   Enough. I won't listen. I have heard too much. Don't expect me to indulge in reproaches and abuse. I will not waste my fury in words. But I repeat, Don Juan: Heaven will punish you. *(Goes out)*

4

Don Juan. **Sganarelle**. *Later the* **boatmen**.

Don Juan   Well, the beauty I wished to speak of is engaged to be married. I caught sight of her a few days ago: the loveliest thing that eye has ever looked upon. She was strolling arm in arm with her betrothed. I have never seen a couple so happy and so pleased with themselves. They made no attempt to conceal their feeling for each other, and that moved me deeply, indeed, it struck me to the heart. I found it utterly intolerable to see them so happy together. To destroy this union that so offended my sensitive heart seemed a voluptuous duty.

Sganarelle   I understand.

Don Juan   You understand nothing. Something has happened that defies understanding. The lady refuses to be parted from her bumpkin.

Sganarelle   Well . . .

Don Juan   So that I find myself obliged to take the necessary steps.

Sganarelle   What about our letters? Our gifts?

Don Juan   All returned.

Sganarelle   What? The lady detests you!

Don Juan   So she thinks. She actually intends to marry the fellow tomorrow. That calls for extreme measures. She must be abducted.

Sganarelle   Oh no!

Don Juan   What! The lout is already playing the husband, planning to entertain her with a boat ride on the sea. I have hired a fast boat and several strong boatmen.

Sganarelle   Oh, my lord! Last night I dreamed of dead fish and cracked eggs, and our cook Seraphine always says that means . . .

Don Juan *(threatens him)*

Sganarelle   Oh, my lord! This is going to be another of your . . .

Don Juan   of my . . .?

Sganarelle   . . . great adventures!

Don Juan   You of course will accompany me. Test your weapons carefully, your life will depend on it. And don't forget the wine.

*(The **boatmen** enter with their oars)*

Don Juan   Let's get going.

5

Don Juan. Sganarelle. Berthelot. Angelot. Colin.

Don Juan   Give these men their instructions.

Sganarelle   Money would be the best instructor, my lord.

Don Juan *(throwing him a purse)*   Here you are. But no more.

Sganarelle *(examines the purse)*   Twenty ducats. That will do it. *(He puts the purse away)* This way, men. We'll pay you two ducats each for your services.

*(The **boatmen** are overjoyed)*

Colin   Many thanks, sir.

Sganarelle   Just a moment. For special pay we expect special services. Can you handle an oar?

Angelot   Nowhere on this whole coast . . .

Sganarelle   Not just this way. *(He makes the gesture of rowing)* This way as well! *(He makes the gesture of striking with an oar)*

Colin   Oh, it's that kind of job!

Angelot   We're peaceful fishermen, sir. If people are going to get hit . . .

Sganarelle *(sternly)*   Oh, so you don't know how to fight. Then I'll teach you.

Angelot   Teach us how to kill people? These men don't seem to have any religion.

Sganarelle   We don't pay two ducats for rowing.

Berthelot   It can't be done, sir. I know him. *(Pointing at **Angelot**)*

Angelot *(to the two others)*   Would you want to kill your fellow men for two ducats?

Berthelot   He's right, sir. Two ducats aren't enough for that kind of thing.

Colin *(to* **Angelot***)*   You wouldn't even do it for three, would you, Angelot?

Angelot *(shakes his head)*

Berthelot *(to* **Angelot***)*   For four?

Sganarelle   Three ducats are out of the question.

Angelot   Four ducats is a lot of money. *(But he continues to shake his head)*

Colin   He's too soft-hearted, you see.

Sganarelle   Trying to gouge three ducats out of us—is that what you call soft-hearted?

Berthelot   Under five ducats nothing doing.

Don Juan *(calling to* **Sganarelle***)*   How about it?

Sganarelle *(furious)*   Very well, I will pay you the outrageous sum of four ducats . . .

Angelot   Five!

Sganarelle   Very well. But you've lost my respect; we're not friends any more. *(Driving the* **boatmen** *upstage)* You might as well show me what you can do. *(Upstage* **Sganarelle** *instructs the* **boatmen** *in "oarsmanship," he himself using his sword. He shouts commands of:* "**Parry** *left!* " "**Parry** *right!* " "*Lunge!* ")*

Sganarelle   My lord, we will do our part, but . . .

Don Juan *(to* **Angelot***)*   Lift up that oar, fellow!

Angelot   No, no, no. My conscience won't let me. *(He runs off)*

Sganarelle   Go to the devil!

Colin   But two of us won't be enough.

Don Juan *(to* **Sganarelle***)*   Raise the pay.

Colin *(calls after* **Angelot***)*   Six ducats. Come back here.

Angelot *(slowly coming back)*   Now it's gone up to six. I'm sorry.

Sganarelle   Let's be going. *(To* **Don Juan***)* Oh, my lord, here comes your father!

Don Juan   Everything seems to be conspiring against me today.

(Enter **Don Luis***. During the following the fencing exercise dies down whenever* **Sganarelle** *is required to wait on* **Don Juan***)*

6

Don Juan. Don Luis. Sganarelle. Boatmen.

Don Luis   I am well aware that my presence is unwelcome to
you. But if you are weary of the sight of me, I am no less weary of
your excesses. How, on top of everything else, can you expect me
to put up with your latest sacrilege? Snatching the only daughter
of our noble friend Don Filipo away from the holy seclusion of the
convent! When will you cease to bring grief upon my head grown
gray in the service of king and country? Must you heap crime upon
crime?

*(Sganarelle discreetly presents **Don Juan** two swords from
which to choose. **Don Juan** imperiously indicates one of them.
Sganarelle goes out)*

Don Luis   To cover up your scandalous doings I am obliged
to wear out the mercy of our king. A time comes when the most
benevolent mercy is at an end. While you gratify your whims, I am
forced to squander the credit my services have built up.

Don Juan   Won't you be seated, sir? It's easier to talk sitting
down.

Don Luis   No, you blackguard, I will not be seated. Ah, how
heedless we are when we beget sons! How passionately I desired a
son, how obstinately I begged for one—here he stands, the son for
whom I importuned heaven with my prayers: a monster! He scoffs
at my remonstrances, laughs at my legitimate wishes!

*(During this tirade **Sganarelle** points smilingly at the performance
of the fencing **boatmen**)*

Don Juan   Not at all, father. Inform me of your wishes regarding
the lady in question, and I shall do my best to comply.

Don Luis   Be still! Don't remind me that I am your father. Too
many people do so to wound me. Are you really not ashamed to be

so unworthy of your birth? What have you ever done to glorify the name you bear?

Don Juan *(while* **Sganarelle** *shows him a basket filled with bottles of wine)*   More of that kind. *(* **Sganarelle** *withdraws upstage)*

Don Luis   You're living on the reputation of your ancestors. But their heroic deeds will not help you. On the contrary, their glory is a torch that shows up your disgrace.

Don Juan   Sir, you will not find me as disobedient as you seem to think. There are situations in which a nobleman has no choice. Certain obligations must be met, regardless of the cost.

Sganarelle *(aside)*   Regardless of the cost to his father.

Don Juan   I will allow Donna Elvira to return to the seclusion from which I should never have snatched her. In view of which change of heart I venture to hope that you will resume your past generosity toward me. My creditors . . .

Don Luis   Wretch, not a word about your creditors! You have more to fear from the wrath of heaven! *(Goes out)*

7

Don Juan. **Sganarelle**. **Boatmen**.

Don Juan *(motions* **Sganarelle** *to approach)*   I want you to have a coach ready when we return in the boat.—How revolting it is to see fathers who live as long as their sons.

Sganarelle *(who has lined up the* **boatmen** *and loaded them with baggage and weapons)*   My lord, you should have thrown the old man out. I admire your patience.

Don Juan   Patience? That is exactly what I haven't got. You rascal, I am thirty-one. Alexander died at the age of thirty-three. He had taken six hundred and eighteen cities. Which means I've got to hurry. Time to get going! The boat! *(They go out)*

Act Two

Ocean beach. Don Juan's and Sganarelle's coats have been hung up to dry.

1

Charlotte. **Pieter**.

Charlotte   It was lucky for them that you happened to be here.

Pieter   Yer dern tootin'. They'd have drowned.

Charlotte   Was it that little squall this morning that upset their boat?

Pieter   I can see I'll have to tell you the whole story from the beginning. Well, the two of us, me and Tubby, were on the beach horsing around, throwing sand at each other, when all of a sudden I see somebody paddling around way out in the ocean. I seen them plain as day and then all of a sudden I seen that I couldn't see nuthin'. Tubby, says I, it looks to me like somebody's swimmin' out yonder. Piffle, says he. Consarn it, says I, there's somebody swimmin' out there. Fiddlesticks, says he, you're seein' ghosts. Do you want to bet, says I, that I'm not seein' ghosts and it's hoomans swimmin' this way. Consarn it, says he, I bet it isn't. All right, says I, this dime says it is. All right, says he, here's my money, says he. I'm nobody's fool, I throw in a dime and then another nickel, I knew what I was doin'. Well, we'd no sooner made our bet than we see these two men plain as day, wavin' like all get-out for us to come and save them. So first I rake in my money. Come on, Tubby, says I, can't you see they're shoutin' for help? Let's get a move on. Naw, says he, they've cost me too much already. Well, to make a long story short, I kept at him till he jumps in the boat with me, and in three shakes we fish them out of the water. They were all blue. So I take them home and sit them down by the fire, they take their clothes off to dry, they're sittin' there mother-naked and then Mathurine comes in, and right then and there one of them starts makin' eyes at her. And that's my story.

Charlotte *(all curiosity)*   But Pieter, didn't you say one was much better looking than the other?

Pieter   That's the master. Must be some bigwig. There's gold all over his coat. *(He points to the coat hung up to dry)* From top to bottom. And his servant looks like a lord too. But bigwig or not, he'd have drowned if I hadn't been there.

Charlotte   You don't say so?

Pieter   Consarn it! If I hadn't been there, he'd have been up split creek.

Charlotte *(burning with curiosity)*   Is he still sitting naked by your fire, Pieter?

Pieter   Naw, his servant dressed him and we all looked on. Bless my soul, I'd never seen one of them fancypants gettin' dressed. The gear they hang on those courtiers! Listen to this, Charlotte. They got hair that don't grow on their head, it's like oakum and they put it on like a great big hat. Their shirts—the two of us would fit into one of the sleeves! Instead of pants they wear an apron that's as wide as from here to Christmas. Instead of a jerkin, they wear a wee little vest that hardly reaches down to their belly button. Instead of a regular collar they wear a neck cloth *(makes a motion)* as big as this, with four big tufts of lace that hang down to their stomachs. *(Sganarelle enters briefly upstage and takes the coats)* On their wrists they got more collars, and on their legs big braided funnels. And they're covered with ribbons, ribbons, ribbons, enough to drive you crazy.

Charlotte   Goodness me, Pieter, I want to get a look at that. *(Stands up)*

Pieter *(makes her sit down again)*   Listen to me first, Charlotte. I've got something else to tell you.

Charlotte *(in a hurry)*   Well, go ahead.

Pieter   Well, Charlotte, you see, I've just got to pour out my heart, as they say. I like you, you know I do, I'm all for our teaming up, but dern it, I'm not rightly pleased with you.

Charlotte   Why? What's wrong?

Pieter   What's wrong? You just make me miserable.

Charlotte   Miserable?

Pieter   Dern it, you don't love me.

Charlotte   Is that all?

Pieter   That's all. Ain't it enough?

Charlotte   Shucks, Pieter, you always come around with the same old story.

Pieter   I always come around with the same old story 'cause it's always the same old story. If it warn't the same old story I wouldn't come around with the same old story.

Charlotte   What do you want of me?

Pieter   I want you to love me, dern it.

Charlotte   Who says I don't?

Pieter   No. You don't love me. I can stand on my head, I buy you ribbons from every peddler that comes along, I dern near break my neck bringin' you blackbirds fresh out of the nest, I pay the organ grinder to play for you on your saint's day—where does it get me?

Charlotte   But shecks, Pieter, I do love you. What do you want me to do?

Pieter   I want you to do what people do when they really love each other.

Charlotte   I really love you.

Pieter   Naw. Anybody can see when it's real. Take Thomasine, she's plumb crazy about her Benjamin. Pesters the life out of him from morning to night, she never leaves him alone. Only the other day . . . he was sittin' on a stool . . . so she sneaks up behind him and pulls it out from under his ass. That's the right way to love somebody. You never do anything like that, you just stand around like a block of wood. I could pass you twenty times, you wouldn't even bother to poke me in the ribs. Consarn it! That's no good. You're cold.

Charlotte   That's the way I am.

Pieter   But you shouldn't be. When you love somebody, you should show it somehow or other.

Charlotte   Well, I love you as best I can. If it doesn't suit you, you can find yourself somebody else.

Pieter   See? What did I tell you? Consarn it, you wouldn't say that if you loved me.

Charlotte   Why must you always keep after me?

Pieter   All I want is a little love.

Charlotte   Don't prod me. Maybe if we stop thinking about it, it'll come all by itself.

Pieter   All right, Charlotte. *(Gives her his hand)*

Charlotte   All right. *(Taking his hand)* There.

Pieter   Try to love me more. Promise.

Charlotte   I'll do my best, but it's got to come by itself. Pieter, is that his lordship?

Pieter *(proudly)*   That's him.

Charlotte   Gracious me, how handsome he is! What a shame if he'd been drowned!

Charlotte. Pieter. Don Juan. Sganarelle.

Don Juan *(motions* **Pieter** *to come closer)*

Pieter *(to* **Charlotte***)*   See? He knows me. *(While* **Pieter***, proudly smiling, approaches the man he has rescued,* **Charlotte** *stares at the nobleman)*

Don Juan   My good man, I'm sure you'd be glad to do me another little service. Run up to the village and give that girl—I believe her name is Mathurine—my best greetings. Tell her I wish to speak to her here on a matter of the greatest importance. And don't tell anyone else. Understand?

Pieter   She'll be here in a minute, your lordship. Yes, your lordship. *(Running past* **Charlotte***)* I'll be right back. I'm running an errand for his lordship. *(Goes out)*

Charlotte. Don Juan. Sganarelle.

Sganarelle We'd better be getting out of here, my lord. Those damned boatmen may have righted their boat and somehow reached the shore.

Don Juan Be still! I'm thinking.

Sganarelle Remember, when the storm was coming up, they wanted to go home and you doubled their pay three times. But the sea has swallowed up our treasury.

Don Juan Sganarelle, we've had bad luck. That storm this morning upset not only our boat but our plans as well. And yet, I must confess, that fisher maiden we saw just now makes up for it all. I discerned charms which, I suspect, will make up to me very amply for our unfortunate accident. That heart must not evade me. And I believe I have already softened it to the point where only a few sighs will be necessary.

Sganarelle I can hardly believe it: here we've escaped death by a miracle and instead of thanking heaven for its mercy you start bringing down its wrath on our heads by your usual . . .

Don Juan *(threatening him)* Hold your tongue! You don't know what you're saying. Your master knows what he's up to. *(Notices* **Charlotte***)* Ah! Ah! Another fisher maiden. Where has she come from? Sganarelle! Have you ever seen anything so charming? Seriously, isn't she at least as beautiful as the other one?

Sganarelle Of course. *(Aside)* Here we go again.

Don Juan *(to* **Charlotte***)* Lovely child, to what good fortune do I owe this delightful meeting? Can it be? Can there really be creatures like you in these remote regions, in the midst of trees and cliffs?

Charlotte Yes, my lord.

Don Juan   Are you from this village?

Charlotte   Yes, my lord.

Don Juan   And you live here?

Charlotte   Yes, my lord.

Don Juan   And your name?

Charlotte   Charlotte, my lord, at your service.

Don Juan   Ah, what a lovely creature! What irresistible eyes!

Charlotte   You make me blush, my lord.

Don Juan   Ah, never blush to hear the truth about yourself! Sganarelle, what do you say? Can you conceive of anything more lovely? Turn around—I beg you. Oh, what a graceful back! The head a little higher—I implore you. Oh, what an adorable little face! Open your eyes. Wider! How beautiful they are! Grant me a glimpse of your teeth—please! Oh, how loving they are! Oh! And the lips, those precious lips! I'm overwhelmed. Never in all my life have I seen so lovely a child!

Charlotte   I don't know if you're making fun of me or not, my lord.

Don Juan   I make fun of you! God forbid! I love you far too much, my words spring from a full heart. Sganarelle, just look at her hands!

Charlotte   Phoo, my lord, they're all black with tar.

Don Juan   What are you saying? They are the most beautiful hands in all the world. Let me kiss them—I beg you.

Charlotte   You do me too much honor, my lord. If I'd only known, I'd have scrubbed them with sand.

Don Juan   Oh! . . . Tell me, lovely child. You're not married yet, I presume?

Charlotte   No, my lord, but soon, to Pieter. He's the son of our neighbor Simonette.

Don Juan   What! A creature like you marry a common fisherman? No, no, that would be a crime against your marvelous beauty. You were not born to spend your life in a village. You are destined to higher things. Heaven has sent me here to prevent this marriage and do justice to your charms. You have only to say the word, my dear child, and I shall save you from a wretched fate and set you in the place you deserve. Perhaps you will say that my love is rather sudden. Ah, but Charlotte, that is the miraculous effect of your beauty; you inspire more love in ten minutes than another in six months.

Charlotte   Really, my lord, I don't know what to say. Your words give me pleasure and I'd like to believe them, but they tell me I should never trust a noble gentleman because all his fine talk is just a trap to take a poor girl in.

Don Juan   I'm not one of those.

Sganarelle *(aside)*   God forbid!

Charlotte   It's no joke to be taken in. I'm only a poor fisher maiden, my honor means a lot to me, I'd rather be dead than dishonored.

Don Juan   By me? I vile enough to dishonor you? No, never. My conscience is much too delicate. Believe me, dear child, I have no other design than to marry you in all honor. I am ready. Whenever you wish. This man here is a witness to my promise.

Sganarelle   No, no, you needn't worry. He'll marry you as much as you like.

Don Juan   Ah, Charlotte, you're not the kind one deceives. Your beauty is your safeguard.

Charlotte   My goodness, I don't know if you're telling the truth or not, but the way you talk makes a body believe you.

Don Juan   Do you wish to be my wife?

Charlotte   Oh yes, if my aunt doesn't mind.

Don Juan   Give me a kiss in pledge . . .

Charlotte   Oh, my lord, wait until we're married. Then I'll kiss you all you want.

Don Juan   Ah, child, I want only what you want. Just give me your hand and on it permit me, with a thousand kisses, to express my ineffable delight.

4

Charlotte. **Don Juan**. **Sganarelle**. **Pieter**.

Pieter *(calling in the distance)*   Your lordship! Your lordship! Mathurine will be . . . *(He comes closer and sees* **Don Juan** *caressing* **Charlotte**. *He pushes* **Don Juan** *aside)*

Pieter   Hey, sir, take it easy! You're all in a lather, you'll catch cold.

Don Juan *(pushing him back)*   How did he get here?

Pieter *(placing himself between* **Don Juan** *and* **Charlotte***)*   I'm telling you to watch your step. Keep your paws off our womenfolk.

Don Juan *(pushes him away again)*   Oh! So much noise!

Pieter   Consarn it! I'll teach you to push me around!

Charlotte *(intervenes)*   Leave him be, Pieter.

Pieter   What? Leave him be? I won't have it.

Don Juan *(menacingly)*   Ah!

Pieter   Dag nab it! Just because you're a lordship do you think you can smooch our women under our nose? Go smooch your own.

Don Juan   What did you say?

Pieter   You heard me. *(***Don Juan** *slaps his face)* Don't you dare touch me! *(***Don Juan** *slaps him again)* Consarn it! Is that a way to repay me for pulling you out of the water?

Charlotte   Don't get excited, Pieter.

Pieter   I want to get excited. And you're a no-good fly-by-night, letting him pet you like that.

Charlotte   Oh, Pieter, you're stupid. It's not what you think. His lordship wants to marry me; that's nothing to get sore about.

Pieter   What? Gee willickers! You're engaged to me!

Charlotte   What of it, Pieter? If you love me, you ought to be glad I'm going to be a lady.

Pieter   No, goldarn it, I'd rather see you dead than married to someone else.

Charlotte   Now now, Pieter, don't worry. When I'm a lady I'll help you make money, you can bring all your fish and crabs to the castle.

Pieter   Consarn it! I won't bring you anything even if you pay double. You going to listen to him? Huh! Holy mackerel! If I'd known I'd have thought twice before pulling him out of the water, I'd have given him one on the bean with my oar.

(**Don Juan** *approaches* **Pieter** *as if to strike him)*

Pieter   Jumping Jehoshaphat! Do you think I'm afraid of you?

Don Juan *(coming toward him again)*   That we shall soon see.

Pieter   I've taken care of better men than you.

Don Juan   Indeed?

Sganarelle   Oh, my lord, leave the poor devil alone. He helped us, you know. *(To* **Pieter***)* Stop hollering, son, and make yourself scarce.

Pieter   But I want to holler.

Don Juan *(raises his hand to slap* **Pieter** *again)*   Ha! Let this be a lesson to you! . . .

(**Pieter** *ducks and* **Sganarelle** *gets the slap)*

Sganarelle *(furious)*   You young snotnose! You can go to the devil! *(Goes to one side)*

Don Juan *(to* **Sganarelle***)*   You asked for that, you humanitarian!

Pieter *(to* **Charlotte***)*   All right, I'll be going. But I'll tell your aunt. *(Goes out)*

Don Juan *(to* **Charlotte***)*   What heavenly bliss when we are man and wife!

5

Don Juan. **Charlotte**. **Sganarelle**. **Mathurine**.

Sganarelle *(catching sight of* **Mathurine**, *laughs)*   Ha ha!

Mathurine *(to* **Don Juan***)*   My lord, what are you doing with Charlotte? Have you been talking love to her too?

Don Juan *(aside to* **Mathurine***)*   No, of course not. She's been buzzing in my ears. She wants to be my wife. I've just told her I was engaged to you.

Charlotte *(to* **Don Juan***)*   What does Mathurine want?

Don Juan *(to* **Charlotte***)*   She's jealous because I was talking to you. She wants me to marry her. But I've told her I was going to marry you.

Mathurine   It's not nice of you, Charlotte, to poach on other people's preserves.

Don Juan *(aside to* **Mathurine***)*   There's no point in talking to her; she won't listen to reason.

Charlotte   It's not nice of you, Mathurine, to be jealous when his lordship talks to me.

Don Juan *(aside to* **Charlotte***)*   You're wasting your breath. She's got an idea in her head, you'll never get it out.

Charlotte   Oh yes, I will. *(Removes one of her clogs)*

Mathurine   You underhanded slut!

Don Juan *(to* **Mathurine***)*   Ignore her. She's possessed by a devil.

Mathurine   Then I'll drive it out of her. *(Also picks up a clog)*

Charlotte   Sneak!

Don Juan *(to* **Charlotte***)*   Don't arouse her. She's dangerous.

Mathurine No, no, I want to give her a piece of my mind.

Charlotte I've got to find out what she thinks.

Mathurine What I think? of you? *(She strikes;* **Charlotte** *strikes back)*

Don Juan *(aside to* **Mathurine***)*   I'll wager she tells you I promised to marry her. *(Aside to* **Charlotte***)* I'll wager she claims that I promised to make her my wife.

Mathurine He saw me first!

Charlotte But then he saw me and promised to marry me.

Don Juan *(to* **Mathurine***)*   What did I tell you?

Mathurine *(to* **Charlotte***)*   He promised to marry me, not you.

Don Juan *(to* **Charlotte***)*   Wasn't I right?

Charlotte Fiddlesticks! He wants me, not you!

Mathurine Hussy! He wants me, not you!

Charlotte Hussy yourself. He'll tell you I'm right.

Mathurine Don't make me laugh! He'll show you who's right.

Charlotte My lord, did you promise to marry her or didn't you? She claims you did.

Don Juan *(aside to* **Charlotte***)*   Let her claim what she likes.

Mathurine My lord, is it true you promised to make her your wife? She says you did.

Don Juan *(aside to* **Mathurine***)*   Let her say what she likes.

Charlotte No, no. I want to know the truth.

Mathurine This has got to be settled.

Charlotte *(to* **Mathurine***)*   Exactly. His lordship will show you that you're still wet behind the ears.

Mathurine Exactly. His lordship will stop your impudent mouth.

Charlotte *(to* **Don Juan***)*   My lord, settle the argument.

Mathurine *(to* **Don Juan***)*   Decide between us.

Charlotte *(to* **Don Juan***)*   Go ahead!

Mathurine *(to* **Don Juan***)*   Speak up!

Don Juan   Ladies, what can I say? You both claim that I promised to make you my wife. Doesn't each of you know what actually happened without my going into details? Everything has been said. I promised marriage. So far so good. If you have my promise, you can rest easy, no need to be put off by idle chatter. The one to whom I have given my promise will be my wife. It's actions that count, not words. When I marry, you will see whom I marry. *(Aside to* **Mathurine***)* Let her think what she likes. *(Aside to* **Charlotte***)* Let her lull herself in hope. *(Aside to* **Mathurine***)* I adore you. *(Aside to* **Charlotte***)* My heart is yours alone. *(Aside to* **Mathurine***)* All beauty pales before yours. *(Aside to* **Charlotte***)* One who has seen you can have eyes for no other. *(Aloud)* I have a little matter to attend to. I'll be back in a moment. Sganarelle, entertain the ladies.

Sganarelle *(with a dismayed look at the one bottle of wine that has been saved)*   I've only saved one.

Don Juan   Knock the neck off. *(Goes a few steps away)*

Charlotte. **Mathurine**. **Sganarelle**. **Don Juan**.

Mathurine *(to* **Charlotte***)*   I say it's me he's going to marry.

Charlotte *(to* **Mathurine***)*   All I say is it's me he loves.

Sganarelle *(offering wine)*   Poor things! Don't let him hornswoggle you. Him! Naturally he can turn your heads. Nothing to it.

(**Don Juan** *comes closer)*

Sganarelle   Give me his coat, his ribbons, and his feathers and I'll seduce you without trying; but then at least you'll get something out of it. Take my advice: don't trust him. *(Sees* **Don Juan***)* Don't trust the fellow who speaks ill of my master . . .

Don Juan   Sganarelle . . . *(Grabs him by the ear)*

Sganarelle   You don't know my master.

(Someone is hurrying in)

Charlotte. Mathurine. Don Juan. Sganarelle. Marphurius.

Sganarelle What's up? What's the hurry?

Marphurius *(panting)* Is this where the duel is to take place? *(Introducing himself)* I am Dr. Marphurius, the medical authority of this humble village.

Sganarelle What duel?

Marphurius Between the noble brothers Don Alonso and Don Carlos on the one hand and the noble Don Juan Tenorio on the other.

Sganarelle Donna Elvira's brothers! Are they here?

Marphurius They will be here in a moment. They combed the village for a whole hour, inquiring after this noble Don Juan Tenorio. Then a young fisherman informed them that he was indeed here. *(To* **Don Juan***)* Is it you, sir? I have come posthaste to offer you my services for the impending duel. I shall be greatly honored to attend your lordship. Foresight is better than hindsight. When the blood flows, we must be prepared. *(To the girls)* Bring shirting and basins of water.

Charlotte Heavens, they're going to stab each other.

Marphurius Yes, they are going to stab each other. *(To* **Don Juan***)* In these humble villages, your lordship, a stab wound is seldom seen nowadays. Ah! The golden age of dueling is past. In those days surgery made greater progress in ten years than in the preceding three centuries. The stab wound flourished, the cleanest, the most elegant of all wounds. Nowadays all they ever bring me is an occasional arm crushed between fishing boats. I am not speaking of the money but of the healer's art. Duels trained the surgeon's hand, they perfected his instruments. With this probe, for example, I treated Don Malaga after his glorious duel with the Duke of Estramadura. The wound was all of two feet long. The family gave me this purse! There were once fifty ducats in it, your lordship. I am not speaking of the money but of the healer's art. How manners have degenerated and the arts with them! *(While pacing off the distance between the duelists)* I can see the day coming when our grandees will belabor each other with fish buckets. They will settle their delicate quarrels with flails and avenge their ladies with butcher knives.

Don Juan   My dears, one of those affairs which honor makes incumbent on those of my class obliges me to remain here alone.

Marphurius   O tempora, O mores! O times, O customs! The stab wound vanishes, the bashed-in skull takes its place.

Don Juan   If it pleases heaven to preserve my life, I entreat you to remember my promise. You will hear from me before nightfall.

Marphurius   A robust but uncultivated population is preparing to force its barbarous ways upon the nation.

Don Juan *(to* **Sganarelle***)*   Escort these sweet young ladies to the village and see to it that no evil befalls them.

Marphurius   Ah yes, those boatmen I just met . . .

Sganarelle   What boatmen?

Marphurius   Three boatmen who escaped this morning's storm by a hair's breadth. They have been going about complaining with the utmost insolence that a noble lord owes them fifty-four ducats. Brandishing their oars in blind fury and letting everyone know that they have been taught how to handle them.

Sganarelle   The rogues! Fifty-four ducats!

Charlotte   Are they looking for you, my lord? You'd better run.

Sganarelle   Yes, my lord, you'd better run.

Marphurius   Cut the knaves down and basta!

Sganarelle *(to the girls)*   Beg him on your knees or we'll all be lost.

Marphurius   Exterminate them! Wipe them off the face of the earth!

Mathurine *(kneeling)*   Run, my lord.

Charlotte *(kneeling)*   Yes, my lord, run! One of them must be that brute Berthelot from the next village. Run, run!

Marphurius *(kneeling)*   And I implore you to cut them down.

Mathurine   Run, my lord. A fine gentleman like you can't let his nose be bashed in.

Sganarelle   They're coming, they're coming!

Marphurius   Do you vulgarians suppose that a Don Juan Tenorio handles his affairs like you loutish fisherfolk? *(He tears linen for bandages and brandishes his instruments)*

Mathurine And Charlotte *(at once)*   Run, my lord. They'll beat you to a pulp.

Don Juan   Indeed, the contest seems too unequal. I will have no truck with brute force. Fate has come between us. Ah, my fair maidens, I cannot ignore your entreaties. Sganarelle, I find myself in a position to fulfill your heartfelt wish. You may put on my coat, give me your rags.

Sganarelle   You are joking, my lord. Do you want me to die in your clothes?

Don Juan   Not if it can be helped. Make ready for the journey home. *(* **Don Juan** *goes out with* **Sganarelle**. *The doctor runs after them)*

Marphurius   Your lordship! Your lordship! The duel! The duel!

(The fisher maidens look at each other, start laughing, and laugh so hard that they have to sit down on the ground)

Act Three

An overgrown park. Among the trees a white building.

1

Don Juan *in* **Sganarelle's** *clothes.* **Sganarelle** *in* **Don Juan's** *clothes.*

Don Juan   Tell me, Sganarelle, haven't we come this way before? These trees, these bushes, these paths look familiar. This ancient tree—was it not a witness to passionate oaths?

Sganarelle   There have been so many trees, my lord, in so many different places. I can't keep them apart. Permit me to sit down a while, my lord. The excitement, the weight of your clothes, not to mention this basket, have tired me out.

Don Juan   Blockhead, why did you have to take the basket? Did I order you to take it? Don Juan does not carry baskets.

Sganarelle   Your clothes have not changed me enough to make me forget my duty of catering to Don Juan's stomach. Shall we eat, my lord?

Don Juan   Knave! A nobleman doesn't bite into a piece of pie on the roadside like a dog. Show my garments more honor. You must behave like me. I will force myself to imitate your manners. And you, knave, will not touch a single bite! (**Don Juan** *eats and drinks*)

Sganarelle *(while* **Don Juan** *eats)*   I'm still thinking about that doctor. Perhaps I should have gone to him for treatment. I feel extremely weak and my stomach is beginning to toss so strangely: from left to right. God knows my health is not of the best, my lord. (**Don Juan** *gives him a severe look*) I think I could really use a doctor.

Don Juan   What for?

Sganarelle To cure me.

Don Juan A doctor to cure you? The time to see a doctor is when you want to die.

Sganarelle Don't you believe in senna leaves?

Don Juan Why should I believe in senna leaves?

Sganarelle *(shakes his head in despair)* All right, never mind medicine. If you don't believe in it, you don't. Let's talk about something else. *(Serves him wine)* What about heaven? Don't you believe in that either?

Don Juan Never mind.

Sganarelle Hm, that means you don't believe in it. And hell?

Don Juan Bah!

Sganarelle So it's no again. And the devil?

Don Juan Yes, yes.

Sganarelle So you don't believe in him either. What about the other world?

(**Don Juan** *laughs loudly)*

Sganarelle But how do you feel about the black bishop?

Don Juan The plague take you!

Sganarelle That's too much. A fact is a fact. Who else do you suppose sucks the blood out of February babies? Who do you believe in if you don't believe in him?

Don Juan What I believe in?

Sganarelle Yes.

Don Juan I believe that two times two is four.

Sganarelle That's a lovely thing to believe. A fine article of faith. So your religion is the multiplication table. As for me, my lord, I haven't studied like you. No man can boast of having taught me anything. But I can see that things aren't so simple. For instance, I'd be glad to have you tell me who made those trees and those rocks; who made the earth and the sky up there. Did they all make themselves? Take yourself, for instance. You're here, aren't you? Well, did you make yourself? Didn't his lordship your father have to get her ladyship your mother pregnant in order to make you? Don't you marvel at how everything in a man works, how everything hangs together—the nerves, the bones, the veins, the arteries, these—these lungs, the heart, the liver and all the trimmings which . . .

Don Juan   Are you almost finished?

Sganarelle   So there is something wonderful about man, whatever you may say. Isn't it a wonder that I'm here? That I have something in my head, something that can think a hundred things at once and move my body the way I want. I want to clap my hands, *(demonstrating)* lift my arm, raise my eyes, lower my head, move my feet, go to the right, to the left, forward, backward, about face! *(Turns around and falls down)*

Don Juan   Lovely. But now we've got to be thinking about how to get to the city.

Sganarelle   Here comes a man. We'll ask him the way. *(Enter a* **beggar***)*

Sganarelle   Hey, you! Hey!

Don Juan   Eat properly at least. Don't forget that you're me. *(* **Sganarelle** *starts to eat. He eats wastefully like* **Don Juan***)*

2

Don Juan. **Sganarelle**. *The* **beggar**.

Sganarelle   Which is the quickest way to the city?

Beggar *(to* **Sganarelle***)*   You just have to take this path, turn right, and then straight ahead. But I advise you to be on your guard, my lord. A little while ago some dangerous-looking men passed by, they were brandishing big cudgels and shouting terrible threats against noblemen.

Sganarelle   I'm very much obliged to you, my friend.

Beggar *(to* **Sganarelle***)*   I am a poor beggar, your lordship. A trifling gift, if you please.

Don Juan   Ha, I see your helpfulness was not entirely disinterested.

Beggar *(to* **Sganarelle***)*   I am a poor man. I shall not fail to pray heaven to send you riches.

Sganarelle   Thank you, my friend.

Don Juan   My foot! Why doesn't he pray heaven to send him a coat without holes in it?

Sganarelle   My friend, you don't know his lordship. He only believes in "two times two is four."

Don Juan   How do you spend your time in the woods?

Beggar *(to* **Sganarelle***)*   All day long I pray heaven to increase the prosperity of the good people who treat me generously.

Don Juan   Then you must be doing very well.

Beggar *(to* **Sganarelle***)*   Oh, your lordship, I'm as poor as a church mouse.

Don Juan   You must be joking. If you pray all day your affairs are sure to prosper.

Beggar   I assure you, your lordship, that most of the time I haven't even a crust of bread for my toothless mouth.

Don Juan *(to* **Sganarelle***)*   Strange, very strange, your lordship. *(To the* **beggar***)* Your efforts are ill rewarded. *(He laughs loudly)* His lordship will give you a louis d'or, his last, but only on one condition: you must curse.

Sganarelle   Your lordship, please!

Beggar *(to* **Sganarelle***)*   Oh, your lordship, don't lead me into temptation.

Don Juan   Make up your mind: do you want to earn a louis d'or or don't you? Here it is. *(To* **Sganarelle***)* In the left-hand pocket, knave. *(He takes a louis d'or from* **Sganarelle's** *pocket. To the* **beggar***)* Go on. Take it, but curse!

Sganarelle   But your lordship . . .

Beggar *(to* **Sganarelle***)*   Your lordship . . .

Don Juan   Or you don't get anything. *(Aside to* **Sganarelle***, giving him a shove)* Sganarelle!

Sganarelle   Just a little curse! There's nothing to it . . .

Don Juan   Go ahead, in the devil's name take it, but curse!

Beggar   No, your lordship, I'd rather starve and go to heaven.

Don Juan *(gives him the louis d'or)*   You idiots! There! I give it to you for love of humanity.

(The **beggar** *takes the gold piece and goes off in a fright)*

Sganarelle   Your lordship, we must be going! Night is coming on.

Don Juan. **Sganarelle**. **Angelica**. *Nurse.*

Accompanied by her nurse, **Angelica**, *a young girl in mourning, steps out of the park carrying a basket of flowers. They go into the mausoleum.*

Don Juan   Oh, what a divine apparition!

Sganarelle *(holds him back)*   Your lordship! Pull yourself together. How can you take the field of love in such a ridiculous outfit?

Don Juan   You're perfectly right. Only a great beauty could make me forget my disguise. Quick, my clothes. Hurry, knave, she'll soon be coming out.

Sganarelle *(begins taking his coat off. Grumpily)*   Oh . . . *(He has barely unbuttoned his vest when a great uproar is heard. Amid shouts the* **boatmen** *are besetting a young nobleman)*

Don Juan   What's this? A noble assaulted by three oafs!

Sganarelle   The boatmen!

Don Juan   The contest is too unequal; such cowardice is more than my eyes can bear. Go to the man's help immediately. I myself do not fight with ruffians who brandish cudgels. Get in there and fight, knave! *(He gives* **Sganarelle** *a kick which sends him into the mêlée, and goes off to one side)*

4

Don Juan. **Sganarelle**. **Don Carlos**. **Boatmen**. **Angelica**. *Nurse.*

Pantomime: Fight. Struck by a **boatman**, *the nobleman falls unconscious to the ground.* **Sganarelle's** *roars put the* **boatmen** *to flight.* **Angelica** *and her nurse emerge from the mausoleum, see the limping half-naked and groaning* **Sganarelle**, *and take flight. While* **Sganarelle** *tries to revive the young nobleman with wine,* **Don Juan** *looks after the fleeing young girl in dismay.*

Don Juan. **Sganarelle**. **Don Carlos**.

Don Juan Hurry, knave, hurry! She's feeding the does in the clearing!

Sganarelle *(busy dressing* **Don Juan***, apologizes to the moaning* **Don Carlos***)* Patience, sir. As soon as his coat is buttoned you shall have wine.

Don Juan Button it properly, he'll come to by himself. *(The coat is buttoned,* **Sganarelle** *wants to go to* **Don Carlos***)* Sash! *(* **Sganarelle** *puts on* **Don Juan's** *sash)* Bandolier! *(* **Sganarelle** *continues to busy himself with* **Don Juan***)*

Sganarelle *(to* **Don Carlos** *who staggers to his feet)* Nothing serious, young sir. You were hit by an oar! I got it in the knee.

Don Juan Wig!

Don Carlos *(to* **Don Juan** *as* **Sganarelle** *adjusts his wig)* Sir!

Don Juan *(whose accoutrement is not yet fully in order, motions him to wait)*

Don Carlos *(when* **Don Juan** *is fully dressed)* Permit me, sir, to tender my thanks for your magnanimous assistance and your . . .

Don Juan *(looking around impatiently)* Sir, I only did what you would have done in my place.

Sganarelle *(aside)* Meaning, nothing.

Don Carlos Indeed, your mere presence sufficed. Your look of authority, your voice accustomed to command. You are wondering, sir, why those devils flung themselves upon me. An unfortunate accident separated me from my brother in whose company I set out this morning to settle a certain affair. While looking for him, I came across these bandits. Though I was a total stranger to them, they importuned me with a story about some nobleman who owed them money, so they claimed, and slandered him most abominably. When I remonstrated with them over their disgraceful maligning of our station, they unleashed such a storm of insults that despite their superior number I resolved to punish them. Their only weapons were oars. But they handled them with such dexterity *(Sganarelle bows complacently)* that I should have succumbed but for your exemplary courage.

Don Juan   Are you on your way to the city?

Don Carlos   No, my elder brother and I are involved in one of those affairs with which our families are so painfully afflicted and which constrain us noblemen to the most extreme sacrifices. O honor, thou inexorable taskmaster!

Don Juan *(to* **Sganarelle***)*   Quick! Run! Find that girl!

Don Carlos   Indeed, the outcome of a duel is bitter in either case. If we do not leave our life on the field, we have to leave the country. We noblemen have a hard lot. Neither caution nor blameless conduct can help us. Our laws of honor make us the victims of other men's transgressions. Our life, our peace of mind depend on the whims of any scoundrel who sees fit to inflict upon us, out of the clear blue sky, one of those insults that a nobleman can expunge only with his sword.

Don Juan   At least we have the advantage of being able to inflict the same inconveniences on anyone who annoys us. If I am not being indiscreet: what sort of affair are you involved in?

Don Carlos   The matter has gone so far that there is no further need of secrecy. Since the insult has become public knowledge, our honor commands us not to overlook it but to avenge it. Accordingly, my dear sir, I need not hesitate to inform you that the disgrace we are resolved to avenge is that of a sister wrested from the holy seclusion of a convent and seduced. The offender is a certain Don Juan Tenorio, son of the venerable Don Luis Tenorio. We have been tracking him since this morning.

Don Juan   Do you know this Don Juan you speak of?

Don Carlos I myself do not. I have never seen him. But my elder brother has given me a description of him. The life he leads is utterly . . .

Don Juan If you please, sir, not another word. Don Juan is my best, to tell you the truth, my only friend. I will hear no evil said of him.

Don Carlos To oblige you I will say no more. That is little enough to ask of a man who owes you his life. But despite your friendship with this Don Juan, I venture to hope that you will frown on his conduct and therefore find it no more than natural that we mean to wreak bloody vengeance on him.

Don Juan I am Don Juan's friend, I cannot alter the fact, but even he may not with impunity transgress against the honor of our station. To spare you the trouble of tracking him down, I shall impel him to give you satisfaction where and when you desire. You have my word of honor.

Don Carlos What high hope you arouse in us! We are most obliged to you, sir, though it would grieve me to see you involved in this affair.

Don Juan I am so close to Don Juan that he would never fight without my consent.

Don Carlos O cruel fate! Why must I owe you my life when Don Juan is your friend?

6

Don Juan. Don Carlos. Don Alonso.

Don Alonso *(speaking to someone behind him, does not see* **Don Juan** *and* **Don Carlos***)* Water the horses and bring them after me. I wish to walk a while. *(He sees the two)* What do I see? You, my brother, with our family's deadly enemy?

Don Carlos Deadly enemy?

Don Juan *(his hand on his sword)* Yes, I am Don Juan. Your superior number cannot move me to conceal my name.

Don Alonso *(drawing his sword)* Ah! Scoundrel! Now you must die!

Don Carlos Stop, brother, stop! I owe him my life. If not for him, ruffians would have killed me.

Don Alonso Will you permit such a consideration to hamper our vengeance? Such gratitude is absurd. Since honor is far more precious than life, if we owe our life to the man who has robbed us of our honor we owe him nothing.

(**Sganarelle** *appears between the trees. He beckons excitedly to attract* **Don Juan's** *attention)*

Don Juan Gentlemen, I have but one request to make of you: that you decide quickly. I am in a hurry.

Don Carlos Brother, I know what I owe to our honor. Shall I permit this gentleman to carry with him to the other world a debt that I have failed to redeem?

Don Alonso Heaven has given us an opportunity to take vengeance here and now. If you do not wish to fight, then go. I alone will make the holy sacrifice.

Don Carlos Brother, I implore you . . .

Don Alonso   No, he must die . . .

Don Carlos *(placing himself in front of* **Don Juan***)*   Stop, brother; stop, I say. I will not suffer you to take his life in this place where he defended mine. If you wish to kill him, you will first have to pierce my heart.

(Pause)

Don Alonso   O unforgiveable weakness!

Don Carlos   Grant me a delay, brother.

Don Alonso   The interests of our family . . .

Don Carlos   Will be safeguarded. Don Juan, you see that I am doing my utmost to repay my debt to you. From which I bid you infer that tomorrow I shall requite your offense with the same zeal as today I requite your succor.

Don Juan   Sir, I have given you my word. Rest assured, I do not fear this encounter, but I must own to you that I should find it rather inconvenient at the present moment. I am thankful to you for the postponement.

Don Carlos   Come at midnight to the dark alley leading to the convent.

Don Alonso   There we shall make amends for our present neglect.

Don Carlos   Let us go, brother.

(Both go out)

7

Don Juan. **Sganarelle**.

Don Juan   Well, knave, where is she?

Sganarelle   Your lordship!

Don Juan   The devil take you, speak! Why are you standing there as if you'd been struck by lightning?

Sganarelle   Your lordship, I have! Do you know what that white building is?

Don Juan   Blockhead, what's a white building to me? Where's the girl?

Sganarelle   Your lordship, that white thing among the trees is— his tomb.

Don Juan   Whose tomb?

Sganarelle   The man you killed according to all the rules . . .

Don Juan   The Commander?

Sganarelle   Heaven protect you!

Don Juan   Oh!—But let's get back to essentials: who is the girl?

Sganarelle   The girl is . . . the Commander's daughter.

Don Juan   His daughter! My word.

Sganarelle   Robbed by you of her father and mother! Your lordship, I implore you, we must leave this place of doom. To stay is to bring the dead man's wrath upon us.

Don Juan   What, coward? Afraid of stones when I'm here beside you? I'll drive this fear out of you. I'll pay the Commander my respects, and you'll come with me.

Sganarelle   Your lordship, please don't go in, please.

Don Juan   I order you not to be afraid! I owe the gentleman a
visit. If he's a gentleman, he'll receive us politely. Come.

(They approach the mausoleum among the trees)

(Music. The mausoleum opens. **Don Juan** *and* **Sganarelle** *stand
before the statue of the* **Commander***)*

8

Don Juan. **Sganarelle**. *The statue of the Commander.*

Sganarelle   There! There he is.

Don Juan   Good Lord! Done up as a Roman emperor.

Sganarelle   Your lordship, he looks so real. As if he were alive and wanted to speak. He's looking at us—I'm . . . *(* **Don Juan** *gives him a menacing glance)* I'd be afraid if you weren't here. You know, your lordship, I think he's unfriendly to us.

Don Juan   That would be most unjust of him. It would suggest that he failed to appreciate the honor I'm showing him. Invite him to dinner at my house.

Sganarelle   I don't think that's of much use to him now, your lordship.

Don Juan   Go on. Invite him, I said.

Sganarelle   You're joking, my lord, a stone can't hear.

Don Juan   Exactly. Do as you're told.

Sganarelle   Lord Commander—*(aside)* this is idiotic!—*(aloud)* Lord Commander, my master Don Juan Tenorio bids me ask whether you will do him the honor of dining with him this evening.

(The statue nods)

Sganarelle   Oh!

Don Juan   Now what's wrong with you? Say something.

Sganarelle *(mimics the statue's nod)*   The statue . . .

Don Juan   Idiot! Speak up!

Sganarelle   The statue!

Don Juan   The statue what? Speak or I'll strike you dead.

Sganarelle   The statue nodded.

Don Juan   The plague take you!

Sganarelle   He nodded. Really. Speak to him yourself.

Don Juan   Blockhead. Lord Commander, will you do me the honor of dining at my house—in pleasant company?

(The statue nods)

Sganarelle   Oh!

Don Juan *(takes a pinch of snuff)*   Time to be going.

(Both go out)

Act Four

The terrace of Don Juan's castle.

1

Sganarelle. **Ragotin**.

Ragotin *(holding a letter in his hand, passes* **Sganarelle***; he is wearing riding boots and breeches)*   This'll be the fourth letter I've taken over there.

Sganarelle   Ragotin! Is she coming or not?

Ragotin   Yes.

Sganarelle   Yes, what?

Ragotin   She's either coming or she's not. How do I know? Why shouldn't she come? You might say she's still in mourning for the commander. But what's that to me? I've got my hands full: knock off a gate keeper, poison a dog, bribe a governess. Letters, letters— back and forth! Two horses worn to a frazzle! Only three left in the stable. Are they my horses? Well then. Is she coming or not? I don't ask, I don't know, my business is riding. *(Goes out)*

Sganarelle.

Sganarelle   Happy man! My trouble is that I know too much. I can feel a terrible tempest brewing over this house, and I'm very much afraid that the lightning will strike the servant along with the master. I'll ask the cook to read my palm. She's good at it. *(Calls)* Seraphine! Seraphine!

Sganarelle. Seraphine.

Seraphine   What is it? I've got a big dinner to cook.

Sganarelle   That's just it.

Seraphine   What's the dinner to you?

Sganarelle   That's just what I want you to tell me. Seraphine, I've got a feeling that a terrible storm is gathering over this house and I want you to read my palm. Seraphine, is my fate tied up with the fate of a great lord? Watch your step.

Seraphine   Let's see!

Sganarelle *(hesitates)*   I want the whole truth.

Seraphine *(taking his hand)*   I always tell the whole truth.

Sganarelle *(withdraws his hand)*   But you can make mistakes.

Seraphine   If you think I can make mistakes, I'll go back to my hors d'oeuvres. I'm sick of reading you people's palms anyway. The other day Josephine fainted and that made Ragotin cut me.

Sganarelle *(suspiciously)*   So you think I'll faint if you tell me the whole truth?

Seraphine   I haven't even looked yet.

Sganarelle   Oh yes, you have.

Seraphine   I say I haven't. And now I'm going back to my carp.

Sganarelle   Damn the carp. Don't be so touchy. Here's my hand. Just tell me if my fate is tied up with the fate of a great lord. Watch your step. *(After a pause)* It isn't, is it? *(Jangles coins in his pocket)* Look carefully.

Seraphine   Your fate is . . .

Sganarelle   Watch your step, now.

Seraphine   Not tied up with the fate of a great lord!

Sganarelle   Right! You really are a good palm reader. *(Suddenly distrustful)* Do you really see that, or are you just trying to make me feel good? I want you to tell me exactly what my hand says. Not what it gives me pleasure to hear. My life line —would you say it was long?

Seraphine *(inspects his hand for some time)*   Long, yes . . .

Sganarelle   What do you mean "long, yes . . ."? Now you're trying to scare me.

Seraphine   I told you you wouldn't be able to take it. Now I'm going back to my ducks in orange sauce. They don't interrupt me all the time.

Sganarelle   Don't try to cut me short when I want to know about my life line. When everybody knows that palm reading is unreliable. If you want to know the truth about the future, what you need is a horoscope. It's expensive but you can rely on it.

Seraphine   You only say that because you're afraid. You're not a man. And it shows in your life line.

Sganarelle   You said yourself it was long.

Seraphine   Yes, long. But thin.

Sganarelle   Hm. Then let it be thin.

Seraphine   It's thin all right.

Sganarelle   But long.

Seraphine   Yes.

Sganarelle   Seraphine, what are we fighting for? All I want you to tell me is this: does it say if there's something special I should watch out for?

Seraphine   But if I tell you you'll start yelling at me again.

Sganarelle   No, I promise.

Seraphine   Veal.

Sganarelle   Don't be silly, Seraphine. Veal doesn't hurt me in the least.

Seraphine   You're Aries, aren't you?

Sganarelle   No, Cancer.

Seraphine   In that case veal really can't hurt you.

Sganarelle   Take another look: should I watch out for stone?

Seraphine   Stone?

Sganarelle   Yes or no?

Seraphine *(hears **Don Juan** coming)*   His lordship! *(She runs away)*

Sganarelle *(shouts after her)*   Stone? Yes or no?

Sganarelle. **Don Juan**.

Don Juan   What's all the shouting?

Sganarelle   Oh, your lordship, I can't get that talking statue out of my mind.

Don Juan   Forget it. Maybe a shadow deceived you, or a blood stoppage could have clouded your eye.

Sganarelle   No, your lordship, you can't deny it, that nod was real. It was a miracle wrought by heaven itself because your way of life has . . .

Don Juan   Listen to me: you stop bothering me with your idiotic sermons or I'll call a stable boy with a whip. Three men will hold you down, or maybe four would be better, and you'll be beaten like a carpet. Understand?

Sganarelle   I understand, your lordship. You express yourself very plainly; that's the best thing about you, you don't beat about the bush, you make things so beautifully clear.

Don Juan   Hm.—What's Ragotin doing?

Sganarelle   Riding.

Don Juan. **Sganarelle**. **La Violette**.

La Violette   Your lordship, Mr. Dimanche your tailor is here; he insists on seeing you.

Sganarelle   A creditor! That's all we needed. Coming to us for money! The idea! Why don't you tell him his lordship is out?

La Violette   That's just what I've been telling him for a whole half hour, but he won't believe me. He's sat down in the antechamber and he's waiting.

Sganarelle   Then let him sit in the antechamber till he rots.

Don Juan   No. That won't do. Bring him in. It's bad tactics to hide from creditors; it's much better to give them something.

(La Violette brings in Mr. Dimanche)

Sganarelle. **Don Juan**. **Dimanche**. **La Violette**.

Don Juan Ah, my dear Dimanche, how kind of you to call!
You are my first visitor since my return. I shall never forgive
my servants for not bringing you in at once. I had given orders
to admit no one, but they ought to realize that such orders don't
include you. To you my door is at all times open.

Dimanche I'm much obliged to you, your lordship.

Don Juan (*to* **La Violette** *and* **Sganarelle**) Scoundrels! I'll teach
you to let Mr. Dimanche cool his heels!

Dimanche It's nothing, your lordship.

Don Juan Nothing? Telling you, my best friend, that I'm out?

Dimanche Your lordship, I have come to . . .

Don Juan Quick, a chair for Mr. Dimanche.

Dimanche I don't mind standing, your lordship, if . . .

Don Juan When you're in my house, I want to see you
comfortably seated.

Dimanche It's quite unnecessary. (*He begins to sit down*)

Don Juan Take that stool away! A chair, I said.

Dimanche Your lordship pleases to joke. I . . .

Don Juan No, no. I know what I owe you. I wish to see no
distinction between us.

Dimanche Your lordship . . .

Don Juan Come, come. Do sit down.

Dimanche It's really unnecessary, I shall be very brief. I've
come to . . .

Don Juan   Sit down, I say.

Dimanche   No, no, your lordship. Don't put yourself out. I only wished to . . .

Don Juan   No, I refuse to listen unless you sit down.

Dimanche   If you insist, your lordship. *(Sits down)* I . . .

Don Juan   You're looking well, Mr. Dimanche.

Dimanche   Thank you, your lordship. Your humble servant. I've come . . .

Don Juan   Your health is your most precious possession—full lips, rosy cheeks, sparkling eyes.

Dimanche   I should like . . .

Don Juan   Madame Dimanche is well, too, I hope.

Dimanche   Tolerably well, your lordship, thank heaven. I thought . . .

Don Juan   An excellent woman!

Dimanche   Thank you, your lordship. I hoped . . .

Don Juan   And your daughter Claudine?

Dimanche   In the best of health.

Don Juan   Ah, the sweet little pigeon. Charming!

Dimanche   You do me too much honor, your lordship. I wished . . .

Don Juan   And Paolo, your little boy? Still making such a hubbub with his little drum?

Dimanche   He's still at it, your lordship . . . I . . .

Don Juan   And Pippo, your little dog? Does he still growl and nip your visitors' legs?

Dimanche   More than ever, your lordship, we can't seem to break him of the habit.

Don Juan   My inquiries seem to surprise you. You forget the deep interest I take in your family.

Dimanche   We're very much obliged, your lordship. I . . .

Don Juan   Give me your hand, Mr. Dimanche. If I have any friend in the world, it's you.

Dimanche   Your humble servant!

Don Juan   And I am yours with all my heart!

Dimanche   You do me too much honor. I . . .

Don Juan   There's nothing I wouldn't do for you. But you know that. Nothing . . .

Dimanche   You are too kind, your lordship . . .

Don Juan   Without thought of my own advantage.

Dimanche   You put me to shame. But, your lordship . . .

Don Juan   Ah, Mr. Dimanche . . . without mincing words . . . will you stay for dinner?

Dimanche   No, your lordship. I really must be going. I . . .

Don Juan *(stands up)*   Servants! Quick! Bring torches. Escort Mr. Dimanche. Four of you, no, five. With muskets.

Dimanche *(likewise stands up)*   Oh but your lordship, it's not necessary, I'll find my way. But . . .

(**Sganarelle** *immediately removes his chair)*

Don Juan   Not a word. I insist on giving you an escort. I always said you'd go far and I mean to see that you do. I am your servant and what is more your debtor.

Dimanche   Oh, your lordship!

Don Juan   I make that clear to anyone who is willing to listen.

Dimanche   If you . . .

Don Juan   Oh, you'd like *me* to escort you?

Dimanche   Oh, your lordship. Now you're making fun of me. Your lordship . . .

Don Juan   Embrace me, I beg you. And once again I ask you to believe that I am always at your disposal, and that there is nothing I wouldn't do for you.

(**Dimanche** *is led away by the armed servants bearing torches)*

Dimanche   Your lordship. I wished . . .

Don Juan *(calling after him)*   Send me two of the usual coats. I'm getting engaged.

Dimanche   Oh! *(Goes out)*

Don Juan   What is it, La Violette?

La Violette   A lady! Heavily veiled.

Don Juan   Bring her in. *(To* **Sganarelle***)* Blockhead! Why are you looking at me like that? Still afraid of that chunk of stone?

7

Don Juan. **Donna Elvira**. **Sganarelle**. **La Violette**.

Donna Elvira   It may surprise you, Don Juan, to see me here at
this late hour and thus attired. But what I have to say cannot be
put off. I have not come in anger as I did yesterday morning. I am
no longer the woman who cursed you and thirsted for vengeance.
Heaven has banished all earthly passion from my heart. What I
feel for you now is a devout tenderness, an affection freed from
the lusts of the flesh, which knows no self-interest and whose sole
concern is for your immortal soul.

Don Juan *(to* **Sganarelle***)*   No, really! I believe you're crying.

Sganarelle   For joy, your lordship.

Donna Elvira   This new love has made me the messenger of
heaven, come to snatch you if I can from the brink of the abyss.
Yes, Don Juan, your crimes are known to me. Heaven has sent me
to say that its patience is worn thin and that its terrible wrath hangs
over your head. You can avert this by repenting before it is too late.
You may have only a few hours in which to escape your doom. As
for me, my fate is decided. I shall withdraw into the holy seclusion
of the convent of Santa Regina. It would be a source of the utmost
grief to me in my retirement if heaven should be forced to make
a terrible example of the man I loved so dearly. But what bliss it
would be for me if I could move you to ward off the fearful blow
that threatens you. Don Juan, grant me this sweet consolation;
don't refuse me the salvation of your soul; spare me the sorrow of
seeing you condemned to the eternal torments of hell.

Sganarelle *(aside)*   Poor woman!

Donna Elvira   I loved you very dearly. Nothing in this world
was so dear to me as you. For you I forgot my duty; for you I gave
all I had to give. And now I ask only one thing of you: don't let
yourself be damned. Save yourself, I implore you, for your sake or

for mine. I beseech you by everything that is capable of touching your heart!

Sganarelle *(aside)*   The heart of a tiger!

Donna Elvira   I'm going now. I have said my say.

Don Juan   It's late, my lady. Don't go. We shall do our best to make you comfortable here.

Donna Elvira   No, Don Juan, don't try to detain me.

Don Juan   My lady, believe me, it would give me pleasure if you stayed.

Donna Elvira   No, there is no time to waste in needless talk. Let me go. No, don't accompany me. And take my words to heart. *(Goes out)*

Don Juan. **Sganarelle**.

Don Juan   Sganarelle, what's to become of our reputation? In love as in war that's what counts the most. A fortress will surrender to the man other fortresses have surrendered to. It accepts surrender as a law of nature. Alexander's reputation conquered more cities for him than his army. A general without a reputation has no other resort but to fight like a madman. Every defeat must be followed by a victory. Have you made the preparations for the dinner as I wished? The musicians? And Belisa, the famous singer? I want her to embellish our banquet with a serenade. And send for those fisher maidens. Have them come in at midnight with their oysters and crabs. I'll sample the wines.

Sganarelle   Oh, your lordship. Heaven forgive you. *(Strange heat lightning on the horizon.* **Sganarelle** *is terrified and* **Don Juan** *laughs)*

Don Juan   Still no news of Ragotin?

Sganarelle *(trembling)*   No.

(Enter **La Violette***)*

Don Juan. **Sganarelle**. **La Violette**.

La Violette   Your lordship, your father is here. On the way he fell in with some boatmen who were turned away by the gate keeper and have been making a disturbance outside. They have been telling him all sorts of stories.

Don Juan *(to* **La Violette***)*   Keep him busy for a few minutes. *(To* **Sganarelle***)* Make me up. A little white.

(**Sganarelle** *makes him up)*

Don Juan   Do you know that I felt a slight surge of feeling for Donna Elvira? That this bizarre new situation has given me a kind of pleasure, and her careless dress, the mildness of her look, and her tears have rekindled the sparks of a flame that was almost spent?

Sganarelle   In short, her words made no impression on you?

Don Juan   A touch under the eyes.

Sganarelle   As you wish.

Don Juan   Sganarelle, we ought to think of mending our ways.

Sganarelle   Oh yes.

Don Juan   Yes, it's a fact, we've got to mend our ways. Another twenty or thirty years of this life and we shall start thinking of our immortal soul.

(Heat lightning in the sky)

Sganarelle   Oh, your lordship, heaven is nodding agreement. Don't harden your heart. There's still time. Repent.

Don Juan   That's just what I mean to do—in a manner of speaking. Go.

(**Sganarelle** *goes out)*

Don Juan. **Don Luis**. *Then* **Sganarelle**.

Don Luis   Scoundrel! What is this new exploit I hear of? How base! How contemptible! Am I to cover such conduct with my name? I can do so no longer. By what right do you enjoy our privileges? What have you done in the world to deserve the name of nobleman? Do you suppose that your blood ennobles you when you lead the life of a villain? Have you forgotten how to blush? Shall it be said that a nobleman is a monster? Shall it be said that the sons of common laborers are more virtuous than ours?

Don Juan   Father, an inner voice must have told you how much I needed you; that must be why you leaped into your carriage. I have had an experience that I can speak of to no one but you. You are a soldier, you are a pious man, you will understand me. Father, you see me miraculously transformed. Let us not speak of the shameful lusts that made me put out to sea to ravish a woman. In the bleak dawn, as the wind howled about my craft, I heard you, my father, crying out to me in a terrible voice: "Turn back!" I fled to the shore.

Don Luis   To the shore! Oho!

Don Juan   Some pious fisher maidens took me in and vied with one another in caring for me. Their simple chatter moved me deeply. *(* **Ragotin** *has entered with a letter)* What is it? *(* **Ragotin** *hands* **Don Juan** *the letter.* **Don Juan** *reads it with every sign of satisfaction and tosses* **Ragotin** *a purse)* Excuse me, father. Heaven has sent me another sign. But let me continue. A little later, deep in the woods, I met a child of angelic beauty who seemed to know me. She took me by the hand and led me to a white mausoleum in the Roman style. We entered. I found myself standing before the stone effigy of the man whom I had robbed of everything he had in the world, his wife, his honor, and finally his life. "My father," said the little girl. "He wishes to forgive you."

Don Luis   Forgive you!

Don Juan   And what do you think it says in this letter? To make his forgiveness complete, that angelic child, the Commander's daughter, announces her visit. I must show myself worthy of her.

(**Sganarelle** *has come back with two jugs of wine*)

Don Luis   Can it be?

Don Juan   Yes, father. Everyone will see my sudden transformation. I will repair the harm done by my deeds and strive for one thing only: full forgiveness. That shall be my life from this day on, and I beg of you, my father, to help me tread the path I have chosen.

Don Luis *(embraces him)*   I came to speak of your latest escapade, which some crude fishermen have brought to my attention. But how quickly a father's reproaches are dispelled by the least sign of repentance! I have already forgotten the cares you've caused me, your words have scattered them to the winds. My cheeks are stained with tears of joy. (**Don Juan** *begins to lead him away*) Persevere in this admirable attitude and you may ask anything you wish of me. But now I must rush to tell your mother; she too must share in this heavenly news. *(Goes out)*

11

Don Juan. **Sganarelle**.

During this scene the servants finish setting the table. Musicians arrive with their instruments and the servants show them their places amid the foliage.

Sganarelle Ah, your lordship, I've been waiting a long time to hear those words. Is it possible? You repent? The Lord be thanked, now I have nothing more to wish for.

Don Juan *(selecting wine)* Idiot!—This one.

Sganarelle Idiot?

Don Juan Did you suppose I really meant what I said?

Sganarelle What? It isn't . . . You're not going to . . . Your . . . Oh, what a man! What a man!

Don Juan If I said I was going to mend my ways, it was only a stratagem, a bit of dissimulation which I must submit to in order to regain the sympathies of my father and certain others whom I need.

Sganarelle What? You believe in nothing and you are going to play the part of virtue! What a man! What a man! What a man!

Don Juan A wise man knows how to exploit the vices of his times. The fashionable vice today is hypocrisy, and when a vice is in fashion it always passes for a virtue. The role of the hypocrite presents marvelous advantages. A grimace or two is all it takes to join the pious club and then, behind the screen of piety, you are free to pursue your own interests. If I run into trouble, no need to stir a finger; the whole pious crew will come to my rescue and defend me against all comers. An honest man is forbidden to blow his nose, a hypocrite can make off with a whole city. Which is just what we're going to do. Listen to me, Sganarelle. Angelica, the Commander's daughter, has consented to come here for dinner. We shall prepare for the meeting with steadfast heart. This is going to be one of the most glorious and delightful feats of my whole career.

Sganarelle   She has consented? But your lordship, does she know who you are?

Don Juan   She will find out. From my lips.

Sganarelle   That you seduced her mother and killed her father? Your lordship, she is the only surviving avenger . . .

Don Juan   Of a dead but, as you suppose, highly indignant father. Ah, to overcome such almost superhuman obstacles, to subjugate a heart that has such good reasons to resist me—there's an exploit that seems worthy of me.

Sganarelle   Your lordship, I have never given up hope that you would be saved, but this is worse than anything you've ever done. Heaven will never stand for such outrageous defiance.

Don Juan   Come, come. Heaven isn't such a stickler as you think. I can see her coming in, light-footed, lovely, blushing ever so slightly. Sorrow for her dearly beloved father casts a charming shadow over her smooth brow. *(To the musicians who have taken their positions among the trees)* Are my little birds all ready in the branches of my trees? Gentlemen, the music! *(The music sounds)*

Don Juan   "My dear señorita, you do not know me. But I know you well, and furthermore I know your family to which I am bound by the closest ties of blood and love. For I am Don Juan Tenorio."

Sganarelle   I hope she scratches his eyes out.

Don Juan   Sganarelle, I would like her to try—"Señorita, spare me nothing. Wound me however you wish, but leave me my eyes; now that I have met you, I need them." Even the dead are moved by flattery, Sganarelle.—"Ah, God is cruel to have created beauty like yours. But He knows what He's doing. Señorita, when I saw you, when I heard who you were, I forgave your father."

Sganarelle   What? You? Forgiving the Commander, the man you killed?

Don Juan   Yes, forgave. Don't interrupt me.—"Alas, señorita, alas, I killed him. There it is again, the reproach he brought upon me by dying. All he had to do to destroy me was die." Ingenious to be sure, but confusing. "If only your father had defeated me in that duel which I did not ask for! I should no longer be alive. How much better for me than to live and be detested by you!" Now the final thrust: "Can you rebuff a desperate man who stands on the brink of nothingness? If you can, then free me at least from a life that has lost all purpose." Something along those lines.

Sganarelle   And honesty is the worst policy, and lies have seven-league boots, and he who laughs first laughs best, and last come first served, and vice is its own reward, and forgive us our innocence, and camels pass through needles' eyes. Ah, to think that a man of your social position can do whatever he pleases and that no power on earth can stop him! Is there indeed no one to do the will of heaven? No one?

Don Juan   Exactly: there's no one.

Sganarelle   To think of all the people who were praying only today that heaven would crush you!

Don Juan   Yes, I could even see it in Mr. Dimanche's eyes. As for my father, it took all my hypocrisy to disarm him. Donna Elvira's brothers are out for my blood. And there must be others who escape my mind. But you're quite right: what can they do?

(Lightning on the horizon. Thunder. The light grows somber)

Sganarelle   Oh, your lordship! That's the third time. And now I'm sure of it. Heaven is speaking to you. Heaven is giving you a sign.

Don Juan   If heaven wants to give me a sign, it should express itself a little more clearly.

(Knocking)

Don Juan   She's come. Go on. Open the door.

(Sganarelle goes)

Don Juan   Bring on the dinner. *(To the musicians)* Twitter, my
dicky birds.

(**Belisa** *sings a serenade.* **Don Juan** *waits in vain for* **Angelica** *to
appear.* **Sganarelle** *returns, pale as death)*

12

Don Juan. **Sganarelle**. *The statue of the* **Commander**.

Don Juan   What is it?

Sganarelle *(nodding like the statue)*   He . . . he's here.

Don Juan   Oh! Not she? Well, I must say, I'm disappointed. Bring him in!

(The statue of the **Commander** *enters)*

Don Juan   My lord Commander, I had hoped that both of you would come. But do be seated.

(The statue of the **Commander** *does not sit down)*

Commander   Don Juan, I have come to invite you to sup with me. Have you the courage to accept?

Don Juan   Yes. Where?

Commander   Give me your hand.

Don Juan   Here it is. If somebody wants to find me, where should he go?

Commander   In the place to which I am taking you you will not be found so easily—should anyone wish to meet you.

Don Juan *(to* **Sganarelle***)*   Bring a lamp.

Commander   No light is needed when heaven leads the way.
(**Sganarelle** *faints)*

Commander   Don Juan, a terrible end awaits those who harden their hearts in sin. To exhaust the mercy of heaven is to invite its lightnings.

(The statue of the **Commander** *leads* **Don Juan** *downstage)*

Don Juan   O heaven! The pain! I am scorched by fire! Stop!
Oh! *(Amid loud thunder the earth opens. One hand in the*
Commander's *clasp, vainly trying to hold his hat with the other,*
Don Juan *sinks into the depths. Tall flames flare from the hole into*
which they vanish. The music has stopped. Various persons rush
out on the stage, one after another)

13

**Sganarelle. La Violette. Seraphine. Angelica. Dimanche.
Elvira's** *brothers,* **Don Alonso** *and* **Don Carlos,** *followed by*
Dr. Marphurius, Don Luis, *the* **boatmen,** *the fisher maidens
accompanied by their fiancés.*

La Violette   What a disaster! He's gone!

Angelica   I'm a little late. *(Sees the hole)* Oh! How awful!

Dimanche *(bringing in two coats)*   It's blackmail! Your two
coats, your . . . Oh! My best customer!

Elvira's Brothers   The scoundrel! Where is he?—Oh! The honor
of our family stained forever!

Seraphine   Oh! Now who's going to eat my ducks in orange
sauce?

Marphurius   Oh! The duel!

Don Luis   Oh! My son! My heir!

The Boatmen   Oh! Where is he?—Fifty-four ducats down the
drain!

The Fisher Maidens   Oh! Who's going to take our oysters?—
The handsome young gentleman!

(All stand at the edge of the hole. Slowly **Don Juan's** *hat flutters
down from above)*

Sganarelle   My wages! My wages!

Trumpets and Drums

Adaptation of George Farquhar's
The Recruiting Officer

Collaborators: B. Besson and E. Hauptmann
Translators: Rose and Martin Kastner

Characters

Captain William Plume
Captain Brazen
Sergeant Kite
Mr. Balance, justice of the peace
Victoria, his daughter
Mr. Worthy, a shoe manufacturer
Mr. Smuggler, a banker
Simpkins, butler to Mr. Balance
Melinda Moorhill
Lady Prude
Rose, a country girl
Lucy, Melinda's maid
Maggie
Sally
Thomas Appletree
Costar Pearmain
Bullock, Rose's brother

William
Mike, a potboy
Mrs. Cobb, a dead soldier's mother
Bridewell, a constable
A Broad-Shouldered Man
An Unemployed Man
The Unemployed Man's Wife
A Miner
The Miner's Wife
A Pimp
Kitty, of Chicken Road
A Pickpocket
A Court Attendant
A Drummer
A Servant

The action takes place in England during the American War of Independence.

Prologue

Spoken by **Sergeant Kite**, *who steps in front of the curtain with his drummer.*

I'm Sergeant Barras Kite, now gathering a company
To help our good King George. For across the sea
In His Majesty's colony America
There's rebellion such as no man ever saw.
If anyone here should crave to join the forces—
Veterans of previous wars, or heroes without horses
Wild about living out of doors
Or footloose, eager to see foreign shores
Apprentices whose masters are too mean
Sons of parents you have never seen
A working man, who leads a hungry life
A husband suffering from a nagging wife—
Come to the Raven, apply to Sergeant Barras Kite
An honest man who'll set you right.
Now, gentlemen: Who among you, in exchange for a handsome
uniform and plenty of fodder
Will defend our dear old England (to the exclusion, of course, of his
sister, his brother, his father and his mother)?

Market place in Shrewsbury.

To one side **Judge Balance's** *house, on the other a recruiting booth.*
Sergeant Kite *steps up to the farm boys* **Pearmain** *and* **Appletree**
who are looking at the pictures outside the recruiting booth.

Kite   Gentlemen, I take it you know the Severn, but do you know
the Mississippi? *(He pulls a small field table from the recruiting
booth and sets a soldier's cap on it)* Gentlemen, observe this cap.
It's a cap of honor; it makes a gentleman out of you as fast as you
can pull a trigger. Anyone who has had the good fortune to be born
six feet tall was born under Uranus and is destined to become a
great man. *(To* **Thomas Appletree***)* Allow me, sir; I just want to
see how your head looks in this cap.

Appletree   There's a trick to this. Won't that cap enlist me?

Kite   No, no, the cap can't do that, and neither can I. *(Since*
Appletree *refuses he turns to* **Pearmain***)* What about you? Come,
let me see how it looks on you.

Pearmain   It's a very nice cap, but I suspect you're up to
something.

Kite   Oh no, friend. Don't be afraid now. *(He manages to get the
cap on* **Pearmain's** *head)*

Pearmain   It stinks of sweat and powder.

Appletree   What's that on the front?

Kite   The golden emblem, two fingers wide, over a G for King
George. A badge of honor, brother.

Pearmain   Brother?—Look 'ere, sergeant; no coaxing and
wheedling. You can't pull the wool over my eyes. Take back your
cap and your brothermanship, because I ain't in the mood today.
Let's be going, Tummas.

(They go off laughing. **Kite** *hangs the cap on the wall of the booth. Sounds of approaching horses.* **Captain Plume** *enters)*

Kite   Welcome to Shrewsbury, captain! From the banks of the Delaware to Severn side.

Plume *(strolling about)*   Shrewsbury! *(Sighs)* How goes the recruiting? What reception has Shrewsbury given her military suitors this year?

*(***Kite*** *makes a disparaging gesture)*

Plume   No luck?

Kite   None to speak of, captain. I ask this rabble, as is my bounden duty: Doesn't your English blood boil in your veins when those American dirt farmers and fur trappers refuse to pay taxes to our good King George?

Plume   Well?

Kite   Their answers weren't nice. I've been here a full week and only recruited five.

Plume   Five. *(Pause)* What sort?

Kite   A poacher. The Strong Man of Kent—once famous as a boxer. A Scottish peddler. A disbarred lawyer and an unfrocked Welsh parson.

Plume   A lawyer? Have you taken leave of your senses?

Kite   Why?

Plume   Mr. Kite, I will have no one in my company who can write. A fellow that can write can draw up petitions and submit complaints—let him go, I say! Discharge him at once!

Kite   What about the parson? He plays the fiddle.

Plume   He can probably write too. Well, keep him for his fiddle. Go on.

Kite   Go on! That's the lot!

Plume   Damnation!

Kite   There's one more recruit, captain. One you didn't expect.

Plume   Who's that?

Kite   One you drummed in last time you were here. You remember Molly at the Raven?

Plume   She's not with child, I hope?

Kite   Not any more, sir, she's got it.

Plume   Kite, it's your duty to father the child.

Kite   I'd rather not, sir. You know I'm married already.

Plume   How many times?

Kite   I haven't got it by heart.—I've put them down here on the back of the muster roll. *(Pulls out the muster roll)* Miss Sheely Snickereyes, she sells fish in Dublin harbor; Peggy Guzzle, the brandy woman at the Horse Guards in Whitehall; Dolly Waggon, the carrier's daughter in Hull; Mademoiselle Van Bottomflat at the Sly Kiss. Then there's Jenny Oakum, the ship's carpenter's widow in Portsmouth, but I don't usually count her, because she was married at the same time to two marine lieutenants and a man of war's boatswain.

Plume   Five. Make it half a dozen, Kite. Is it a boy or a girl?

Kite   A boy.

Plume   Put the mother down on your list and the boy on mine. Enter him as Francis Kite, grenadier on unlimited furlough. I'll allow you a man's full pay for his keep. But now go comfort the poor wench in the straw.

Kite *(with a sigh)*   Yes, sir. Have you any further commands?

Plume   Not for the present.

Kite   There comes someone you must remember from last year. Mr. Worthy, the shoe manufacturer. *(Goes out)*

Plume   For a fact, it looks like Worthy—or maybe Worthy's ghost.

Worthy   Plume! Back again safe and sound?

Plume   Safe from the battlefields of the New World and sound, I hope, from London's ale houses.

Worthy   You're a happy man, Plume.

Plume   What's wrong? Has your father risen from the dead and climbed back into the business?

Worthy   No. No.

Plume   Married?

Worthy   No, no.

Plume   Well then, who is it? Do I know her?

Worthy   Melinda.

Plume   Melinda Moorhill? But she began to capitulate a year ago, and, if I recall correctly, offered to surrender on honorable terms. I believe I advised you to propose an elopement to suit her romantic nature.

Worthy   And so I did. She asked for time to consider. But then suddenly, and most unexpectedly, the fortress received fresh supplies and I was forced to turn the siege into a blockade.

Plume   Details, if you please.

Worthy   Her aunt in Flintshire died, leaving her twenty thousand pounds.

Plume   My dear Worthy, I see you haven't mastered the rules of warfare. Your blockade was foolish. You should have redoubled your attacks, taken the fortress by storm, or died on the ramparts.

Worthy   I did make one general assault, throwing in all my forces. But I was repulsed with such vigor that I had to abandon all hope of making her my mistress. For the past six months, I have been courting her with the utmost tenderness and devotion: my intention is marriage.

Plume   And while you worship her like a goddess, she treats you like a dog. Is that it?

Worthy   Exactly.

Plume   My dear Worthy, if you want to give her a better opinion of you, you must bring her to a lower opinion of herself.

Worthy   How?

Plume   Let me think.—My first thought would be to sleep with her maid. Or I might hire three or four wenches in the neighborhood to spread the rumor that I'd got them all with child. Or, we could run verses in the gazette about every pretty woman in Shrewsbury, and leave her out. Or we could arrange a ball, neglecting to invite two or three of the town's worst scarecrows, and overlooking Melinda as well.

Worthy   Those would be telling blows, I admit. But Shrewsbury is such a dull Tory stronghold—balls or verses in the gazette are out of the question.

Plume   And bastards as well? With all these recruiting officers in town? I thought it was our principle to leave as many recruits behind as we carry off.

Worthy   My dear captain, no one questions your determination to serve your country with all you've got. Molly at the Raven can testify to that.

(Kite has re-entered)

Plume   What now?

Kite   You sent me to comfort that poor woman in the straw—Mrs. Molly, my wife, Mr. Worthy.

Worthy   Splendid! I wish you joy, Mr. Kite!

Kite   Well you may, sir, seeing as how I came by wife and child in half an hour. Captain, sir, someone else had been comforting her before I got there.

Plume   In what respect?

Kite   Early this morning, a butler in green livery brought her a basket of baby clothes.

Plume   Who in the world could have done that?

Kite   It was Simpkins, Miss Victoria's butler.

Plume   Victoria?

Worthy   Victoria Balance? Impossible!

Plume   Who is Victoria Balance?

Worthy   Don't you remember Miss Pritchett's boarding school on Walnut Road?

Plume   Ah, yes! The little sixteen-year-old!

Worthy   Who almost fell out the window when you waved to her.

Plume   Yes, she was very funny. She sent me a note at the Raven but there was no time. But why should she make Molly presents? A grown woman might do that, not a schoolgirl. And only one woman in a thousand, one who's above jealousy, so to speak.

Worthy   At that age a year makes all the difference. She's almost grown-up.

Plume   What a noble gesture! I should say she deserves to be remembered. Worthy, who serves the best wine? That's the place to discuss our business.

Worthy   Yes, that's what I've come for. Where do you propose to buy boots for your grenadiers? From Worthy and Co., I trust?

Plume   First I must find grenadiers for your boots, Worthy. I shall pay my respects to Mr. Balance at once. Kite, have the drummer proclaim my arrival. Starting tomorrow, I order you to stir up such a commotion that Shrewsbury will stand on its head and salute with its feet.

(**Plume** *and* **Worthy** *depart to the* **Raven**. **Kite** *salutes*)

2

At the home of Mr. Balance.

Mr. Balance *is reading a school notebook. Drumming and shouts are heard from the street.*

Drummer   Latest news from the Raven! The hero of Bunker Hill has arrived from overseas! His Majesty's Captain William G. Plume presents his greetings to the glorious city of Shrewsbury.

*(***Mr. Balance** *hides the notebook behind his back as his daughter* **Victoria** *enters)*

Victoria   Father, a Sergeant Kite was here. He says Captain Plume has arrived from London and wishes to pay you his respects.

Balance *(sarcastically)*   To *me?*—Victoria—

Victoria   Sir—

Balance   What was in that basket you had Simpkins take to a certain Molly Fastspittle?

Victoria   A few cakes, sir.

Balance   Indeed! Baby clothes were in it.

Victoria   How horrid of Simpkins.

Balance   Of course you had no idea that Captain Plume was the father of Miss Fastspittle's illegitimate child? *(She is silent)* What are Captain Plume's illegitimate children to you, will you tell me that?

(A trumpet sounds)

Victoria   Not children, there's only one child.

Balance   What is it to you?

Victoria   Father, when lovers are separated by this war in the colonies . . .

Balance   Lovers!—Victoria, how old were you when your mother died?

Victoria   Four.

Balance   Have I ever denied you anything? Haven't I always treated you with indulgence and loving care?—Well. Your brother's death has made you sole heir to my estate. That means an income of twelve hundred pounds for you. Get that captain out of your head!

Victoria   Sir, Captain Plume has never been in my head . . . And he would never offend a man in your high position by . . .

Balance   . . . seducing you? He would, though. I know the thoughts and feelings of young officers because I remember my own thoughts and feelings when I was a young officer. I'd have given my right arm to seduce the daughter of a worthy old squire on whom I was billeted . . .

Victoria   I'm surprised at you, sir.

Balance   I should hope so.

Victoria   You may be justified in your opinion of English officers; but perhaps you have more confidence in English girls, father.

Balance   None whatever! Any English girl with any spirit—your case, I hope—will let herself be seduced by an English officer. I suspect the two of you have . . .

Victoria   Father, you're beastly. *(Icily, as* **Balance** *produces the notebook)* Sir, have you been reading my diary?

Balance   Not yet, but don't oblige me to. Tell me the truth.

Victoria   There's nothing to tell, father. *(As her father is about to open the notebook)* Next to nothing. Last Whit Sunday Captain Plume was here for dinner. He didn't even speak to me. Except to say: "Little girl, a blue ribbon would be even more becoming," as he was passing me the pudding. That same evening I went back to school and I haven't seen him since. *(***Balance** *again makes a motion to open the notebook)* Except once. He came strolling by with Mr. Worthy as I was standing at the window with some friends, and he waved to me. There's really nothing else. *(**Balance** threatens again to open the diary)* Only the note I sent him, wishing him a pleasant journey. It would have been rude not to.

Balance   Very well. *(Hands her the diary)*

Victoria   Only last Sunday you said the recruiting wouldn't get off the ground until Plume arrived. You praised him to the skies.

Balance   And I still think highly of him as a recruiter of soldiers, not of my daughter. In short: put Captain Plume out of your mind. Or any captain, for that matter. Sit down, Victoria. *(**Victoria** sits down)* Captains are paupers. You own forests. Captains are notorious for turning everything they can lay hands on into cash. They have an inborn aversion to anything green; they can't bear to leave trees standing. Old Hambleton down in Cheshire showed me a patch of land two miles square that had been stripped bare of trees. A captain of the Wimbleford Dragoons had acquired it by marriage. Two weeks after the wedding, a builder appeared on the scene; and every oak and elm, even the hundred-year-old beeches, were turned into sills, portals and sashes, or auctioned off to provide the noble captain with money for one of those fancy houseboats that have come into fashion on the Thames. *(He walks to the door and shouts at the top of his lungs)* Simpkins. The coach-and-four! *(To **Victoria**)* Victoria, I speak to you not as a father, but as a friend. I would rather advise than command. Your Uncle Harry has invited me to a pheasant shoot. Be sensible; go on ahead of me.

*(**Simpkins** comes in)*

Simpkins   The coach will be ready in ten minutes, sir, and Captain Plume is here to pay his respects.

Balance   Show him into the library. *(**Simpkins** goes out)* Pack your bag, Victoria.

Victoria   Are you speaking as a father or as a friend?

Balance   Whichever you prefer . . .

Victoria   Is that your last word?

Balance   Yes.

Victoria   Thank you. *(She goes out)*

Balance *(shouting)*   Victoria!—Simpkins!—Show the gentleman in.

(Plume *comes in)*

Balance *(with outstretched arms)*   Captain Plume!

Plume   Mr. Balance.

Balance   Welcome to Shrewsbury! The gates of our city are open wide to you.

Plume   Thank you, Mr. Balance.

Balance   You must again regard this house as yours.

Plume   You are very kind. And how is your charming daughter, Mr. Balance?

Balance   Let me wish you every success in your efforts to carry off . . .

Plume *(startled)*   Sir? . . .

Balance   . . . a splendid company of grenadiers.

Plume   Quite so, sir. Quite so.

Balance *(sits down)*   You must give me a detailed account of our military situation over there, captain.

Plume   Our situation over there is a situation . . . how shall I put it? . . . an unusual situation. From a military point of view. From a military standpoint.—May I inquire whether your daughter . . .

Balance   I have to admit that six months ago I trembled for England. Bunker Hill has restored my confidence.

Plume   I have something to show you. As a lawyer you may be interested in this rubbish they're handing out all over America.

(Simpkins *comes in with whiskey)*

Balance *(reading)*   "Draft of a Declaration of Independence."
The gall! "When in the course of human events it becomes
necessary for one people to dissolve the political bonds which have
connected them with another hitherto . . ." High treason!

Simpkins   Scoundrels.

Balance *(reading)*   "All men are created equal . . ." Where does the
Bible say that?—"Liberty and the pursuit of happiness . . ." So here
it is in black and white; these new ideas we've heard so much about.
It's base greed, that's what it is! *(**Simpkins** shakes his head sadly)*

Balance   Do these rebels—these Franklins, Jeffersons, and
Washingtons—really think the English crown will stand for such
ideas?

Simpkins   Pah!

Balance   On the pretext that it costs too much, they refuse to
import our tea. More than ten thousand cases of unsold tea are
rotting in Liverpool docks at this very moment. At the same time,
these lawyers and backwoods generals, reared in equality, want to
sell their cotton, which we need here, to God knows who, merely
because they get better prices. Imagine a colony presuming to trade
with the whole world. Whoever heard of such a thing!

Simpkins   Tsk, tsk.

Balance   Is something wrong, Simpkins?

Simpkins   I beg your pardon, sir.

Balance   Imagine, sir, if your tenants suddenly proclaimed their
independence and, instead of sending you their eggs, decided to
send them to town and let you perish for want of albumen?

Plume   I have no tenants, sir, but of course you're right.

Balance   What's more, these "new ideas" are contagious—they
spread like the plague. The whole civilized world must join forces
against these rebels. The Germans, I hear, have already come
forward, with thirty thousand Hessians.—Have our losses been
considerable?

Plume   Considerable. You could make my work here a good deal easier, Mr. Balance, by taking the example of most other counties. Instead of sending the shiftless riffraff to jail, send them off to war.

Balance   I don't hold with such practices. There's no need for them in Shrewsbury. Our people know what they owe our king.

Simpkins   Thank God!

(**Balance** *stamps his foot.* **Simpkins** *goes out*)

Plume   I hope you're right, sir. So far I must admit . . .

Balance   Your presence will change all that, Plume. A bit of martial music in the square, a captured flag or two, a patriotic speech, not too high-flown for our good country folk, and, of course, you can always count on the ardent support of our fair sex. Shrewsbury will give you everything you need, captain, everything!

(**Victoria**, *in traveling attire, comes in, followed by a servant carrying her bags. She nods briefly and goes out*)

Plume   Your daughter, Mr. Balance?

Balance   Yes. On her way to visit her uncle in the country, Captain Plume.

Plume   Oh.

3

At Melinda Moorhill's house.

Melinda *sings, accompanying herself on the harp.*

Melinda

Chloe in the forest glade.
Achilles from behind a tree
Stepped, "Oh could you, pretty maid
Favor me?"
 Fearfully the maiden gazed
 Hid her features in the meadow grass.
 Said the hero, mournful and amazed
 "Don't you care then for my gold cuirass?"

As Achilles turned to go
Birds fell silent in the brake.
Listening to the brook's bright flow
Chloe spake.
 Said the maid: "It's easy to resist
 Lion, stag, and strutting peacock, too.
 Golden armor leaves me unimpressed
 But I have noticed that your eyes are blue."

(**Victoria** *rushes in followed by her servant with her bags. The servant puts the bags down and leaves)*

Victoria Can I stay with you, Melinda? For a week. Father wanted me to go to Uncle Harry's in the country. But I can't leave Shrewsbury at the moment.

Melinda Of course. You know you are always welcome here *(They embrace)*

Victoria I'm so unhappy!

Melinda I'm so miserable!

(They both burst into tears)

Victoria   Dearest Melinda!

Melinda   Dearest Victoria! *(Calling)* Lucy, bring the tea! *(To Victoria)* Is it your captain? I hear he's back.

Victoria   This time I shall make sure he doesn't go off again. How are things between you and Worthy?

Melinda   Oh, Worthy! I must have made some mistake. Now he wants to marry me.

Victoria   Well?

Melinda   I don't know.

Victoria   But you love him.

Melinda   Yes, but . . .

Victoria   And he loves you. To be sure, he's not a hero . . .

Melinda   What do you mean? Everyone can't go dashing around the world like your Captain Plume. What have you got against Worthy?

Victoria   Against Worthy? Nothing. On the contrary, I fail to see why you treat the poor man so cruelly. He's a gentleman of rank and fortune. Besides, he is friends with my Plume, and if you're not nicer to him . . .

Melinda   Heavens, Victoria! Must we talk about Worthy and me? I only said that he was getting rather stodgy.

Victoria   Small wonder when you've trained him like a dog.

Melinda   Worthy is not a dog, Victoria. And now let me tell you what I think of your Captain Plume! He's a depraved, lazy, importunate fop!

Victoria   My dear Melinda, your opinion only proves how well suited you are to your stodgy Worthy now that you've inherited twenty thousand pounds. You treated him like a man as long as you were trying to extract five hundred pounds a year from him. Without success, of course.

Melinda   What do you mean by that?

Victoria   My meaning is perfectly clear.

(Pause)

Melinda   Without success! I don't envy you your success. Such success is easily come by.

Victoria   You think so?

Melinda   Besides, you don't stand a chance.

Victoria   Really?

Melinda   You poor deluded goose! Do you think a dashing young officer, who in the past six months has had half the world at his feet and has a girl in every town, is going to settle down in a God-forsaken hole like Shrewsbury for the sake of the insignificant daughter of a justice of the peace?

Victoria   What do I care how many girls he's got waiting for him! I wouldn't want a man with nothing on his mind but me!

Melinda   Victoria, have you lost all pride, throwing yourself at the first rowdy rake of an officer . . . ?

Victoria   There you go again! Unfortunately, this is your house, Melinda . . .

Melinda   I wouldn't have taken it amiss if you had stayed in yours, Victoria . . .

Victoria   Don't worry, Melinda, I'll take your gentle hint.

Melinda   The sooner the better.

Victoria   I am always quick to follow my inclinations. Your humble servant, madam. *(Flounces out)*

(Her servant picks up her bags and follows. **Lucy** *brings in the tea)*

Melinda   Impudent hussy.

4

Market place.

*The recruiting officers have arranged a band concert. A platform
has been set up in front of* **Mr. Balance's** *house. The recruiting
booth is decorated with captured flags. A broad-shouldered man
is sitting at a table outside the* **Raven.** *The band strikes up a
military march.* **Kite** *steps out of the inn and stops in front of
the broad-shouldered man, eyeing him admiringly.* **Pearmain**
and **Appletree** *are looking at the pictures on the wall of the
booth.*

Kite *(to the broad-shouldered man)* Oh! Allow me to
congratulate you on your chest development.—Mike!—Money's
no object to our good King George. *(***Mike** *the potboy has come out
of the inn)* Mike! Ale for the gentleman. *(He catches sight of the
farm boys and walks toward the recruiting booth)* Gentlemen, may
I invite you to drink a pint of ale with me this evening?

Appletree When it comes to that, we'll take on the best of them.

*(***Plume**, **Balance**, **Melinda**, *and* **Worthy** *come out of* **Mr.
Balance's** *house. They step up to the platform to a flourish of
trumpets)*

Kite Shrewsbury salutes the hero of Bunker Hill!

*(***Plume** *waves to the crowd in all directions)*

Kite Three cheers for Captain Plume! Hip, hip, hurrah!

(The farm boys join in)

Kite Let's have a cheer for the king and the honor of
Micklesbury! *(He goes into the inn with the laughing farm boys)*

(The guests of honor take their places on the platform. **Simpkins**
serves them whiskey)

Balance   Ladies and gentlemen! You have just seen one of the men who are making it possible for England to pursue her policy of strength throughout the world.

Worthy   A herculean task! *(He listens to the music)*

Balance *(points to the square)*   The ice is beginning to melt; Shrewsbury is yielding to the martial strains of Höchstedt and Blafontaine. The blare of brass is injecting a little heroism into the anemic souls of our citizens. Plume! I insist on an account of the battle of Bunker Hill.

Plume   This is rather embarrassing, Mr. Balance. One battle is very much like another.

Simpkins   Ahem!

Balance   Did you say something, Simpkins?

Simpkins   Begging your pardon, sir, but we know all about Bunker Hill here in Shrewsbury, sir. Indeed we do, captain.

Balance   What do you know?

Simpkins   The river is called the Hudson, Mr. Balance. Upstream there's a dam and a mill pond, sir; downstream, barley fields. The rebels had managed to cross the Hudson but under cover of night, Captain Plume—begging your pardon, sir—maneuvered eighty grenadiers and a field-piece through their lines. A single well-aimed shot—am I right, captain?—sweeps the dam away and the water starts flooding their barley fields. To be sure, our brave soldiers were decimated by murderous musket volleys, but then it happened as Captain Plume had anticipated. Those rebels are no soldiers, they're common dirt-farmers who've forced themselves into uniform. At the sight of a good-sized flood, such people soon revert to being dirt-farmers, he he he! That night a whole corps of dirt-farmers ran off to repair the dam and save the drowning livestock on their flooded farms. At eight o'clock in the morning we attacked. The outcome is common knowledge. Pardon, sir. Pardon, captain.

Balance   Thank you, Simpkins.

*(Simpkins *goes out)**

Balance *(to* **Plume***)*   What would you say was our main base of operations at present?

Plume   Boston.

Balance   Boston? You'll have to explain that.

Plume *(using whiskey glasses to illustrate)*   Boston, Howe, Washington. *(He makes a sign to* **Worthy** *and during the following explains the battle to* **Balance***)*

Worthy *(to* **Melinda***)*   Madam, I am obliged to express my astonishment at your coldness to my friend Plume. You know how highly I regard him.

Melinda   Is that a reprimand? Are you finding fault with my manners?

Worthy *(meekly)*   Not at all. I am merely making an observation.

Melinda   Whatever has been the matter with you these last few days? The day before yesterday, no sign of you. Where were you? Yesterday you sent your servant for the novels you had lent me, which I hadn't even read! Today . . .

Worthy   Today?

Melinda   You seem to have fallen under some bad influence. Have you come here for the sole purpose of insulting me?

Worthy   I had no intention of either insulting you or seeing you. I came, I must admit, in the hope of meeting someone else.

Melinda   Oh!

(**Brazen** *comes in)*

Balance   Who is that overdressed fellow with the sash? Never saw him before! What regiment is that anyway?

Worthy   I'll wager he knows you, though. He knows everybody and his brother. It's Captain Brazen. He's a Caesar with the ladies;

veni, vidi, vici, and there you have it. No sooner has he talked to
the maid than he's slept with the mistress.

Brazen *(approaching with outstretched arms)*   Mr. Worthy,
your humble servant, and so forth. Listen, my dear fellow . . . *(He
whispers in* **Worthy's** *ear)*

Worthy   Don't whisper. When company's present . . .

Brazen   Mort de ma vie! I beg the lady's pardon. Do introduce
me, my dear fellow.

Worthy   Captain Brazen—Miss Moorhill.

Brazen   Moorhill! *(Strikes himself on the forehead)* The Sussex
Moorhills or the Welsh Moorhills? Lovely lady, your servant, and
so forth. And who might that be?

Worthy   Ask him.

Brazen   So I will. Your name, sir.

Balance   Most laconic, sir.

Brazen   Laconic! A very fine name, indeed. I've known several
Laconics abroad, splendid chaps. Poor Jack Laconic. Killed in the
battle of Peshawar. On the Ganges. Well I remember that fateful
day, he was wearing a blue ribbon on his cap and all we found in
his pocket afterwards was a piece of dried ox tongue. Malaventura!
I have good reason to remember: on that very day, twenty-two
horses were killed under me.

Balance   You must have ridden mighty hard, sir.

Brazen   Torn to pieces by cannon balls, they were, all but six that
were gored to death on the enemy's chevaux-de-frise.

Balance   Do you know Plume? Captain Plume?

Brazen   Plume? No. Is he related to Dick Plume, who was
with the East India Company? He married the daughter of
old Tonguepad, chairman of the Lord Raleigh shipyards. An
exceptionally pretty girl, apart from a slight squint in her left eye.
She died giving birth to her first child. The child survived. A little

girl, it was. But whether she was called Margaret or Margery, upon my honor, my dear fellow, I can't remember.

Melinda   Mr. Worthy, would you see me home? It's rather noisy here.

Worthy   Not at all. The band plays these marches beautifully, Mr. Balance.

Melinda   I asked you to see me home, Mr. Worthy.

Worthy   I should be delighted to, madam, if, as I mentioned before, I hadn't arranged to meet someone here.

Melinda   I do hope there's one gentleman here who will be good enough to see me home.

Brazen (*putting his arm around her waist*)   Dear child, here is my hand, my life-blood, and so forth. Your servant, Worthy. Ditto, Laconic.

*(**Brazen** and **Melinda** leave)*

Kite (*from the taproom*)   Ladies and gentlemen: long live our good King George! Hip, hip, hurrah!

Balance (*laughing*)   Veni, vidi, vici!—What's come over you, Worthy? (*Goes into the house*)

Worthy   Plume!

*(**Kite** comes out of the taproom. The broad-shouldered man lifts his glass; it is empty)*

Kite   Mike! Another pint for the gentleman. (*He goes out*)

Worthy   Plume! She's thrown herself into the arms of another man!

Plume   She's all yours, man. (*Follows **Balance** into the house. **Worthy** in consternation follows them*)

Kite (*back in the taproom*)   Long live our good King George! Hip, hip, hurrah!

(The light changes. More shouts of "hip, hip, hurrah" are heard from the darkened taproom. The stage is dark and empty. **Pearmain** *and* **Appletree***, slightly tipsy, and* **Kite** *emerge from the* **Raven***. The broad-shouldered man is still sitting outside the taproom.)*

Kite   Hey, boys. That's the soldier's life! Plenty of grub and plenty of ale. We live, as the saying goes—we live—how can I describe it? . . . we live like lords. *(To the broad-shouldered man)* May I ask, sir, how you enjoyed the king's ale, sir?

Broad-Shouldered Man   Couldn't be better, sir.

Kite   You'd enjoy the king's service even more, sir.

Broad-Shouldered Man *(drains his glass)*   Don't make me laugh, sir. I've been sitting here all day at your expense. *(Gets up to leave)*

Kite   One moment, sir. You know the Severn, but do you know the Mississippi? *(The man clumps off. We see that he has a wooden leg)* What's this! *(Calling after him)* Where's your leg?

Broad-Shouldered Man   Bunker Hill.

Appletree   He's lost a leg.

Kite   For the king, though. Hats off, boys!—All right; he's lost a leg. But so has some damned rebel over there.

Broad-Shouldered Man   For himself, though. *(Goes out)*

Pearmain   For himself, though. *(Laughs)*

Kite *(stares after the broad-shouldered man)*   This is a case for the constabulary.—Now listen to me!—The swine!—Have you ever seen a picture of the king?

Both   No.

Kite   I'm surprised at you. I happen to have two of them with me, set in gold; the spitting image of His Majesty, God bless him. Here, both of them set in pure gold. *(He takes two gold coins from his pocket and holds them up)*

Appletree *(looks at the coin)*   A miracle of nature! *(He looks at it earnestly)*

Pearmain   Pretty!

Kite   I'll make you a present of them, one each. *(Hands them the coins)* Think nothing of it. One good turn deserves another. *(Laughing, they pocket the coins.* **Plume** *and* **Worthy** *come out of the judge's house)*

Plume   Chin up, Worthy!

*(***Worthy** *takes his leave and goes out)*

Kite   Atten-shun! Off with your hats! Damn your souls to hell! Off with your hats! It's the captain, your captain!

Appletree *(laughing)*   We've seen the captain before. I'll keep my cap on.

Pearmain   There ain't a captain in all England I'd take my hat off to, sir. My father owns five acres of land.

Plume   Who are these jolly lads, sergeant?

Kite   A couple of farm lads from Micklesbury. I've just enlisted 'em as volunteers in your command, captain.

Pearmain   Tummas? Art tha' enlisted?

Appletree   Not I, damn me. Art tha', Costar?

Pearmain   By Jesus, no! Not I! *(They both laugh)*

Kite   What! Not enlisted!—Ha ha ha! That's a good one, by God, very good.

Pearmain   Come on, Tummas, let's go home.

Appletree   Aye, come on. *(They start to leave)*

Kite   Gentlemen, watch your manners in the presence of your captain!—Dear Tummas!—Honest Costar!

Appletree   No, no; we must be going.

Kite   I command you to stay! You're in the army now. I'm putting you both on sentry duty here for the next two hours. And the first one who dares to leave his post before he's relieved gets this sword in his guts! There.

Plume   What's the trouble, sergeant? Aren't you being a little harsh on these two gentlemen?

Kite   Too soft, sir, much too soft. These fellows are refusing to obey orders, sir; one of 'em ought to be shot as an example to the other.

Pearmain   Shot, Tummas?

Plume   Gentlemen, what's this all about?

Pearmain   We don't know. The sergeant has talked himself into a proper rage, sir. But . . .

Kite   They refuse to obey orders and they deny that they're soldiers.

Appletree   No, no, sergeant, we don't deny it outright; we wouldn't dare, for fear of being shot. But as humbly and respectfully as you please, we'd like to go home now.

Plume   That's easily settled. Has either of you received any of the king's money?

Pearmain   No, sir.

Kite   Turn out your pockets.

Pearmain   Nothing there, sir; only the king's picture. *(Produces the coin)*

Kite   You see? A gold piece, and what a gold piece; three and twenty shillings and sixpence. The other one's got the king's money in his left trouser pocket.

Plume   Gentlemen, you are enlisted.

*(**Kite** goes to the recruiting booth and gets the muster roll)*

Appletree   We're enlisted, Costar!

Pearmain   Damnation, that we ain't, Tummas! I want to be brought before the justice of the peace. It was a present, captain!

Plume   A present! *(Aside to* **Kite***)* You and your damned tricks! *(Pretending to hit him)* I won't stand for it. You scoundrel, you whoreson, I'll teach you to trick an honest man! Cutthroat! Villain!

Pearmain   There's a captain for you!

Plume *(turning to them)*   What a shabby way to treat two lads like you.—I come to you as an officer to enlist soldiers, not as a kidnapper to carry off slaves.

Appletree   Hear that, Costar? Ain't that nice?

Plume   It's true, gentlemen, I could take advantage of you; the king's money was in your pocket and my sergeant is ready to swear you've enlisted. But I don't believe in using force. Gentlemen, you are free to go.

Pearmain   Thankee, captain. You're a real gentleman.

(They turn to leave)

Plume   Wait, boys, just one more thing. You're first-rate chaps, both of you, and—believe it or not—the army is the one place to make real men of you. The world is a lottery; every man has his ticket and you've got yours. Look at me: a little while ago I carried a musket; today, I'm commanding a company.

Pearmain   I'd follow him to the ends of the earth!

Appletree   Better not, Costar.

Pearmain   Captain, I'd follow you to the ends of the earth!

Appletree   Costar, don't be daft!

Plume   Here, my young hero, here are two real English guineas. That's only a taste of what I'll do for you later on.

Pearmain   Gimme!

Appletree   Don't take it, don't take it, Costar. *(He begins to cry and tries to pull* **Pearmain** *back by the arm)*

Pearmain   I will, I will!—Damn ye, don't hold me back when something tells me I'll be a captain yet.—I'll take *your* money, sir.

Plume   There. And now you and I will go marching across the world, and wherever we set foot, we shall be the masters.

Pearmain   To the end of the world!

Plume *(aside)*   Bring your friend with you, if you can.

Pearmain   Yes, sir. Tummas, must we part?

*(**Appletree** undergoes an inner struggle)*

Appletree   No, Costar! I can't leave 'ee—I'd rather come along, captain.

Plume   Here, my boy. *(Gives **Appletree** the money)* There. Now: your name?

Appletree   Thomas Appletree.

Plume   And yours?

Pearmain   Costar Pearmain.

Plume   Look after them, Kite. *(Goes into the **Raven**)*

Kite *(beckons them to come over)*   A fine pair you turned out to be. I bet you've tried to talk the captain into giving me the boot and making one of you sergeant. Which one of you wants my sergeant's pike?

Both   Me.

Kite   Here.—In your guts!—Get a move on, you bastards!

(Drives them off)

5

Market place.

Plume *and* **Kite** *are sitting in the recruiting booth. They are bored.* **Workless**, *an unemployed laborer, passes by.*

Kite   Sir, you know the Severn, but do you know the Mississippi?

Workless   Nope. *(Goes out)*

Kite   We're getting no place fast!

Rose's Voice   Pullets! Young and tender! Fresh Picklewood pullets! Get your pullets!

Plume   Look what's coming!

Kite   Look at the strapping farm boy with her.

Plume   That concert cleaned out the company's funds and only bagged us two recruits. Both yokels. Perhaps we ought to pay more attention to the rural population.

Kite   We'll give another concert next Sunday.

Plume   What will we use for money?

*(***Rose*** and her brother,* **Bullock***, approach.* **Rose** *is carrying a basket of pullets)*

Plume   Here, chick, chick! Here, pretty child!

Rose   Buy a chicken, sir?

Kite   Show the captain all you have!

Plume   You tend to your own knitting, Mr. Kite.

*(***Rose*** laughs)*

Kite *(leads* **Bullock** *to the recruiting booth)*   Sir, you know the Severn, but do you know the Mississippi?

Plume   Come, child; I'll take all you have.

Rose   All I have is at your service, sir. *(She laughs)*

Plume   Let me see. Young and tender, you say. *(Chucks her under the chin)* What is your name, pretty creature?

Rose   Rose, sir. My father's a tenant farmer. We're always here on market day. I sell chickens, eggs, and butter; my brother Bullock sells the corn.

Plume   May I touch, my pretty?

Rose   Touching is buying, sir.

Bullock   Hurry up, Rose!

Rose   Twelve shillings, sir, and it's all yours.

Plume   Here's a pound, my dear.

Rose   I can't make change, sir.

Plume   Oh, but you can. My lodgings are two steps from here. You can make change there, my pretty. Tell me, have you many admirers in Picklewood?

Rose   Yes, six admirers, and one intended.

Plume   Wouldn't any of them want to join the army?

Rose   No.

Plume   We'll have to talk that over too. Come along.

*(**Plume** and **Rose** disappear into the **Raven**. **Bullock** is looking at the pictures on the recruiting booth)*

Bullock   Would you be needing a drum major, for instance?

Kite   No, only grenadiers.

*(**Bullock** looks at the display again)*

Bullock   What's that?

Kite   It's the Sultan of Okk's harem.

Bullock   Okk? Is that in America?

Kite   Where else?

Bullock   And you pay money for it?

Kite   Of course.

Bullock   I'd get seasick.

Kite   Where are you from?

Bullock   Picklewood.

Kite   Picklewooders don't get seasick.

Bullock *(looking again at the display)*   There isn't even a shop in all Picklewood. I'm yer man, sergeant.

Kite   And here's your money. Your name?

Bullock   Bullock.

Kite   Bullock, you're in the army now.

Bullock   Rose! Where did Rose get to? Rose! Rose!

Kite   Stop that noise. She's probably gone off with your captain.

Bullock   To hell with you and your harem! *(Runs off)*

Kite   Wait till you see those harems—you're in for a big surprise.

*(**Victoria** enters, disguised as a young squire)*

Victoria   I must see Captain Plume at once.

Kite   Hmmm.

Victoria   Where is he?

*(**Kite** doesn't answer. **Victoria** hands him some money)*

Kite   He's at the Raven. But you can't see him now. He'll be back.

Victoria   Is Captain Plume busy?

Kite   I should say so. He's working himself to a frazzle.

Victoria   May I ask what he's busy with?

Kite   The rural population, sir. The rural population. Right now we've got our eye on the rural population.

Victoria   Quite so. The rural population is a breed apart. How long do you think your captain will be busy?

Kite   A good fifteen minutes.

Victoria   Then I'll wait.

(**Brazen** *approaches the booth)*

Brazen   Sergeant, where's your captain? I've got to shake his hand. What's his name again?

Kite *(standing at attention)*   Captain Plume, Captain.

Brazen *(catching sight of* **Victoria***)*   Stop! Let me look at you. *(***Victoria** *shrinks back)* Would you believe it! Mort de ma vie! But that's . . . Like two bullets from the same barrel! The spit and image of Charles! Charles! *(He embraces* **Victoria** *and whirls her around)*

Victoria   Sir, what's the meaning of this?

Brazen   The very image of Charles! Even the voice! Except for a slight modulation to minor, E–G sharp–A, don't you know.

Victoria   My name's Wilful, sir, Victor Wilful.

Brazen   The Kentish Wilfuls or the Devonshire Wilfuls?

Victoria   Both, sir, both. I am related to all the Wilfuls in Europe. At present I am head of the whole Wilful family.

Brazen   Splendid. *(To* **Kite***)* Where's Frank?

Kite   Captain Plume is engaged in business . . .

Brazen   I see. Business and so forth . . . *(Looks at his watch)* A scoundrel, that's what I am! See you later, gentlemen. Wilful, your servant and so forth. *(Goes out)*

Victoria *(mopping her forehead; subdued)*   My name *is* Wilful.

Kite   Of course, sir.

(Enter **Lady Prude** *with* **Bullock***)*

Prude   Where is your captain, sergeant? This young man, the son of my tenant, tells my Captain Plume has abducted his sister. What do you know about this?

Kite   Nothing, madam.

Bullock   But he was there. He showed me the pi . . . *(***Lady Prude** *looks at him sternly)* . . . pictures. And meantime the captain disappeared with the slut!

Kite   Atten-shun! Why don't you take better care of your sister?

Prude   Are you Turks? Where is the girl?

Bullock   He told me himself that she went off with the captain.

Kite   Shut up!

Prude   Where *is* the captain? By your mother's immortal soul, where is he?

Kite   Madam, by that same immortal soul, I swear I don't know.

Prude   Turks!

Victoria *(to* **Kite***)*   Busy! With the rural population! *(Crosses the square and goes into the* **Raven***)*

Prude   Who was that young man? *(To* **Bullock***)* Fetch the justice! *(* **Bullock** *leaves)*

Kite   You're wasting your time, madam.

Prude *(looks at the pictures)*   Disgusting! You are an evil man.

Kite   Why?

Prude   Because you lie like Caiaphas. You may think you're doing it for your captain, but it's lying all the same. Where's the girl?

Kite *(reproachfully)*   Madam!

(Loud voices are heard from the inn)

Landlady's Voice   You know very well you're not allowed into the officers' quarters.

Rose's Voice   I was only selling my chickens.

Landlady's Voice   Chickens indeed! I know that kind of chickens. This isn't a bawdyhouse. Get out!

(**Rose** *runs out of the inn. She is met by* **Lady Prude***)*

Prude   Rose!

Rose   Oh, Lady Prude! I've sold the lot. At two shillings a piece! Begging Your Grace's pardon, what would this lace be worth a yard? *(Shows her a piece of genuine lace)*

Prude   Mercy me! Creole lace! Where did you get it, child?

Rose   I came by it honestly, my lady

Prude   I doubt it very much. What did you give in return? Look me in the eye!

Rose   Why? I'm giving my brother for a soldier. And Cartwheel, my intended, as well. And two or three of my admirers from the village. That's what the captain wanted. Would you believe it, my lady; he took me into his own quarters, and he made me a garter out of a band off his sleeve, and put it on with his own hands. He was dreadfully sorry, he told me so, when the landlady knocked at the door and said she had to speak to him. But we're going to see each other again.

Prude   Turks!

(**Balance** *enters with* **Bullock***)*

Balance   Lady Prude . . .

Prude   Mr. Balance, you are the justice of the peace in this town, but what has become of the peace in this town?

Balance   Are you, perchance, referring to the officer who is honoring Shrewsbury with his presence?

Prude   He's a scoundrel—that's what he is!

Balance *(grandly)*   Lady Prude, you cannot stop England's daughters from giving England's fighting men their proper due.

Prude *(dryly)*   Perhaps you ought to think of your own daughter when you say that, Mr Balance.

Balance *(dryly)*   I have thought of her, Lady Prude.

6

Billiard room at the Raven.

Victoria *is waiting for* **Plume**. *After a short while* **Plume** *appears.*

Victoria   I hope I haven't disturbed you in a delicate situation, captain. The landlady seemed upset when she learned that you were not alone in your room. I'm so sorry.

Plume   What brings you here, Mr . . . .

Victoria   Wilful.—I have a letter for you. *(Hands him a letter.* **Plume** *sits down)* You may be wondering how I come to have this letter. Well, the other day, as I was returning from a morning canter extra muros, a carriage suddenly came thundering in my direction. My horse shied. The coachman tried to rein in his horses, but they reared. A cry of fright from inside the carriage, the sound of a wheel splintering against the curbstone. I leapt from my horse to offer my assistance. You will appreciate my relief at finding that the beautiful young person gazing wanly at me from the cushions was unharmed. While the driver changed the wheel I kept the fair stranger company. I learned that she was the daughter of Balance, the justice of the peace, who, for some whim, had sent her off to the country. She soon confided that this had separated her from someone she loved dearly, of whom she then spoke at some length. Sitting on the very curbstone that had brought about this happy encounter, she hastily penned a note. "For Captain Plume," she said simply, got back into the carriage, and drove off.

(**Plume**, *who has been sipping his whiskey all through* **Victoria's** *account, opens the letter and reads it. He bursts into loud laughter)*

Victoria   Why are you laughing?

Plume *(laughing)*   Read it yourself, young man.

Victoria *(reads)*   "A young friend will reveal the true reason for my departure. With the fervent hope that you will remain in

Shrewsbury forever this time. Yours, Victoria Balance." Captain, you're a lucky man!

Plume   Priceless! She expects me to resign my commission for her!

Victoria *(with a forced laugh)*   How perfectly naive!

Plume   I could die laughing.—How about a game?

(They go over to the billiard table)

Victoria   On the other hand, captain, the young lady's sentiments seem to be of a serious nature. Of course your profession stands in the way of serious commitments and I can see you would never want to give up your noble calling. Though there are men who would, if the reasons were important enough.

Plume   Quite so.

Victoria   And there are such reasons, captain. There are men who, for one reason or another, would not take up this profession in the first place. I suppose you would advise them to put a bullet through their heads.

Plume   Not at all.

Victoria   Why not?

Plume   After all, there *are* other professions.

Victoria   Indeed? For instance?

Plume   Well, all sorts.

Victoria   Yes, of course. But which would you choose? Justice of the peace?

Plume   Justice of the peace? Never!

Victoria   Trade perhaps?

Plume   No, not trade.

Victoria *(whose eyes are filling with tears)*   Artist?

Plume   You can't be serious, Mr. Wilful!

Victoria   In short—no other profession.

Plume   It must be admitted that civilian professions have certain disadvantages.

Victoria   And the military profession has none?

Plume   No, I wouldn't say that.

Victoria   What disadvantages? (**Plume** *seeks vainly for an answer)* Do you mean that an officer can't marry?

Plume   Not if he's a man of principle. Of course there are compensations.

Victoria   I see.

Plume   Incidentally, when will you be seeing Miss Balance?

Victoria   You mean that an affair with Miss Balance is *your* compensation for not being able to marry?

Plume   Why not?

Victoria   Indeed. Why not? (**Victoria** *viciously jabs the cue into the table, tearing the cloth)*

Plume   Anything wrong, Mr. Wilful?

(**Mike** *the potboy comes in)*

Mike   Bull's-eye. *(He examines the damaged table)*

Victoria   Surely you can mend that.

Mike   Mend it! The table's ruined. That will be two pounds.

Plume   Charge it!

Mike   How are you going to pay for it when you still owe for last Sunday's ale?

Plume   Don't make a fuss, Mike! Put it on the slate!

Mike   And the room where you receive your ladies? You haven't paid for that either! Put it on the slate! No more of that!

Victoria   Idiot! Is that a way to talk to one of England's heroes? Here are five pounds for last Sunday's ale and for the room. Where do you expect the captain to receive his ladies? Now get out!

Mike   A brand new billiard table. *(Goes out)*

Plume   Young man, I hope you haven't over-extended yourself.

Victoria   A mere trifle. By the way, Miss Balance hopes her little attention to a certain Molly at the Raven didn't strike you as presumptuous.

Plume   By no means. I admire her generosity; a rare display of worldly wisdom in one so young.

Victoria   In any event mother and child are well provided for.

Plume   I hope she didn't give her any money?

Victoria   I wouldn't know.

Plume *(calling out)*   Kite! *(To* **Victoria***)* The mother, my dear Wilful, happens to be my sergeant's wife. The poor creature spread the tale that I was the father in the hope that my friends would come to her assistance. She succeeded. *(* **Kite** *comes in)* Mr. Kite, I hope there wasn't any cash in the basket that was sent to Molly—I mean Mrs. Kite?

Kite   Yes, captain, there was. I only heard about it this morning. Those greedy people . . .

Plume   How much?

Kite   Twenty pounds. Old Mrs. Fastspittle goes right out and buys a hat shop. What can I do with a hat shop, tell me that?

Victoria   You'd rather she'd bought a helmet shop, I suppose.

Plume   Kite, you are to return the money to Miss Balance at once.

Kite   Me? You want me to pay out money on top of everything else?

Plume   All right, you haven't got it. Very well, I shall pay your debts. I admire Miss Balance's solicitude, but money, no—that I can't permit. Wilful, lend me thirty pounds.

Victoria   I'll be glad to. *(Takes out her wallet and hands him thirty pounds)*

Plume   I'll give you my note payable in three days. We'll have plenty of cash after the inspection.

Victoria   That's not necessary.

Plume   Ah, but it is. Excuse me now. *(Goes out)*

Victoria   Three days? *(To* **Kite***)* Will you be leaving in three days?

Kite   Three days and we're off to the New World. How would a little trip to America strike you? You know the Severn, but do you know the Mississippi? *(He produces some pictures)* Boston— Philadelphia—Baltimore.

Victoria   I don't believe, Mr. Kite, that the Bunker Hill area is quite the thing for tourists.

Kite   For soldiers, though!

Victoria   You think I ought to join the army?

Kite   You've got money to burn. Why not buy an ensign's commission?

Victoria   Where?

Kite   In our company.

Victoria   How much would it be?

Kite   About twenty pounds, I'd say.

Victoria   I could afford that, but . . .

Kite   Twenty pounds and a few more for extras—and you can come along with us!

Victoria   I must admit, one little chat with your captain has convinced me that a military career offers unparalleled pleasures, deeper satisfactions than love.

Kite   Than what?

Victoria   Than love.

Kite   I should think so. Uniform, boots, sword belt, cocked
hat,—you'll get the lowest prices if you buy them through me.
You're sure to get nicked if you don't. Say twenty-five pounds—
no, twenty-four—no, better make it twenty-five. *(Since* **Victoria** *,
who has been listening in amusement, seems to hesitate)* Cold feet?
Balderdash. People die in bed, too, you know. True, Bunker Hill
cost us eleven thousand men, but . . .

Mike *(busy tearing the torn cloth off the billiard table)*   Eleven
thousand? Did you say eleven thousand, sergeant?

Kite   What are you hanging around for? What have you heard?

Mike   Nothing, sergeant, by St. Patrick.

Kite   You were listening when I was talking about Bunker Hill,
weren't you? What exactly was said?

Mike   Something about eleven thousand men—that's all.

Kite   And what did I say about them?

Mike *(after a pause)*   That they were lost *(as* **Kite** *threatens him)*
and found again.

Kite   Get out! Scoundrel! *(* **Mike** *goes out in a panic)* In round
numbers, ensign, twenty-five pounds, everything included. But for
that you'll find out what a man is.

Victoria   Of course, I'd be glad of that.

Kite   Take me, for instance: born in the gutter, grew up with the
dregs to the age of ten. That's where I learned that the main thing
in life is filling your belly. It's not the whole story, mind you, but
it's the first step. My mother, Cleopatra, sold me for three gold
florins to a gentleman who'd taken a fancy to my beauty. That's
where I learned that a man's got to obey his master, body and
soul. I was sacked because I took a liking to the master's fine
linen and my lady's liqueurs. Then I worked as a bailiff. That's
where I learned how to bully and hold out my palm. It was only
after learning all that that I was found fit for military service. I
had nothing more to learn but boozing and whoring. And marrying,
of course.

Victoria   What do you mean by that?

Kite   Marrying in soldier fashion without benefit of parson or license. Our sword is our honor. We lay it on the ground. First the young hero jumps over it, then the girl. The buck leaps and the whore jumps. A roll of drums and off to bed. That's how we get married.

Victoria   What about the captain—can he do all that?

Kite   He hasn't an equal.

Victoria   I must own that I felt a certain liking for your captain even before I heard that. Perhaps he could do with a guardian angel while performing his strenuous duties in the New World. Sergeant Kite, I'm at your service *(They shake hands)* (**Plume** *comes in)*

Plume   My note, Wilful.

Kite   Ensign Wilful, sir. (**Plume** *looks at her with astonishment. She makes a besitant gesture)* It's all settled, captain. Mr. Wilful wants to see the New World.

Victoria   What do you say, Captain Plume? Would you be willing to take me with you to the New World?

Plume   I'm afraid I must decline to have a gentleman in my company.

Victoria   Oh.

Kite   Ensign Wilful will be glad to contribute five pounds to the next recruiting concert, captain.

Plume   Learned to fence?

Victoria   Yes, sir.

Plume   Whist?

Victoria   A little.

Plume   I suppose half a bottle of port puts you under the table.

Victoria   No, sir.

Plume   Make it ten pounds—If there wasn't a certain je-ne-sais-quoi about you that appeals to me . . . Your treatment will depend on your conduct. Here's your note, Wilful, and kindly pass this letter on to your pretty friend. *(Hands her a letter)*

Kite   That makes it forty pounds.

Victoria   That's enough now, Mr. Kite. Thirty-five, and get out.

Plume   Let's get some breakfast, ensign.

Victoria *(hesitates)*   Captain Plume, I have a confession to make. I hope it won't throw you into a rage. That country lass has made quite an impression on me. Are you very much involved?

Plume   Ah, ensign. In such matters we can easily come to terms. I'll exchange a woman for an able-bodied man any time. Suppose we discuss it over breakfast. *(Both go out)*

Interlude before the Curtain

Victoria *(with her uniform under her arm)*   Ladies and gentlemen, your Victoria is faced with a hard decision. She has joined the army to be near the man she loves! Can she really mean to cross the ocean? Be that as it may, I cannot bear to leave his side during his last days in England, no matter how foolhardy this may be. How does the song go? *(She sings)*

At certain times in life we're driven
Head over heels to make a painful choice:
Whether to fate and passion we should give in
Or let ourselves be guided by reason's prudent voice,
    But the bosom swells with emotion
    And the mind hasn't got much to say
    The sail fills with wind on the ocean
    And the ship doesn't ask long; Which way?

Sister, what metal are you made of?
Where is your modesty and where your pride?

There's hardly any plight or peril you're afraid of
Once love has caught you up in its tumultuous tide
    The doe runs after the stag
    And the lioness follows her lord
    And to be with her lover a maid
    Will go to the ends of the world.

7

Market place.

Plume *and* **Kite** *are sitting in the recruiting booth.* **Jenny Mason** *and old* **Mrs. Cobb** *are standing outside.*

Mrs. Cobb   Well, I've come for his things.

Jenny   That's old Mrs. Cobb. They say her son Bert was killed at Bunker Hill.

Plume   I see.

Kite *(rummages about and finds a watch)*   The captain has brought this for you: his watch.

Mrs. Cobb   Thank-ee.

Jenny   It's been a blow to her. But now that I have the good fortune to see the captain, could I inquire about my husband, Jimmy Mason?

Kite   Jimmy Mason. He's even picked out the farm he's going to buy when it's all over. He's doing fine or I'm a worthless rogue.

Jenny   It's only that I've had no news of him for almost six months.

Kite   The bloody post, it's always the same thing. Don't you worry, Mrs. Mason, he's all right. Good evening to you!

Mrs. Cobb *(to* **Jenny***)*   Did Bert have a watch?

(Both women go out. **Kite** *mops his forehead)*

Plume   The devil take them!

Kite   She'll be all over Shrewsbury, driving everybody crazy.

Plume   How many have we recruited so far?

Kite   Nine, captain.

Plume   We had that many three days ago. Then there's the two Picklewooders that girl—what's her name again?—dragged in. Eleven in all. It's terrible! What's wrong with this place?

Kite   Recruiting's been slow in the last few days, captain.

Plume   Why?

Kite   It's the rumors about the losses at Bunker Hill. *(Captain Brazen comes in)*

Brazen   We meet again! How are you, my dear old boy? What's your name, dear fellow?

Kite   This is Captain Plume, Captain Brazen.

Brazen   Right. Plume, you're just the man I was going to ask for five pounds.

Plume *(laughs and makes a gesture of regret)*   Me? *(They sit down)*

Plume   How's your recruiting, old boy?

Brazen   I beg your pardon?

Plume   How many have you recruited?

Brazen   Shh!

Plume   What's that?

Brazen   Shh! That's my last word.

Plume   What's that you're holding?

Brazen   Two plans—for getting rid of twenty thousand pounds.

Plume   Mightn't it be better to find a way of raising twenty thousand pounds?

Brazen   My dear fellow, you may find it hard to understand why a man like me should want to get rid of twenty thousand pounds. In the army I spend twenty times that much every day. But now, I want your advice. The building fit is on me. Which would you advise: a pirate ship or a theater?

Plume   Pirate ship or theater—that's an odd question. Takes a bit of thinking. Brazen, I'm for the pirate ship.

Brazen   I don't agree with you, my dear fellow. A pirate ship can be badly built.

Plume   So can a theater.

Brazen   But a pirate ship can also be badly manned.

Plume   So can a theater.

Brazen   A pirate ship can founder without a trace.

Plume   A theater is even more likely to.—Consequently my advice to you is still the same—stick to the pirate ship.

Brazen   Very well!—But what if I don't get the twenty thousand pounds?

Plume   Where do you propose to get these twenty thousand pounds?

Brazen   It's a secret, my dear fellow. A lady I've ferreted out lately. At first I hung back. But now I really think I'll marry her. Twenty thousand pounds . . . She's to meet me next Sunday on the river bank half a mile out of town, and so forth. I must be off this minute.—Mum's the word, my dear fellow. *(Is about to leave. Turns back once more)* Twelve shillings?

(**Plume** *repeats the gesture of regret)*

*(***Brazen*** *goes out)*

Kite   We're pretty well cleaned out ourselves, sir.

Plume   You don't say so?

Kite   We haven't raised a company. We've still got the ensign's ten pounds for next Sunday, but no ideas. I think I'll have to fall back on my old household remedy. Boots off, door bolted, six large beers, a bit of bread to munch in between. I remember in Bengal, when I'd been trying for three whole weeks to make the colonel's wife's maid and not getting anywhere, my favorite remedy gave me the answer.

Plume   What was it?

Kite   To settle for the colonel's wife! Never fear, sir, right here
by the Severn I'll come through again. Your company will be up to
strength.

Plume   Kite, what do you make of that little Balance girl who
writes those letters? Doesn't she strike you as the sort who goes the
limit on paper but calls for the preacher and wedding bells before
she'll let you kiss her on the forehead? Not for us, eh? I don't
remember her very well, damn it! Somehow she reminds me of our
ensign—what do you think? Has she got a brother? (**Kite** *shrugs
his shoulders sullenly)* What a bore Shrewsbury is this year. Admit
it. Wilful may be stinking with money but I'll have to tell him
it's not my way to give up a woman without getting something in
return. He'll just have to produce the Balance girl. I'm not going to
turn monk for his sake. Lord, is this Shrewsbury tedious!

Kite   Will you be by the Severn on Sunday, captain?

Plume   For the concert? Yes, I think so. But I don't know if I'll
have any time for you.

Kite   We may need you, sir. The inspecting officer from London
will be here any day.

(**Victoria** *comes in wearing the king's uniform)*

Victoria   Ensign Wilful reporting for duty.

Plume   Speaking of duty, what have you done with that wench
from Picklewood, Wilful? Rose.

Victoria   I've arranged to meet her, sir.

Plume   Where?

Victoria   By the Severn.

Plume   When?

Victoria   Sunday. Sunday afternoon.

Plume   Afternoon! To feed the swans? Hold hands? It may be
none of my business, but if I find out that you lack enterprise in

these matters, I'm through with you. You come around whining, I hand you a juicy morsel and you lock it up in the pantry. Furthermore, I'd have expected a man of your breeding to return the favor. What about the Balance girl?

(Victoria hurriedly produces a letter from her back pocket)

Plume *(angrily)*   No more letters! I want something tangible! And not next week but tomorrow, Sunday. Is that clear?

Victoria   Yes, captain.

Plume   Dismiss!

(Victoria salutes)

8

By the Severn.

Plume *is sitting on a bench, waiting. In the distance the strains of a military band.*

Kite *(disguising himself behind the bushes. To **Plume**)* You're in for a surprise, captain. This may turn out to be the biggest idea I've ever had. If this doesn't bring Shrewsbury around, my name is mud. *(Steps out of the bushes, disguised as a flower seller)*

How do I look, captain?

Plume Terrible.

Kite *(shuffles off, his feelings hurt)* Lilacs! Fresh lilacs!

*(**Victoria** comes in dressed in the uniform of an ensign)*

Plume All alone?

Victoria Captain Plume, I don't quite know how to explain it. Yesterday she was all set to come. Today she just couldn't make up her mind. Are you dreadfully disappointed?

Plume Nothing can disappoint me any more in Shrewsbury.

Victoria She's not like Shrewsbury.

Plume But why wouldn't she come?

Victoria Perhaps it's because she doesn't trust herself. She's a woman of spirit, you know.

Plume She's obviously well able to control that spirit of hers.

Victoria That's not fair.

Plume I beg your pardon?

Victoria Perhaps if you gave her more time . . .

Plume   A soldier lives at a fast pace, Wilful. He's got to take his meals on the run. He must dispense with certain dishes. A chunk of bread and into the saddle. Have you arranged to meet with—what's her name again—Rose? This is an order: tell her to come to my quarters at the Raven tonight. And keep your proper distance, two paces, ensign. Is that clear?

Victoria   Yes, captain. *(Angrily)* Then you shouldn't write such letters.

Plume   So you've been reading letters entrusted to you by your superior officer?

Victoria   Not at all. But when they're being read, I can tell if they were dictated by true sentiments or if they ring false.

Plume   I'll thank you to keep your opinion of my technique to yourself, ensign.

Victoria   You've got no heart and you can count me out. *(She steps aside)*

*(**Worthy** comes in)*

Worthy   Lost! Irrevocably lost! Plume, your stratagem has been my ruin. To hell with all strategists! Melinda and Brazen are to meet here by the river and they're rowing out to that notorious island.

Plume   Who told you that?

Worthy   Her maid.

Plume   So you called on her again. In spite of my warning. And were shown the door.

Worthy   Nothing of the sort, worse luck. Her maid came to me.

Plume   Then she was sent. To arouse your jealousy. And you want to throw up the game? Worthy, if you give in now—you'll lose everything. Melinda's maneuvers, clearly born of desperation, must be thwarted! She is only meeting Brazen because of you. I admit it may be unpleasant for you to watch them disappear into the bushes . . .

Worthy   Unpleasant? Unbearable!

Plume   Unbearable! Nonsense! We sacrifice a town in order to win a country. You accept a setback to ensure final victory. Worthy, your faint-heartedness will make you miss the greatest chance of your life.

Worthy   What! Am I to look on while the woman I love and that scoundrel . . .

Plume   By all means. And with perfect composure. You must give her an opportunity to find out for herself what a worthless rascal your rival is.

Worthy   But . . . in my presence?

Plume   How else?

Worthy   Plume, it's more than I can bear.

Plume   Nonsense. Come along to my quarters and have a toddy with plenty of rum. I'll have one myself.—Stop looking like a sick calf. You've never been closer to victory. *(To* **Victoria***, who is still standing about)* What are you waiting for?

Victoria   On my honor, captain, I don't understand you. Isn't Victoria worthier of you than all these Mollys and Roses and whatever their names may be in all the taverns of England and the New World?

Plume   Undoubtedly. But she's not here. And Rose will be. You'll see to that. *(Goes out with* **Worthy***)*

Victoria   Never, never, never. *(Goes out)*

*(***Mike** *and* **Lucy** *come in.* **Lucy** *carries a picnic basket. She curtsies to* **Worthy***)*

Mike   Why that big smile for the shoe business?

Lucy   He gave me a pound.

Mike   He gave you a pound?

Lucy   I was nice to him, so he gave me a pound.

Mike   What's the story?

Lucy   Miss Moorhill sent me to tell Mr. Worthy that she was going to the Severn with a dashing captain and that if nobody stopped her something dreadful would happen. Mr. Worthy went white as a sheet and gave me a pound.

Mike   Is she really up to something with that captain?

Lucy   Naw. She only wants to make Mr. Shoe Business jealous.

(They move toward the river. **Mike** *spies a swan in the distance)*

Mike *(pointing)*   There's Felix.

Lucy   Kitchie-kitchie. Ten more errands like that one and we'll have the money for the fare. "America, here we come."

Mike   But not the way they want us to be going, me as a grenadier and you as a you-know-what. Oh no, we're going into the hotel business. *(The swan swims close; they feed it)*

Lucy   I'll write to Aunt Emmy in New York tonight.

Mike   What for? That hole! We're going to Boston.

Lucy   Hole, you say! It may be a small town now, but it's got a future.

Mike   Too small for another hotel, Shh!

(**Appletree** *in uniform comes in with his girl* **Maggie**, **William**, *a young blacksmith, and his girl* **Sally***)*

Maggle   Let's sit here—there's somebody here already.

Sally   And here's the swan. I've got bread for him. Do you mind, Tummas?

William   Who cares if he minds?

Sally   He eats out of my hand.

Mike *(furious)*   He does that.

(**Mike** *and* **Lucy** *go out. The others look after them with surprise)*

William *(to* **Sally***)*   You're making eyes at him because of his uniform.

Appletree   I only wish I could get rid of it.

Maggle   William is staying on in Micklesbury. What'll you have. William, an egg or some sausage?

Appletree   An egg. *(takes one)*

Maggie   William!

Appletree   You haven't said a word about the shoes and the pretty furs I'm going to bring back to you.

Maggie   It's easy to know who's going, but you can never tell who's coming back.

(Music)

Sally   They're playing "When I Leave You." Sing it for me, Tummas.

Appletree *(sings with the music)*

When I leave you for the war, dear
Leave you standing on the shore, dear
On the queen's great ship as out of port we sail
Find another sweetheart. Minny
For this ship goes to Virginny
And when I'm gone, my love, my love for you will pale . . .

Maggie *(sings)*

I'll be cheering with the others
For our husbands, sweethearts, brothers
When the queen's great ship goes sailing with the ride.
Jimmy dear, you must believe me
Memories of you will grieve me
When I'm walking with another at my side.

(**Kite** *comes in disguised as a flower girl)*

Kite   Lilacs, fresh lilacs! Forget-me-nots, violets! Buy some violets for your sweetheart before he leaves for America. *(To*

Sally*)* I can see your friend is a real fighting man. I've got seven of my own, all in the army where they belong.

Maggie   He's staying right here. He's a blacksmith.

Kite   Go on with you. *(To **William***)* Here, let's look at your hand. Blacksmith. A violent man by profession. You were born under Biceps.

Maggie   Biceps? What's that?

Kite   One of the signs of the zodiac. There's Leo, Sagittarius, Biceps, Anvil, Boston, Massachusetts, Kentucky, Philadelphia, Mumps, and so on. Twelve in all.—Let's see. Have you ever made bombs or cannon balls?

William   Not I.

Kite   Either you've made them or you're going to make them. It's scientific. What's more, it's in the stars—Oh! What a future! In exactly two years, three months, and two hours you will become a captain.

Sally   A captain!

(The farmers listen in, some attentively, some skeptically)

Kite   In the artillery. You'll have two batmen and ten shillings a day. It's written in the stars, the fixed stars.

William   What do the stars say about my smithy?

Kite   What's that?

William   What'll happen to my smithy?

Kite   Where would the fixed stars be if they started worrying about every filthy village smithy?

William   In that case, shit on your fixed stars.

Kite   You'll pay for that once we're away from home. *(Aside, in leaving)* I'll get that man or I'm not a . . .

*(**Victoria** comes in)*

Kite *(salutes)*   The trumpeter won't play his solo. He wants another pound. Scum.

*(**Victoria** hands him money)*

Sally   She's a funny one.

William   Did you see her salute?

*(**Kite** goes out. **Victoria** walks toward a boat. **Appletree** salutes)*

Sally   How smartly he does it!

William   He's got to.

Appletree *(eager to go)*   Come, let's go.

*(The farmers leave. **Victoria** has sat down on the side of the boat)*

Maggie   But I've still got bread for Felix! *(She gathers her things and runs after the others. **Victoria** remains sitting on the boat. Suddenly **Rose's** voice is heard)*

Rose's Voice   Chickens! Fresh Picklewood chickens!

Victoria *(jumps to her feet)*   Damn it. Here come the chickens!
*(**Rose** and her brother **Bullock** emerge from the grove. **Bullock** is in uniform)*

Rose *(to **Bullock**)*   Who's that officer over there?

Bullock   That's our new ensign.

Rose   Go and ask him where the captain is.

Victoria *(to herself)*   Up and at 'em, Victoria. You're wearing breeches now.

*(**Bullock** approaches her)*

Bullock   Where's the captain, sir?

Victoria   Attention! Didn't they teach you to salute an officer? About turn! Right leg, raise! Left leg, raise! About turn! At the double, march! Double mark time! Left, right, left, right! Halt! On the face, down! Up, down, up, down! How do you recognize an ensign?

Bullock *(still lying on the ground)*   By his uniform and bearing, sir.

Victoria   Up, man!—Do you know the difference between a horse cart and a cart horse, you old dungfork?

Bullock   Yessir!

Victoria   About her, now. Who's she?

Bullock   My sister Rose. She's got to see the captain.

Victoria   Come here, child, and give me a kiss.

Rose   But I don't know you, sir.

Victoria   What's that got to do with it? We soldiers have to cat on the run.

(Rose is kissed)

Victoria   I am Captain Plume's ensign, Rose. It's my job to look after you, the captain is busy today.

Rose   But I was to see him personally.

Victoria   What for? You can see me instead.

Rose   He wanted to give me something, sir.

Victoria   I'll give it to you all right.

Rose   Please, sir, tell him I'll come tonight.

Victoria   Where?

Rose   Why, to the Raven.

Victoria   You'd go to the Raven? At night? How can you make yourself so cheap?

Rose   He'll get what he wants from me, and I'll get what I want from him.

Bullock   On the up and up, sir. Have a care what you say, Rose, don't shame your parents.

Rose   I'm doing it for Charles too, you know.

Victoria   Charles?

Bullock   Charles Cartwheel, her intended.

Rose   He's to be a drum major!

Victoria   Doesn't he mind your going to see the captain?

Rose   Why should he? "If the captain's good to you," says
Charles, "he's sure to be good to me when I'm his soldier."
Whatever I do, I'm doing it for the village and for Charles.

Victoria *(takes* **Rose** *aside)*   Look here, child, the captain isn't
going to be at the Raven at all tonight.

Rose *(stubbornly)*   Then I'll wait in the hall.

Victoria   You will not wait in the hall. You will wait in my room.
Aren't I a handsome fellow? A kiss, this minute.

Rose   Yours to command. *(Kisses her; to* **Bullock***)* If the ensign
wants . . .

Victoria   Here's a pound for your chickens, child. Now let's be
off to the dance. And you, there, carry the chickens. *(* **Victoria**
pulls **Rose** *away.* **Bullock** *follows.* **Melinda** *comes in)*

Melinda *(looking around)*   Heaven help me! A hazardous
enterprise, if I'm found out the whole town will condemn me. Ah,
Worthy, there is nothing I wouldn't do to make you mine! Worthy!

(**Brazen** *comes in)*

Brazen *(catches sight of* **Melinda** *and looks at his watch)*   As
punctual as the bugler! Madam, I am your humble servant and
so forth.—Nice little river, the old Severn.—Do you like fishing,
madam?

Melinda   A pleasant, melancholy pastime.

Brazen   I'll fetch the fishing rods at once.

Melinda *(aside)*   Where can Worthy be?

Brazen   You must know, madam, that I have fought in Flanders
against the French, in Hungary against the Turks, in Tangiers

against the Moors, but I have never been so much in love before. Slit my belly, madam, if you will; in all my campaigns I have never met so fine a woman as your ladyship.

Melinda   And of all the men I have known, none has ever paid me so fine a compliment. You soldiers are the best-mannered of men, that we must allow.

Brazen   Some of us, madam, not all! There are brutes among us too, sad brutes, ah yes, madam. As for me, I've always had the good fortune to prove agreeable. I have had splendid offers, madam. I might have married a German princess, worth some fifty thousand pounds a year. But her bathroom disgusted me. Shall we repair to the woods? (**Melinda** *makes a negative gesture*) The daughter of a Turkish pasha fell in love with me when I was a prisoner among the infidels. She offered to steal her father's treasure and run away with me. But I don't know why, my time had not yet come. Hanging and marriage, you know, are governed by fate. Fate has preserved me for one of the most seductive ladies in all Shrewsbury. And, so I am told, one of the wealthiest as well. What would you say to a stroll in these delightful woods, my little nymph? (**Melinda** *tries to run away, but* **Brazen** *catches up with her and pulls her into the wood*)

(The swan swims closer to the shore as **Lucy** *and* **Mike** *reappear)*

Lucy   The one thing I'll miss when I'm over there is Felix.

Mike   He'll miss us too on Sunday afternoons. *(Takes out a slip of paper)*

Lucy   What's that?

Mike   From the New World. It was given to me by a coachman who got it from a Liverpool sailor. Listen! Run along, Felix! Down with the king. Down with the archbishop, down with the lords. We in the New World need no more kings and no more lords, who grew fat on our sweat. We in the State of America wish to be an English colony no longer. Signed: Franklin.

Lucy   When did you learn to read, Mike? *(She takes the paper from him)*

Mike   Oh, Fred showed me yesterday how it's done.

Lucy   It says something entirely different.

Mike   What does it say?

Lucy   "Declaration of Independence."

Mike   Sounds good too. Read it.

Lucy   "That all men are created equal, that they are endowed by their . . ." I can't make out that word . . . "with certain . . . rights: Life, Liberty and the Pursuit of Happiness . . ."

Mike   Lucy, that's the place for us.

Lucy *(as if announcing)*   At the Sign of the Swan, Proprietors Mr. and Mrs. Mike W. Laughton. *(Play-acting)* Don't take in any more guests, Mike W. Laughton. All I've left on the spit is two sides of beef.

Mike   Right, Mrs. Mike W. Laughton. I'll just have to turn away the lord mayor of Philadelphia. But first, let's have a little dance, in the kitchen. After all, we've paid the musicians. *(They dance)*

Lucy   Bolt the doors, Mike W. Laughton, the redcoats are coming!

Mike   Load my musket, woman! Those god-damned English! Bang—bang! These muskets aren't oiled properly, Mrs. Mike W. Laughton!

Lucy   My best salad oil!

Mike   Bang. Bull's-eye. *(He stretches out on the ground)*

(Enter the **Farm Boys**, followed by **Kite** disguised as a preacher)

The Farm Boys *(walking up to the swan)*   Kitchie-kitchie.

Kite *(who has followed them)*   Kitchie-kitchie.

(The swan swims away hurriedly)

Kite *(preaching)*   Brothers and sisters in Christ! My visits to the sick have chanced to bring me to your lovely Severn on this fine day. And I feel I should say a few words to you. I said to myself: What do my dear sisters and brothers in the villages know about the great recruiting campaign for our good King George's army, which has been going on these past few weeks in town and country? In these weeks when England's glory and prestige in the world are at stake. In these weeks His eye is upon us. It is written in Deuteronomy, Book 2, Chapter 27, Verse 14: The Lord sees the black ant on the black stone in the black night. Dearly beloved, are there any questions that torment you? Speak up, my son.

William   Your Reverence, is it not true that a man may do his duty by staying home as well?

Kite   A most intelligent question, a question that deserves an answer. Dearly beloved, it has come to the attention of the church that there are some in these parts who shrink back from defending English liberty in America because their flesh is weak and afraid. Nonsense, say I. Flesh is dust and shall return to dust, but England is England and will be England for all eternity. Not only here, but in that godforsaken America as well, ye shining lights of Micklesbury!

Mike   But isn't it true, Your Reverence, that the people over there are people just like us?

Kite *(thundering)*   What about geographology, you snotnose? What about the Ninth Commandment, you slopjar? Is it not written: "Thou shalt not covet thy neighbor's wife and house"? And hasn't America belonged to our good King George of England ever since the Lord created it? And now it is being coveted by those Americans, the devil take every last one of them, begging the ladies' pardon.

Mike   Isn't it true, Your Reverence, that there are no lords or kings in America?

Kite   Whoever put that into your head, you whiskey thief? According to the latest census, there are 44,302 lords in America and no less than seven kings, and not a one of them is any good.

Appletree   That's a fact.

Mike   And isn't it true, Your Reverence, that you aren't a reverend gent at all and that you're Mr. Kite, son of Cleopatra the Gypsy, jailbird and lifelong sergeant?

(**Maggie** *cries out; the farm boys look at* **Kite***)*

Kite   What a bunch of creeps you turned out to be. *(To* **Appletree** *who salutes him)* Deserters will be shot on the spot. *(* **Kite** *departs amid loud laughter)*

William   I'll be damned.

Sally *(rising)*   Who'll come to the woods with me? I know where to find raspberries!

(**Appletree***, slightly embarrassed, follows her)*

Mike *(getting up)*   Let's go. *(He and* **Lucy** *go into the woods)*

Maggie *(in tears)*   William, take me home. *(* **William** *leads* **Maggie** *into the woods)*

*(***Melinda** *comes out of the woods, followed by* **Brazen** *who is playing a panpipe)*

Melinda   Oh, Worthy, my dear Worthy, save me from this madman!

Brazen   As you see, madam, the king's service has preserved my vigor, enabling me to serve the most ardent of English women with undimished powers of body and soul. Confidentially, madam, you see before you a warrior who longs to lay his laurel-crowned head on a loving bosom. Which explains why I am offering you the opportunity of accepting my hand.

(**Pearmain***, wearing a uniform, comes in)*

Pearmain   Stand by, captain!

Brazen   On Sunday?

Pearmain   Yessir, captain. The inspecting officer from London, sir!

Brazen   I'm busy!

Pearmain   Yessir, captain! *(Goes out)*

Brazen   Melinda!

Melinda   Captain Brazen, how can I accept your tempting offer? Surrender myself to a soldier whom the king may take away from me at any time? I've sworn not to. And I shall keep my oath. I shall never marry a soldier.

Brazen   Never marry a soldier?

Melinda   Never, captain. Your uniform will always be a barrier between us.

(**Worthy** *storms in with pistols)*

Melinda *(overjoyed)*   Worthy!

Worthy   Fickle woman! And all for this gaudy fly-by-night who has the audacity . . . Here, take your choice! *(Holds out the pistols to* **Brazen***)*

Brazen   Pistols? Are they loaded?

Worthy   Each with its charge of death.

Melinda   What has this to do with you, Mr. Worthy? I didn't know you took the slightest interest in my affairs.

(Drumroll)

Brazen   Harkee. Stand by. Besides, I'm a foot soldier. I don't favor pistols.

Worthy   I am here to fight for the honor of Shrewsbury. We men of Shrewsbury will not stand idly by while our women throw themselves at men who tomorrow will be gone over the hills and over the sea.

Brazen   Fire and brimstone! Sir, I've tasted the smoke from the cannon's iron mouth. *(He picks a pistol and takes a dueling stance)*

Melinda *(to* **Worthy***)*   Monster! *(She sobs)* How can you! It's all over between us. *(Runs out)*

Worthy   That's it! Run away! Leave me here to die alone. *(Takes his place and counts paces)* One, two, three . . .

Brazen   Stop! Where's the lady?

Worthy *(darkly)*   Gone.

Brazen   In that case, why fight? Embrace me, my dear fellow, life is short enough as it is. *(Drops the pistol and walks over to the bench.* **Worthy** *sits down beside him.)*

Worthy   Turning tail! And in the king's uniform!

Brazen   Come, come, Worthy, the uniform doesn't make the man.

Worthy   How can you say that? You who owe your despicable triumphs entirely to your uniform?

Brazen   On the contrary, Mr. Worthy. I've learned different My uniform stands in my way. Excuse me, my dear fellow. *(Goes out)*

*(***Kite*** drives all the soldiers out of the woods. The girls are trying to hold them, calling out their names piteously)*

Kite   Inspection! All in uniform back to town! Get going, you sons of bitches! *(Turning to the girls)* Civilians can stay. *(To* **Sally***, sobbing and clutching at* **Appletree***)* Stop bawling!

Girl *(calling after the drummer)*   Jonathan!

Worthy *(who has remained sitting on the bench)*   Bandits!

9

At the house of Mr. Balance.

Same evening. **Balance** *is reading a letter; he is very upset.* **Simpkins** *is holding a candle.*

Simpkins   Bad news, sir?

Balance   Frightful.

Simpkins   I'm sorry, sir.

Balance   The sun is setting on the British Empire.

(**Worthy** *comes in)*

Balance   How is the inspection coming along, Worthy?

Worthy *(shrugs his shoulders)*   I'm afraid that lot of recruits in the market place won't empty my warehouse for me. It's not enough to have boots for the soldiers; we must have soldiers for the boots. Here comes Plume.

Balance   Dreadful! *(* **Plume** *comes in)* How are things, Plume? I hope the inspecting officer from London found your company up to strength.

Plume   The inspecting officer from London found exactly eleven recruits.

Balance   Terrible.

Worthy   If it will do you any good, Plume, I'll join your company. There is nothing to keep me here any longer.

Balance   What's got into you, Worthy? You're a shoe manufacturer, not a soldier. You might as well ask me to shoulder a musket.

Plume   Mr. Balance, my mind is made up. I'm asking for a transfer to East India. Give your daughter my respectful regards.

Balance   Captain Plume!

Plume   Mr. Balance?

Balance   Be seated.

Plume   I am seated.

Simpkins   He is seated.

Balance   Captain Plume, you can't go to the East Indies, your place is in America. I shall not be divulging military secrets if I tell you the bad news that has precipitated the inspector general's visit. Boston has fallen to the rebels.

Simpkins   Impossible!

Balance   I beg your pardon? *(He motions* **Simpkins** *to leave the room)*

Plume   All right. We've lost Boston. Do you expect me to retake Boston with my bare hands?

Balance   Plume, you can't let England down in this fateful hour, and neither can Shrewsbury. Until now I did not think it necessary to resort to compulsory recruitment. Now I see that it is necessary. *(Takes a law book from the bookcase)* Recruitment Act, 1704.

Worthy   But this is 1776. There was a scandal when they tried to enforce these laws in Welshpool.

Balance   But they yielded two full companies of able-bodied convicts. Are we to allow undesirable elements to grow fat in our prisons or defile our streets? Put them in the army! In a way you could even call it cruelty to leave these people in jail, or let the unemployed vegetate in the streets, when they could be dying a hero's death for English liberty in the New World. It is in every respect our patriotic duty to give them this opportunity. Come with me to the prison, Captain Plume.

(**Melinda** *comes in)*

Melinda   Uncle! Will you permit me to speak to Mr. Worthy in private?

Balance   Gladly, my child. Do speak to him, he's got a bee in his bonnet. Make yourselves at home, Simpkins will bring you tea. Come along, captain. *(Goes out with* **Plume***)*

Melinda   Surely you understand, Mr. Worthy, that after what has happened I find it intolerable that my letters should be in your possession.

Worthy   I shall return them to you before I embark, madam. Permit me to bid you farewell, Miss Moorhill.

Melinda   How long have you been in this traveling humor?

Worthy   It is only natural, madam, for us to avoid what disturbs our peace of mind.

Melinda   I should interpret it rather as a desire for change, which is even more natural in men.

Worthy   Change would seem to have a special attraction for women as well, madam; why, otherwise, would you be so fond of it?

Melinda   You are mistaken, Mr. Worthy! I am not so fond of change as to leave home. Nor do I think it wise of you to fling yourself into danger and expense in the slender expectation of questionable pleasures.

Worthy   The pleasures awaiting me abroad are indeed questionable, madam, but one thing I am sure of: I shall meet with less cruelty on the battlefields of the New World, amongst the barbarous cowboys and fur trappers, than I have found here, in my own country.

Melinda   Mr. Worthy, you and I have wasted enough words. I believe we would come to an agreement sooner if each of us were to tender his accounts.

Worthy   Indeed, madam. If we do, you will find yourself very much in my debt. My fears, sighs, vows, promises, assiduities, and anxieties have accrued for a whole year without eliciting the slightest return.

Melinda   A whole year! Oh, Mr. Worthy! What you owe me cannot be repaid by less than seven years of servitude. How did you treat me last year when, taking advantage of my innocence and poverty, you tried to make me your mistress, that is, your slave? Add to that your shameless behavior, your loose language, the familiar tone of your letters, your ill-mannered visits—do you remember all that, Mr. Worthy? *(Sobs)*

Worthy   I remember well. Too bad nothing came of it.—But you for your part must take into account . . .

Melinda   Sir, I'll take nothing into account. It's to your interest that I should forget. You have treated me barbarously; I have only been cruel to you. Weigh the one against the other. And now, if you wish to turn a new leaf, stop acting like an adventurer and behave like a gentleman. How could you leave me standing in the market place the other day like a leftover sack of wool?

Worthy   I only did that to test you, and, believe me, I regret it more than anything I have ever done. But you and that captain, before my very eyes . . . *(His voice breaks)*

Melinda   I was only trying to arouse your jealousy. That was the only reason; can't you believe me?

Worthy   Melinda.

Melinda   Worthy. *(They go toward each other, arms outstretched)*

*(***Simpkins*** comes in)*

Simpkins   Captain Brazen!

Brazen *(pushes him aside) Mister* Brazen! *(He stands there beaming in a shabby civilian frock coat)*

*(***Melinda*** looks at him in consternation)*

Brazen   Melinda! Your wish is fulfilled. For you I did what I've never done before. One word from you and I laid down my weapons. Darling, come to my arms! *(He puts his arm around her waist)*

Melinda   How dare you? Can't you see Mr. Worthy? *(Slaps his face)*

Brazen   No, no. I'm blinded. Worthy! 'Sbodkins! My lady has wit in her very fingertips. Deplorable blunder. I beg your pardon, madam, the ways of an old warrior, don't you know. Worthy! So you're the lucky man! Have I got it straight?

Worthy   Heaven forbid! Rather say unlucky. I've got more than enough proof of that now.

Melinda   Worthy!

Worthy   Your letters will be returned to you, madam. If you care to read them over, you will see what you have done to me.

Melinda   Albert!

Worthy   No, it's all clear to me now, only too clear.

Melinda   No!

Worthy   No? Yes. Can your fickleness go so far as to deceive this man who has sacrificed his career to you at your bidding? If you do that, there's no gentleman on earth who will have anything to do with you.

Melinda   This is too much. Mr. Worthy . . .

Worthy   This is too much. What's too much? Stick to this dubious chameleon, since you obviously prefer outward glitter to a true heart. No, I'm not the lucky one, Mr. Brazen. But I don't envy you your luck if your great sacrifice earns you such striking favors.

Melinda   My favors were bestowed on the wrong man, Mr. Worthy. From now on you can expect nothing better, if you should ever cross my path again. I beg your forgiveness, Mr. Brazen.

Brazen   Granted.

Melinda   Would you see me home and . . .

Brazen   And so forth, madam.—Courage, my dear fellow. The fortunes of war, you know. *(Goes out with* **Melinda***)*

Simpkins *(entering)*   Tea, Mr. Worthy?

Worthy *(bellows)*   Whiskey!

Simpkins   Sir, I must beg your pardon for these little oversights. *(His voice breaking)* Boston has fallen to the rebels.

(Simpkins goes out)

(Balance and Plume enter in a dejected mood. They sit down without a word)

Balance *(calling)*   Simpkins!

Simpkins *(entering)*   Mr. Balance!

Balance *(shouts)*   Whiskey!

Simpkins   You must forgive me today. *(Goes out)*

Balance   What's the matter with him?

Worthy *(over his shoulder)*   Boston.

(Pause)

Balance   Why are you looking out the window so gloomily, Worthy?

Worthy   You don't seem too cheerful yourself, sir.

Balance   Worthy, we've been too lenient in Shrewsbury these last few years. The jail is empty. One solitary prisoner. A sex maniac, and that's all. A drop in the bucket.

Simpkins *(comes in)*   Lady Prude. Mr. Smuggler.

Balance   Lady Prude? I have an idea. Show them in.

(Lady Prude and Mr. Smuggler come in)

Prude   Balance, one more Sunday like this and I shall leave Shrewsbury forever. The behavior of those soldiers on the banks of our fair Severn would have put Sodom and Gomorrah to shame. Mr. Smuggler, the banker from London, was here for lunch. His hair stood on end.

Smuggler   Your servant, Mr. Balance.

Balance   Your servant, Mr. Smuggler.

Prude   I see one of the main culprits right here in your parlor. Molly Fastspittle can tell you all about him. And so can Rose, my tenant's daughter.

Plume   Sir, since this town has showered me with insults instead of soldiers, I beg to take my leave. *(Goes out)*

Balance   Captain Plume!—*(To* **Lady Prude***)* I do wish you would learn to control your unfortunate prejudice against the only people who can hope to give England a certain measure of order and discipline.

Prude   For the last ten days I have been battling the military rabble; to no avail.

Balance   Do you call the heroic sons of England military rabble? They are risking their lives for you, my lady.

Prude   I'm paying them for it. A fifth of my income goes toward their upkeep. But I'm not paying them to sing bawdy songs and sin in the bushes on the Sabbath.

Balance   My lady, it is not my habit to scrutinize the bushes on the Sabbath.

Smuggler   In London we have special houses for such things.

Prude   We have them here too, Mr. Smuggler. I could tell you a thing or two. Chicken Street!

Smuggler *(to himself)*   Chicken Street!

Prude   And not only in Chicken Street. In the taverns and inns! This town is overrun with disreputable elements of all ages, drunkards, pickpockets, and unemployed, who flaunt their sins with impunity. Will the authorities never . . .

Balance *(who has been listening with growing interest, now raises his hand)*   You're perfectly right, my lady, and the authorities *will*. We shall teach the rabble patriotism. We shall give justice and morality free rein, even if it means filling Shrewsbury's prison to the bursting point!

Prude   You are contemplating a cleanup?

Balance   A most thorough cleanup, Lady Prude.

10

At the Raven.

Victoria *is asleep on a chair. She has taken off her sword, boots, and coat. Commotion in the inn. Loud knocking and shouts of "Open up," "The constables."*

Victoria   What's going on?

Rose *(from behind a screen)*   There's a rumpus down in the hall.

Victoria   Five in the morning. The night has passed without trouble; I've slept soundly, but I'm afraid my companion is less pleased. Poor Rose! *(To* **Rose***)* Good morning, my pet. And how are you this fine morning? *(Starts to pull on her boots)*

Rose   Same as yesterday. You've made me neither better nor worse.

Victoria   Didn't you like your bed-fellow?

Rose   I don't know if I had one or not. Ruining a poor girl's reputation for nothing!

Victoria   I saved your reputation. You didn't get your lace frock, but don't fret. I shall give you much nicer things than the captain.

Rose   You can't. Now I know.

(Knocking at the door)

Voice   Open up! The constables!

Victoria   Good God. I'm half naked.

Voice *(outside)*   Open the door or we'll break it down!

Victoria   Just a minute!—Rose, my hat, give me my hat.

(Constable **Bridewell** *forces his way in)*

Victoria   What's the meaning of this?

Bridewell   Two more lovebirds! *(To* **Victoria***)* This is a raid. You're under arrest.

Victoria   Get back, fellow! If you come any closer you're a dead duck.

Bridewell   Put away that sword, pipsqueak, or I'll knock out your milk teeth, in the name of the king!

Victoria   Just try it, flatfoot!

Bridewell   That's an insult to His Majesty! Insult me and you insult the king. You're under arrest, pipsqueak.

(**Sergeant Kite** *comes in)*

Bridewell   Another haul, Mr. Kite, Goose and gander, both in the trap.

Kite   Blarney!

(**Lady Prude** *comes in)*

Prude *(sees* **Rose***)*   Rose! Rose! My poor child! Did he . . .

Victoria   I protected her, Lady Prude. Captain Plume was going to . . .

Bridewell   And you did instead.

Rose   He hasn't done a thing.

Kite   That's our ensign, Mr. Wilful. Our job is to jail civilians, my lady.

Prude   Our job is to jail monsters and he's a monster! Constable, take him away.

Kite   Hands off. You can't arrest an officer without the consent of his superior. Just a minute. *(Goes out and is heard calling out "captain")*

Victoria   My lady, I don't think there's any need to get Captain Plume . . .

(**Plume** *comes in without coat or sword, followed by* **Kite***)*

Plume   Ensign Wilful . . .

Rose *(runs over to* **Plume***)*   I've been wanting to talk to you, captain. I was waiting for you here.

Bridewell   In the ensign's room. Caught in flagrante.

Prude   Rose, come here!

Plume *(going toward* **Victoria***)*   So this is how you carry out my orders, ensign? Boston has fallen and you amuse yourself—like this. There's never been anything like it in all military history. Why do the likes of you join the army, that's what I'd like to know. For no other reason than to f . . . fulfill your desires. Man, I don't know what to think of you.

Rose   Man! Ha! I wouldn't be too hard on him, captain. He's quite harmless.

Plume   Harmless? Hmm. An uncontrolled satyr. *(* **Rose** *giggles)* This is no laughing matter.

Rose   It is, though!

Plume   What are you anyway? No ensign would behave like that, only a . . . Harmless? *(A light dawns on him)* I'll speak to you later. *(To the audience)* Victoria Balance! Well, I'll be jiggered! She herself never shows up, but she keeps every other girl away from me. I'll show her! *(To* **Lady Prude***)* My lady, I cannot but agree with you. Constable, take the ensign to jail!

Kite   Captain, sir, what's the good of this idiotic raid? We were looking for grenadiers, and now we're even losing our officers.

Prude   You don't understand, sergeant. Your captain intends to clean up not only Shrewsbury but the king's army as well. Constable, do your duty.

Plume *(virtuously)*   Exactly, Lady Prude. The law makes no distinction between civilians and soldiers.

Prude   Well said!

Plume *(to* **Victoria***)*   You have defiled the king's uniform; off to prison with you!

Bridewell   Come on, pipsqueak. *(Grabs her)*

Victoria   Captain!

Plume   One more thing. Rose, my child, come here. *(He puts his arms around her)* I swear, before these witnesses, to make up for all the wrong this scoundrel has done you. And now, take him away.

Prude   Stop! Just a word. It seems to me that we've caught the pike, but what about the shark? Sir, behind that cloak of moral indignation I detect your own lust, naked and unabashed.

Victoria   How discerning of you, Lady Prude, You libertine! But I'll put a spoke in your wheel. This note bears your signature, Captain Plume. It fell due at midnight. Can you meet it? I demand immediate payment!

Plume   Wilful!

Victoria   You can't pay? Very well! Constable, take this man to debtors' prison at once. I demand it.

Prude   Quite so! Gets them with child, and won't marry; borrows money, and won't pay it back! Take him away too!

Kite   'Sblood!

Bridewell   But I can't arrest a man for debt without a warrant. I'm sorry, my lady. Besides, he's an officer.

Kite   Exactly!

Victoria   I thought the law made no distinction between officers and civilians.

Prude   Take him away!

Kite   Hands off! I'll bite off my leg before I let you arrest my captain.

Prude   Sergeant, you have shown the most commendable zeal all night. Don't weaken now, let virtue be your captain.

Plume   Dismiss, Mr. Kite. Farewell, Rose, we must part. Never accept money from strangers.

(Plume goes out, followed by Bridewell and Victoria)

Kite   Now we've got a company and no captain. *(Goes out)*

Rose   What's going to happen now?

Prude   Nothing, my child. You will go back to Picklewood.

Rose   But there's not a man left there.

Prude   Thanks to you, my poor misguided lamb!

11

Jailhouse.

Plume *is busy with his toilet.* **Victoria** *is sitting on a bench.*

Plume   We wouldn't want to waste our time here, Wilful. Let me teach you the favorite song of our glorious company. Two —three! *(Sings)*

Seventeen reservists from Z Battery
Stand eyeing the women of Gaa.
Then each reservist pushes
One of them into the bushes
Where they take a close look at the evening star.
  And that will be the only star
  She'll see in Gaa
  It stays there for an hour or two, then au revoir.
  Aha.

(**Plume** *motions to* **Victoria** *. Under* **Plume's** *direction she sings the stanza over)*

Plume   Second verse! *(Sings)*

In the morning you won't find Z Battery
They ride off at first light.
But on leaving each reservist
Has a fig to give his dearest
—Which makes a pound of figs, if I am right.
  That fig will be the only thing she'll get to see
  A fig is all she ever gets, apparently.
  Dear me.

(**Victoria** *repeats the stanza)*

Victoria   Dear me . . .

(Through the bars of the door one sees the prisoners being driven by)

Bridewell *(outside)*   Eleven shillings and I'll turn you loose.

Pickpocket *(outside)*   Eleven shillings? That's highway robbery.

Bridewell *(outside)*   Lock him up!

Miner *(outside)*   I've got at least fifteen shillings in the house. Send for my wife.

Bridewell *(outside)*   Lock him up!

Plume   Filthy scum!

Victoria   You may find it hard to understand, but having you arrested was an act of real friendship, Plume. You are better off here than falling into the snares of the Mollys and Roses who pursue you without appreciating a man of your fine qualities. (**Plume** *remains silent)* The money doesn't matter to me. I've proved that I'm not petty in these matters. But why should I always be the one to finance your debaucheries? (**Bridewell** *comes in with fresh water for* **Victoria***)*

Bridewell *(gleeful)*   Come on, pipsqueak. Time to wash! You're appearing in court.

Victoria   I don't want to wash.

Bridewell   What?

Victoria   I have a cold.

Plume   He has a cold.

Victoria   Yes, I have a cold. *(She sneezes)*

Plume   Whatever made you join the army? I mean, if you're so delicate and inclined to colds.

(**Bridewell** *pours the water into the pail)*

Victoria *(shouting at the constable)*   I told you I have a cold!

Bridewell   I can't make out why these people never want to wash.

Plume *(cruelly)*   I suppose you just sprinkle powder on it. Cleanliness is the hallmark of a good soldier. Before washing, a soldier removes his clothes. With soap, and, if necessary after field drill, with pumice, he cleanses all parts of his body.

Bridewell   Take off your coat and wash!

Victoria   No.

Plume   He likes dirt, that's what it is.

Bridewell   In the name of the king, off with your coat and wash!

Victoria   Not as long as I live. *(She eludes* **Bridewell** *and he chases her)*

Victoria   Captain!

Plume   No rough stuff, constable. *(Motions him to stop)*

Bridewell   Fusses like a blooming woman.

Plume   Doesn't he, though? *(* **Bridewell** *goes out)* It's not just a question of physical cleanliness, Wilful; you're a deplorable character in every respect. You malinger, you squirm out of things, and you try to deceive your superiors. You are neither honest nor straightforward. Your motives for joining the army are obscure. How do I know you're not a common spy?

Victoria   That's not fair, captain.

Plume   How dare you! And where's your soldierly bearing? I'll teach you discipline. On duty and off, I set the tone around here, understand? Altogether, your behavior is an offense to the moral standards of our profession. No back talk! Let one example suffice: an ensign keeps his fingers out of his captain's love affairs, even if it kills him. Now I shall have to see how I can make it up to that poor girl. To top it all, you seem to have disappointed her. She didn't seem very enthusiastic about you this morning, Wilful. But in spite of all that, because I still feel an inexplicable liking for you, I'll make you a fair proposition. Tear up that note. For two pounds the constable will let you go.

Victoria   No. Besides, you haven't left me two pounds.

Plume   Then you'll stop at nothing?

Victoria   That's right. You must pay your debts.

(In the background more prisoners are led past)

Unemployed Man *(outside)*   You've no right to lock me up just because I can't find work.

Another Prisoner *(outside)*   The mills have shut down.

Bridewell *(outside)*   But the barracks are open. Get in there!

Unemployed Man *(outside)*   It's a bloody shame!

Bridewell *(outside)*   Halt! Who said that? You've insulted the constabulary. I'm turning you over to the dragoons.

(**Kite** *brings in another prisoner, the banker* **Smuggler**, *wearing a lady's dressing gown over his fine underwear)*

Smuggler   For the last time I'm asking you to return my clothes. *(He smiles and bows to* **Plume** *and* **Victoria**) A mistake, gentlemen.

Kite   Were you or were you not in Chicken Street? *(Goes out)* *(Smuggler offers cigars.* **Victoria** *declines.* **Plume** *takes two)*

Smuggler   Gentlemen! Boston has fallen, and with it the stock-market. Obviously firm measures are in order. The decimated ranks of our regiments must be replenished—but not with bankers! If you start putting *us* in the army, we may decide to let the New World go. What would that do to your profession, young man?

(**Worthy** *bursts in)*

Worthy *(to* **Bridewell***)*   Open up, you blockhead! *(* **Bridewell** *unlocks the door)* Mr. Smuggler. Some subordinate has blundered. Come with me. A thousand pardons. Hello, Plume.

Smuggler   Captain Plume, your servant.

(Leaves with **Worthy** *and* **Kite***)*

(**Plume** *offers* **Victoria** *a cigar. They smoke in silence for a while)*

Plume   Wilful, I find it hard to understand how Victoria could choose a messenger of your stamp.

Victoria   Perhaps she couldn't get any other. ("Loch Lomond" *is heard from backstage*)

Plume   It's the same old story, Wilful. Miss Balance and I have failed to make contact again.

*(Tears well up in **Victoria's** eyes, she steps aside with dignity)*

Plume   Since it's "marriage or nothing" in these latitudes, as it should be, I suppose nothing will come of it, except that I'll go wandering through the foggy forests of Massachusetts, the corn fields of Virginia, the swamps of Delaware, and the burning prairies of Maryland with the image of a wonderful girl in my heart.

Victoria *(angrily)*   I should have thought Miss Balance deserved a better fate than to have her image carried through burning cities along with the drunkards, thieves and desperadoes of all sorts that you will be in command of from now on. Aren't you ashamed of such a company? I shall discard my uniform without delay, and I urge you to do the same.

Plume *(wearily)*   Go right ahead. (**Victoria** *takes fright)* Let me tell you something; a cheese on the shelf wants to be paid for before it's eaten. But one thing it doesn't do—it doesn't bite the customer in the leg.

*(Enter **Bridewell** with **Plume's** hat and sword)*

Bridewell   The justice of the peace wants you in court right away, captain. He is furious about your being arrested.

Victoria   What about the note?

Plume   Look here! I'm riding off in the morning and embarking the day after, note or no note. Our brief acquaintance has now come to an end. When I come back in a year or two, if I do come back, I hope I find you less designing.—Your servant, Miss Victoria Balance. *(Goes out)*

Victoria   Go to the devil, you beast! *(Starts bawling)*

Interlude before the Curtain

Worthy *leads* **Mr. Smuggler** *past quickly, covering him with his coat. They are followed by* **Bridewell***, who is pulling a number of prisoners along on a rope. The last prisoner is the miner, who sings loudly.*

Miner *(sings)*

Everybody paid—more or less
When the king was in distress
Armies cost a lot each day
All paid up without delay
All except for E.N. Smith

Bridewell   Quiet!

Miner

But the king got very tough
Didn't think they gave enough
Plucked them out of bed and alehouse
Packed them all off to the jailhouse
All except for E.N. Smith.

In the house of Mr. Balance.

The library, where Simpkins is waiting with the judicial robes.
Balance *receives* **Plume** *in the adjoining ball, which has been converted into a courtroom.*

Balance Captain Plume! Excuse this unfortunate incident.
Do permit me to advance you the thirty pounds. Bridewell!
(**Bridewell** *comes in and* **Balance** *gives him the money)* Give
this to the ensign—what's his name again?—in return for the note.
(**Bridewell** *goes out)*

Plume Thank you, Mr. Balance.

Balance Your ensign seems to be a rather peculiar fellow. The
impudence of the man!

Plume Yes, indeed. Just between you and me, sir, a most unusual
person, obstinate and totally unfit for military service. I've had to
discharge him.

Balance Aren't you being a bit too hard on him? My dear captain
You will sit beside me on the bench. Captain Brazen ought to be
here before long. *(He goes into the library)*

Plume Thank you, Mr. Balance. *(He glances through the list of
names)*

Simpkins *(in the library, helping* **Balance** *on with his robe)* I
understand the raid last night was rather productive, sir.

Balance Yes. There are always plenty of rogues.

Simpkins I presume that not a few of them will be put to the
sword.

Balance Don't be so bloodthirsty, Simpkins.

Simpkins Yes, sir. Shrewsbury expects a good deal of today's trial.

(**Melinda** *and* **Lucy** *come in)*

Melinda   My life is shattered, sir. Captain Brazen, whom an incomprehensible caprice led me to encourage, has resigned from the army, and I feel obligated to him.

Balance   What about Worthy?

Melinda   That's just it!

Balance   What's this about quitting the service in the midst of a war? Just when Boston has fallen! I won't stand for it. What would become of England?

Simpkins   Monstrous!

Balance   I beg your pardon?

Melinda   But uncle, how can you make him stay in the service?

Balance   Leave that to me, my child. *(Ponders for a moment)* Civil law—false representations concerning non-existent dowry.

Melinda   Uncle, you *must* send him off to America!

Balance   Don't worry. Lucy, what do you know of your mistress's intimate affairs?

Lucy   Nothing, sir.

Balance   In other words, everything. Lucy, go and find Captain Brazen. Tell him you've been sent by your mistress, who is at home, choking with tears. Tell him her entire fortune was invested in a cargo of tea, which the rebels have wantonly dumped into Boston harbor.

Lucy   My wages!

Balance   Tell him that in view of her misfortune Miss Moorhill feels she can no longer expect the captain to abandon his glorious military career. If Captain Brazen shows any signs of chivalry, self-sacrifice or sincere devotion, which seems unlikely, you must ask him for two pounds for the household That should bring him to his senses.

Lucy   Is the money really gone, sir?

Balance   Run along now, Lucy, and trust your masters.

Lucy   Very well, sir. But in money matters, I like to know where I stand. *(Goes out)*

Melinda   Uncle, I don't know how I shall ever repay you.

Simpkins *(to the departing* **Balance***)*   God be with you, sir.

(**Kite** *and* **Pearmain***, the latter carrying bundles of uniforms, come into the adjoining courtroom.* **Bridewell** *brings in the* **Pickpocket** *and puts him under the measuring rod;* **Pearmain** *takes his measure. The public enters from the other side of the hall)*

Unemployed Man's Wife   They got my husband. Did they get yours?

Miner's Wife   Yes, they got mine too.

The Broad-Shouldered Man   They want to put them all in the army.

Jenny   They've gone through all the taverns.

Mrs. Cobb   And certain other houses as well.

Unemployed Man's Wife   I hear they've nabbed a banker and an officer.

The Broad-Shouldered Man   You won't see them here, you can lay to that.

Bridewell   Silence!

(**Balance** *has come into the courtroom in the meantime, and has walked up to the table)*

Balance   The court is in session.

Plume   Name?

Pickpocket   Billy Pickpocket.

Kite   If it please the court, I would like to testify in this case as king's counsel.

Balance   You have the floor, sergeant.

Kite   Bridewell, where's the watch? *(Turning to the pimp)* Freddy, this individual stole a gold watch from you, am I right?

Pimp   It's the gospel truth, mister.

Pickpocket   Beg your pardon, Your Worship. It's my watch.

Kite   Can you prove to the court that this is your watch, Freddy?

Pimp   Tell 'em, Kitty.

Kitty   Your Worship, I gave Freddy a watch for his birthday. It's got a scratch on the back.

Kite   That's the one!

Kitty   "Kitty," he says to me, he says: "Kitty, if I ever have to wallop you, just say: 'Freddy, the watch!' "

Pimp   She's too free with her money, Your Worship. And don't talk so much.

Balance *(to the* **Pickpocket***)*   A clear case of pickpocketing. That man is fit for military service.

Kite   Absolutely.

Plume   Take him away.

(The **Pickpocket** *is led away;* Freddy *starts to leave too)*

Jenny   They're picking up everybody they can lay their hands on.

Kite *(calls out)*   Just a minute, Freddy. *(Addressing the bench)* Name: Freddy Big. *(To* **Kitty***)* Kitty, is this wretched watch the only thing you ever gave your protector?

Kitty   You don't know my Freddy, Mr. Kite. Whatever I takes in, he takes offa me. Ouch!

(The pimp has slapped her face)

Kite   Your Worship, I believe that does it. I can't save you after that, Freddy, that's pimping.

Pimp   Bartholomy, that ain't fair.

Kite   In the name of the king, I declare this man to be a brutal, lazy and greedy element, and consequently fit for the army.

Balance   Take him away.

(The pimp falls down in a faint. He is measured and dragged off)

Kitty *(as the* **Court Attendant** *leads her out)*   Freddy, I didn't do it on purpose.

The Broad-Shouldered Man   Fine grenadiers they're getting.

Miner's Wife   Good enough for over there.

Unemployed Man's Wife   It's only the scum that's going over now.

(**Brazen** *comes in wearing civilian clothes)*

Balance   There's Brazen!

Brazen   You'll have to excuse me, Mr. Laconic, I'm retiring into private life. I'm getting married.

Balance   You don't say! In spite of everything? Amazing! Permit me to prepare Melinda.—Bridewell, who's next?

Brazen   Is she here? *(Runs after* **Balance***)*

Balance *(goes into the library; to* **Melinda***)*   I'm so sorry, my dear, I was mistaken.

Brazen *(has followed* **Balance** *into the library)*   Melinda! *(In the courtroom the miner is brought in and measured)*

Miner's Wife   Bob!

Brazen *(in the library)*   My nymph! The parson is waiting, we must leave this instant, my love.

(**Melinda** *faints)*

Brazen *(to* **Balance***)*   Happiness, my dear fellow.

Unemployed Man's Wife *(in the courtroom)*   Where did they nab him?

Miner's Wife   At the Blue Bear; peacefully drinking his ale. Be sensible, don't make a fuss.

(Lucy hurries through the courtroom into the library)

Lucy   I've looked all over for you, Mr. Brazen—at the inn, at the hat shop . . .

Brazen   Hahaha! I was at the flower shop.

Balance   Ah, you missed him, he knows nothing. The world's beginning to make sense again. Tell him.

Lucy   Mr. Brazen, Miss Moorhill is beside herself. We have to ask you for two pounds for household expenses. All Miss Moorhill's money was invested in a cargo of tea. The rebels have dumped it in Boston harbor.

Brazen   All of it?

Lucy   All of it.

Brazen   Damnation! The scoundrels! It goes without saying that this relieves you of any obligation to me. Your servant, madam. *(Goes out)*

Balance   Simpkins! *(Simpkins comes in)* Take Miss Moorhill to the parlor.

(Balance returns to the courtroom. Simpkins and Lucy leave the library with the unconscious Melinda)

(In the courtroom Bridewell steps forward with the miner)

The Broad-Shouldered Man *(to The Miner's Wife)*   Your husband has visible means of support. Which means they can't put him in the army. That's the law.

Plume   Name?

Miner   Bob Miner, sir.

Balance   What have you got on him, Bridewell?

Bridewell   Nothing, Your Worship, except that he's a very decent fellow.

Balance   Then why have you brought him here?

Plume   Mr. Balance, let me at least have *one* decent fellow in my company.

Balance   Trade?

Miner   Miner. I work in the colliery.

Miner's Wife   See! My husband has visible means of support. *(Pause)*

The Broad-Shouldered Man   See?

Kite   If it please the court, this man's means of support is not visible; he works underground.

Miner's Wife   It's work, though.

Balance   You can't be a miner any more, you shall be a grenadier. Thanks to you, other miners will be able to remain miners.

Miner   But I'm a married man.

Balance   Don't you know that we've lost Boston?

Miner   No, Your Worship. I don't know the gentleman.

Balance   You mean you don't even know what Boston is? Is that all the fate of England means to you? Into the army with you!

Plume   Take him away.

Miner   Pack of skunks! *(He is led away)*

Miner's Wife *(as she is being dragged off)*   You can't do this! Bob! I'm going to have a child!

Unemployed Man's Wife   What's Boston got to do with him!

Jenny   The whole thing is illegal.

The Broad-Shouldered Man   It's legal, but . . .

Wife Of Unemployed Man   They make the laws to suit themselves.

The Broad-Shouldered Man   That's it!

Bridewell   Silence!

Mrs. Cobb *(to* **Bridewell***)*   Stop shouting.

(Enter **Victoria** *in the uniform of an ensign)*

Victoria *(to* **Balance***)*   My name is Wilful, sir. Captain Plume, the gentleman sitting beside you, must not be permitted to leave England under any circumstances. The wrong he has done is so appalling that I can speak of it only if you clear the court, sir.

Balance *(under his breath)*   Victoria, have you lost your mind?

Victoria   Oh, you've recognized me?

Balance   What is the meaning of this ridiculous masquerade? Go into the library at once! *(* **Victoria** *goes out)* Next!

Mrs. Cobb   They're bringing one in.

Unemployed Man's Wife   John!

Bridewell   Silence in the court!

Jenny   You're worse than wolves.

Balance *(to* **Victoria** *in the library)*   So you ran after him.

Victoria   You must stop him leaving England.

Balance   Is that all?

Victoria   You must marry us at once.

Balance   Are you out of your mind?

Victoria   Do you want your daughter to become a camp follower, creeping after an officer, abandoning herself to him in some ditch? She has done everything in her power to resist her emotions. All in vain. She can't go on much longer; not another minute!

Balance   Great God! That damned Plume. *(Calls into the courtroom)* Plume!—Bridewell, send for Captain Brazen.

Jenny   What's up with the ensign?

(**Plume** *goes into the library)*

The Broad-Shouldered Man *(referring to* **Plume** *who walks into the library)*   Looks like the captain's nose isn't quite clean either.

Balance *(to* **Victoria** *in the library)*   So you've been pulling the wool over my eyes. Hiding a criminal love affair under the king's uniform. Captain Plume, I know all. What have you got to say for yourself?

Plume   Well, Mr. Wilful . . .

Balance   Mr. Wilful! You persist in speaking of a Mr. Wilful to me?

Plume   Yes, sir. Mr. Wilful.

Balance   Mr. Wilful?

Plume   Yes, Mr. Wilful and . . . *(To* **Victoria***)* I'm surprised to see you in this uniform. Haven't I told you explicitly that I forgo the pleasure of having you in my company?

Victoria   William, we mustn't deceive father any longer. Forgive your Victoria; at this juncture she must tell the truth. Father, we are married.

Balance   Ah!

Victoria   We are married in soldier fashion. We soldiers need no preacher, marriage bells, or license. Our sword is our honor. We lay it down on the ground. First the young hero jumps over it, then the amazon. The buck leaps and the whore jumps. A roll of drums and off to bed. That's how we get married. The ceremony is brief and dignified. And now your daughter is bearing twins.

Balance   This is too much!

Plume   On my honor, sir . . .

Victoria   Yes, yes, William, defend your honor and deny everything, dishonor me a second time and deal me the finishing blow by saying "There has been nothing between us."

Plume   I'm surprised at you, Victoria.

Balance   Is that all you have to say?

Plume   Surely you don't believe all this?

Balance   I believe it. I know my daughter.

Plume   There has been nothing between us, sir.

Victoria   Nothing! Do you call this nothing! You induce me to put on a uniform and charge me forty pounds for it, you lure me to America to keep me near you! Nothing?!

Balance   Nothing indeed! You'll have to get married at once!

Victoria   Marry a soldier? Never! Captains are notorious for turning everything they can lay their hands on into cash. They have an inborn aversion to anything green. Sir, I own forests!

Balance   Quite right. Plume, you will have to quit the service at once.

Plume   That's ridiculous.

Balance   What's ridiculous?

Plume   It's my profession, sir!

Balance   Your profession! And my reputation?

Plume   And my duty to England?

Balance   And your duty to my daughter?

(The loud voices in the library have caught the attention of the people in the courtroom)

The Broad-Shouldered Man   What's going on in there?

Kite   Shh!

Balance   You have unlawfully pressed a female into service with the object of abducting her to America. I'll give you five minutes to think it over. It's a father's blessing: my daughter plus twelve hundred pounds a year—hm, let's say one thousand pounds— or the full force of the law: bread and water in a dungeon. *(To Victoria)* Take off those rags.

(Victoria goes out)

(**Balance** *returns to the courtroom*)

Balance *(calling through the window)*   Mike!

The Broad-Shouldered Man *(to* **The Unemployed Man's Wife***)*
Your husband had better not say he's out of work or they'll nab him for sure.

Unemployed Man's Wife   They'll be in for a big surprise.

Balance *(at the window)*   Mike! A jug of ale! *(To* **Bridewell***)*
Where *is* Captain Brazen? Next! *(Sits down)* Name?

Unemployed Man   John Workless. Unemployed.

Balance   Well, constable, what are the charges against this man?

Bridewell   With your permission, sir, there are no charges against this man.

Unemployed Man's Wife   That's right.

Balance   What did you bring him here for?

Bridewell   Please, Your Worship, I don't know.

The Broad-Shouldered Man   What does it say in the warrant?

Bridewell   I can't read.

Kite   May it please the court. The country can spare this man, the army needs him. Besides, he's cut out by nature to be a grenadier.

The Broad-Shouldered Man   He's chicken-breasted.

Unemployed Man   Do you want a punch on the nose?

Bridewell   Silence!

Kite   In wrestling and boxing he'll take on all comers. He's the quickest man with a knife in the whole county. Every Saturday night he gets drunk and beats up his wife.

Unemployed Man's Wife   That's a bloody lie. He's the kindest, most considerate man in the parish. My five young ones will bear me out.

Mrs. Cobb   There's one with five kids!

Balance   Tell me, my friend, how do you provide for your wife and five children?

Unemployed Man   I don't.

Unemployed Man's Wife   That's the truth.

Kite   Poaching, sir. The man has picked off every hare and partridge for five miles around. He's got a gun.

Balance   A gun! If he likes to shoot, he ought to be picking off rebels.

Mrs. Cobb   A woman with five children!

Unemployed Man's Wife   Yes. That's why they want to send my husband away. They know I get one every year and they're afraid they'll be a burden to the parish.

Kite   Mr. Balance, this honest woman has hit the nail on the head. Won't the township be better off taking five children under its wing now than six or seven next year? With his nutritious, stimulating diet, this man is capable of saddling you with two or three little poachers at a go.

Unemployed Man's Wife   Look here, sergeant. The parish won't get on any better by sending my John away. As long as there's a man left in this town, I'll saddle you with kids.

Balance   Put that woman in the workhouse! Take her away! (**Bridewell** *leads her off*) As for the husband . . .

Kite   I'll take care of him, Mr. Balance.

Mrs. Cobb   What about the children?

Balance   Clear the court! (**Bridewell** *and the* **Court Attendant** *clear the court*)

Mrs. Cobb   There must be somebody we can complain to.

The Broad-Shouldered Man   There is—the justice of the peace.

Jenny   But he's the one who's sending them to the army.

The Broad-Shouldered Man   That's just it.

Balance   Bridewell, call the next. *(Goes off into the library)*

Balance   Your answer, sir?

Plume   All this is unlawful, sir. You can't do a thing to me.

Balance   I've asked you for your answer.

Plume   Now that my company is up to strength.

Balance   Your answer, sir?

Plume   So far I have never seen your daughter dressed in a manner that would make marriage conceivable.

Balance   It's either my daughter, or debtors' prison.

Plume   Did you say twelve hundred pounds?

Balance   One thousand.

Plume   Twenty-four hundred.

Balance   Never.

(Returning to the courtroom, he sees **Mike** *bringing in a jug of ale and gives him a strange look)*

Balance   Look here, Mike, why aren't you in the army?

Mike   I can't go, Your Worship, I'm under eighteen.

Balance   You never knew your father or mother; you grew up in the orphanage. How would you know how old you are? I decide on your age, you oaf! That's the law. Eighteen and a half. Take his measure.

(**Mike** *is measured and led away)*

Balance   All orphans are in my care. Bridewell, next!

Bridewell   There aren't any more.

Balance   No more? There were twelve a minute ago.

Bridewell   They're all gone now.

Balance   Usher!

Attendant   Mr. Balance?

Balance   I understand they're all gone?

Attendant   Please, Your Worship, Bridewell let them go after they'd each paid him eleven shillings. As usual.

Balance *(to* **Bridewell***)*   You're discharged! No, you're not discharged, you're being handed over to Mr. Kite. Take his measure.

Bridewell *(reaches in his pocket)*   Just a minute, Mr. Balance. I intend to buy my discharge. I'll go as high as two pounds.

Balance   Two pounds? All you've got.

Bridewell   All?

Balance   All. On the table!—All! Including what you took from the ensign. *(* **Bridewell** *pays)* Excellent. Take his measure.

Bridewell   But I've paid up, sir!

(**Pearmain** *puts him under the measuring rod)*

Bridewell *(waves him aside)*   Five foot. *(He is led away)*

Balance   Mr. Kite, Shrewsbury wishes to provide your new company with a flag. *(* **Kite** *pockets* **Bridewell's** *money)* Now let us compare your roll with my record. *(They sit down and compare lists)*

*(***Victoria** *comes into the library dressed as a woman.* **Plume***, smoking his cigar, looks at her silently)*

Victoria   Are you angry with me?

(**Plume** *does not answer)*

Victoria   Is that all you have to say?—Since you hate me that much . . . I shall withdraw my charges. I don't want to force you . . .

Plume *(grinning)*   I understand.

Victoria   William.

Balance *(in the courtroom)*   Correct.—Read the Articles of War!

Kite   Captain Plume will have to do that.

Balance   You won't be seeing him again. *(Goes into the library)*

Victoria   What is it you don't like about me, William? Is it my hair style? Is it my dress? All that can be changed.

Balance   So it can.

Plume   I've made my decision.

Victoria And Balance   Yes?

(**Brazen** *comes in, still in civilian clothes)*

Brazen   Mr. Laconic.

Balance   Still in civilian dress?

Brazen   I'm dreadfully upset. The tailor has made a child's coat out of my uniform.

Plume *(takes off his coat)*   Take mine, old boy.

Brazen   You're quitting?

Victoria   William!

Brazen   Eureka!

Balance   The solution!

Brazen   Is she the one? Congratulations! Hold on, I've seen that face before. *(They toss each other their coats)*

*(***Victoria** *helps* **Plume** *and* **Balance** *helps* **Brazen** *put them on)*

Plume   Mr. Balance, I've decided in favor of the twenty-four hundred pounds.

Balance   Never!—Captain Brazen, read the Articles of War.

Brazen   At once, sir! Who to?

Plume   Haven't you any recruits at all, man?

Brazen   Not a one.

Plume   Take my company.

Brazen   Plume, brother, do you mean that? Where is it?

Plume   In my left-hand pocket.

Brazen *(pulls out a document)*   I'm your man forever!

*(**Brazen** rushes into the courtroom and bellows at **Kite**, who in the meantime has lined up the recruits)*

Brazen   I shall now read the Articles of War!

Balance *(in the library)*   And herewith I empower you as her husband to punish her as you see fit.

Victoria   William!

Brazen *(in the courtroom, begins to read the Articles of War)*   Whosoever . . . *(Mumbles)*

Plume *(in the library)*   Sir, a town besieged by a regiment may defend itself.

Brazen *(in the courtroom)*   . . . will be shot! Whosoever . . . *(mumbles)*

Plume *(in the library)*   Faced with an army, it hands over the keys.

Brazen *(in the courtroom)*   . . . will be shot! Whosoever . . . *(mumbles)*

Plume *(in the library)*   Safe from battlefield injuries, I look resolutely forward to the prospect of gout.

Brazen *(in the courtroom)*   . . . will be shot! Whosoever . . . *(mumbles)*

Plume *(in the library)*   To your love, Victoria, I sacrifice my ambition.

Brazen *(in the courtroom)*   . . . will be shot!

Plume *(in the library)*   More glorious to be defeated by your charms than to conquer all America.

Victoria   William!

Brazen *(in the courtroom)*   In short: all will be shot. Everybody about turn—quick march! *(Led by* **Brazen**, *the recruits leave)*

(Outside, the round of drums and marching feet)

*(***Simpkins** *enters the library)*

Simpkins   That's the recruits from Welshpool. Shrewsbury is trailing behind!

Balance *(shouts at him)*   Pull yourself together, Simpkins. And fetch the champagne.

(**Simpkins** *goes out)*

Lucy *(who has meanwhile rushed into the library through the courtroom)*   Mr. Balance! *(She pulls him back into the courtroom)* They're taking my Mike.

Balance   England needs him.

Lucy   What about me?

Balance   What about you?

Lucy   I need him too.

Balance   Get the boy out of your head, he's going to be a grenadier.

Lucy   Mike W. Laughton has other plans, sir, and if you don't set him free

Balance   What then?

Lucy   Then everybody is going to find out who gets to be an ensign around here.

Balance   Lucy!

Lucy   Mr. Balance . . .

Balance   Usher, bring back the potboy. *(* **Court Attendant** *brings back* **Mike**. **Kite** *follows)*

Kite   What about this man, Mr. Balance?

Balance   For the last time: how old are you, Mike?

Mike   I think I'm seventeen, Your Worship.

Balance   Do you think you can drag off children to America, sergeant? The boy is only seventeen. This is an outrage! Discharge him at once.

Lucy   The uniform will be handed in, *(She helps* **Mike** *take off the coat. Assisted by* **Lucy***,* **Mike** *totters over to the bench.* **Lucy** *hands* **Kite** *the coat)*

Kite   Please, Mr. Balance! Now we're short *another* man!

Balance   We almost forgot this one. *(To the attendant)* How much did you get from that rogue Bridewell? Shut your mouth! Enlist him in the company!

Kite   Thank you, Mr. Balance. *(He hands the uniform to the* **Court Attendant** *; both leave)*

(Worthy comes in)

Worthy   Thank you, Mr. Balance. Where's Melinda?

Melinda *(rushes into the library)*   Here!

Worthy *(also rushing into the library)*   Melinda!

Melinda   Albert! *(They embrace)*

*(***Lady Prude** *arrives with* **Mr. Smuggler***, the banker)*

Prude   My respects, Mr. Balance. A historical day for Shrewsbury!

Smuggler   England's on the march again. I take my hat off to you, Mr. Balance.

(All have gathered in the courtroom. **Simpkins** *has brought in champagne and glasses. From outside the departing recruits are heard singing a soldier's song)*

Recruits

Come on Johnny, take your gear
In Virginia you won't hear
Children's screams or woman's plea
Over the hills and over the sea.

Balance *(lifts his glass)*   To good old England!

Mike *(to **Lucy** , aside)*   To a *new* one, a better one!

Smuggler   Long live English liberty, at home and overseas.

Lucy *(aside to **Mike**)*   To us.

Prude   Prosperity to our colonies over the sea!

Mike *(aside to **Lucy**)*   May they be free!

Simpkins   Let God prevail!

(A cork pops)

Recruits

Our King George is older now
Care and worry crease his brow
His empire's gone for a cup of tea
Over the hills and over the sea.

Brazen *(calls up from the street)*   Mr. Laconic, your servant and so forth.—Good day, Mr. Smuggler. *(To **Plume**)* Congratulations on a fine catch, Plume.

Plume *(at the window)*   Kite!

Kite *(from the street, coldly)*   A pleasant evening to you, *Mister* Plume.

Recruits

Sweetheart, if I'm left to die
Happiness will have passed us by
While good King George reigns immovably
Over the hills and over the sea.

(The song fades away)

Simpkins *(sobbing)*   England, England, first and always!

Balance   And now: off to the pheasant shoot!

All Together   Ah!

Balance   Simpkins! The coach and four!

Notes

THE TUTOR

Texts by Brecht

Notes to *The Tutor*

Result of the Rehearsals

The Berliner Ensemble's production of *The Tutor* was directed by a collective consisting of Brecht, Neher, Monk, and Besson. Neher's episodic sketches served as a basis for the arrangements, while most of the suggestions put forward by the collective and by the actors were tested out, usually in accordance with instructions shouted from the stalls, even at the most delicate moments. This testing meant that the usual psychological discussion could be dispensed with, while the shouts hampered the (equally usual) establishment of a "creative climate," in which consciousness comes off second best. The rehearsals lasted for nine weeks, and for at least five hours each day. Under R. Berlau's direction photographs and descriptions of the production were prepared for a "Model Book," from which the following extracts come.

Prologue

The prologue in front of the curtain was spoken to the delicate sound of a music box. As the speaker was being made to stand for the entire historical species known as Hofmeister [or household tutor to a noble family], he was given something of the mechanical quality of a figure on a performing clock; the movements of his head and limbs were jerky and his speech clipped. The impression given was by no means dainty, more on the sinister side, not least because of the cynical grin accompanying the words "Those nobles made me only too willing," together with the cynically discreet shielding of the mouth at "the sorry state of Germany." Despite a certain snapping of the jaw, and a double jerk at every bow, as is usual with automata, the whole thing was not pressed too far but remained in the realm of suggestion, never obscuring the fact that the actor was alive. In later performances, however, he developed the same doll-like quality further, and we had a high enough regard for his virtuosity to allow this.

1. Bowing and scraping

The scene is the street outside the privy councillor's garden gate. It shows Läuffer* working his beat, as it were. He lies in wait for the major as the latter takes his customary walk accompanying the privy councillor home after their morning glass. The two brothers pause in conversation while still a few paces from the gate, and only move on when Läuffer approaches, pretends to be surprised at the encounter, and begins while still at a distance to execute his first long-drawn, careful bow. They walk past him without acknowledgment; none the less he hurriedly makes two further bows, likewise while walking. Chilled by his reception, he gives the brothers a nasty look over his shoulder, then turns round and performs a fourth bow to their backs, cursing the while under his breath. (It took us five rehearsals to realize that he must utter his curses during the bow and not after it, which shows how easy it is at the outset to overlook the most obvious and essential points.) Meanwhile the brothers speak of Läuffer in the most indifferent manner, as the privy councillor fishes out one of his many keys and opens the gate. Laughingly saying "He may be good enough for that," he gives the major a pat on the shoulder and lets him into the garden, where the major pauses and studies a plant at the foot of the wall. The fern in question interests him only mildly, but it is enough to overshadow whatever interest he has in Läuffer; he is far more deeply concerned by its history than by that of the man who is to be in charge of his children's education. This scene will not work properly unless the privy councillor puts his question "But tell me, brother, do you know . . ." with sudden concern, to be answered by the major with a great vague shrug of the shoulders.

---

* [In these notes the characters are referred to by the names given them by Brecht, which are generally the same as in Lenz's original. As these are in many cases fabricated word portraits (cf. Sir Toby Belch, Captain Brazen, Lady Dumbello, etc.), in our English version of the text they have been translated as follows:

Läuffer (from *laufen,* to run, and *läufig,* in heat)—Hasty
Pätus (from Latin *paetus,* cross-eyed)—Squint
Bollwerk (bulwark)—Buttress
Jungfer Rehhaar—Miss Swandown
Jungfer Watten—Miss Cotton
Jungfer Rabenjung—Miss Gosling
Gustchen (Lenz's diminutive of Augusta) has been anglicised into Gussie.]

2. The lovers' parting

The privy councillor, who, being better off than his brother "wouldn't want anything cheap," is not prepared to make do with a tutor for his son Fritz but sends him to Halle university instead—which of course allows a tutor to have undisputed access to his girl Gustchen. Their parting scene must show delicately how the young von Berg fends off his cousin; she wants him to take her into the summer-house, but he takes her through Klopstock instead, until he finds the latter filling him with irrepressible feelings and flings her on the bed as he swears his oath: a literary detour. The lovers are separated by his olympian father, with the result that, having been parted in the name of reason, they end up just as remote from one another as at the beginning. He goes off in order to become worthy of her, and by so doing makes certain that she will become unworthy of him.

3. Engaging a tutor

The trail has been laid. The daughter of the house has been sensually aroused, and this has been further aggravated by the fact that her lover's departure deprives her of him. The family is vulnerable, the tutor can be taken on. As he performs one or two minuet steps to the major's wife the poor devil is fighting for his life, the eye which she keeps on his feet is no sharper than his own. He wipes the sweat from his forehead ("My son will not require any other dancing master for the time being"), while she calls for one more *pas*. Meanwhile Leopold, the son he is applying to educate, is catching flies against the wall; he has seen so many employees engaged. Läuffer grunts with pleasure as the major's wife sings her minuet; he has hurried over to turn the pages for her. Then some Prussian provincial French. When, after chiding him for kissing her hand—it's not done in France—she none the less grins graciously and stretches out her paw for a further kiss, Läuffer's success so goes to his head that a faux-pas is bound to follow. He comes forward, between the major's wife at the keyboard and the count on the sofa, and lets the latter know his opinion of the dancer. (Incidentally, this scene failed to work until Läuffer made a distinctive movement to express his "daring to step forward." He had to move down to the centre of the stage; the words alone were not nearly enough.) The gentry freeze; deadly lorgnettes are levelled at him. He stammers out some excuse—the man had been booed off the stage at Koch's theatre—and is dismissed from the room. In his nervousness he nonetheless turns round once more in the doorway on hearing himself talked about, thereby inviting another swipe. After his departure there is a moment's pause. The major's wife sails over to the sofa, the count gets up, walks past her in counter-motion; they approach one another with constrained smiles, then let the smile drop, hurriedly reassuming it as they once more turn towards each other. As he mulls over the scandalous incident, already planning how to present it to further houses, he mechanically pinches the cheek of the maid who serves him his chocolate, before going on to pinch the handle of the cup. The major's wife's final remark answers the question why Läuffer is not sacked: he is cheap.

4. Insterburg rebuffs

Once Läuffer has been put in his place indoors we turn to him again and show that his position also prevents him from finding pasture outside. If necessary this scene can be cut, but it does present Läuffer's situation in a good exteriorized way. It calls for a refined virtuosity (special figure-skating skills on Läuffer's part, an enchanting but simple stage set and so on). We showed Läuffer severely handicapped by his obligation to look after the half-witted Leopold, who at once tumbles over and as soon as the young ladies appear is parked by Läuffer against one of the posts for the lights. When Läuffer runs over to the rear after his vain attempt to establish contact he bares his teeth as evidence of the savage feelings which he is finally to turn against himself. Immediately thereafter he becomes an object of utter ridicule; on getting him back his pupil clumsily pulls himself up, bringing Läuffer to the ground.

5. A new pupil

Now Läuffer can be thrown the bait; we have isolated him both inside and out; he is starved and kept short, and we are now about to lock him in with the eatables and make them tasty and ripe. He must not realize his "good fortune" at once, let us give it to him as an additional exploitation, as overtime work. First we shall reinforce the foundations, thicken the atmosphere of hostility and boredom. Mime can be used to develop the relationship between Läuffer and his pupil Leopold: the very sight of the latter makes Läuffer yawn; by infection Leopold follows suit. There is no chalk for the blackboard; Leopold has it and pushes it over to Läuffer with his foot. The tutor reciprocates with uncontrolled hatred, then starts copying the word "agricola" from the book, but he is so badly prepared that he has to check the spelling after the first two syllables. The major is in a bad mood because he wants the fellow to perform a service which he himself cannot pay for. His efforts to educate his son are a miserable failure.

He charges at him like Zieten's hussars charging the Austrians, renewing the attack in silent desperation when the first effort fails to make Leopold sit up as straight as he wants. Eventually it turns out that he only launched this offensive because he wished to get Leopold out of the room. He then spends some time going round the awkward subject, and his sense of having made a tactical error in arguing about Läuffer's salary is apparently such that when the latter asks for a horse he promises to look into the matter. This is too much for Läuffer. Having resentfully lain down under all the haggling and the imposition of new tasks, he had put his request with every expectation of being refused. Now he outdoes himself in bows, and hastens to display his drawings. The major merely looks at the first of them and shoves the second aside. Standing in the doorway, he warns Läuffer that he must "be gentle with" his daughter.

6. Philosophy and physiology

Now let us have a look at the new pupil's far-away lover, and let us wheel in Halle on our revolving stage. It is here, at the university, that the young store up experiences both on the intellectual and on the physical plane. We see our man Fritz von Berg poised between sacred and profane lovers, between Pätus and Bollwerk. Pätus is scared of his landlady but not of his professor; Bollwerk favours crawling to the professor but has the landlady under his thumb. Fritz opts for philosophy, but goes off to look at girls with Bollwerk. Fritz needs to be presented as the observant guest.

7. Catechism lesson

The daughter of the house is not disinclined to play with fire, and we have seen to it that such playing is made easy for her. Thus Läuffer must not be made to fall in love; he is lost from the outset ("he loves because he wants to go to bed"). Accordingly he seems all the more rigid, a cat among the pigeons, though a cat who is his own trainer. Nonetheless, this scene provides a chance to display Gustchen's social superiority. She combines the resources of her body and of her social position to get him dancing. At the beginning of the scene the teacher is gazing at a smiling pupil, and the story goes on in such a way as to make us believe that this is her attitude to Läuffer's teaching. He successfully stares her down. Guiltily she begins reciting the Creed. "I believe that God created me." When she gets stuck, Läuffer starts moving towards her with loud, measured, deliberate steps which seem to tick off the seconds of the silence between them. As he circles round her, looking down at her derisively, she restarts the sentence in a kind of panic and then, with the man behind her, gets stuck again. Then suddenly she smiles and looks up at him, repeating the last words "created me" with a shift of emphasis from "created" to "me": the graceful and unashamed triumph of the female. From this instant his advance proves to have been an error which leads straight to defeat. The examination conducted by him quickly turns into an examination conducted by her; it is no longer he who helps her out with the right word, but she him. (She openly mocks the schoolmasterly pedantry of his diction [. . .], delivering her "From all perils, and guards and defends me" with her head on one side in such a way as to suggest that it is he who has lost the thread and needs a helping hand. His "protects" is spoken with hopelessness, and his "Without any merit or worthiness in me" contains a childish reproach.) Then comes the row over her drawing lesson. Her haughty assurance that she had no time calls for the utmost self-control on his part. He paces restlessly and painfully to and fro, twists round like a top as on the skating rink, stops abruptly with his ruler tightly gripped between his elbows behind him as if to fetter himself. She looks him over as though he were some intriguing insect and for a moment is almost touched; she goes up to him and apologizes for having disappointed him. He lets this opportunity slip and looks stubbornly away. At once she resumes the employer's mantle and imitates her mother, ("It was quite impossible,") in order to put him in his place. What makes him finally lose control is her teasing remark that drawing is the one thing she enjoys doing. She is genuinely frightened by the savagery of his outburst. Once he has rushed out she stretches self-indulgently: he is a plebeian, with a plebeian's strength.

8. My kingdom for a horse!

Wanted: an outlet. Society's imperious finger points to the brothel. But the unhappy victim of the conflagration cannot get at the sole permissible cooling draught unless his employer first hands him the ladle. Läuffer, abandoned, armed only with a promise (i.e., unarmed), has to choose a mediator, his father, who must in turn address himself to a mediator, the employer's brother.

The eighth scene takes place in the privy councillor's garden, which we already know (from outside) from scene I. In his shirtsleeves, wearing a rustic gardener's apron and broad-brimmed straw hat, the privy councillor, after refusing the pastor's request, bends his knees in order to clip a box tree. Greatly to the disadvantage of Läuffer, who gets no chance to state his practical demand, an ideological argument develops between the two elderly gentlemen, conducted on the pastor's side with irascibility, on the privy councillor's with the infuriating self-control of a man of the world.

The latter too on one occasion gives a look typical of his class ("interesting to see how people like this behave") as the pastor bellows out the words "a shepherd of souls" in a vain attempt to make the authority of the church tell on his side. When Läuffer cannot contain himself his father intervenes, out of concern for his son's dignity. Thus he has to wrestle with his father to get his request for mediation across. His father's presence prevents him from letting the privy councillor have it straight; he feels forced to deny the real objective of the proposed visits. Brutally, the privy councillor states it. Läuffer, a broken man, follows his agitated father to the garden gate, only to turn round once more, stare at the privy councillor with a snort and warn him darkly that something terrible may happen. Then father and son go off in haste, gesticulating angrily as they pass along the garden wall. The privy councillor has raised his voice for just one sentence: "Been feeling your oats?" He carefully now and again clips an overgrown shoot from the box tree with his big shears.

9. The abandoned vacation

While in Insterburg his Gustchen finds herself abandoned to a sex-starved tutor who has been deprived of any outlet, far away in Halle Fritz von Berg undergoes an experience which prevents him from hastening to her rescue, while at the same time giving him the intellectual equipment finally to understand her situation and to forgive it. He sacrifices his holiday money for Mistress Rehhaar, who had slept with the student Bollwerk while thinking allegedly of the student Pätus. What needs to be lightly and comically shown here is the peculiar form of self-castration adopted by German intellectuals of middle-class background, who are capable of experiencing not only other people's revolutions but also their own private life on an exclusively "intellectual plane."

Details

The transition to Pätus' big outburst (from "There are times when I feel almost weary" to "Bollwerk, Bollwerk") needs to be abrupt and utterly unexpected.

Fritz von Berg's attitude in this scene is freer, and he has also begun wearing a Schiller-style shirt. When he thumps his fist on the table after remarking "I too have developed in this Halle of yours" it is out of a sense of having become "one of the boys." With a gesture of freedom he announces his intention not to sleep with his girl. It is the moment of his self-castration, and it bears the same heroic stamp as will the unfortunate Läuffer's.

A good gesture by Fritz: at "Your duty is my duty," his hand is on his heart in true romantic style. A little hesitantly, it creeps down to his waistcoat pocket: "Command my purse."

Pätus counts the twenty thalers out on the table, coin by coin, lending the operation a symbolic significance.

10. *Sooner or later it had to happen*

Lenz had Läuffer sitting by the bed. We thought it would help the development of the story if we showed him and Gustchen in bed together. This needs to be the next thing one sees after seeing how he was denied a horse for his excursions to Königsberg. First and foremost it is the solution to a problem; only then do scruples begin to appear, together with the shadows of difficulties to come. The scene is a difficult one for the actor playing Läuffer. He must never let himself be harsh, merely lost in other thoughts. On top of that he is physically relaxed, sated, even though he finds, poor devil, that reflecting on the possibility of unpleasant consequences sours the long-awaited sensual pleasure. His occasional cynicism (as in the sentence about his over-nourishment, with which he bears out the privy councillor's "Been feeling your oats?") has something helpless about it. He has got up to help himself to Gustchen's morning chocolate on the table. On his return to the bedside his broody mood deepens. Every minute the chasm between the two of them grows wider. Quickly it becomes evident that they have simply been using one another.

So far as Gustchen is concerned the subject of "love by proxy" has already been introduced in the previous scene. At first she is relaxed, stretches out comfortably and speaks with a lazy frivolousness, as if from another planet. She takes his hand briskly as if picking up a prop, puts it on the edge of the bed before her and ponders over it, stroking the air above it as if contact might destroy the illusion that it is Fritz's. Nonetheless there is an underlying sexual satisfaction to the frivolous tone of the first sentences, and when she makes up to Läuffer using the *Romeo and Juliet* monologue she had been saving for Fritz, it is because she is at the same time nervous that he may draw away as soon as he begins thinking. Läuffer's departure is hurried and undignified, and not on his part alone. Reproaching him for having stayed too long, she hands him his vest, which has been lying on the bed, a witness of their union. There is one touching moment for Gustchen in this scene, where she reacts to his "I'm not Romeo, I'm Läuffer" by sitting up, staring at him as if she were seeing an unknown man in her bed, then falling back and weeping. But whatever element of tragedy enters into this must be on Läuffer's side. Where she for him still stands proxy for an anonymous Nature, he for her has to stand proxy for a quite specific man: Fritz.

11. The discovery

Frau von Berg's passion for singing is evidence that ugly and beautiful sentiments are entirely compatible; after all, didn't that Gestapo butcher Heydrich adore his Bach? What makes her performance ugly is not so much her voice as her unbridled energy. When she upbraids her husband the major, meanwhile playing the "Largo," she does so because he is coming from work; he for his part sees music as a source of slovenly conduct, and sweeps the music off the spinet with his hoe. The major's wife's angry lamentations over the family disgrace are made all the more piquant by the audience's knowledge that this is a family where the mother is trying to steal her daughter's suitor (though that is as far as the comic aspect must go). The parts of the major and his wife should be given to actors with vitality; Europe has had two hundred years in which to learn how horribly vital their class is.

12. Läuffer finds a refuge

Läuffer's dark premonitions have been fulfilled. We see him seeking refuge in a village school, hunted like a criminal. Here, in the gutter, everything will be repeated—his aggression, his reduction to impotence, his persecution—except that this time the persecutor is himself. The refuge turns into a rat-trap. The schoolmaster Wenzeslaus' mistrust yields to a recognition that he has found a cheap slave in this victim of persecution who is ready to do anything in exchange for shelter. Soon he has him sitting down at the table correcting exercise books, and is able himself to lean back in his chair and take things easy. The victim has to eat, work, smoke, and listen to self-satisfied homilies all at the same time, and he does all this with crawling humility. The element of exploitation here is so naive and so coated with morality that Läuffer still calls the schoolmaster his benefactor a year later—something that needs to be brought out by the actor. We must combine Wenzelaus' worst features—his appalling sense of humour, his thirst for freedom that can be slaked by beer and cheap gin, his combination of pedantry and high-flying base thoughts, etc.—with as much approach at humanity as can be managed. At the same time the model in whose image he brings up children must be such as to inspire terror.

When the feudal mob bursts in it is a good idea to have the wounded Läuffer lying as long as possible uncared-for: the injustices inflicted on and by him get debated across his bleeding body. The major charges into the room in search of his daughter, then goes on marching to and fro, so as to carry on the search for her by this movement. The privy councillor merely demonstrates fear of scandal. Dramaturgically speaking, the twelfth scene is a seesaw, a plank laid across a beam. The tutor steps on to the plank in the most profound distress, prior to walking further and further up it until his weight makes it tip over and drop him into the bottommost depths.

13. Gustchen at the lake

Leaving Läuffer to a confused fate (which still has one or two things up its sleeve for him) we observe his employers setting their affairs in order. The life-saving scene by the lake will bear a certain amount of comedy; it may be a disaster, but there are servants at one's call. However, true though it may be that tragedy leads a precarious existence wherever the standard of living is high, it would be wrong to strip Gustchen and the major of any kind of seriousness. It should of course be shown how Gustchen waits for her rescuers before wading into the lake, how she takes off her shoes in order to leave them a clue, how she turns round once more in order to add her carefully folded shawl, then steps into the water with her face averted; all this, however, is really because she knows that in their circles anything can be arranged and straightened out, given a little good will. There is more comedy in the count, who has forgotten his status as a suitor and has simply come along to glean impressions for his chronique scandaleuse, likewise in the privy councillor who, being in no position to lift a finger himself, makes do with "organizing" the rescue operation and putting forward observations of an appropriately general kind. The major's accents are entirely serious, as are his wild cursing of the domestics who fail to hand him the pole quickly enough, and the sermon which he reads his daughter. At the end of the scene, when she is in her father's arms, we allowed her to give a contented little waggle of the feet.

14. The self-castration

The fourth act is one of the most subtle ever written, and the whole of it needs to be clearly lifted out of the rest of the play and to have its poetry underlined in such a way that the audience can transfer the self-mutilation from the sexual to the wider intellectual sphere. For it we changed the lighting; by omitting the projections normally used to indicate locality we made a very dark and unfamiliar background without otherwise altering the harsh lighting of the set. In addition we enclosed the three scenes in a musical framework, using Mozart's "Turkish March" scored for harpsichord, cymbals, and piccolos. For the rest we took particular pains to bring out the realistic element in the acting. After all, if this episode is left uninterpreted, presented in its own terms, i.e., signifying nothing more than the dilemma of a poor devil forced to opt for a sexual life or a professional one, it will still be typical enough of the social order in question.

14 a.

This scene shows Läuffer undergoing a nightmare. Once more his sex rises up against him. The arrangement accordingly needs to hark back to scene 7, the catechism lesson. The same way of stalking the victim, of trying to get behind it. The escape to the window. The unsteady walk thence to the wall, as if an invisible storm were blowing a leaf to perdition. The slaps he gives himself with a ruler.

One or two further details: when Lise comes back with the coffee pot and knocks, Läuffer has his pen poised to make a correction. Still holding it thus poised he walks over to the door as in a dream, opens it, takes the pot from Lise, pushes her away, closes the door, comes back to the table, puts the pot down, then finally makes the correction. Lise, as her guardian is dragging her off at the end of the scene, breaks away from him, goes back to the table with averted face and fetches her lamp.

14 b.

Läuffer delivered his soliloquy standing in front of the blackness of the open window. In it the element of speculation predominated, but there was something like an explosion with the phrase "in the presence of her creation," while the decision seemed to be reached with "Shall I pluck out the eye that offends me?" When he ripped off his coat at the end one saw the wildness that marks counter-revolution.

14 c.

For this scene we created total silence; the stormy night of its predecessors was intended purely to let us achieve a silence that should be almost audible. Overturned furniture, scattered clothing provided evidence of the wildness that had gone before. At the end of the scene the snow which was to fall throughout the fifth act became visible for the first time on the cyclorama. Some such mixture of realistic and poetic elements seemed to us absolutely necessary at this point. The big problem for the actors is the breathtakingly swift transition from Läuffer's tragic admission that he has castrated himself to the schoolmaster's hymn of praise. The audience hardly has time to feel sorry for the wretched man before it is once again being asked to feel contempt for him. No sooner has the poor tutor's persecution achieved its goal than the playwright attacks him too. This rapid transition, which is necessary for the development of the comedy since it is only in this way that we can erase the individual, surgical element, works if the actor playing the schoolmaster gives full effect to his emotional shock and likewise to his natural fright, then allows this fright to tinge his "Say no more. You shouldn't have done it!" and calls him a "second Origen" as if he were announcing a discovery.

An alternative solution was suggested by the Swiss playwright Frisch: to start with "You shouldn't have done it!" leaving the audience to wonder nervously what had happened, and in the reading of the letter insert after "by my own decision—a cruel one, I can assure you—" the words "to castrate myself."

In any case it is essential for the actor playing the schoolmaster to remain as realistic as possible, as did Friedrich Maurer in the Berlin production. He said "What, regret it?" with the mild incredulity of someone who observes a hero at a moment of weakness and smilingly recalls him to himself. At the end of the scene, however, he slightly overstressed the note of hearty, optimistic encouragement, as if he still had some faint private doubts.

15. End of an Italian journey

Everything has now been prepared for the ending. The abnormal has been recognized as such; normality once again comes into "its own." The sacrificial rites have been performed; the survivors can get married off.

Now that all is open and above-board we change the set for this last act, without drawing the curtain, against a sky still full of gently falling snow.

The philosopher pats his discreet little tummy and slyly narrates his treachery: that accounts for the first couple. Fritz von Berg remains uneasy. Pacing the room with great strides he describes an Italian journey whose artistic experiences have become increasingly clouded by concern about his Gustchen. Fritz dare not open his letter from home, and when Pätus reads it out to him he collapses in a faint near the stove. Pätus runs for some cold water. Back in his easy chair he offers his "realistic" opinion of women. Karoline Pätus, entering at this point, knows no misfortune whose memory cannot be blotted out by a good cup of coffee. Staggering, Fritz hastens away from the wreckage of his friend to seek the tomb of his beloved.

16. Engagement in the snow

From the outset the second of the closing scenes dispels any fears on the part of the audience and of Fritz von Berg. The von Berg family is tragedy-proof. There is only one brush with the play's more disturbing events: when the young lover, after intellectually reconciling himself to his beloved's unfaithfulness, is led up to the cradle and sees the flesh and blood result. He hesitates for a second or two.

17. Lise gets Läuffer

Finally the most difficult of the endings: that for Läuffer. The scene is set on a Sunday morning and has many festive features. Lise is spreading a snowy-white tablecloth, while the two men concentrate on a dignified subject, the sermon. Läuffer sits and speaks with new-found authority, also with the false modesty that goes with it. None the less he has been robbed of his force. He absorbs the schoolmaster's suggestions that the old Adam is still active in him with nothing more than distaste, Lise's readiness to marry him without particular surprise.

[*Große kommentierte Berliner und Frankfurter Ausgabe* [henceforth BFA], vol. 24, pp. 357–71, also in *Versuche 11* (1951); scenes 13–15 in *Theaterarbeit*. These and the following scene-by-scene notes were written during rehearsals with the Berliner Ensemble in 1950. It was Brecht's intention to make a "Model Book" (an annotated photographic record of a given production) of this production. Insterburg, now called Chernyakhovsk, is near Königsberg (Kaliningrad) in the part of East Prussia annexed by the USSR at the end of the Second World War. The University of Halle near Leipzig was founded in 1694; it is now the Martin Luther Universität Halle-Wittenberg. The Swiss novelist-playwright-architect Max Frisch had seen much of Brecht during the year and a half which he spent based in Zurich.]

On poetry and virtuosity

For some time to come we shall need to talk about the poetry of a play and the virtuosity of its production, something that seemed of little urgency in the recent past. It seemed not merely to lack urgency but to be a positive distraction, and this less because the poetic element had been inadequately developed and appreciated than because it had been used as a pretext for maltreating reality, in that people imagined they would find poetry wherever reality was made to take a back seat. Lies masqueraded as inventiveness, imprecision as lavishness, slavery to prevailing forms as mastery of form, and so on. This made it necessary to test images of reality in the arts for their truth to reality, and to examine the artists' intentions towards it. As a result we were forced to make a distinction between truth and poetry. More recently we have almost given up examining works of art from their poetic (artistic) aspect and made do with works lacking any appeal as poetry and productions from which virtuosity is absent. Such works and such productions may be effective on some level or other, but it cannot be a deep one, nor take a political direction. For it is a peculiarity of the means employed by the theatre that they communicate insights and impulses in the form of pleasures, and that the depth of the latter corresponds to the depth of the former.

What follows is a description of some elements of virtuosity in the performance of *The Tutor* which accompany poetic factors in the play. The fact that the latter in turn accompany social factors is herewith to be noted, but should not hinder anybody from dwelling on those making for poetry and virtuosity.

1

The four bows executed by Läuffer, the first on seeing the two brothers, then a hurried pair of twin bows as he passes them, and a final one, spiced by a curse, to their backs, are, if precisely executed, a piece of virtuosity that gives rhythmical and plastic expression to Läuffer's social subservience, choreographic training, and under-nourishment, not to mention the awkwardness peculiar to him. Setting the scene outside the garden gate of the privy councillor's town residence is poetic, for it helps the spectator to become aware of the brothers' morning glass, of their well-entrenched habits and their comfortable standard of living. With Shakespeare this might have been a bit too much; not so however with Lenz's intimate, small-scale, comedy of manners. None the less the setting is not designed to achieve illusion, this being impeded from the outset by the projecting of a hand-coloured steel engraving in the taste of that time.

2

The realization that people can be drawn together by poetry is itself poetic. A masterly description of the seductiveness that arises from the reading of a love poem can be found in the fifth canto of Dante's *Inferno*. A touch of this poetry, mildly alienated by comic allusions, should enter into the reading of Klopstock by the two lovers. A further factor is the way in which the couple's position at the outset of the scene matches that at the end: both times they are seen in profile, at the same correct distance, except that the second time they have her father sitting between them; it is thanks to him that this distance has been restored. You may ask if such subtleties are noticed by the audience, but it is an unworthy question. Another subtle point is that the audience's attention is drawn to Gustchen's bed when her young lover leads her over to it to swear eternal devotion; in due course we shall see her lying in it with the tutor. At a first seeing of the play, the effect may simply be to suggest that they are only drawn to the bed by the thought of eventual unfaithfulness, but the ensuing tenth scene will become all the more effective, and when the play is seen a second time the former will also gain added significance—one should always reckon with a second visit.

3

For this scene we arranged the lighting effects in a way that can be called poetic. Generally speaking we were not using effects but full lighting. In this case, however, the projections prevented us from making full use of the lighting equipment, while a particular consideration led us to keep the walls at the back noticeably in the dark. The actor playing Leopold caught flies so well and so amusingly as to distract attention from the simultaneous cross-examining of Läuffer. Not having the heart to cramp the young actor's style, we felt forced to take the light off him. This had the poetic advantage that for the rest of the scene only the people of rank, the count and the major's wife, stood out plastically, while Leopold and the maid provided the background, and Läuffer only came into the full light on making his faux-pas, after which he was thrust into the half-darkness again. The little mime in which major's wife, count, and maid change position after the tutor has been thrown out, so that the two persons of rank can be on their own, is a virtuoso element which is described in the notes [see extract 3 above]. Läuffer's examination, where the sweat gathers on his brow as he has to give evidence of his gracefulness, was of course likewise carefully performed as a virtuoso "turn."

4

Scene 4 shows Läuffer in all the loneliness which makes a normal love life impossible for him. He is the cock of the walk being treated as a cat among the pigeons. He shows off his arts, performing the most hazardous leaps. (Läuffer, of course, must under no circumstances be made to appear vain. He is far too busy trying to impress the girls to be carried away by his own impressiveness.) He is brought down by the clumsiness of his pupil, with whom he is already fed up, and this puts the lid on his failure, for which he himself is in no way responsible. For the group of girls we took on a new actress who knew how to giggle. In the event this giggling in itself was evidence of the girls' sexual awareness and inhibitions.

5

It is a poetic factor when Läuffer, having been forced in his loneliness to take on Gustchen as an extra pupil, in return tries bargaining for permission to use a horse to go into Königsberg for "study." This deal is evidence of his initially innocent attitude with regard to Gustchen, but also of the famine from which he suffers.

6

Our demonstration that the freedom in question was thoroughly limited must not be allowed to detract from the account given of the freedom-loving atmosphere in university towns at that time. Even Bollwerk's dirty jokes tend to represent extreme daring. The light needs to be shown here, as well as the bushel that hides it. The costumes were particularly beautiful, with their black breeches and white linen shirts, and there was rhythm and grandeur in the gestures and the movements. It was not so much that the portrayal of the students was romantic as that their romanticism was portrayed.

7

The flame kindled in the sixth scene spread to the seventh in the person of the ex-student Läuffer. Prior to his outburst, admittedly, Läuffer keeps a tight rein on himself. His fate is settled as soon as the audience sees his new pupil sitting there with a smile on her face. The twisting movement by which he at one point recovers himself, and which Gustchen greets with a "I never saw you so deep in thought," recalls the skating figures of scene 4. It is a first-rate poetic invention. So is his use of his schoolmaster's ruler, as he pins himself to it as to a cross-beam, jamming it under his armpits, or raps himself with it to punish his sexual longings. The same rapping process in the fourteenth scene will tell the audience that his sex has once more risen against him.

8

The privy councillor praises freedom's sweetness and necessity, while at the same time clipping back his box trees.—His argument with the pastor about intellectual principles not only blocks Läuffer's request but develops into an agitated dispute between the pastor, who is now full of all kinds of forebodings, and his son; they are seen gesticulating as they walk off behind the garden wall.—And Läuffer's frantic demands (his desperate "my kingdom for a horse!") allow the audience to infer the danger now menacing Läuffer's pupil. (Meanwhile the privy councillor has no idea that his strict stand for morality has delivered his son's fiancée into the tutor's hands.)

9

The second of the Halle scenes once again calls for a certain fire, which must of course be felt to be that of the characters, not of the actors. Though the emotional extravagances of their "intellectual adventures"—a veritable Catalaunian battle whose fallen victims go on fighting in the air—need to appear comic, neither Pätus' despair nor von Berg's spirit of self-sacrifice should be made to seem anything but genuine (e.g., by exaggeration). Nor should Bollwerk and Rehhaar cease to be likeable just because Bollwerk has deceived Pätus while Mistress Rehhaar's predicament forces her to flirt. Young people's problems carry an element of helplessness which makes them touching.

Both Halle scenes were brought round on the revolving stage as the half-curtain opened, so as to allow the happenings in "far-away Halle" to be visibly adduced.

10

The question, what in the narrative should come after what, is a poetic one. We debated whether the second Halle scene should be played between the catechism lesson and the request for a horse, or between the request for a horse and the love scene. We opted for the second, but others may take a different view. It is fine if Läuffer can be seen in Gustchen's bed directly after being refused the horse. On the other hand it is also a good thing if the love scene can be immediately preceded by the second Halle scene with its posing of the problem of love by proxy.

This scene needs to be very much like a real love scene, even though the only yearnings which it satisfies are Gustchen's for Fritz, and Läuffer's which could equally well be satisfied in Königsberg. The union has induced proximity; such distances as remain are due to the disparity of the couple's social positions.

11

We are once again in the realm of beautiful feelings when disaster suddenly irrupts. The major's wife's attempt to woo Count Wermuth—that contrived approach on wings of song—is a grotesque counterpart to the reading of Klopstock in scene 2. Poetic parallels are Tolstoy's *Kreutzer Sonata* and Dante's *Inferno*. The poetic element will be destroyed if the major's wife's performance is so caricatured as to lose *all* charm. It is an act of virtuosity designed to achieve a poetic effect when she plays Handel's "Largo" during her bickering with the major. A certain aesthetic and social-critical piquancy is added if the actor performing the latter can give a superficial flavour to the outraged father's outburst, so that it becomes the banal expression of a social convention. The audience must presume that it will fail. The background to this scene is furnished by the maid's infatuated attentions to the count.

12

One or two anticipated effects: the fact that it is entirely by the power of the human spirit that the schoolmaster succeeds in beating off the first attack of the feudal gang, before naked force bursts in and the shot is fired; the way his initial suspicion of having to deal with a criminal is transformed into confidence in a serf who can be made use of because he has committed a crime and needs a refuge; the way Läuffer's complaint that his victim was forced on him is directed to his next victim.

It also seems legitimate to let the spectator take a certain pleasure in understanding the construction of this pivotal scene which links the two halves of the play. Expelled from the feudal world, Läuffer takes refuge in that of the petty bourgeoisie. He swaps tyrants, his examination is repeated, as is his faux-pas too: having aired his views of the arts in the one, he now raises the question of pay in the other. His trade will be even more lowly than before, his calling definitely nobler.

13

The confused sounding of the tocsin from the village tells the audience that the search operation has begun. We quickly realize that it is going to succeed.—While the girl is being fished for, privy councillor and count indulge in some profound reflections. The former prepares consoling remarks in case she is dead, the latter, being unable to swim, washes his hands of all responsibility.—For an instant or two at the beginning of the scene, however, what was said above about young people's problems still needs to apply.

14

Before a stage of largely bare boards one has the impression of a terrible station on the road to Calvary. The gentle movements to and fro of the confused child, the cup that will not pass. The horse-blanket round Läuffer's shoulders, showing how cold the room is, with a coldness that stimulates the need which it cannot subdue. The teacher raps himself again. Then the victim of seduction turns into a violator.—The violator turns into an avenger. The soliloquy remains a total revolt, the action to which it leads is a blind suppression of revolt of any kind, the action to end all actions.— The greyness of the next morning brings utter weakness, along with its canonization.

Interlude

Letting the stage revolve visibly, bringing on the different settings in such a way as to fix the existing state of everything and show the developments of the next twelve months, is a device that also allows the play's three conclusions to be brought together by having the stage rotate once more, this time with fully performed scenes.

15

The philosopher has arrived, not on Parnassus but beside a warm stove; his drink is thin red wine, not the hemlock. It is true that we are dealing with mediocrities for whom the tragedy has involved no personal loss, but that makes the sight all the more depressing. Pätus' dream world may be comic, but his awareness of reality is pathetic. One wonders with indifference whether he will leave his whip behind when he goes to the rector's daughter; he certainly doesn't fail to conceal his Kant.—Fritz's mild disappointment, buried among his other worries, is a key point of the part. Another poetic factor is the way in which his account of the interruption of his Italian journey (the classic educational operation of that time) betrays that it was in fact an escape.—As for Karoline, both by her speech and by her appearance she should prompt the reflection that it may well be better to be deceived by someone like Mistress Rehhaar than married by someone like Karoline.

16

It is tempting to sacrifice the opening of this scene, the little family ceremony with the privy councillor's short speech about the snow, to the instinct to speed up the three concluding scenes (three endings) in order to polish them off. To permit this is to lose a poetic element. The snow whose beauty (purity) is thus praised is the same snow as had such a ghastly significance at the end of scene 14, in the gray morning light following the tutor's act of self-castration. Their mockery of the self-mutilator concludes logically enough with a great roar of laughter at his letter of request.—The maid's story and Fritz von Berg's speech must be performed as bravura pieces; both characters are glad to abandon themselves to the general atmosphere of cosiness.

17

The castrated man's little tummy is of course a piece of poetic licence; like his red cheeks it represents a distortion of the character in the direction of cosy contentment. On top of that we have the fairy-tale note in the answers given by the admirable Lise, which recall Grimm's Hans in Luck. Nor is this all that can be done to create an atmosphere of calm. The whole picture must be beautiful. In our production the black of the men's and Lise's clothes, together with the white of the tablecloth, gave an impression of purity, while the grouping round the table was agreeable to the eye.

[BFA, vol. 24, pp. 379–87, also in *Versuche 11* (1951). Introduction and descriptions of scenes 15–17 included in *Theaterarbeit*. Leopold was acted by Joseph Noerden; photographs of his fly-catching performance are on p. 103 of the latter volume.]

Details of the production

The Rebellious Minuet

The major's wife is examining the candidate Läuffer to see if he is a suitable tutor for her son Leopold. She is sitting at the spinet, Leopold in the background catching flies against the panelling. Läuffer downstage left by the footlights bows greedily in response to the rapidly intoned demands which have presumably already been put by the major's wife to a whole host of tutors. He claims a little hoarsely to have had "at least five" dancing masters in his life. She calls for a *compliment* from the minuet. Instantly she starts pounding the delicate keys. Läuffer is unprepared; for an instant it looks as if he cannot dance at all, then we see that it is his confusion, and he just needs a few seconds to collect his thoughts. Holding himself very upright, with his fists supported on his hips, he executes a few finished steps across the front of the stage, raising his legs very high and carefully apportioning the space available to him for this dance figure. His head looks rather twisted, screwed round on his shoulders. It is as if he were skirting thin ice; at the same time the way he carries his shoulders is a bit challenging, he strides like a caged tiger, as it were, with savage grace. Halfway across he turns towards the major's wife and executes a *compliment* so elaborate in conception that it would call for an entire corps de ballet. She appears satisfied. ("Well, well, not bad.") The young master, before whose eyes the examination is being conducted, boredly goes back to catching flies. Läuffer pulls out his handkerchief and mops the nervous sweat from his brow; he thinks he has made it. But the major's wife is thirsty for more sweat. "Now, if you please, a *pas*." Making a face, which the audience can see since Gaugler turns his head round again, he goes on to perform a *pas*, after which he stands there completely exhausted. In her excitement the major's wife graciously plays him a minuet, letting the spinet as it were feel the weight of her fists. Läuffer briefly pulls himself together, then goes over to the spinet with long gliding steps, continually wiping the sweat from his face, there to deliver a deep, animal-like noise of pleasure and bend greedily over the major's wife's meaty hand. What gave the scene its meaning was Gaugler's ability to reveal the low-born Läuffer's brutal and rebellious vitality strapped into the corset of feudal etiquette. The rudiments of the tragicomedy have herewith been hinted at.

> [BFA, vol. 24, pp. 390–91. This additional note on scene 3 was written for *Theaterarbeit,* 1952. Gaugler is the Swiss actor Hans Gaugler, who had acted in Brecht's *Antigone* in Chur in 1948 and came to Berlin to play Läuffer.]

End of an Italian Journey (Scene 15)

1

The beginning of the scene shows how Pätus, now that he is a married man, can only read his Kant in secret. The little book, once so openly and provocatively displayed on his table, now has to be fished out from behind a barricade of other, more officially acceptable writings. Kant has gone underground. Though Pätus still reads him on occasion he will no longer be seen with him in public.

2

The Latin word "matrimonium" needs to be rolled appreciatively round the tongue in just the same way as the privy councillor's "farra communis" or Wenzeslaus' "nervi corrupti" (in scene 12). But whereas the privy councillor perceptibly acts the educated man in the presence of his more uncouth brother, and Wenzeslaus produces his diagnosis with philistine pomposity, Pätus dwells only slightly on his "matrimonium." He is the least anxious of the three to show off his knowledge.

3

Once again the Kant quotation is rapidly reeled off. The only passages to be specially brought out are those calculated philosophically to underline

Kant's restrictive influence on Pätus (". . . no arbitrary contract, but one made *necessary* by the laws of mankind," "they *must* of necessity marry, and this necessity follows from the laws proscribed by *pure reason*.")

4

"Only in public. How else could I . . ." is brought out hurriedly and with more emphasis than necessary. Pätus is entrenching himself. He knows that Kant is a black spot on his career. There is a chance here for the actor to display bad conscience.

5

Pätus has put his Kant on the footstool before him. At the words "and as you see right here, I had to" he points down at it.

6

Fritz's "So your favorite philosopher has proved to you" is not merely an answer to what Pätus has been saying but also his first faint realization of the inadequacy of all human endeavour. On the one hand Pätus' desertion shows that even the gnarled oak may be riddled with worm, while ceaseless dripping will wear down stone; on the other hand it confirms his own sudden exasperation with the world and its ways. Fritz is maturing, and the process has reached the stage of a gloomy recognition of what our world is like.

His hurried, absent-minded nodding at Pätus' big speeches, together with his nervous way of playing with the letter at the start of the scene, have already combined to show that Fritz is not entirely with us. It is only his politeness that prevents him from coming out with his fears then and there. He is just waiting for the right moment to unload his worries.

7

The brief "What was the subject of your thesis?" momentarily paralyzes Pätus. This innocent question touches him on a very sensitive spot. A point has been reached when no further philosophical explanation is possible, and when not even Kant can offer anything to justify his betrayal. His feeble answer, with its self-revealing cleverness, needs to be spoken as such. It has to be made clear that Pätus himself is not entirely easy at his carefree reply. He can laugh in places where there is nothing to laugh at, be over-emphatic where it would really be better to speak in an undertone, and so on.

8

Pätus may make a large gesture to accompany his exclamation, "Karoline is very different," but the sour face he pulls at the ensuing "made for marriage" suggests that marriage with the well-upholstered Karoline has its drawbacks. His "Incidentally, she's the rector's daughter" really is remarked incidentally. Pätus no longer has inhibitions about specifying the amount of his bribe.

9

Fritz's "So the two of you live here beside the stove" is a mixture of contrasting thoughts and feelings. This final balance-sheet of Pätus' "roaring youth" is somewhat depressing. It strikes Fritz as peculiar that the sum total of so many heroic actions can equal nought. None the less there is something to be said for the warm stove.

Back from his Italian journey, the traveller is not entirely unmarked by self-pity either. The sight of Pätus' placidity relentlessly reminds him of the enormous billows and tempests he must still survive on the oceans of life.

10

"I find that I've rather cooled toward him" is most haughtily spoken. Pätus leans back in his chair with his whole weight, blows a thick blue cloud of smoke up at the ceiling, then starts to speak with the slightly grating voice of a budding lecturer.

11

After Pätus' "How was Italy?" Fritz jumps into the fray. He deals summarily with the obligatory part ("Divine. It's made a man of me.") His speech shows that he too has changed. His gait has become smooth and dignified, his voice has developed a steely edge. The actual situation may not be quite like that, but the words themselves emerge nicely turned. Like a connoisseur he negligently drops in the titbits (such as "olives," "Pompeii," and "headlong journey"), thereby adding to their effectiveness.

12

We tried two alternative approaches to Fritz's collapse. First we made him fall by the door-jamb in the centre of the stage, but abandoned this because here Fritz's slow crumpling attracted too much attention. So we settled for a faint by the window.

13

When Pätus pauses in his reading of the letter after the words "uncle's house" Fritz impatiently says "Go on!" and stamps his foot. The criminal refuses to be blindfolded and begs the judge to deal with his case according to the rule-book.

14

At this point Pätus makes his voice hard as steel. This is supposed to encourage Fritz to take what is coming to him like a man.

15

Fritz's furious self-criticism must be performed with the utmost Sturm und Drang. The two men have swapped parts. Where in Scene 9 it was Pätus who beat his breast in despair it is now Fritz. But now that Pätus is compromising more and more with the establishment, the friends' lofty sentiments no longer coincide. Fritz alone survives as an idealist relic.

16

Pätus' advice is thoroughly realistic. His vocabulary suggests that he already has his own beer-drinking circle. Such phrases as "women have got to be kept in hand" and "Women! we know what they are" show that he has progressed a good way along the road from Kant to Nietzsche. These middle-class platitudes need to be delivered in a voice redolent of beer.

17

The sound of Karoline's footsteps takes Pätus by surprise. He quickly pops Kant into a tobacco jar. Not even the conjugal bedroom is immune from the long arm of the social hierarchy. One sees the drawbacks of a rational marriage.

18

Karoline Pätus is a very important character. When she enters the room, Rococo, Biedermeier and Art Nouveau all appear together. A paralyzing atmosphere of coffee-cups seeps in. There's nothing else for it: it's farewell to rebellious youth.

19

The scene originally ended with Fritz staggering off, leaving the tableau of Pätus and Karoline. The spuriousness of their idyll was underlined by the subsequent addition of "Sad, but it's no concern of ours." The ensuing "Come and warm yourself by the stove" is just the final nail in the coffin of the Sturm und Drang with which Pätus' career began. The quondam moral giant and subsequent traitor withdraws to a life of bourgeois heroism.

20

As the lights dim and the stage begins to revolve, Karoline goes over to the stove and sits down.
[From *Theaterarbeit,* pp. 90–92, headed "Examples from the production notes." These notes would appear to be Brecht's, though they are not signed. Brecht's term for "a life of bourgeois heroism" is "das bürgerliche Heldenleben," an allusion at once to Richard Strauss's tone-poem and to Carl Sternheim's cycle of plays.]

The choice of play

In order to provide plays for the German theatre (its classical repertoire having shrunk alarmingly in these troubled times) and at the same time to create a link with Shakespeare, without whom a national theatre is hardly feasible, it seemed a good idea to go back to the beginnings of classicism, to the point where it is both poetic and realistic. Plays like Lenz's *The Tutor* allow us to find out how Shakespeare might be staged here, for they represent his initial impact on Germany. In them substance has not yet been raped by ideology but develops handsomely in every direction, in natural disorder. The audience is still involved in the great debate; the playwright is putting forward ideas and provoking them, rather than offering the whole work as their embodiment. This forces (or enables) us to play the incidents that take place between his characters and keep their remarks separate; no need to make them our own. In this way the characters, instead of being either serious *or* comic, are sometimes serious, sometimes comic. The tutor himself claims our sympathy for being so utterly crushed, together with our contempt for letting this happen.

[BFA, vol. 24, p. 388. Written for *Theaterarbeit*, 1952.]

Aspects of taste in the production

Lenz's play, with its crude subject matter, calls for unusually elegant treatment. Moreover the view given of the German Misère could not be allowed to depress the spectator, but must inspire him to help overcome it. Everything depended on the gracefulness of the movements and the musicality of the words. Colour and cut of the costumes had to be first rate, as had the furniture and any architectural elements shown. The Ensemble looked to tasteful old engravings, etc., for ideas. What emerged was by no means an idealization of the period. Its standard of taste was in fact relatively high. The maggot had not yet grown up into a dragon. Students' rooms, village schools, and country houses still looked very different from what they do now.

The sets and costumes for *The Tutor* were by Caspar Neher, the projections by Hainer Hill.

[BFA, vol. 24, pp. 391–92. Written for *Theaterarbeit*.]

Is *The Tutor* a "negative" play?

The Tutor has been criticized in some quarters for being a "negative," or unconstructive, play. In the opinion of the Berliner Ensemble this play, containing as it does three portraits of schoolmasters (privy councillor, Wenzeslaus, and Läuffer) and three of students who intend to become schoolmasters (von Berg, Pätus, Bollwerk), and being set in the period when the German bourgeoisie was evolving its educational system, offers a stimulating satirical view of this aspect of the German Misère. The production was a perfectly valid contribution to the great process of educational reform which is currently being undertaken in our republic. As can be seen from such works as *Tartuffe*, *Don Quixote*, *Candide*, and *The Inspector General*, satire is not normally concerned to set up exemplary characters as a contrast to those which it mocks; in the concave mirrors which it uses to exaggerate and emphasize its targets the "positive" character would not escape distortion. The positive element in *The Tutor* is its bitter anger against inhuman conditions of unjustified privilege and twisted thinking.

[BFA, vol. 24, p. 392. Written for *Theaterarbeit*. The fact that the privy councillor also belongs in the educational system—at its top—emerges more clearly from the original than from Brecht's adaptation.]

Editorial Note

Adapting Lenz

To judge from the surviving typescripts, Brecht seems to have begun with a first adaptation "by the Berliner Ensemble" which bears no marks of his own hand and could well have been prepared by his collaborators. This was very much closer to Lenz's original than is our text, and took in large tracts of it uncut. The main differences came in the second half of the play, and were concerned above all with clearing away unnecessary characters and entanglements. Lenz, for instance, made Gustchen go away for a whole year after being caught in bed with Läuffer (which occurred in Act III, scene 1), have her child, leave it to be brought up by an old blind woman, then come back and stage her suicide in the lake. The old woman brought the child first to Läuffer, then to the Bergs, who found that by a strange chance she was Pätus' grandmother; old Pätus, another Insterburg dignitary, had quarrelled with her (as also with his son), but in the end the family were reconciled all round. As a further complication Lenz introduced a Herr von Seiffenblase and *his* tutor, who visited the three students in Leipzig, carried home discreditable reports about them, and seem to have had nebulous designs on Gustchen and Miss Rehhaar alike.

All these extra characters are eliminated in the first adaptation, as is also Miss Rehhaar's father, who in Lenz had given Fritz lute lessons and fought a ridiculous duel with Pätus over his daughter: she herself first appearing in Königsberg, where Seiffenblase had taken her and made her pregnant. The events too are tightened up. Gustchen goes into the lake immediately after being caught with Läuffer, while the three scenes in the village school—Lenz's III, 2, where Läuffer seeks refuge and Count Wermuth looks for him, his III, 4 with Wenzeslaus tediously expounding his rules of life, and his IV, 3 with the shooting of Läuffer a year later—are strung together into one enormous scene preceding Gustchen's wetting, finishing with a new reference by Läuffer to the horse problem and his sex life. Then where Lenz had made Läuffer reveal his self-mutilation to Wenzeslaus before ever seeing Lise (servant, not ward, to Wenzeslaus in the original), the adaptation moved the dialogue with Lise about her suitors, etc., from the beginning of V, 10 to before the castration, adding the monologue for Läuffer virtually as in the final scene 14 b.

The other principal new passages, apart from the prologue, were the major's remarks about Läuffer's view of the "Hero-King" (added to I, 4); the catechism lesson at the beginning of Gustchen's first scene with Läuffer

(II, 2); the major's wife's singing at the start of her scene with the count (II, 6, now moved forward to follow II, 2); the introduction of Bollwerk at the beginning of the first student scene (in Lenz's II, 3 he only appears at the end) and his references to Kant; further reference to Kant early in the second student scene (V, 6, now shifted to the beginning of Act V); a new ending to the scene where Läuffer reveals his self-castration (V, 3), which cites his letter to the major and shows his anxiety about his job; and the new festive beginning and ending to the last scene, in which Fritz and Gustchen reunite over the baby (V, 11 and 12 after the elimination of old Pätus), so that the play finishes on the song "Oh silent winter snow." Besides the castration monologue there is also one other entirely new scene, which replaces the original II, 4. Here Lenz had two girls, Jungfer Hamster and Jungfer Knicks, reporting to Frau Hamster on the absurd sight of Pätus rushing off to the theatre in a wolf-skin with three dogs after him. Instead the adaptation introduces Miss Rehhaar, and shows Pätus being made ridiculous in her eyes by Bollwerk's cruel exploitation of his limp.

This first (or at any rate first surviving) version was heavily reworked by Brecht in a second adaptation using about one-third of its pages as they stood, and otherwise making many changes, cuts, and transpositions. Dated "22. 12. 49" on its last page, the new typescript established the text very much as we now have it. Apart from making some massive (and necessary) cuts, what Brecht did here was partly to get the episodes into a more logical narrative sequence, incidentally scrapping the new scene just described, together with the original II, 7 (Fritz going to jail for Pätus' debts), and throwing II, 6 and III, 1 into a single scene; partly to bring out certain elements in the situation which he had found hints of in Lenz—for instance, the notion of Fritz as philosopher and the major as would-be rustic, the sexual basis of Läuffer's plea for a horse, Gustchen's use of Läuffer as a surrogate for Fritz, and Pätus' ultimate choice of the cosy life. He also introduced further quotations from Kant and, for the first time, Klopstock, and devised some good openings for the actors: e.g., the skating scene, first conceived as an episode on the Insterburg promenade, and the maid's speech in the last festive scene.

To start with Act I, he rewrote scene 1 in more or less its final form, moved the lovers' parting (Lenz's scenes 5 and 6, which had been telescoped to make scene 4 of the first adaptation) forward to become scene 3, then added a note:

Position of scenes 2 and 3
With this kind of construction everything depends on the sequence, on what precedes what in the story. So the LOVERS' PARTING needs to come

before TAKING ON A TUTOR; the lover has left before the educator moves
in. Another reason for putting the departure scene at the beginning is
that it does not carry the story further but merely sets out a situation
which is decisive for what follows (daughter of the house ready for a
man). Gustchen's erotic inclination towards Fritz, aggravated by their
parting, is interpreted as awakening her erotically rather than as tying
her hands.

So the two were switched, after Count Wermuth's inquiry about Gustchen,
and the major's wife's answer, had been added to the end of the earlier
scene. Most of the major's closing speech in scene 4 (the present scene
5) was new, and the skating scene followed as the first of the second act.
Then came the catechism scene and the first student scene, much as we now
have it, with its new references to girls, to the unfortunate effect of Kant on
university examiners, and its invocations of "Pätus, the just," etc., building
up the philosopher's figure; the first mention of Miss Rehhaar was also
inserted here. The garden scene followed virtually in its final form, with
Läuffer's two new interruptions about the horse and the privy councillor's
"Been feeling your oats?" inserted in Brecht's writing. The act finished
with the bedroom scene, more or less in its final form, and Gustchen's
exclamation "My Romeo!"

The second student scene, which introduced the third act, was new,
though still lacking its opening Klopstock quotation (see our scene 9); Miss
Rehhaar now appeared for the first time, together with the quite new notion
that she had been made pregnant by Bollwerk as a kind of stand-in for
Pätus. In the telescoped II, 6 and III, 1, which now followed (scene 11,
the discovery scene), the references to farming and the major's talk about
Berlin banks and ballets were likewise new. The long composite scene with
Wenzeslaus (12) was severely cut, eliminating *inter alia* the appearance
of the village barber to dress Läuffer's wound. Lise, now more clearly
identified as Wenzeslaus' "daughter," made her appearance with the beer—
an afterthought of Brecht's—flung herself in front of Läuffer and repeated
Gustchen's message about the pond as in the final text, leaving the von
Berg party to rush out. After the pond scene itself (13), which has Gustchen
"throwing herself into the pond" with no hesitation and no backward
glances, and omits the Berg servants, there is the interlude much as in the
final version, but with no mention of Karoline, merely of Pätus "*skating
with a new girl.*"

For his fourth act Brecht made a new scene 14 by taking the three
consecutive village school scenes of the previous version and treating
them as (a), (b), and (c), though almost without changes apart from the

addition of Wenzeslaus' encouraging remarks about Läuffer's qualifications just before his letter. The fifth act then began with scene 15, third and last of the student scenes, with its new references to Fritz's Italian journey (an allusion to Goethe's book of that name) and to Pätus' marriage and heating arrangements; Karoline initially being described as "née Rehhaar," a detail which was changed in a further version which also introduced her offer of coffee. The present final scene came next, very much as now and extensively cut by comparison with the previous version, and was followed by the festive finale at the Bergs', in which the central section was new with its speech for the maid and its long speech for Fritz; an incidental point later dropped is that the latter announced his intention of becoming a schoolmaster. The play still ended on the song, and there was no epilogue.

This second adaptation was completed some four months before the première. Leaving aside those changes which were made in rehearsal (described in Egon Monk's notes which follow) there were few further developments. Leopold was brought into the skating scene, which was moved forward into the first act, and Pätus' remarks on "German servility" were added to scene 6. In the bedroom scene (10) Läuffer, who had hitherto sat on the bed, was shown lying in it, while the confusion with Fritz was further underlined (e.g., by Läuffer's "I'm not Romeo, I'm Läuffer" and the final "Oh Fritz, my love!"). The von Berg servants were brought into the shooting and pond scenes (12, 13), as were the count's and the privy councillor's reactions to them in the latter. In 15, the last student scene, Pätus was shown dismissing Miss Rehhaar in his pride at having married the rector's daughter; his final invitation to sit by the stove was also new. So we can briefly summarize what survived of Lenz's play in the final text, scene by scene as follows:

Act One

1. The bows come from Lenz's I, 1 and 2, and the suggestion that Läuffer's father was too poor to complete his son's education.
2. The middle of the scene (after the Klopstock quotations) and the gist of the privy councillor's intervention are from I, 5 and 6.
3. Nearly all from Lenz's I, 3.
4. Nothing.
5. Well over half from I, 4, including the argument over pay.

Act Two

6. Pätus and Bollwerk, and the episode of Frau Blitzer and the coffee are in II, 3, as is the lure of the theatre.
7. The second half from Lenz's II, 2.
8. More than half from II, 1, including the lines "I was promised a horse to ride to Königsberg every three months."

Act Three

9. Nothing, apart from the figure of Miss Rehhaar.
10. About half from II, 5, including the *Romeo and Juliet* quotation and Gustchen's remark "Your father forbade you to write to me," which shows the identification with Fritz.
11. About half is from the combined II, 6 and III, 1, notably almost the whole of the ending after the major's wife irrupts.
12. The greater part comes from the fusion of III, 2 and 4 and IV, 3, including all Wenzeslaus' pedantry.
13. About half is from the combined IV, 4 and 5.

Interlude

Nothing.

Act Four

14. (b) is new, but about half each of (a) and (c) come from V, 3 and 10, including Wenzeslaus' applause for Läuffer's action.

Act Five

15. Less than half is from V, 6. The reference to Seiffenblase (Soapbubble) is a loose end.
16. V, 11 and 12 provide the major's appeal to Fritz's philosophical disposition, and Fritz's ensuing acceptance of the child.
17. Nearly all is from a fusion of V, 9 with the second half of V, 10, notably Lise's love for Läuffer and Wenzeslaus' reaction to it.

Changes during rehearsal

Notes by Egon Monk

During rehearsals the order of the scenes was quite often changed, shortened or added to. In most cases these alterations were not the result of any theoretical considerations but arose from the continual growth of the arrangement, the increasing elegance of the narration, the noting of social inaccuracies, the attempt to give lightness to the performance, and so on. Where the rehearsals revealed new and unsuspected potentialities in such characters as Pätus we tried to follow them up. [. . .]

1. In scene 1 the audience learns from the privy councillor that Läuffer cannot get a job at the local school because he is not educated enough. In the privy councillor's view he is just about adequate to "drum a little knowledge and good manners" into the major's son, so that he may become a soldier like his father. This judgement is subsequently confirmed when scene 5 (the school scene) shows Läuffer stumbling pathetically over the simple Latin word "agricola." It took one or two rehearsals for us to realize that it wasn't enough just to establish that Läuffer was unqualified. If we wanted to explain his behaviour in terms of his situation in society we must give some indication of his origins. So we made the privy councillor follow up his remark "but he's not trained for it" by adding "his father's purse gave out before his finals."

The reason why the production of *The Tutor* made so complete an overall impression was its accumulation of a large number of details, some of them very small.

2. So as to show how much more interested the major was in the origins of his fern than in those of his son's prospective tutor (an idea that only evolved during the rehearsals) we had him add "'Sblood! Enough about that lout, we were talking about your fern here."

3. Changes in the scene order usually led to changes in the text. In the first version of *The Tutor* Fritz von Berg in Halle renounced his holidays *after* Gustchen at Insterburg had allowed herself to be seduced. During rehearsal we realized what the right order of events had to be: it is because Fritz in Halle high-mindedly gives up spending the holidays at Insterburg with his Gustchen that she feels herself abandoned by him and so lets the tutor seduce her (she is taking a substitute). But since the play had contained no previous reference to Fritz's wanting to come to Insterburg in the holidays

we made Gustchen add, when plighting her troth to her Fritz by the bed in scene 2: "That you'll always fly to the arms of your Gussie at holiday time and come back from the university in three years." Fritz breaks his promise and Gustchen turns to the tutor. However, his experiences in Halle, where he sacrifices his holiday money for Miss Rehhaar, put him in a position to understand his Gustchen and forgive her.

4. We also wanted to show that Läuffer's bodily needs arose from a lack of understanding on society's part. [. . .] He has to ensure that he can now and again get away from Insterburg. During the rehearsing of scene 5 we accordingly added the dialogue from "Major, would it be too bold of me" to "for two or three days?" Having put his request in the most obsequious possible way, Läuffer acknowledges the major's half-assent with lavish motions of gratitude. He executes several marked bows in rapid succession, and in exchange for the faint prospect of a horse is prepared to shoulder any other burden the major puts on him. That is to say, not only the reduction which has just been effected in his salary but also the doubling of his responsibilities as tutor. The major fails to keep his promise and Läuffer, after a most desperate attempt to get the privy councillor to understand, allows his pampered body to commit a sin.

5. During rehearsal the student Pätus emerged as the most interesting character in the play after Läuffer. Where Läuffer castrates himself physically—which of course at the same time stands for a spiritual castration: the abjuring of rebellion—the self-castration practised by Pätus can only be understood in a spiritual sense. Pätus in *The Tutor* goes the opposite road to Schiller's: his Misère declines from extravagance to banality in the course of the play. To make this development clear we had first to lead Pätus to the highest summits before letting him fall headlong into the pit of philistine self-satisfaction. An opportunity was provided by the Kant quotation in the first student scene. Initially we chose a passage about apodictic and assertive sentences [. . .] with the result that Pätus, whom we meant to play a considerable part in our play, seemed not merely to Bollwerk but also to such spectators as occasionally came to rehearsals to be a muddleheaded clown whom nobody could possibly take seriously. We replaced it with an extract about the Ding an sich, but this made matters no better. Stage and auditorium alike confirmed that Bollwerk was right to ridicule Pätus' Kant-worship; which was not at all what we had intended. Finally we picked a passage from Kant's work "Zum ewigen Frieden," which had the desired effect. Pätus had to attain a genuine ethical high point before writing his thesis on war as the father of all things. He achieves something like

greatness by his stubborn loyalty to Kant's truly progressive views. He is tellingly subversive, even if only in his ideas. He explains his stubbornness in another sentence added later: "And my 'No'... to some supreme leader." Bollwerk doubts whether such views are useful, but nobody supports him, Fritz too having said "It doesn't seem so wrong to me."

So we had the high point from which the fall could take place. [...]

6. In scene 12 we tried to show how Wenzeslaus the schoolmaster, once he has been so generous as to open his house to the fugitive Läuffer, realizes his protégé's potential as cheap labour and, after overcoming his initial mistrust, decides to exploit Läuffer's predicament for his own advantage. At rehearsal it became clear that miming alone was not enough to make his intention evident. So we introduced an extra sentence after Wenzeslaus' big speech on the obligations of a German schoolmaster, to be spoken when he had sunk back in his armchair, exhausted by this effort: "I assume, young man ... yes, that's how it is." Wenzeslaus has shielded Läuffer as one shields the ox that is due to pull one's cart.

7. We found in the course of rehearsal that in scene 14, where Lise says that her guardian would not give her to an officer because of the unsettled life and lack of possessions, we had to make Läuffer exclaim "And me? What have I got?" Subsequently, when Wenzeslaus asks him how he means to support her, Läuffer is telling the truth when he says he has told her already. As long as he remains capable of embarking on marriage he is hampered by his bad social position, and only his incapacity for marriage, after once castrating himself, puts him in a position to support his wife. [...]

8. Castration of the body is followed by castration of the mind. When Läuffer writes his letter to Major von Berg, begging him for God's sake not to deprive him of an existence for which he has made certain sacrifices, we added a postscript in which he promises "always to teach the martyrdom of our Hero-King without omissions."

9. Right up to the dress rehearsal we were uncertain whether the play ought to end with Fritz's return to Insterburg after the Pätus sub-plot has been rounded off, and his reconciliation with Gustchen, or with the castrated Läuffer's engagement to the schoolmaster's daughter. Till then the ending had been the phony idyll of the von Berg family reunion, complete with punchbowl and tears of joy over the happy turn of events as brought about by God. It was only after the dress rehearsal that we decided to end the play with Läuffer. For the tutor's splendours and miseries are the subject of the

story, and it was he who had been the pretext for an evening spent probing the causes of the German Misère.

[From the previously unpublished "Hofmeister Textänderungen währendder Probe" written up by Egon Monk from his rehearsal notes after discussion with Brecht in the summer holidays of 1950. These and Herr Monk's other unpublished notes on the production appear to have been destined for a "Model Book" which was never published. For Brecht's conception of the German Misère see p. xii.]

CORIOLANUS

Texts by Brecht

Enjoying the hero

As for enjoying the hero and the tragic element, we have to get beyond a mere sense of empathy with the hero Marcius in order to achieve a richer form of enjoyment. We must at least be able to "experience" the tragedy not only of Coriolanus himself but also of Rome, and specifically of the plebs.

There is no need to ignore the "tragedy of pride," or for that matter to play it down; nor, given Shakespeare's genius, would this be possible. We can accept the fact that Coriolanus finds it worthwhile to give his pride so much rein that death and collapse "just don't count." But ultimately society pays, Rome pays also, and it too comes close to collapsing as a result. While as for the hero, society is interested in another aspect of the question, and one that directly concerns it, to wit the hero's belief that he is indispensable. This is a belief to which it cannot succumb without running the risk of collapse. Thereby it is brought into irreconcilable conflict with this hero, and the kind of acting must be such as not only to permit this but to compel it.

[BFA, vol. 24, pp. 402. Written in 1951 or 1952.]

Plan of the play

Brecht often wrote documents in lower case, and his practice has been preserved here [Editor].

I

1   ROME caius marcius is prepared to quell a revolt of the starving plebs, but the threat of war with the volsces leads the senate to make the plebs concessions: they are given tribunes.
2   ANTIUM aufidius is advancing on rome at the head of the volsces.
3   ROME mother and wife see caius marcius off to the war.
4   CORIOLI caius marcius takes corioli, a volscian city. caius marcius is dissatisfied with his troops because they fight less well when taking it than when defending their own city.

II

1   ROME the city welcomes caius marcius as a conqueror. the tribunes are worried that he will put up for consul.
2   ROME the senate asks coriolanus to solicit the citizens' votes according to custom.
3   ROME coriolanus goes begging and is elected. the tribunes expose his plans for the plebs.

III

1   ROME coriolanus rejects the plebeians' demand for grain and attacks the tribunes.
2   ROME coriolanus is persuaded by his mother volumnia that it is worth apologizing to the people for the sake of power.
3   ROME instead of apologizing coriolanus loses control, insults the people, and is banished.
4   ROME volumnia and some senators accompany coriolanus to the city gate.
5   ROME volumnia curses the tribunes.

IV

1   CORIOLI a roman and a volscian discuss the situation.
2   ANTIUM coriolanus hires himself out to aufidius as leader of an army against rome.

3   ROME rome is seized by panic when it is learnt that coriolanus is moving on rome at the head of the volsces.

4   CORIOLI aufidius is merely waiting for rome to surrender before taking action against coriolanus.

V

1   ROME the senate sends menenius out to negotiate with coriolanus. it is not going to risk arming the plebs.

2   CORIOLI coriolanus packs menenius off without listening to his reasoned arguments.

3   ROME the tribunes call on the people to arm itself.

4   CORIOLI volumnia moves her son to turn back.

5   ROME rome receives volumnia without thanks on her return.

6   ANTIUM coriolanus is killed by the volsces.

7   ROME rome gives certain patrician ladies leave to wear mourning for coriolanus.

[Bertolt Brecht Archive [henceforth BBA] 1769/02–3. This characteristic dissection of the story, emphasizing and at times adjusting what Brecht regarded as the points of interest, exists in at least three versions in the Brecht Archive, all identical except that one of them is amended so as to cut III, 1. The plan presumably dates from an early stage of the work on the play.]

Four short notes

(1) General

I don't believe the new approach to the problem would have prevented Shakespeare from writing a *Coriolanus*.

I believe he would have taken the spirit of our time into account much as we have done, with less conviction no doubt, but with more talent.

(2) The first scene

It is only by studying *the unity of opposites* that a proper disposition of the opening scene of Coriolanus becomes feasible; and this is the foundation on which the entire play rests. How else is the director to bring out the difference between Menenius Agrippa's phony *ideological* attempt to unify patricians and plebeians, and their real unification as a result of the war?

(3) A question arising from the first scene

What is the relationship between Marcius and the Senate? The patricians flatter Marcius ("'tis true that you have lately told us, /The Volsces are in arms."). Marcius stifles his unease at the concession of the tribunate, as he is anxious to get a command in the war. But Marcius is made subordinate to Cominius, and the fact that Cominius has to remind him of his former promise suggests that he is at first none too pleased at this.

(4) Act IV, scene 4

In Act IV, scene 4 the citizens shouldn't change their opinions (as in Shakespeare) so as to regret Coriolanus' banishment; the nobility, however, should be clearly shown to be afraid (not for Rome, but for their own lives).

This can be brought out

(i) by having the citizens remark that it is better to have a vulture like Coriolanus *against* them than fighting in their ranks;

(ii) by letting the nobility fall into a panic, like a lot of flustered hens whose cock has flown off to a neighbouring farmyard. They tremble to such an extent before their social equal that the weapons they are collecting fall from their hands.

[(1), BFA, vol. 24, p. 403; (2), BFA, vol. 24, p. 402, and are attributed to1951–52. (3) no longer appears in print. (4) is an unpublished note (BBA 1769/06) headed "Suggestions by Brecht." The result will be seen in the adaptation, where only one of the suggestions was carried out, and that in modified form.]

Study of the first scene of Shakespeare's Coriolanus

B. How does the play begin?

R. A group of plebeians has armed itself with a view to killing the patrician Caius Marcius, an enemy to the people, who is opposed to lowering the price of corn. They say that the plebeians' sufferance is the patricians' gain.

B. ?

R. Have I left something out?

B. Are Marcius' services mentioned?

R. And disputed.

P. So you think the plebeians aren't all that united? Yet they loudly proclaim their determination.

W. Too loudly. If you proclaim your determination as loudly as that it means that you are or were undetermined, and highly so.

P. In the normal theatre this determination always has something comic about it: it makes the plebeians seem ridiculous, particularly as their weapons are inadequate: clubs, staves. Then they collapse right away, just because the patrician Agrippa makes a fine speech.

B. Not in Shakespeare.

P. But in the bourgeois theatre.

B. Indeed yes.

R. This is awkward. You cast doubt on the plebeians' determination, yet you bar the comic element. Does that mean that you think after all that they won't let themselves be taken in by the patricians' demagogy? So as not to seem more comic still?

B. If they let themselves be taken in I wouldn't find them comic but tragic. That would be a possible scene, *for such things happen,* but a horrifying one. I don't think you realize how hard it is for the oppressed to become united. Their misery unites them—once they recognize who has caused it. "Our sufferance is a gain to them." But otherwise their misery is liable to cut them off from one another, for they are forced to snatch the wretched crumbs from each other's mouths. Think how reluctantly men decide to revolt! It's an adventure for them: new paths have to be marked out and followed; moreover the rule of the rulers is always accompanied by that of their ideas. To the masses revolt is the unnatural rather than the natural thing, and however bad the situation from which only revolt can free them they find the idea of it as exhausting as the scientist finds a new view of the universe. This being so it is often the more intelligent people who are opposed to unity and only the most intelligent of all who are also for it.

R. So really the plebeians have not become united at all?

B. On the contrary. Even the second citizen joins in. Only neither we nor the audience must be allowed to overlook the contradictions that are bridged over, suppressed, ruled out, now that sheer hunger makes a conflict with the patricians unavoidable.

R. I don't think you can find that in the text, just like that.

B. Quite right. You have got to have read the whole play. You can't begin without having looked at the end. Later in the play this unity of the plebeians will be broken up, so it is best not to take it for granted at the start, but to show it as having come about.

W. How?

B. We'll discuss that. I don't know. For the moment we are making an analysis. Go on.

R.   The next thing that happens is that the patrician Agrippa enters, and proves by a parable that the plebeians cannot do without the rule of the patricians.

B.   You say "proves" as if it were in quotes.

R.   The parable doesn't convince me.

B.   It's a world-famous parable. Oughtn't you to be objective?

R.   Yes.

B.   Right.

W.   The man starts off by suggesting that the dearth has been made by the gods, not the patricians.

P.   That was a valid argument in those days, in Rome I mean. Don't the interests of a given work demand that we respect the ideology of a given period?

B.   You needn't go into that here. Shakespeare gives the plebeians good arguments to answer back with. And they strongly reject the parable, for that matter.

R.   The plebeians complain about the price of corn, the rate of usury, and are against the burden of the war, or at any rate its unjust division.

B.   You're reading that into it.

R.   I can't find anything against war.

B.   There isn't.

R.   Marcius comes on and abuses the armed plebeians, whom he would like to see handled with the sword, not with speeches. Agrippa plays the diplomat and says that the plebeians want corn at their own rates. Marcius jeers at them. They don't know what they are talking about, having no access to the Capitol and therefore no insight into the state's affairs. He gets angry at the suggestion that there's grain enough.

P.   Speaking as a military man, presumably.

W.   In any case as soon as war breaks out he points to the Volsces' corn.

R.   During his outburst Marcius announces that the Senate has now granted the plebeians people's tribunes, and Agrippa finds this strange. Enter senators, with the incumbent consul Cominius at their head. Marcius is delighted at the idea of fighting the Volscian leader Aufidius. He is put under Cominius' command.

B.   Is he agreeable to that?

R.   Yes. But it seems to take the senators slightly by surprise.

B.   Differences of opinion between Marcius and the senate?

R.   Not important ones.

B.   We've read the play to the end, though. Marcius is an awkward man.

W.   It's interesting, this contempt for the plebeians combined with high regard for a national enemy, the patrician Aufidius. He's very class-conscious.

B.   Forgotten something?

R. Yes. Sicinius and Brutus, the new people's tribunes, came on with the senators.

B. No doubt you forgot them because they got no welcome or greeting.

R. Altogether the plebeians get very little further attention. A senator tells them sharply to go home. Marcius "humorously" suggests that they should rather follow him to the Capitol. He treats them as rats, and that is when he refers them to the corn of the Volsces. Then it just says, "Citizens steal away."

P. The play makes their revolt come at an unfortunate moment. In the crisis following the enemy's approach the patricians can seize the reins once more.

B. And the granting of people's tribunes?

P. Was not really necessary.

R. Left alone, the tribunes hope that the war, instead of leading to Marcius' promotion, will devour him, or make him fall out with the senate.

P. The end of the scene is a little unsatisfactory.

B. In Shakespeare, you mean?

R. Possibly.

B. We'll note that sense of discomfort. But Shakespeare presumably thinks that war weakens the plebeians' position, and that seems to me splendidly realistic.

B. Beautiful things.

R. The wealth of events in a single short scene. Compare today's plays, with their poverty of content!

P. The way in which the exposition at the same time gives a rousing send-off to the plot!

R. The language in which the parable is told! The humour!

P. And the fact that it has no effect on the plebeians!

W. The plebeians' native wit! Exchanges like "Agrippa: Will you undo yourselves? Citizen: We cannot, sir, we are undone already!"

R. The crystal clarity of Marcius' harangue! What an outsize character! And one who emerges as admirable while behaving in a way that I find beneath contempt!

B. And great and small conflicts all thrown on the scene at once: the unrest of the starving plebeians plus the war against their neighbours the Volsces; the plebeians' hatred for Marcius, the people's enemy—plus his patriotism; the creation of the post of people's tribune—plus Marcius' appointment to a leading role in the war. Well—how much of that do we see in the bourgeois theatre?

W. They usually use the whole scene for an exposition of Marcius' character: the hero. He's shown as a patriot, handicapped by selfish plebeians and a cowardly and weak-kneed senate. Shakespeare, following Livy rather than Plutarch, has good reason for showing the senate "sad and confused by a double fear—fear of the people and fear of the enemy." The bourgeois stage identifies itself with the patricians' cause, not the plebeians'. The plebeians are shown as comic and pathetic types (rather than types who bear misfortune with humour), and Agrippa's remark labelling the senate's granting of people's tribunes as strange is used for the light it casts on Agrippa's character rather than to establish a preliminary link between the advance of the Volsces and the concessions made to the plebeians. The plebeians' unrest is of course settled at once by the parable of the belly and the members, which is just right for the bourgeoisie's taste, as shown in its relations with the modern proletariat. . . .

R. Although Shakespeare never allows Agrippa to mention that his parable has managed to convince the plebeians, only to say that though they lack discretion (to understand his speech) they are passing cowardly— an accusation, incidentally, that's impossible to understand.

B. We'll note that.

R. Why?

B. It gives rise to discomfort.

R. I must say, the way in which Shakespeare treats the plebeians and their tribunes rather encourages our theatre's habit of letting the hero's hardships be aggravated as far as possible by the "foolish" behaviour of the people, and so paving the way in anticipatory forgiveness for the later excesses of his "pride."

B. All the same Shakespeare does make a factor of the patricians' corn profiteering and their inclination at least to conscript the plebeians for war—Livy makes the patricians say something to the effect that the base plebs always goes astray in peacetime—and of the plebeians' unjust indebtedness to the nobles. In such ways Shakespeare refrains from presenting the revolt as a piece of pure folly.

W. But nor does he do much to bring out Plutarch's interesting phrase: "Once order had been restored in the city by these means, even the lower classes immediately flocked to the colours and showed the greatest willingness to let the ruling authorities employ them for the war."

B. All right; if that's so we'll read the phrase with all the more interest: we want to find out as much about the plebeians as we can.

P. "For it may be a question of characteristics of famous ancestors."

R. There's another point where Shakespeare refrains from coming down on the aristocratic side. Marcius isn't allowed to make anything of

Plutarch's remark that "The turbulent attitude of the base plebs did not go unobserved by the enemy. He launched an attack and put the country to fire and sword."

B.   Let's close our first analysis at this point. Here is roughly what takes place and what we must bring out in the theatre. The conflict between patricians and plebeians is (at least provisionally) set aside, and that between the Romans and the Volsces becomes all-predominant. The Romans, seeing their city in danger, legalize their differences by appointing plebeian commissars (people's tribunes). The plebeians have got the tribunate, but the people's enemy Marcius emerges, *qua* specialist, as leader in war.

B.   The brief analysis we made yesterday raises one or two very suggestive problems of production.

W.   How can one show that there has been opposition to the plebeians uniting, for instance? Just by that questionable emphasis on determination?

R.   When I told the story I didn't mention their lack of unity because I took the second citizen's remarks as a provocation. He struck me as simply checking on the first citizen's firmness. But I don't suppose it can be played in this way. It's more that he's still hesitating.

W.   He could be given some reason for his lack of warlike spirit. He could be better dressed, more prosperous. When Agrippa makes his speech he could smile at the jokes, and so on. He could be disabled.

R.   Weakness?

W.   Morally speaking. The burnt child returns to its fire.

B.   What about their weapons?

R.   They've got to be poorly armed, or they could have got the tribunate without the Volsces' attacking; but they mustn't be weak, or they could never win the war for Marcius and the war against him.

B.   Do they win their war against Marcius?

R.   In our theatre, certainly.

P.   They can go in rags, but does that mean they have to go raggedly?

B.   What's the situation?

R.   A sudden popular rising.

B.   So presumably their weapons are improvised ones, but they can be good improvisers. It's they who make the army's weapons; who else? They can have got themselves bayonets, butchers' knives on broom-handles, converted fire-irons, etc. Their inventiveness can arouse respect, and their arrival can immediately seem threatening.

P.   We're talking about the people all the time. What about the hero? He wasn't even the centre of R.'s summary of the content.

R.   The first thing shown is a civil war. That's something too interesting
     to be mere background preparation for the entrance of the hero. Am I
     supposed to start off: "One fine morning Caius Marcius went for a stroll
     in his garden, went to the market place, met the people and quarrelled,"
     and so on? What bothers me at the moment is how to show Agrippa's
     speech as ineffective and having an effect.

W.   I'm still bothered by P.'s question whether we oughtn't to examine the
     events with the hero in mind. I certainly think that before the hero's
     appearance one is entitled to show the field of forces within which he
     operates.

B.   Shakespeare permits that. But haven't we perhaps overloaded it with
     particular tensions, so that it acquires a weight of its own?

P.   And *Coriolanus* is written for us to enjoy the hero!

R.   The play is written realistically, and includes sufficient material of a
     contradictory sort. Marcius fighting the people: that isn't just a plinth
     for his monument.

B.   Judging from the way you've treated the story it seems to me that
     you've insisted all of you from the first on smacking your lips over
     the tragedy of a people that has a hero against it. Why not follow this
     inclination?

P.   There may not be much pretext for that in Shakespeare.

R.   I doubt it. But we don't have to do the play if we don't enjoy it.

P.   Anyway, if we want to keep the hero as the centre of interest we can
     also play Agrippa's speech as ineffective.

W.   As Shakespeare makes it. The plebeians receive it with jeers, pityingly
     even.

R.   Why does Agrippa mention their cowardice—the point I was supposed
     to note?

P.   No evidence for it in Shakespeare.

B.   Let me emphasize that no edition of Shakespeare has stage directions,
     apart from those presumed to have been added later.

P.   What's the producer to do?

B.   We've got to show Agrippa's (vain) attempt to use ideology, in a purely
     demagogic way, in order to bring about that union between plebeians
     and patricians which in reality is effected a little—not very much—
     later by the outbreak of war. Their real union is due to *force majeure*,
     thanks to the military power of the Volsces. I've been considering one
     possibility: I'd suggest having Marcius and his armed men enter rather
     earlier than is indicated by Agrippa's "Hail, noble Marcius!" and the
     stage direction which was probably inserted because of this remark.
     The plebeians would then see the armed men looming up behind the

speaker, and it would be perfectly reasonable for them to show signs of indecision. Agrippa's sudden aggressiveness would also be explained by his own sight of Marcius and the armed men.

W. But you've gone and armed the plebeians better than ever before in theatrical history, and here they are retreating before Marcius' legionaries. . . .

B. The legionaries are better armed still. Anyway they don't retreat. We can strengthen Shakespeare's text here still further. Their few moments' hesitation during the final arguments of the speech is now due to the changed situation arising from the appearance of armed men behind the speaker. And in these few moments we observe that Agrippa's ideology is based on force, on armed force, wielded by Romans.

W. But now there's unrest, and for them to unite there must be something more: war must break out.

R. Marcius can't let fly as he'd like to either. He turns up with armed men, but his hands are tied by the senate's "clemency." They have just granted the mob senatorial representation in the form of the tribunes. It was a marvellous stroke of Shakespeare's to make it Marcius who announces the setting-up of the tribunate. How do the plebeians react to that? What is their attitude to their success?

W. Can we amend Shakespeare?

B. I think we can amend Shakespeare if we can amend him. But we agreed to begin only by discussing changes of interpretation so as to prove the usefulness of our analytical method even without adding new text.

W. Could the first citizen be Sicinius, the man the senate has just appointed tribune? He would then have been at the head of the revolt, and would hear of his appointment from Marcius' mouth.

B. That's a major intervention.

W. There wouldn't have to be any change in the text.

B. All the same. A character has a kind of specific weight in the story. Altering it might mean stimulating interest that would be impossible to satisfy later, and so on.

R. The advantage would be that it would allow a playable connection to be established between the revolt and the granting of the tribunate. And the plebeians could congratulate their tribune and themselves.

B. But there must be no playing down of the contribution which the Volscian attack makes to the establishment of the tribunate; it's the main reason. Now you must start building and take everything into account.

W. The plebeians ought to share Agrippa's astonishment at this concession.

B. I don't want to come to any firm decision. And I'm not sure that that can be acted by pure miming, without any text. Again, if our group of plebeians includes a specific character, it wouldn't any longer be taken to stand for half of plebeian Rome, i.e., as a part standing for the whole. But I note your astonishment and inquisitiveness as you move around within this play and within these complex events on a particular morning in Rome, where there is much that a sharp eye can pick out. And certainly if you can find clues to these events, then all power to the audience!

W. One can try.

B. Most certainly.

R. And we ought to go through the whole play before deciding anything. You look a bit doubtful, B.

B. Look the other way.—How do they take the news that war has broken out?

W. Marcius welcomes it, like Hindenburg did, as a bath of steel.

B. Careful.

R. You mean, this is a war of self-defence.

P. That doesn't necessarily mean the same thing here as usually in our discussions and judgements. These wars led to the unification of Italy.

R. Under Rome.

B. Under democratic Rome.

W. That had got rid of its Coriolanuses.

B. Rome of the people's tribunes.

P. Here is what Plutarch says about what happened after Marcius' death: "First the Volsces began to quarrel with the Aequi, their friends and allies, over the question of the supreme command, and violence and death resulted. They had marched out to meet the advancing Romans, but almost completely destroyed one another. As a result the Romans defeated them in battle. . . ."

R. I.e., Rome without Marcius was not weaker, but stronger.

B. Yes, it's just as well not only to have read the play right through before starting to study the beginning, but also to have read the factual accounts of Plutarch and Livy, who were the dramatist's sources. But what I meant by "careful" was: one can't just condemn wars without going into them any further, and it won't even do to divide them into wars of aggression and wars of defence. The two kinds merge into one another, for one thing. And only a classless society on a high level of production can get along without wars. Anyhow this much seems clear to me: Marcius has got to be shown as a patriot. It takes the most tremendous events—as in the play—to turn him into a deadly enemy of his country.

R.   How do the plebeians react to the news of the war?

P.   We've got to decide that ourselves; the text gives no clue.

B.   And unhappily our own generation is particularly well qualified to judge. The choice is between letting the news come like a thunderbolt that smashes through everyone's defences, or else making something of the fact that it leaves them relatively unmoved. We couldn't possibly leave them unmoved without underlining how strange and perhaps terrible that is.

P.   We must make it have tremendous effects, because it so completely alters the situation, if for no other reason.

W.   Let's assume then that at first the news is a blow to them all.

R.   Even Marcius? His immediate reaction is to say he's delighted.

B.   All the same we needn't make him an exception. He can say his famous sentence. "I'm glad on't; then we shall ha' means to vent/Our musty superfluity," once he has recovered.

W.   And the plebeians? It won't be easy to exploit Shakespeare's lacuna so as to make them seem speechless. Then there are still other questions. Are they to greet their new tribunes? Do they get any advice from them? Does their attitude towards Marcius change at all?

B.   We shall have to base our solution on the fact that there is no answer to these points; in other words, they have got to be raised. The plebeians must gather round the tribunes to greet them, but stop short of doing so. The tribunes must want to lay down a line, but stop short of it. The plebeians must stop short of adopting a new attitude to Marcius. It must all be swallowed up by the new situation. The stage direction that so irritates us, "Citizens steal away," simply represents the change that has taken place since they came on stage ("Enter a company of mutinous citizens with clubs, staves and other weapons"). The wind has changed, it's no longer a favourable wind for mutinies; a powerful threat affects all alike, and as far as the people goes this threat is simply noted in a purely negative way.

R.   You advised us in our analysis to make a note to record our discomfort.

B.   And our admiration of Shakespeare's realism. We have no real excuse to lag behind Plutarch, who writes of the base people's "utmost readiness" for the war. It is a new union of the classes, which has come about in no good way, and we must examine it and reconstitute it on the stage.

W.   To start with, the people's tribunes are included in the new union; they are left hanging useless in mid-air, and they stick out like sore thumbs. How are we to create this visible unity of two classes which have just been fighting one another out of these men and their irreconcilable opponent Marcius, who has suddenly become so vitally needed, needed for Rome as a whole?

B. I don't think we'll get any further by going about it naïvely and waiting for bright ideas. We shall have to go back to the classic method of mastering such complex events. I marked a passage in Mao Tse-tung's essay "On Contradiction." What does he say?

R. That in any given process which involves many contradictions there is always a main contradiction that plays the leading, decisive part; the rest are of secondary, subordinate significance.—One example he gives is the Chinese Communists' willingness, once the Japanese attacked, to break off their struggle against Chiang Kai-shek's reactionary régime. Another possible example is that when Hitler attacked the USSR even the émigré White Russian generals and bankers were quick to oppose him.

W. Isn't that a bit different?

B. A bit different but also a bit the same thing. But we must push on. We've got a contradictory union of plebeians and patricians, which has got involved in a contradiction with the Volsces next door. The second is the main contradiction. The contradiction between plebeians and patricians, the class struggle, has been put into cold storage by the emergence of the new contradiction, the national war against the Volsces. It hasn't disappeared though. (The people's tribunes "stick out like sore thumbs.") The tribunate came about as a result of the outbreak of war.

W. But in that case how are we to show the *plebeian-patrician* contradiction being overshadowed by the main *Roman-Volscian* contradiction, and how can we do it in such a way as to bring out the disappearance of the new plebeian leadership beneath that of the patricians?

B. That's not the sort of problem that can be solved in cold blood. What's the position? Starving men on one side, armed men on the other. Faces flushed with anger now changing colour once more. New lamentations will drown the old. The two opposed parties take stock of the weapons they are brandishing against one another. Will these be strong enough to ward off the common danger? It's poetic, what's taking place. How are we going to put it across?

W. We'll mix up the two groups: there must be a general loosening-up, with people going from one side to the other. Perhaps we can use the incident when Marcius knocks into the patrician Lartius on his crutches and says: "What, art thou stiff? stand'st out?" Plutarch says in connection with the plebeians' revolt: "Those without any means were taken bodily away and locked up, even though covered with scars from the battles and ordeals suffered in campaigns for the fatherland. They had conquered the enemy, but their creditors had not the least pity for them." We suggested before that there might be a disabled man of this sort among the plebeians. Under the influence of the naïve patriotism that's so common among ordinary people, and so often shockingly abused, he could come up to Lartius, in spite of his being a member of the class that has so maltreated him. The two war victims could recall their common share in the last war; they could embrace, applauded by all, and hobble off together.

B.   At the same time that would be a good way of establishing that it is generally a period of wars.

W.   Incidentally, do you feel a disabled man like this could perhaps prevent our group from standing as *pars pro toto*?

B.   Not really. He would represent the ex-soldiers.—For the rest, I think we could follow up our idea about the weapons. Cominius as consul and commander-in-chief could grin as he tested those home-made weapons designed for civil war and then gave them back to their owners for use in the patriotic one.

P.   And what about Marcius and the tribunes?

B.   That's an important point to settle. There mustn't be any kind of fraternization between them. The new-found union isn't complete. It's liable to break at the junction points.

W.   Marcius can invite the plebeians condescendingly, and with a certain contempt, to follow him to the Capitol, and the tribunes can encourage the disabled man to accost Titus Lartius, but Marcius and the tribunes don't look at each other, they turn their backs on one another.

R.   In other words both sides are shown as patriots, but the conflict between them remains plain.

B.   And it must also be made clear that Marcius is in charge. War is still his business—especially his—much more than the plebeians'.

R.   Looking at the play's development and being alert to contradictions and their exact nature has certainly helped us in this section of the story. What about the character of the hero, which is also something that must be sketched out, and in precisely this section of the story?

B.   It's one of those parts which should not be built up from his first appearance but from a later one. I would say a battle-scene for Coriolanus, if it hadn't become so hard for us Germans to represent great wartime achievements after two idiotic wars.

P.   You want Marcius to be Busch, the great people's actor who is a fighter himself. Is that because you need someone who won't make the hero too likeable?

B.   Not too likeable, and likeable enough. If we want to generate appreciation of his tragedy we must put Busch's mind and personality at the hero's disposal. He'll lend his own value to the hero, and he'll be able to understand him, both the greatness and the cost of him.

P.   You know what Busch feels. He says he's no bruiser, nor an aristocratic figure.

B.   He's wrong about aristocratic figures, I think. And he doesn't need physical force to inspire fear in his enemies. We mustn't forget a "superficial" point: if we are going to represent half the Roman plebs with five to seven men and the entire Roman army with something like nine—and not just for lack of actors—we can't very well use a sixteen-stone Coriolanus.

W.   Usually you're for developing characters step by step. Why not this one?

B.   It may be because he doesn't have a proper development. His switch from being the most Roman of the Romans to becoming their deadliest enemy is due precisely to the fact that he stays the same.

P.   *Coriolanus* has been called the tragedy of pride.

R.   Our first examination made us feel the tragedy lay, both for Coriolanus and for Rome, in his belief that he was irreplaceable.

P.   Isn't that because the play only comes to life for us when interpreted like this, since we find the same kind of thing here and feel the tragedy of the conflicts that result from it?

B.   Undoubtedly.

W.   A lot will depend on whether we can show Coriolanus, and what happens to and around him, in such a light that he can hold this belief. His usefulness has got to be beyond all doubt.

B.   A typical detail: as there's so much question of his pride, let's try to find out where he displays modesty, following Stanislavsky's example, who asked the man playing the miser to show him the point at which he was generous.

W.   Are you thinking of when he takes over command?

B.   Something like. Let's leave it at that for a start.

P.   Well, what does the scene teach us, if we set it out in such a form?

B.   That the position of the oppressed classes can be strengthened by the threat of war and weakened by its outbreak.

R.   That lack of a solution can unite the oppressed class and arriving at a solution can divide it, and that such a solution may be seen in a war.

P.   That differences in income can divide the oppressed class.

R.   That soldiers, and war victims even, can romanticize the war they survived and be easy game for new ones.

W.   That the finest speeches cannot wipe away realities, but can hide them for a time.

R.   That "proud" gentlemen are not too proud to kowtow to their own sort.

P.   That the oppressors' class isn't wholly united either.

B.   And so on.

R.   Do you think that all this and the rest of it can be read in the play?

B.   Read in it and read into it.

P.   Is it for the sake of these perceptions that we are going to do the play?

B.   Not only. We want to have and to communicate the fun of dealing with a slice of illuminated history. And to have first-hand experience of dialectics.

P.   Isn't the second point a considerable refinement, reserved for a handful of connoisseurs?

B.   No. Even with popular ballads or the peepshows at fairs the simple people (who are so far from simple) love stories of the rise and fall of great men, of eternal change, of the ingenuity of the oppressed, of the potentialities of mankind. And they hunt for the truth that is "behind it all."

[From *Versuche* 15, 1957; reprinted in BFA, vol. 23, pp. 386–402, and translated in *Brecht on Theatre*, 1964. This essay in dialogue form, that is not an accurate transcription of a discussion, was written in 1954, after the project had apparently been put into mothballs, then used by Brecht as the opening (and most substantial) item of the mimeographed collection of new theoretical writings which he made in 1956 under the title *Dialectics in the Theater.* Of the four participants B. is of course Brecht himself, while P. is Peter Palitzsch, R. Käthe Rülicke, and W. Manfred Wekwerth, the eventual director of the Berliner Ensemble production and also of the 1971 National Theatre production in London, which attempted to show that virtually the same interpretation of the play could be based on the original text.

P.'s mention of "famous ancestors" refers to Brecht's poem, "Literature will be scrutinized." Ernst Busch, whom Brecht expected to cast as Coriolanus, played Galileo and other leading parts (see Volume 5, p. xix) for the Ensemble, but Coriolanus was finally played by Brecht's son-in-law Ekkehard Schall.]

Editorial Note

Adapting Shakespeare

Brecht seems to have used *Coriolanus* as something of a training-ground for the younger dramaturgs and assistant directors, some of whose names appear in the note to the study of the first scene. They were divided into groups of two or three, says Peter Palitzsch, and set to analyse the story, check the translation, and suggest cuts and changes. It was in answer to the very radical nature of some of their proposals that Brecht made his dictum about amending Shakespeare, the emphasis in his answer being of course on the word "can." A great deal of his concept of the dispensability of the hero and the role to be given the plebeians was in fact already there in Shakespeare's text, so that gradually more modest ideas prevailed and the original play began to re-emerge. However, he felt that the play could not be left entirely unamended so long as the masses lacked self-awareness and their sense of history remained undeveloped, with the result that there are still some major alterations in the early outline plan of the play printed above (pp. 448–449): notably Coriolanus' criticism of his troops in I, 4; the fact that the demand for grain in III, 1 is not just past history but something to be dealt with now; the whole business of arming the people in Act V (though Shakespeare's Sicinius provides a peg for this by his allusion in V, 1 to "the instant army we can make"); finally the *un*enthusiastic reception of Volumnia in V, 5 and the addition of the last scene.

The other notes which we print underline his intentions with regard to I, 1 and to IV, 4 (his eventual IV, 3), and most of the proposed alterations were in fact carried out. They would certainly have been more extensive if he had not preferred to leave it open what he would do to the battle scenes in Act I; thus Elisabeth Hauptmann's note when the play was finally published three years after his death in 1956:

> It was Brecht's intention to combine scenes 4 to 10 of Shakespeare's play to make one big battle scene, which would have formed his Act I, scene 3 [or scene 4 in the outline plan for the Berliner Ensemble acting version]. Brecht wanted to write this scene during the rehearsals, since he felt it essential to work out the text simultaneously with the positionings and movements.

Indeed Manfred Wekwerth and Joachim Tenschert did just this when they eventually staged the play for the Berliner Ensemble in September 1964; (they also restored a shortened version of I, 2). In the published text,

however, which our translation necessarily follows, the original seven
scenes have been merely renumbered 3a, 3b, etc., but are otherwise left as
they stood in the old standard Schlegel-Tieck translation, here rendered in a
modified version of Shakespeare's English.

This translation by Dorothea Tieck was the one from which the
adaptors worked, and to some extent it survives in Brecht's final text
even apart from the scenes in question. His was, in fact, not so much a
new translation as a radical reworking of the old one, which underwent
much the same roughening-up process as did A. W. Heymel's version of
Marlowe's *Edward II* some thirty years earlier. Many of the Tieck lines
and phrases have been taken over unchanged or still remain recognizable;
some passages have been paraphrased and condensed; others have been
entirely rewritten, sometimes for dramaturgical reasons, sometimes to bring
them closer to the English. Thus Cominius' report in II, 2, which Tieck
for some reason made finish up "and strikes with sudden reinforcement/
The city like divine might" returns to something very near the original
"And with a sudden re-enforcement struck/Corioli like a planet," while
the "heart-hardening spectacles" of Coriolanus' speech on leaving Rome
have become, not Tieck's "herzhärtend Schauspiel" but "herzhärtende
Spektakel." It could also be more "gestic" (in Brecht's sense) to restore
something like Shakespeare's word order and rhythms, as in Coriolanus'
raging speech after his banishment in III, 3 (Brecht's III, 2), starting "You
common cry of curs! whose breath I hate," where Brecht's version is
altogether more forceful, rendering the final "There is a world elsewhere"
not by Tieck's lilting "Noch anderswo gibt's eine Welt" but by an abrupt,
challenging "s'gibt/Noch eine Welt woanders."

Brecht's cuts, which include the whole of Shakespeare's II, 2 and V, 5,
are no more drastic than in any other modern production of this long play.
Nor are his additions and interpolations all that lavish, the only heavily
affected scenes being II, 3, where Coriolanus solicits the plebeians' votes,
IV, 3 (the highway) and V, 4. Their extent and direction can be judged from
the following scene-by-scene summary (Shakespeare's scene numbers
being given each time in parentheses):

Act One

1. (I, 1) The man with the child is new, also the appearance of the
    armed men accompanying Marcius, whose entry has been brought
    forward by some sixteen lines. The messenger's entry has likewise
    been advanced. The citizens' applause for their tribunes is new, as is

Marcius' expression of contempt for them ("And the newly baked/ Tribunes"). The last twelve lines of the scene are new, and replace all Shakespeare's ending after Marcius' exit: Brutus now finds Marcius essential on military grounds, and the citizens, provided with a reason for leaving, no longer "steal away."

2. (I, 3. I, 2 is cut) Shakespeare's scene with some cuts.
3. (I, 4–10) Shakespeare's seven scenes in the old Tieck translation.

Act Two

1. (II, 1) The opening exchanges between Sicinius and Brutus are new, as far as Menenius' entry. His speeches have been cut to bare essentials, as far as the tribunes' exit, eliminating all discussion of Marcius' pride. At the end of the scene, when the tribunes are left alone, their exchanges are mainly new up to the point where Brutus says "I heard him swear,/ Were he to stand for consul, never would he/Appear i' the marketplace." Their ensuing proposal (just before the messenger's appearance) to tell the plebeians how Marcius hates them is cut.
2. (II, 2) Shakespeare with a few cuts.
3. (II, 3 followed by III, 1) The allusion to Marcius' indispensability is new at the end of the first citizen's second speech, together with the exchanges immediately following, as far as "Here he comes." So is everything from the entry of the man with the child up to that of three more citizens—Shakespeare's "two other citizens." So is Coriolanus' very Brechtian song. Then once Coriolanus has asked if he can change his clothes the rest of II, 3 is cut, so that the plebeians are no longer induced by the tribunes to revoke their votes ("almost all/Repent in their election"), and a new bridge passage inserted leading into III, 1 after the tribunes' entrance, where Menenius says "Be calm, be calm." This passage, from "Yes, that you may" to "Noble Marcius, what/Will you do with this grain if chosen consul," confronts Coriolanus with the question of whether to distribute the new grain, and it is his refusal to do this that now makes the plebeians change their minds, on plain materialistic grounds (the fourth citizen's "Where, Coriolanus, are the spoils /Of Corioli?"—another interpolated speech).

The attempt to arrest him follows, as in III, 1, but more violently and on different grounds, his offence in Shakespeare having been that quickly over; almost as soon as the tribunes have called for his arrest he draws his sword, then is protected by the patricians and hustled out before worse can happen. Tribunes and people are accordingly not "beat in," as in Shakespeare, while all else that follows—the tribunes' threat to kill Coriolanus, their argument with Menenius and his offer to intercede—is cut.

Act Three

1. (III, 2) Virtually as in Shakespeare.
2. (III, 3) Ditto, except that Brecht adds the interpolated comments by the citizens, cuts Sicinius' suggestion that the people should vote "For death, for fine or banishment," and instead of Shakespeare's "Have you collected them by tribes?" substitutes the more modern concept of "chairmen of the electoral districts."
3. (IV, 1) Close to Shakespeare, with cuts.
4. (IV, 2) Ditto.

Act Four

1. (IV, 3) In Shakespeare's scene too "a Roman and a Volsce" meet on the highway and discuss Coriolanus' banishment, but Brecht has rewritten it entirely in his own way, reminiscent in its mundane details of some of the dialogue in *Lucullus*.
2. (IV, 4 leading to IV, 5) Close to Shakespeare, with the one scene prefacing the other as there. The comic ending with the three servants, after Coriolanus' and Aufidius' exit, is cut, though Brecht must surely have regretted losing their Schweykian comments on war and peace.
3. (IV, 6) This is the IV, 4 of Brecht's plan, though in the event the changes are less radical than proposed there. In Sicinius' opening speech "without the hero" is a gloss. The citizens' remark at the end about Coriolanus' scorched-earth policy is new, while the second citizen's final question and Sicinius' curt "Yes" take the place of the original first citizen's "I ever said we were i' the wrong when we banished him" and the second citizen's reply "So did we all. . . ."
4. (IV, 7) Aufidius' closing speech is a paraphrase of the original, and the reference to the smoke signal is new (as are those in succeeding scenes); otherwise the scene is as in Shakespeare.

Act Five

1. (V, 1) Brutus' speech is new, with its order to distribute arms to the people. Otherwise Shakespeare's scene differs in having the tribunes on stage throughout, and its opening and closing speeches have been cut.
2. (V, 2) Shakespeare with cuts, notably of the closing exchanges.
3. (part of V, 4) The first half of the scene is new, with its evidence that a minority of the patricians are ready to join the plebs in defending the city. The ensuing exchanges between Comlnius and Sicinius are a shortened form of the Menenius-Sicinius dialogue at the beginning of the original V. 4. But Brecht's conclusion, again, is new, with its important statement by Brutus in lieu of Shakespeare's "the ladies have prevailed" and the jubilations that follow.
4. (V, 3) Two speeches by Coriolanus and one by Volumnia have been cut, during which Shakespeare makes him kneel to her, then refuse to let her kneel to him. Volumnia's first long speech ("If silence were possible") has had its beginning paraphrased, while her second, which shows her making use of every possible ground of appeal, has been entirely rewritten apart from its last three lines, so as to bring out (a) Coriolanus' dispensability, (b) the people's armed resistance, and (c) the patricians' dilemma whether to use the Volsces to defeat this resistance or vice versa. In Shakespeare Coriolanus' exclamation "O mother, mother" is followed by

> Behold the heavens do ope,
> The gods look down, and this unnatural scene
> They laugh at. O my mother, mother! O!
> You've won a happy victory for Rome . . .

Aufidius admits to being moved, and the scene ends, in flat contradiction to Brecht, with the lines "all the swords/In Italy, and her confederate arms,/Could not have made this peace."
5. (V, 5, showing Volumnia's triumphal return to Rome, has been cut) New scene, in which Brutus' couplet recalls the interscene verses in *Galileo*. It takes the place of the altered V, 5 proposed in Brecht's plan.
6. (V, 6) The scene has been simplified by eliminating Aufidius' "three or four conspirators" (who incidentally provided Christopher Isherwood with the title of his first novel) and instead having his officers kill Coriolanus with no preliminary instructions. The senators, a little confusingly, replace Shakespeare's lords of the city (of Antium, that

is), and then everything after Coriolanus' death is cut: Aufidius helping to bear away the body, while the lords resolve "Let's make the best of it."

7. Entirely new. The suggestion in Brecht's plan is here reversed, and the ladies are *not* allowed to wear mourning.

THE TRIAL OF JOAN OF ARC AT ROUEN, 1431

Texts by Brecht

Dialectical factors in the adaptation and production of
The Trial of Joan of Arc at Rouen, 1431

(B) Interest common to occupying power and collaborationist clergy: destroy Joan. Clash of interests: the English wish to destroy her *qua* rebel, the clergy *qua* heretic.

(A) When Joan calls for the expulsion of the English her spiritual judges sheepishly lower their heads. They know what they do.

(A) In the second scene (opening of the trial) the clergy are all battling against Joan, but at the same time they are battling against one another for the honour of being the one to win the battle. They interrupt each other; one of them will contemptuously read the documents while another is examining the accused; Manchon, having been sent back to his place after a foolish question of his has given Joan an opening to launch an attack, thereafter sits and sulks, without taking any interest in the progress of the case.

(B) Cut off from the people, Joan *suddenly* breaks down (in the eighth scene). But it can be observed (in the sixth) how her isolation keeps undermining her resistance.

(B) The fourth scene (market day in Rouen) shows how the people are divided and confused by the clergy's ingenious solution of libelling the great patriot as a heretic; but also how this causes the clergy to lose ground.

(A) Fear (at the sight of the executioner) stimulates Joan to make particularly bold answers. The more the church needs and uses such people, the less inclined she is to submit to its authority.—It is not the church's threats but her own mistaken assumption as to the people's passivity that temporarily breaks down Joan's resistance.

(A) (B) Once she hears of the popular unrest in Rouen of which she is the centre, her anger is directed against the Bishop of Beauvais, and it is anger at herself. For having lost faith in the people.

[BFA, vol. 24, pp. 404–5.]

The last crowd scene

We took an astonishingly long time to work out the right attitude for the English soldiers, in fact we had quite a few performances behind us. They need to be brutal and on edge. When they turn their backs on the crowd they feel their backs and necks threatened even though the crowd is held off by a rope. Then when they thrust the crowd back (the rope having been coiled up) there is a characteristic instant. The crowd has collected in front of the peasant's son, the loose woman is hysterically screaming "Henry, go home!" One of the soldiers has given ground; he lowers the point of his pike. Will he run the wine merchant through? For three seconds everything stops. Then the soldier holds it level across his body once more, and growling "Back, back" continues to push back the crowd.

It is important to have fifteen seconds' pause as the burning starts, after the loose woman has softly remarked "Now!" and the prayers of the kneeling nuns have come to a stop in the middle of the Hail Mary. And it is likewise important that everyone should stare towards the stake (assumed to be on the apron), even right through the episode with the executioner and the peasant's son.

[BFA, vol. 24, p. 407. The last-mentioned episode is not in our text.]

Editorial Note

Adapting Anna Seghers

Anna Seghers' radio play, which provided eleven of the seventeen scenes, together with the bulk of their dialogue, was first broadcast by the Belgian (Flemish-language) radio in 1935 and subsequently published in the Moscow *Internationale Literatur.* In 1950 it was broadcast by the East German radio. By using crowd noises and shouts, together with anonymous voices, it provided a feeling of the popular presence all through. The effect of this on Joan is much more lightly suggested than in the adaptation; the key which Brecht seized on is Joan's "Why are the people so gay" after her interrogation by La Fontaine (in Brecht's Scene 4), which the adaptation shifts to follow the threat of torture (two scenes later). Joan hears the crowd's shouts when she recants, and "draws in her breath"; nothing else is said to explain why she puts on men's clothes again during the ensuing popular riots. Altogether Seghers' court proceedings take up a far larger proportion of the play than those in the adaptation, while her crowd is more of a collective force and less differentiated, with none of Brecht's genre scenes.

The problem, then, for Brecht and Besson was (a) to make a full length play of this, (b) to bring out Seghers' implication that Joan's mystical voices somehow became the voice of the tangible people, and (c) to establish those people not as radio sound effects but as a group of individuals on the stage. This was done by taking the eleven sections into which the radio play falls—they are separated by clearly marked pauses or breaks—making separate scenes of them, and adding three entirely new crowd scenes (8, 10, and 11); which means that the second half of the cast list (i.e., all the characters after "English soldiers") are likewise new. At a later stage the opening and closing scenes in the Touraine countryside were added, with Jacques Legrain as a symbol of the French wine-growing peasantry recurring right through the play. The girls' song in these scenes was new, as was the mocking verse about Bishop Cauchon in the crowd scenes, the former being very freely derived from Christine de Pisan's poem of 1429: the first stanza from verse 35 and the third from verse 46. A second key remark was introduced in Cauchon's last interview with Joan (13) after she has put on a man's clothes once again; discussing her recantation she confesses "But then I doubted the people; I thought they wouldn't care if I died, and just go on drinking their wine. But they knew all about me the whole time!"

To take the scenes briefly:

1. New, not in Seghers.

2. Developed from anonymous crowd remarks at the opening of the radio play, which provide about half the dialogue.

3. Far the greater part comes from the radio play, with some rearrangement. The new passages tend to stress the role of the English as occupiers—e.g., the opening exchanges, and other use of the English language in Brecht's original play—together with the subservience of the French authorities towards them.

4. The middle section is new, including the exchanges about Catherine of La Rochelle and her visions.

5. Built round the exchanges between several (anonymous) assessors a little later in the radio play about Gerson's affidavit. Here the remarks are shared among identifiable characters. The market setting and whole first half of the scene (with the fishwife and company) are new, as are the closing speculations about Joan's virginity.

6. Almost entirely from the radio play.

7. From the radio play, but shifted back to come between the sight of the torture instruments and Joan's recantation.

8. New. The phrase of the scene title "Joan thinks the people have forgotten her" (penned by Brecht on one of his lists of scenes) can only refer back to the previous scene.

9. In the radio play Joan's recantation takes place in the audible presence of the crowd, and while the bishop begins reading the sentence and the executioner holds a burning torch ready to light the pyre. Maître Érard and his role are new. The condemnation read here by the bishop is that read by Chation in Seghers; virtually all the rest of the dialogue is new apart from the sentry's final remark. The English anger at Joan's escape is less laboured in the radio play.

10. New.

11. New.

12. Apart from the first two remarks about collaboration with the English and the final hand-washing, this is virtually as in the radio play.

13. Like all the other scene titles and locations, this, with its "Joan has heard the voice of the people" is Brecht's. The scene is from the radio play, except the allusions to the people between the Bishop's "But you have publicly recanted" and his "In other words you are obstinate and guilty of a relapse." Here Anna Seghers simply had Joan say "Because I didn't know what a recantation meant."

14. Mainly from the radio play.

15. The crowd remarks here are partly from the end of the radio play, partly from the recantation scene (when the pyre was about to be lit). Brecht

has shuffled them and distributed them to his individual characters. In the radio play the man who lit the flames is seized with remorse, and dominates the ending with his cries.

16. New.

DON JUAN

Texts by Brecht

On the adaptation

Notes on the Production

1

As setting, preferably Molière's original stage with its splendid perspectives, chandeliers, bare indications; the world as the grandees' ornamental fishpond.

2

The acting to be utterly serious, i.e., this is a society which takes itself very seriously indeed.

3

The great seducer never demeans himself by using specific erotic tricks. He seduces by means of his costume (and his way of wearing it), his position (and his barefaced abuse of it), his wealth (or his credit), and his reputation (or the self-assurance given him by his fame). He appears as a sexual Great Power.

4

Certain incidents can be accompanied by Lully's music. The conversations with Donna Elvira in the first and last acts are thereby made to lose their tragic character and become more suitably melodramatic. A flourish (mort) on the horns goes very well with the avenging brother's (Don Alonsa's) appearance in the third act.

[BFA, vol. 24, pp. 412–13]

Don Juan *as a Character*

Don Juan is not an atheist in any progressive sense. His unbelief is not a militant one, calling for people to act. It is just a lack of belief—Don Juan may even believe in God, he would merely rather He was not mentioned, since this might disturb his own life of pleasure.—He will make use of any argument that gets a lady on her back, and equally any that gets her off his.

We are not on Molière's side here. His vote goes to Don Juan—the Epicurean (and follower of Gassendi) supporting the Epicurean. Molière ridicules heavenly justice, he feels this dubious arrangement for repressing *joie de vivre* is right up heaven's street. The only opponents he allows Don Juan are cuckolded spouses and so on.—We are against parasitic *joie de vivre*. Unfortunately the only bon vivant we can point to is the tiger.

[BFA, vol. 24, p. 413–14]

Besson's Production of Don Juan *with the Berliner Ensemble*

When seventeenth-century German companies played Shakespeare, it was a vulgarized, bowdlerized Shakespeare in fancy dress. It was not till the classical revival that the texts were again straightened out and the significance of his works discovered. (Though it would be a mistake to assume that this led to a genuine Shakespearean tradition which could still be drawn on, since this splendid stream in turn rapidly stagnated, degenerating into routine banalities.) The bourgeois German theatre disposed of Molière without wrecking the text; he was broken in by being "interpreted in depth," "humanized," "supernaturally charged." The miser became a "virtually" tragic figure, the "victim" of superhuman greed. Dandin, whom snobbery made a cuckold, became a kind of Woyzeck, whose wife is stolen by an aristocrat. Don Juan became the "perhaps positively tragic rake," "ever insatiably seeking and yearning."

The text before us offers no justification for such an interpretation, which betrays a total ignorance of the age Molière lived in and of his attitude towards it. We suffer today from a peculiar notion of progress which greatly hampers the theatre in its efforts to resuscitate great works from the past. According to this view, progress consisted in artistic creation becoming less and less naïve and primitive as time progressed. It is a view which is also extremely popular in the bourgeois camp, which is where it properly belongs. When the English actor Olivier made his film of Shakespeare's *Henry V* he started off with a portrayal of the play's première in the Globe Theatre. The acting was represented as emotional, stilted, primitive, virtually half-witted.

Then "modern" acting took over. The crude old days were put behind us, the acting became elegant, superior, full of subtleties. I have hardly ever seen a film that irritated me so much. Fancy thinking Shakespeare could have been so much cruder and stupider a director than Mr. Olivier! Of course, I do not hold that the last century, or for that matter our own, has contributed nothing new to the portrayal of human social life or to the depiction of individuals. But there is not the least justification for giving older works "the benefit" of this, if they happen to be masterpieces. We mustn't impose features of Goethe's Faust on Marlowe's; it would not make him Goethean, nor would it help him to be more Marlovian. Old works have their own values, their own subtleties, their own scale of beauties and truths. Our job is to find these out. This doesn't mean that Molière has to be performed as he was in seventeen-something, only that he must not be performed as he was in 1850 (and for that matter in 1950). The variety of perceptions and beauties in his works is just what allows us to derive effects from them that are in tune with our own time. The old interpretations of Molière's *Dom Juan* are more use to us than the new (which are likewise old). We get more from the satire (closer to Molière) than from the semi-tragic psychological study. We find the glamour of this parasite less interesting than the parasitic aspects of his glamour. Leipzig philosophy students discussing Besson's production found the satirical presentation of the feudal concept of love as a hunt so topical that they burst out laughing and told us of present-day ladykillers. I hope and believe that they wouldn't have been nearly so interested by supernatural destroyers of souls.

There is in fact a double significance to Benno Besson's production of *Don Juan*. He restored the comic aspect of the character of Don Juan—justified, incidentally, by the original casting in Molière's theatre of the actor who usually played the comic marquis—by restoring the play's social message. In the famous begging scene, which had hitherto served to present Don Juan as a free-thinker and progressive, Besson simply showed a libertine, too arrogant to admit any obligations, thus revealing how offhandedly the ruling clique treated the beliefs licensed and enforced by the state. He took a slight formal liberty by abandoning the play's division into five acts, a piece of period formalism, undoubtedly adding to the audience's entertainment by this simple measure, without at all detracting from the sense of the play. Another point of significance for the German stage was the extremely happy use Besson was able to make of the unique traditions of the French theatre. The audience was delighted to observe the broadly universal quality of Molière's comic sense, that hazardous mixture of the finest chamber-music comedy with extreme farce, interrupted by those short, exquisitely serious passages which are unequalled elsewhere.

Our theatre is at a lovely stage of learning. That is why its experiments matter and its errors can perhaps be forgiven.

[BFA, vol. 24, pp 414–16. Dated 1954, it appeared that year in nos. 5–6 of the monthly *Sinn und Form*.]

Editorial Note

Adapting Molière

Don Juan is one of the less radical adaptations made by the Berliner Ensemble, and seems to be one of those with which Brecht himself had least to do; indeed there is less material in the Brecht Archive relating to it than even to some of the adaptations not normally credited to him, such as Gerhart Hauptmann's *Biberpelz* and Johannes R. Becher's *Winterschlacht*. Since he was relatively unfamiliar with French writing, the initiative and the bulk of the work on this play are almost certainly due to his bilingual collaborator Benno Besson, who directed its first production in November 1953. Besson had been co-translator of the French version of *Mother Courage* performed by the Théâtre National Populaire under Jean Vilar two years earlier, and they also staged *Dom Juan* (in its original version) at Avignon in 1953. That was the summer when Brecht was concentrating largely on his own last play *Turandot* and also wrote the cycle of poems called the "Buckow Elegies."

A note in BFA says that "the translation of the adaptation of the stage version was due to Bertolt Brecht, Benno Besson and Elisabeth Hauptmann," which would suggest that the adaptation itself may first have been made in French. A considerable number of its scenes are more or less straight translations from Molière, though there are also some dramaturgical changes, while the anti-aristocratic satire is strengthened (evidence of the Don's cowardice, extra references to his debts, etc.), and there is a new love adventure with the commander's daughter Angelica, who does not figure in the original at all (though there are other versions of the legend where Donna Elvira is his daughter, as in Da Ponte's libretto). To resumé the principal differences, in their order of occurrence:

Title

Molière's play is called *Dom Juan* while its non-hero is Don Juan. Its sub-title "le Festin de Pierre" has been dropped.

Act One

Scenes 1–3 are virtually I, 1–3 of the original, but 4 is a new scene, made from the conclusion of I, 2 (which deals with the proposed abduction at sea) and introducing the three boatmen, who are not in Molière at all. Hence scene 5 is entirely new. Scenes 6 and 7 are then made by bringing forward Don Luis' first appearance from IV, 4–5 together with parts of the dialogue, and adding the references to Donna Elvira and to the creditors.

Act Two

Scenes 1–6 are virtually Molière's II, 1–4, though 2 is an extra scene introduced to make the encounter with Mathurine more explicit, while in Molière Pieter (Pierrot) and the girls are peasants rather than fisherfolk. The dispute between the two girls is made more violent; in Molière they neither take off their sabots nor strike one another. Seven however is a new scene, replacing Molière's brief concluding scene 5, in which a bravo called La Ramée arrives to warn the Don that twelve horsemen are on his track. It omits La Ramée but introduces the comic doctor Marphurius, with the evident function of showing Don Juan to be a good deal more frightened of a beating from the infuriated boatmen than of any aristocratic duel.

Act Three

In his scene 1 Molière had Sganarelle disguised as a doctor, which allowed him to make some characteristic jibes at that profession, leading into the discussion of Don Juan's own scepticism about medicine: "Don't you believe in senna leaves?" and so on as in the adaptation. Scene 2 with the beggar is close to Molière's, except that the repeated indication that his remarks are addressed *"to Sganarelle"* have all been inserted; in the original there was a direct relationship between Don Juan and the beggar, with the former giving his own money. Scene 3 with Angelica's appearance and scene 4 with Sganarelle rather than Don Juan putting Don Carlos' attackers to flight (they being here identified with the boatmen) are both new, as is Don Juan's change of clothes at the beginning of the following scene, which introduces new references to the boatmen and their grudge against the aristocracy but is otherwise close to the original III, 3. Then 6, with Don Alonso's entry, is much shortened from III, 4, while 7 and 8 are carved out of III, 5, with additional references to Angelica as the commander's daughter.

Act Four

This combines acts IV and V of the original, apart from the shifting forward of Don Luis' first entry (as above). Scenes 1–3 here are new, Seraphine not figuring in Molière's play at all, while Ragotin has only one line in it. Then 4–6 are IV, 1–3, the main difference being that the closing episode between the tailor and Sganarelle, who also owes him money, is cut. Scene 7 with Donna Elvira is IV, 6; scene 8 is entirely new; while in 9 the references to Elvira's effect on Don Juan come from IV, 7. The farcical meal here has however been cut, where Molière had Sganarelle stealing the Don's dishes while the lower servants stole his; and so has IV, 8, where the statue makes its brief second appearance.

Scene 10, Don Luis' second entrance, ends with a shortened version of V, 1, in which Molière had Don Juan "faisant l'hypocrite" to his father, an instruction that provides one of the clues to his play. Some of Don Luis' opening remarks derive from IV, 4, though Don Juan's account of the boat episode and the appearance of Angelica are of course new. Then scene 11 starts with part of V, 2, Don Juan's speech on hypocrisy being drastically shortened, but the preparations for the meal are new, together with the Don's rehearsal of his speech to the expected lady guest. V, 3 is cut, where his new-found hypocrisy is shown failing to work on Elvira's brother Don Carlos, who thus virtually drops out of the adaptation after the third act. The meal having been held back till now, the ghosts in V, 4 and 5 are eliminated and the commander's appearances in IV, 8 and V, 6 rolled together to make scene 12, whose conclusion with the Don dropping down the flaming hole is from the original.

After that, however, instead of Sganarelle's brief musings there is the new scene 13, with its parade of characters, including the tardy Angelica. Molière provides Sganarelle's concluding cry.

As for the actual translation, Molière's style has been largely allowed to go by the board. E.g., Sganarelle's "Je trouve fort vilain d'aimer de tous les côtés comme vous faites" becomes "Dieses Herumgeliebe ist was furchtbares" ("This indiscriminate loving is abominable," p. 194); Donna Elvira's "Vous plaît-il, Don Juan, nous éclaircir ces beaux mystères?" becomes "Don Juan, dürfte ich Sie um eine Erklärung dieser rätselhaften Erklärung [sic] bitten?" ("Don Juan, may I ask you to explain your puzzling explanation?" p. 197); while Charlotte's "Que veux-tu que j'y fasse? C'est mon himeur, et je ne me pis refondre" becomes "Ich bin nun mal so" ("That's the way I am," p. 206). It is not clear how far this kind of verbal clumsiness is deliberate, intended perhaps to be anti-aristocratic. In addition, of course, many speeches have been condensed in translation, rather than cut.

TRUMPETS AND DRUMS

Texts by Brecht

Plan of the play

1. Headquarters

Plume, the recruiting officer who has arrived from London, is informed by his sergeant Kite about the state of the market for recruits and love. Recruiting is going badly, but Victoria, the justice's daughter, who a year earlier had been in pigtails, has been visiting a girl put in the family way by Plume. Plume gives his friend the shoe manufacturer Worthy a word of advice in matters of the heart. In return Worthy offers him a handsome commission on boots, which Worthy needs soldiers to fill.

2. The justice's house

To shield her from Plume, Balance sends his daughter Victoria away to the country. A true patriot, he then receives Plume with open arms.

3. Melinda's house

Victoria finds no asylum at Melinda's.

4. Market place

Band concert and promenade. Shrewsbury salutes England's heroes. Worthy follows the strategy recommended by Plume, and gives Melinda the cold shoulder. She instantly consoles herself with one of the heroes, the fiery Captain Brazen. With Plume's assistance Kite manages to gaff two young fellows.

5. Headquarters

A young gentleman called Victor is looking for Captain Plume, who has just gone inside the inn with Rose, a country girl, for a business discussion. Her brother calls in the landowner Lady Prude. She cross-examines Rose, who emerges from the inn with some lace.

6. Billiard room at the inn

Victor hands Plume a letter from Victoria. The young gentleman has pots of money, and stands treat to Plume and Brazen In a conversation with Plume he establishes the fact that the former cannot live without the excitements of the battlefield. He resolves to be recruited, and chooses Plume. The casualty lists for the victory at Höchstätt are made public.

7. Room at the inn

The recruiting drive has come to a standstill. Kite does his pathetic best, disguised as a fortune-teller. Worthy makes it up with Melinda. She agrees to leave Brazen.

8. Picnic by the Severn

Victor steals the country girl Rose away from Plume. Melinda tells Brazen that she is going to marry a civilian. The alarm is sounded. Couples emerge from the bushes. Kite drives them all to headquarters.

9. The justice's house

Lady Prude denounces Plume and Victor for immorality. Balance's attitude, as he opens the post from London, is "Thou shalt not muzzle the ox that treadeth out the corn": i.e., the town's defenders are entitled to the town's daughters. The post contains the Act of Impressment. But the prisons prove to be empty. How are they to be filled? A meeting of notables decides on a grand moral clean-up. Brazen presents himself to Melinda in civilian clothes.

10. Room at the inn

During the cleaning-up operation Victor and Rose are arrested as lovers. Victor demands Plume's arrest, which is effected, much to the delight of Lady Prude, by a weeping Kite. [. . .]

11. The justice's house

Among Plume's fellow prisoners is a business man who speaks enthusiastically to him of the excitements of the city. Victor refuses to wash in public and is led away. Then Balance starts forcing the malefactors into the army. On Plume's appearing before him he becomes enraged at Kite's lack of patriotism, and invites Plume to join him on the bench. Summoned out of the courtroom, however, he encounters Victoria. In his anger he cashiers Plume. At this Victoria, who is determined to fight for her beloved man, pretends to commit suicide. She announces that she is pregnant and forces her father to order Plume's release from the army. The latter now sees Victoria for the first time and is thrown into confusion. Buzzing round Melinda are Brazen (in civilian clothes) and Worthy (in uniform). But a bugler recognizes in Brazen a detested sergeant, and so Balance is able to make him take over Plume's battalion. Plume will become a stockbroker in the city and multiply Melinda's twenty thousand pounds for her. While a battalion from the neighbouring town is marching past on its way to embark, that great patriot Balance shoves into the army whatever he has no personal need for at home.

[BBA 651/01–2. This scheme, which follows the eventual division into scenes, apart from the subsequent insertion of the prison scene (11), dates from after the decision to call Farquhar's Silvia Victoria, but before the transposition of the whole play to the period of the War of Independence. The last scene in particular is very different.]

The love story

Victoria was sixteen and a pupil at a boarding school, when she had a brief "love affair" with Captain Plume lasting barely three days: letters (in which she insisted on marriage), a hasty rendezvous, a painful leavetaking. When Plume comes back he hardly remembers anything about it, but is told that she has stood by a girl whom he had put in the family way. Her father, the justice of the peace, is told so too; he sends her away to the country as Plume arrives.

Then a young man appears in Plume's quarters with a letter from Victoria. Plume is absent on business (with Rose). The young man, whose name is Victor, witnesses the scandal over Rose. Victor/Victoria finds the wartime climate unhealthy. At the same time a conversation informs her that Plume is entirely committed to his profession because it satisfies his love of excitement. Victor/Victoria agrees to enlist as an ensign [. . .] in order to be able to remain by Plume's side as his guardian angel. She asks Plume to abandon Rose to her. She does not, however, trust him when he wants to finish off his business with Rose. She herself arranges a rendezvous—with Rose—at Haughton's Hotel. The rendezvous [. . . proves] a failure.

Rose asks for Plume. Victor meanwhile is arrested during the police raid and brought before her own father. Luckily Plume is arrested too. Victoria asks her father to reduce him to the ranks (I am carrying his twins). Plume now sees her for the first time, as she offers herself, her money, and the excitement of London.

[BBA 983/71–72. The typescript is torn and partly illegible. "Haughton" for the hotel proprietor is presumably Farquhar's Horton, but may have helped suggest the name Laughton for the potboy in the final version. Charles Laughton's family were of course also in the hotel business.]

Three notes

a) Contradictions

The field within which characters and plot move displays, *inter alia*, the following contradictions:

An officer's profession and vocation.

An officer does his best to defend his own country, wherever he happens to be fighting, and to live off the country wherever he happens to be stationed; it too may be his own.

He provides himself with local girls, irrespective whether he is in his own country or abroad.

The conqueror gets himself conquered.

The ruling class find that patriotism and egotism coincide.

b) First scene

War as a universal concern and as a private one. On arriving Captain Plume is told how Shrewsbury is reacting to its "military suitors." Not many recruits have applied, but a girl has applied for the captain.

The war however is distasteful to the captain, whose job it is to get recruits for it. He is throwing soldiers into a battle with civilians.

Reluctant to fight as a soldier for civilian interests, the captain will transfer to civil life in the course of the story (thereafter to do his exploiting in England rather than America). Sergeant Kite's report indicates a conflict of interests between the young people of Shrewsbury and the Crown.

What sort of alienations are going to bring out these contradictions apart from an alienating style of acting?

c) Captain Plume

There is no reason why an English recruiting officer in a restoration comedy should be given any higher social status than, say, a traveller in wines in early twentieth-century Prussia. It was not what you might call a profession for the aristocracy, whose sons had regiments of their own by the age of eight. Plume is a farmer's boy who has worked his way up by his native wit, possibly combined with courage, and has no need of fine manners. The story of the play requires him to be reasonably well-built, and no one in the audience need share Victoria's feelings for him. Nor on the other hand does his rank have to be held against him. A subordinate, he is at the same time a plebeian.—As for his outward appearance: smartness or elegance of bearing should be avoided. Plume may wear a pretty uniform, but he neither poses as an aristocrat nor moves about like a flamingo.

[BFA, vol. 24, pp. 417–18. Ribbentrop, Hitler's foreign minister, was once a traveller in wines.]

Editorial Note

Adapting Farquhar

The main work on the adaptation seems to have been done in March and April, 1955, though the play was not produced till the following September. The first complete script in the Brecht Archive is marked "1955 brecht besson" in Brecht's hand, which suggests that Elisabeth Hauptmann's contribution came later. Initially the period of the play was to have been that of the Marlborough Wars, as with the original, while the heroine's name Silvia was also to be retained. However, a number of major dramaturgical changes seem to have been decided on from the outset, to judge from Brecht's early plans noting what he regarded as the main points of the story, some being Farquhar's and some new ideas of his own. Thus, to take the original scene by scene, the following is a rough summary of how Brecht proposed to use it:

I, 1. (Brecht's scene 1.) Worthy was from the first made into a shoe manufacturer with a vested interest in recruiting, summarized in the phrase "soldiers for boots." Plume's previous knowledge of Silvia was more extensive in Farquhar; Brecht reduced it to a minimal recollection.

I, 2. Melinda's apartment. (Originally 2, shifted to 3.) Brazen's letter is cut. Brecht's first idea seems to have been to bring on Brazen himself here, but this was abandoned.

II. 1 and 2. An apartment in Justice Balance's house and *Another apartment,* (Run together to make scene 3, shifted to 2.) All reference to the death of Silvia's brother—the occasion for a fine display of family indifference in the original—was omitted, also the exchanges between Plume and Silvia indicating a certain degree of previous devotion. At an early stage Brecht switched round the two halves of the composite scene so as to make Plume appear *after* Silvia's exit.

II, 3. The street. Included more or less intact in Brecht's scene 4, though there seems to have been an original intention to make Pearmain the potboy and allow him, before his recruitment, to overhear Balance discussing the war casualties, possibly however in a new scene.

III, 1. The market place. (Scene 5.) In the event, Brazen's first appearance was brought forward merely by one scene. (Brecht originally thought of making him a sergeant who masquerades as an officer and is recognized by Balance, but this was dropped). The episode between Plume and Rose was observed by Silvia, who is not in Farquhar's scene at all, and also by a new character, Lady Prude, in lieu of Balance. Prude, says a note, was to "complain to Balance about the decline of morality in Shrewsbury," and later to take part in a "meeting of Shrewsbury notables" where she would denounce Plume and call for police action; this was effected in Brecht's scene 9.

III, 2 and IV, 1. The walk by the Severn side. (Scene 8.) There seems to have been no intention to follow Farquhar in letting the two recruiting officers compete for Silvia's military services. Brecht's notes say: "Disguised as a young man, Silvia lets herself be recruited so as to be near Plume"; "Brazen confesses his war-weariness to Melinda" (not in Farquhar); and "Silvius [i.e., Silvia in male attire] steals the farmer's daughter Rose away from Plume." In the original the actual recruiting of Silvia only occurs when the justices order her into the army in the last act.

IV, 2. It looks as if nothing from this scene was ever meant to be kept, since Lucy has no role in the adaptation *qua* maid to Melinda (whereas Farquhar here has her trying to blackmail her mistress), while the advancing of the duel eliminates the Worthy-Brazen quarrel.

IV, 3. A chamber. Kite's fortune-telling act played no part in Brecht's plans, though part of the scene was in fact taken into scene 8.

V, 1. An anteroom adjoining Silvia's bedchamber. (Scene 10.) "A raid on the inn leads to the arrest of Silvius and Rose as lovers," says an early note. In Farquhar the only other characters to appear here are Bridewell and Bullock; Plume, still ignorant of "Wilful's" identity, is not present.

V, 2. Justice Balance's house. Once again, nothing in this scene, which brings the freshly arrested Silvia (still unrecognized) before her father, seems to figure in Brecht's schemes, though there is a very approximate equivalent in Lady Prude's reactions in the second half of scene 10, which also includes Rose's reference to her bed-fellow as "the most harmless man in the world."

V, 3. Melinda's apartment. Brecht's notes suggest that he has no interest in Worthy except as a shoe manufacturer. However, a good part of the exchanges between Worthy and Melinda in his otherwise new scene 9 come from here.

V. 4. The market place. Another scene of no dramaturgical use to Brecht, though Plume's and Brazen's discussion about how best to lay out twenty thousand pounds was taken into the otherwise new scene 7.

V, 5. A court of justice. Incorporated in scene 12, as described below.

V, 6. The fields. The mock-duel has been taken into Brecht's scene 8. As for Lucy's weakness for Brazen, like her whole role in the intrigue around Melinda it has gone.

V, 7. Justice Balance's house. Fused with V, 5 to make scene 12. Brecht's interpretation of justice here follows the early note which says "Having just received the Pressing Act from London, Balance imagines he can go to work in a big way. The prisons being relatively empty, it is decided to fill them. This means going along with Lady Prude, Plume's old enemy," the ground for this now being prepared in the new scene 9, which makes the play's relation to the Mutiny and Impressment Acts (promulgated when Farquhar himself was a recruiting officer in Shrewsbury) that much more explicit. The prisoners Workless and Miner are drawn from Farquhar (though he gives them no names), likewise the arrest of Bridewell. Silvia, however, is tried too in Farquhar's V, 5, and sent into the army to the accompaniment of Plume's reading of the Articles of War. She is only recognized and released in V, 7, after which, as one of Brecht's notes puts it, "Brazen condemns Plume to civilian life."

In the "1955 brecht besson" script the references were originally to the battles of Marlborough's time—Plume, for instance, was "the hero of Schellenberg" (i.e., Donauwörth, 1704)—but they have been amended, often in Brecht's own hand, and remarks about America, the colonies, Boston harbour and so forth worked in (though by an evident oversight Kite's list of heavenly bodies in scene 8 was left with "Dixmude, Namur, Brussels, Charleroy," as in Farquhar, instead of the "Boston, Massachusetts, Kentucky, Philadelphia" of the final script). This version contains the twelve scenes in their final order, also the prologue and three of the songs: "When I leave you for the war, dear" from scene 8, "E.N. Smith" from the interlude after scene 11, and "Over the hills and over the sea," though instead of concluding the play this was sung by Kite in scene 4, and in a version much closer to Farquhar's original in the corresponding II, 3.

Besides Lady Prude, it introduced another new "notable" in the shape of Mr. Smuggler, the London banker, who was given rather more to do than in the final version. Thus in scene 11 he had to tell Plume and Kite of a city coup in wool which he claimed was as exciting as any military encounter, after which he gave Plume his card, saying, "If I can be useful to you at any time . . ." while in the last scene he recognized Brazen as his absconding cashier Jack. The butler Simpkins, however, figured on many pages of this version as "a servant," with virtually nothing to say, though there are additions which build the part up slightly, and retyped pages which give him his name. The Mike-Lucy sub-plot too is barely started (Mike being called George and Maggie Minnie, which explains the use of that name in the scene 8 song); while the other two justices, Scale and Scruple, still make their unnecessary appearance as in Farquhar. As for Silvia, she has become (anachronistically) Victoria, but is still not recognized by Plume in the prison scene. Apparently it comes as a complete surprise to him when, as he starts to sign her release (as in Farquhar), she exclaims "Father, I can no longer deceive you. William, pardon your Victoria if she now tells the truth," then goes on very much as on p. 318.

The Worthy-Melinda relationship is left unresolved at the end of the play (Worthy in this version having actually enlisted under Plume in scene 9), and the two lovers only come together as the company takes its bow. The two scenes that differ most from the final text, however, are scenes 8, *By the Severn,* and 12, the concluding court scene. The first of these was evidently conceived as consisting of two settings "wooden bench by the copse" and "punt in the reeds," which would have alternated on a revolving stage; also the blacksmith was an extra character called Flock, later to be merged with William. In scene 12, which showed the court and an antechamber, the sequence of episodes was as follows (showing their present order in parentheses):

Balance with Melinda and Lucy (2)
Plume invited to join the justices (1)
Trial of Workless (9)
Trial of Miner (5)
Victoria pleads for Plume's arrest and is recognized by Balance (6)
Victoria with Balance and Plume in the antechamber (7)
Lucy's report to Brazen (4)
Question of Plume's and Victoria's marriage (8)
Balance instantly sentences five anonymous prisoners for having no visible
    means of support (—)
Trial of prostitute, pimp, and pickpocket (3)
George (Mike) and Bridewell sentenced (10)
Plume accepts Victoria, hands his uniform to Brazen who reads the Articles
    of War (11)
Balance sentences three unemployed men (—)

Lucy gets George (Mike) discharged (12)
Brazen marches off with recruits. Balance, Victoria, and Plume leave for the
    pheasant shoot (13)

This left considerable changes to be made in the play before the present
text was arrived at, notably the further development of the references to the
American War of Independence and the repeated insertion of Kite's catch-
phrase about the Mississippi. The broad-shouldered man was introduced in
scene 4 and the court scene, where it was decided to give more prominence
to the crowd; hence the former's comments, together with those of the
wives, Jenny, Mrs. Cobb, etc. Simpkins the butler was further built up,
possibly using elements from Charles Laughton's *Ruggles of Red Gap* and
a few Wodehouse recollections, to fill in the new American background
(as by his account of the battle of Bunker Hill in scene 4) and at the same
time perhaps to give a good if anachronistic role to the actor Wolf von
Beneckendorff. Scene 6 in the billiard room was amended to start with yet
another account of Bunker Hill, this time from the potboy, but this was then
dropped. In scene 8 by the Severn the swan was introduced and the Mike/
Lucy passages built up so as to show their sympathy for the colonists. Scene
10 (the bedroom scene) was likewise lengthened, showing *inter alia* that
Plume recognizes Victoria. The songs were added to, initially by Melinda's
song (scene 3) and the second and third verses of "Over the hills and over
the sea" in the last scene. Victoria's song at the end of scene 6 came later, as
did the Kiplingesque "Women of Gaa" (? Goa. Scene 11) and the first verse
of "Over the hills." Other late additions were the exchanges between Lucy
and Mike (now surnamed Laughton) about their hotel in New York and its
defence against the redcoats, and a number of Simpkins' patriotic comments
and interjections.

Thus Brecht's new scenes additional to Farquhar are: 6, the billiard
room, which may derive from Brecht's early note that "Silvius tries to find
out how strongly Plume is committed to the military profession. Plume
can't imagine either himself or Silvius having any other"; 7 on the market
place; most of 9, culminating in the meeting of notables; and 11 in prison.
Significant points taken from the original include the personalities of Kite
and Brazen together with much of the latter's dialogue – for instance such
expressions as "my dear" and "Mr. Laconic" – and his interest in Melinda's
twenty thousand pounds; likewise Balance's warning against predatory
captains [p. 257], the episodes with Rose (and her chickens) and Appletree
and Pearmain, the cases of Workless and Miner in the last scene and, above
all, the whole central notion of magistrates sending men into the army.